FINANCIAL POST

GUIDE TO | **INVESTING**
AND PERSONAL FINANCE

KEY PORTER BOOKS

Canadian Cataloguing in Publication Data

Main entry under title:

Financial post guide to investing and personal finance

Rev. ed.
ISBN: 1-55263-344-6

1. Investments – Canada. 2. Finance, Personal – Canada.

HG5154.F56 2001   332.63'2   C00-933225-1

THE CANADA COUNCIL | LE CONSEIL DES ARTS
FOR THE ARTS | DU CANADA
SINCE 1957 | DEPUIS 1957

The publisher gratefully acknowledges the support of the Canada Council for the Arts and
the Ontario Arts Council for its publishing program.

We acknowledge the financial support of the Government of Canada through the Book
Publishing Industry Development Program (BPIDP) for our publishing activities.

Key Porter Books Limited
70 The Esplanade
Toronto, Ontario
Canada M5E 1R2

www.keyporter.com

Revisions to this edition were compiled by Bruce Cohen, Bud Jorgenson and Beth Marlin.

Cover illustration: Nicholas Vitacco
Illustrations: Nicholas Vitacco, Tony Smith and David Middleton
Electronic formatting: Beth Crane, Heidy Lawrance Associates

Printed and bound in Canada

01 02 03 04 05 6 5 4 3 2 1

CONTENTS

ome of the specifics may have changed over time, but the thrust of successful investing and prudent asset management remains the same. Published three years ago, the *Financial Post Guide to Investing and Personal Finance* has been a runaway hit. We have received positive feedback on the book as both a tool to understanding the markets and as a manual on using the *Financial Post* when making all-important decisions about money.

As a result of this feedback, we are pleased to bring you the second edition of the guide — complete with updated tables, graphs and information. While many of our long-time readers are seasoned investors with considerable knowledge of financial markets, others are new to the game. Some may be active equity investors but have no idea of how currencies, for instance, are traded. This guide covers equity, mutual fund, debt and currency markets and explores how they are affected by both government policy and the economy. We have called on some of our top writers, including William Hanley, Patrick Bloomfield and Sonita Horvitch to provide overviews in their areas of expertise. Throughout, tables and graphs found in the *FP* Investing section of the *National Post* are used to illustrate how the myriad of investment vehicles work.

While it is important to make money, it is equally important to preserve it. That's where the personal finance portion of the book comes in. Along with a series of overviews by Jonathan Chevreau and Arthur Drache, we have dipped into our storehouse of already published articles to provide a package that spans the personal finance spectrum—from tax and retirement to insurance and investment planning.

At the back of the book is a helpful glossary, defining the hundreds of investment and personal finance terms mentioned. We hope you enjoy the updated version of the book and find it useful. Happy investing and saving.

Douglas Kelly
Executive Editor, *National Post*

CHAPTER 1

GETTING STARTED

- How to define your investment goals and get into the stock market

- How to read stock tables and company reports

- How to set up an account

- Understanding dividends

IMPROVING YOUR ODDS

IN THE LOTTERY OF LIFE | BY WILLIAM HANLEY

THE FIRST KNOWN RECORD of the saying "a penny saved is a penny earned" is from 1640. And it pops up regularly in slightly different guises throughout English literature, from Dickens to P.G. Wodehouse to Alison Lurie. It is a compelling theme through the ages and one that is even more compelling today. If you work hard and work smart to earn a living, try to hang on to as much of it as possible. And what you hang on to, put to work. Indeed, as we enter 2001 and as millions of Canadian baby boomers begin to face retirement, saving and investing has become a national pastime, if not an obsession, for many people concerned that state and company pensions may not provide them with the "golden years" lifestyle they expect. But despite a maelstrom of information from every possible source about investment products and plans, studies show that many Canadians start investing too little, too late, with the consequence of facing older age with not enough to show for a lifetime of hard work.

WHEN INVESTING WAS SIMPLER

While the investment universe has exploded during the past decade, with Canadians forsaking traditional investment vehicles such as GICs for the juicier returns on mutual funds, most people's investing "careers" began when they were children with that first bank account: Your mom or dad took you down to the bank with that birthday cheque from granddad or with the precious proceeds from your piggy bank and you opened a savings account. You added a few dollars here and there, and every time you went to the teller window, the bank book was updated and regularly there was a bit extra added to the total, as if by magic.

Back in the 1950s and '60s, that magic amounted to about 3% per year on a savings account, less on a chequing/savings account. Back then, bank interest and Canada Savings Bonds were basically the known investment universe for two or three generations of Canadians. Many of the ideas on investing held by those generations were forged in

There are two rules of investing. First, don't lose any money.
Second, see rule No.1.

the Dirty '30s of the Great Depression, when deflation made cash king and a penny saved was indeed a penny earned.

In the '60s, for instance, the Canadian stock market seemed a strange hybrid of widows' and orphans' stocks such as Bell Canada and spectacular speculative scams like Windfall Mines. Mutual funds, such as they were, were soon to fall from grace via the IOS scandal.

INFLATION TRIGGERS THE RISE AND FALL OF INTEREST RATES

But that era also brought two watershed personal financial developments for Canadians: Canada Pension Plan (CPP) and registered retirement savings plans (RRSPs). CPP, now undergoing a desperately needed overhaul, was a good idea badly executed. It gave many a false sense of security about retirement and the monies put into it were squandered on general government spending. RRSPs were a fine idea, a tax shelter for everyman and everywoman who could manage to put something aside.

After the relative stability of the '60s, Canadian investors were thrust into the scary new inflationary world of the 1970s, which was marked by a falling stock market and rising interest rates. By the end of the decade the inflation rate was in double digits, mortgage rates were approaching 20% and some five-year guaranteed investment certificates were paying an astounding 21% a year. Investors didn't quite know how well they were doing, and whether they were on track.

It took much of the 1980s to unwind the great inflationary spiral. The stock market recovered, only to crash in October 1987. But the groundwork was painstakingly being laid for a new era of investing in a relatively inflation-free environment, even though many retirees yearned for the days of 15%-plus returns on their fixed investments.

The 1990s and the very early 21st century felt a lot like the '60s in terms of investing. Interest rates have fallen to their lowest level in 40 years, slashing returns on term deposits to levels last seen in the 1950s. And tame inflation provided a vibrant backdrop for the stock market, which in turn has produced what can only be described as a mutual funds mania.

SOME INVESTORS PREFER TO PLAY IT SAFE WITH GUARANTEED RETURNS

By early 2001, though, the action in stocks started to look like a bear market. Broad averages churned and the technology-heavy Nasdaq composite index was well down from record levels set in the spring of 2000.

Warren Buffett, one of the world's richest private citizens, has been a relentless acquisitor of stocks through his Berkshire Hathaway Inc. holding company, providing investors with returns approaching 25% a year for almost 30 years. While the Wizard of Omaha's investment strategies may seem beyond the realm of everyman and everywoman, he dispenses much down-to-earth advice in Berkshire's annual report. "There are two rules of investing," Buffett says. "First, don't lose any money. Second, see rule No. 1."

As glib and folksy as that might sound, keeping what you save is an essential cornerstone of any investment plan. And that's why some people, especially those retired or approaching retirement, are not comfortable with the risk-reward equation in equities, preferring to stick with a guaranteed fixed return even if it means missing out on a bull market in stocks.

PICKING THE RIGHT INVESTMENT CAN SEEM LIKE A GAME OF LOTTERY

Over the long term, stocks can provide exceptional returns to those who buy and hold. But that doesn't mean the formula works all the time.

The most prescient and luckiest Canadian investor would have bought stocks in the '60s, switched into real estate in the '70s, bought gold bullion in 1979, then GICs in 1980, switched back into stocks in 1982, bought some real estate in 1985, sold it in 1989, and then concentrated on picking and holding stocks until the bond market rally in 2000. And all the above as much as possible in an RRSP.

This, of course, would have been the equivalent of winning the lottery. While Generation X has struggled with rising taxes and falling real incomes, it can be argued that the generation of Canadians born after the Second World War actually did win in the lottery of life. The baby boomers grew into adulthood in a period of unparalleled prosperity in the world in general and Canada in particular. Most should have been able to save, invest and build assets as a bulwark against any eventuality.

It's ironic that the Xers, immersed in the new investment culture despite tighter times, are far more attuned to the need to save than were their profligate boomer parents.

THE KEY TO SUCCESS IS AN INVESTMENT STRATEGY

Meanwhile, there's still time for laggard boomers to get it right even though, for many people, getting that penny to save and earn is more difficult. There's no excuse for not having a strategy, a plan to live by and with.

Read on. And become your own best investment counsellor.

WHO ISSUES STOCKS AND BONDS, AND WHY

Securities are the fibres that knit together the economy. Stocks represent an ownership stake – literally a share of a company. Bond-holders are lenders.

Those who need money companies and governments – are issuers of securities. Private companies are those in which equity is closely held, either by one or more individuals or by other companies. Going public means giving up some control, in part because the owner-ship is spread more broadly but also because corporations that sell securities to the public are subject to rules on disclosure of information and other matters.

After a stock is listed on a stock exchange, investors are free to sell their new shares, and trading begins. The company doesn't make money when these shares are traded, although the higher visibility generated through open trading can enhance its profile and credibility.

Companies raise money for a variety of purposes, such as expansion projects or to take over another company, and this can be done with equity or debt.

Governments can't issue stock but they too need funds to finance major public works, such as public buildings and highways. Issuing bonds is a way of spreading the capital cost of these projects over their useful life. Crown corporations, such as electric utilities, are an extension of governments and their debt financings are a guaranteed obligation of taxpayers.

When large corporations and governments need cash for short-term needs, they may use a line of credit from a bank. But often they go to the money market and issue trade-able securities with terms up to one year. The most common money market term is three months. When governments go to the money market, their securities are called treasury bills. Corporate money market securities are commercial paper and banks issue bankers' acceptance notes. For longer-term borrowing, bonds are the preferred route.

But interest on debt is an unyielding obligation and too much debt can cripple a company. So, a growing company will issue stock to maintain a healthy balance between debt and equity. Common stockholders, even those who hold only a tiny fraction of total shares issued, still have a legal right to a say in a company's business.

Bondholder rights are governed by the terms of the contract under which the bond is issued. Bondholders stand ahead of shareholders if a company is in distress.

INVESTORS IN STOCKS HAVE TWO BASIC OBJECTIVES
• Income from dividends provides investors with a portion of a company's earnings.

MARKET SUMMARY | TABLES AND CHARTS

The summary tables on the front of the FP Investing section of the *National Post* cover the daily highlights of key markets – **stocks, bonds, commodities and foreign exchange.** The information in these tables is available in greater detail within the Investing section, but these tables provide an overview at a glance on general trends in these markets. An important feature of this series are the charts showing trends over the last 12 months and the previous two weeks.

These tables show benchmark indexes (except for the currencies and three high-profile commodities). For all of the entries, the close is for the latest trading day and there is a range of trading values for the last 52 weeks. Other columns track the changes over the last 12 months and the calendar year to date.

Index	Close	Net chg	% chg	52W high	52W low	−Yr over yr− net chg	% chg	−Yr to date− net chg	% chg
TSE 300	8886.37	−122.26	−1.36	11401.97	8018.57	+788.18	+9.73	+472.62	+5.62
TSE 200	476.43	−3.11	−0.65	551.66	443.31	+28.39	+6.34	+13.18	+2.85
TSE 100	550.66	−8.06	−1.44	717.25	493.49	+51.46	+10.31	+31.61	+6.09
S&P/TSE 60	526.33	−8.07	−1.51	698.58	472.29	+45.05	+9.36	+30.47	+6.14
Toronto 35	553.44	−1.35	−0.24	610.98	457.08	+86.76	+18.59	+73.28	+15.26
CDNX Index	2774.17	−59.37	−2.10	4526.06	2152.95	+589.47	+26.98	+436.72	+18.68

Dividend policies are set by a company's directors and payments are stated in a specific amount for each share. Most blue chip companies pay regular dividends but the board is under no obligation to pay. The boards of many companies prefer to keep most or all of the profits to reinvest in the growth of the firm.

• Buying shares at a lower price and selling high provides investors with a capital gain. Start-up companies provide investors with the opportunity for big gains if growth prospects are realized.

INVESTORS IN BONDS HAVE ESSENTIALLY THE SAME GOALS BUT THE MECHANICS ARE DIFFERENT
• Interest income is fixed with conventional bonds and cannot be changed.
• Buyers of new bonds get the face value returned when the bonds mature but those who buy bonds in the secondary market can have capital gains or losses. Because the interest payment is fixed, the price of a bond will rise or fall as interest rates change. When rates go up, the price falls. When rates decline, the price rises.

Tax treatment is among the many factors that go into an investment decision. Capital gains have a different status than dividend or interest income and stocks can be treated differently from bonds. Securities trade in markets that are regulated by tradition and law. Most stocks are traded through recognized exchanges, which are public markets that bring together buyer and seller. Companies must conform to certain listing standards, which vary from exchange to exchange. Thus the reputation of the exchange is an important factor in stock selection by investors.

Bonds mainly trade over-the-counter, which means the market is a network of banks and investment dealers. But there is a move to greater transparency in bond trading and public markets are slowly accumulating bond listings. National government bonds are the benchmark securities in this market and governments are among the direct participants in bond trades. Both governments and corporations rely on the dealer network in raising money but government treasury agencies do more of the work in-house.

Distribution of government securities is through a group of "primary dealers," which includes the major banks and brokerage firms. When a company goes to the market for funds, it usually picks one or more of the investment dealers for advice on the size and price of the securities issue. The dealers act as underwriters – buying the new shares and then selling them to the public. The dealers' profit, or underwriting fee, is the difference between their buying price and selling price.

PREPARING A PROSPECTUS IS THE FIRST STEP TO ISSUING NEW SHARES
Once the conditions of the offer are established, the company and the investment dealer must make sure the offer complies with provincial securities regulations. Requirements include preparation of a prospectus – a document that provides potential investors with the information they need to make an informed investment decision. Once the prospectus has been accepted by provincial securities commissions, sale of the new shares can begin.

ECONOMIC SIGNPOSTS TO INVESTMENT

When setting out to invest, the road map is a chart of the economy. Stocks that are good investments in boom times may get marked down more than the average when a slow-down arrives. At a more fundamental level, identifying the stage of the business cycle helps determine whether to emphasize equities or fixed income securities when making changes to a portfolio.

Throughout the industrial era there has been an ebb and flow to economic activity. Central bank management of monetary policy has created a sense of confidence that the modern economy can avoid boom-and-bust excesses but few will maintain the business cycle has been eliminated. Conventional economic analysis divides the business cycle into five stages; they are expansion, peak, contraction, trough and recovery. They can be defined in the following terms:

Expansion: This is a growth period characterized by stable prices, rising corporate profits, healthy job creation and a bullish sentiment for stocks. Interest rates begin to creep higher, which means a decline in bond prices.

Peak: As an expansion progresses, signs of excess begin to show up in the economy. Business inventories or construction activity get too far ahead of demand and a tight labor market leads to inflationary wage demands. Overstocking leads to price cutting and labor unrest leads to strikes. The result of these developments is falling profits and a weakness in stock prices. Interest rates rise as the economy peaks, so bond prices fall.

Contraction: Too much of a good thing at the peak causes a correction and a severe correction is a recession. Household confidence suffers during this phase and people save more. A higher savings rate means the use of money shifts away from consumption and toward investment.

The practical result of a bigger pool of savings is a decline in interest rates. An erosion in corporate profitability affects stock prices. Falling interest rates during this part of the cycle means that bond prices rise.

Trough: The slowdown means business has much less room to raise prices, inventory levels are run down and wage demands moderate. But, eventually, deferred spending by consumers and businesses creates pent-up demand and at the bottom of the cycle there is a shift toward greater consumption. Interest rates stabilize and stock prices begin to anticipate a rebound in profits.

Recovery: This is the preamble to a new expansion. Economists define the recovery period to mean the length of time it takes for the total value of goods and services produced by the economy (gross domestic product) to reach its pre-recession peak. Employment grows and inventory is restocked during this period. Interest rates remain stable and stocks start pricing in rising earnings.

Within the business cycle, prices of certain stock groups will behave differently. "Cyclicals" have a special relationship to swings in the economy. For example, resource stocks tend to lead the cycle.

Demand for basic commodities precedes an upturn in economic activity because corporate managers in processing industries will stock up on the raw materials when they see signs of improving demand.

FIRST OF ALL, DO SOME SECURITIES CHECKS

 Making money on the stock market is easy – buy low, sell high. Deciding when to buy or sell is the difficult part and that involves research and experience. Investors can rely on professionals for these attributes but it is always a good idea to know where to find basic information and analyze the significance of that information. Research on securities is divided into two broad categories – fundamental and technical.

Fundamental analysis involves careful study of an issuer of a security – past records of sales, earnings, assets, markets, management performance and other factors. The issuer can be a company or a government. When looking at provincial government bonds, for example, "sales" could mean revenue from a dominant industry in the province. A study of the fundamentals also includes an analysis of the issuer's performance compared with similar issuers. Another aspect of the fundamentals is how the issuer is affected by economic trends.

TECHNICAL ANALYSIS MEASURES MARKET PERFORMANCE

Technical analysis is the study of the security itself or the indexes that measure market performance – the patterns of past price moves and their predictive ability. In simple terms, it's a study of momentum and how to spot the turning points in price moves. Trading volume is an important element and technicians also make extensive use of averages in price or volume to smooth out day-to-day variations.

QUANTITATIVE ANALYSIS MAKES USE OF SPREADSHEETS AND DATABASES

A third category of research is "quantitative analysis," which is an invention of the computer age. This approach crunches huge volumes of numbers with spreadsheets and databases, using both technical and fundamental factors.

High-tech methods of analyzing securities tend to be the preserve of those who trade frequently, sometimes in and out of a stock on the same day. But heavy trading is for those with big portfolios because transaction fees eat up the profits from small trades.

For many small investors, the best approach is to buy the shares of good companies for the long term. Basic information is readily available. Financial newspapers are a key resource. They follow major corporate stories as well as routine developments.

Shareholders receive regular financial reports on a company's operations but prospective shareholders are well advised to review recent disclosure documents. They can be obtained from a company's investor relations office, a brokerage firm or a large

COMPANY MEETINGS | TABLE

Annual and special meetings are events that give ordinary shareholders a chance to see senior managers in a public forum and ask questions. The agenda for the meeting is set out in advance in an information circular. Most of these meetings include a report from the chief executive.

COMPANY MEETINGS

Listings supplied by Toronto Stock
Exchange, Montreal Exchange

Tues., Nov. 14, 2000

Axia NetMedia Corp. (Annual Special)	
Hyatt Regency Hotel, Calgary	3 p.m.
Intrawest Corp. (Annual General)	
Waterfront Hotel, Vancouver	11 a.m.
Neurochem Inc. (Annual)	
Queen Elizabeth Hotel, Montreal	10 a.m.

COMPANIES IN THE NEWS | INDEX

On the second page of the Financial Post section, a Companies in the News index directs readers to stories that mention companies in that day's Financial Post. Shareholders use this index to monitor news developments affecting companies whose shares they own.

COMPANIES IN THE NEWS

360networks Inc. D2	Global Election Systems ...D2	Qwest Communications ...C2
ADAC......................C2	Global TeleSystems Inc. C2	S.D. Myers Inc. C9
Advanced Micro Devices ..C6	Hemosol Inc. C2	SSL International PLC C2
Archer-Daniels-Midland ..C2	Henkel C2	Sears Canada Inc. D1
BASF C2	Hewlett-Packard Co. ...C1, C7	Sierra Wireless Inc. C8
BCE Inc. C2, C4	Honeywell C13	Smithfield Foods Inc. C9
BellSouth Corp. C2	Hollinger C1	Southwest Airlines Co. C2
Bertelsmann AG C14	IBP Inc. C9	Streamline.com C2
BioChem Pharma Inc. C1	Jitec Inc. C3	Sun Life Assurance Co. C8

Page number

public library. Most corporations have Internet sites. Newswire services on the Web disseminate corporate press releases.

The latest editions of the annual report, the annual information form and the quarterly statement all contain an array of information on the company that is both financial and operational. Other useful documents in doing research on a company are a prospectus, if a company has done a recent financing, and reports from credit rating agencies on the company's securities.

INDEXES MEASURE A MARKET'S PROGRESS

On the question of "How high is high?" the answer in the stock market comes from what is known as an index.

Most equity indexes are designed as a proxy for trends and magnitude of price changes. If an index goes up by 10%, that means stock prices have gone up by roughly 10% and dividends that arrive during a period of rising prices are a bonus.

Bond indexes generally are designed to measure total return, which is a combination of interest income and changes in bond prices. There are a few total return indexes for stocks but most people watch those indexes that track capital gains or losses.

SOME INDEXES ARE MORE INFLUENTIAL THAN OTHERS
AND THERE ARE TWO BASIC REASONS FOR FOLLOWING AN INDEX

• For the average investor, the reason is the index is seen as a broad indicator of market direction in a national market. In Canada, the Toronto Stock Exchange 300 composite index fills that role. The venerable Dow Jones average of 30 industrials has long been watched around the world as a guide to the U.S. market. More recently, however, there has been a high correlation between trends in the Nasdaq composite index and changes in U.S. consumer confidence.

• For professionals in the securities industry, the key indexes are those on which futures and options are traded. For them, these indexes are an investment class as well as market indicators. In North America, the most widely followed index in this category is the Standard & Poor's index of 500 U.S. stocks. The Toronto Stock Exchange has developed a series of derivative-backed indexes in an agreement with S&P and they hope to develop a similarly wide Canadian following for the S&P/TSE 60 index.

THE DOW | IS DIFFERENT

Computers now calculate stock indexes on the run and the high/low points for the day represent real prices at that time. The Dow Jones average is an exception. The Dow is the oldest stock index in use and the reason for the difference is historical. In the early days – long before computers – Dow index values were calculated once a day. From 1884 to 1915, prices of the stocks in the index were stated as a percentage of the par value, and at that time US$50 was a standard par value. Thus, the early index numbers were averages of these percentages. Calculations of highs and lows for the Dow didn't begin until Oct. 1, 1928. Those numbers were calculated by using the average of the high price and the low price for each stock during the trading day. Now the indexes are calculated with computers, the tick-by-tick calculation method adjusts for the highs and lows for component stocks as they are set during the day.

THE PERFORMANCE OF A STOCK IS TRACKED IN SUBINDEXES

Broad-based indexes like the TSE 300 have subindexes – 14 in the case of the TSE 300 – and these classifications allow investors to track the performance of a stock of one company in relation to the general trend for its sector. Often, those subindexes will also be divided into categories.

In the U.S., the S&P 500 fills the role of sector benchmark.

The TSE 300 is designed to broadly mirror the composition of the Canadian economy but weightings of the various sectors also reflect the popularity of certain stock groups among investors. For example, the TSE gold subindex accounted for more than 10% of the composite index when the price of gold was above US$400 an ounce in the early 1990s. But the weighting had dropped to just 2.8% at the start of 2001, when gold was down to US$265 and gold miners were out of favor with investors. Technology stocks shone as gold faded and going into 2001 tech heavyweight Nortel Networks Corp. had an 18% weighting in the TSE 300.

WATCHING THE PERCENTAGE CHANGES OF AN INDEX ALLOWS FOR COMPARISONS

Changes in the level of an index are measured in points but the significance of a change of, say, 100 points will vary. A move of that size is substantial if the starting point is 500 but negligible if it is 10,000. For that reason, people watch for percentage changes, especially when making comparisons among markets.

The Dow Jones industrial average is the world's most widely watched stock market index, in part because it goes back to 1884. The modern structure of the Dow index dates to 1928, but it still has value as a measure of stock market performance over more than a century and technical analysts follow the Dow for its historical patterns.

The TSE 35 index is roughly comparable with the structure of the Dow because it includes 35 large-capitalization frequently traded Canadian stocks. But the short history of the TSE 35 – it was begun in 1987 – makes it less useful than the TSE 300, which was begun in 1977. The TSE has used old trading records to backdate the 300 to 1956.

Other Canadian exchanges have indexes that reflect general direction. They include the Canadian Venture Exchange index, CDNX, the new benchmark for small cap stocks in Canada.

In the U.S., the S&P 500 index is a more comprehensive measure of national corporate activity than the Dow. The Nasdaq composite index is weighted to technology stocks and regional companies that represent the broad base of U.S. industry.

Among widely followed overseas stock indexes are two from the Financial Times – the index of the 100 largest companies listed on the London Stock Exchange and the index of the top 100 continental European and Irish shares on the exchange's SEAQ services. Other important overseas indexes are the Nikkei 225-stock average in Tokyo, the Dax 30-stock index in Frankfurt, the CAC 40-stock index in Paris and the All-Ordinaries 330-stock index in Australia.

North American and international index tables provide a broad overview of trends in markets around the world. Toronto and Montreal index listings also include breakdowns of subindexes and the TSE 300 list shows all the industry categories within the sector subindexes.

THE HIGH AND LOW points for each trading day during the past 52 weeks is the intraday reading. The 52-week high is usually different from the closing high or low for that period. Computers track each change in the combined value of the basket of stocks in each index as it constantly changes throughout the trading day (in the jargon of the investment community, there is a tick-by-tick change in the index).

VOLUME is the number of shares traded in stocks in the index. Volume is stated in board lots, which means units of 100 shares. Most exchanges count a buy or sell of 100 shares as a volume of one board lot. But Nasdaq, the U.S. interdealer network, counts a buy and a sell of 100 shares as a volume of two board lots.

North American indexes

52W high	52W low	Index	% Yield	P/E	Vol 00s	High	Low	Close	Net change	% change
Toronto Stock Exchange										
11401.97	7519.45	TSE 300	1.25	25.07	785569	9170.89	8969.27	9115.05	-84.01	-0.9
4051.75	3206.56	Metals & Minerals	1.90	12.66	70390	3536.47	3477.75	3536.47	-0.75	nil
5594.58	3476.88	Integrated Mines	1.90	11.80	68990	3853.07	3788.72	3853.07	+1.22	nil
1517.57	881.76	Mining	1.97	n.m.	1400	1487.10	1419.50	1477.68	-12.94	-0.9
5601.87	3469.45	Gold & Precious Mnrl	1.42	n.m.	21069	3703.53	3654.50	3654.50	-10.08	-0.3
8679.37	5358.22	Oil & Gas	0.60	15.03	75887	7450.69	7405.39	7441.39	+34.90	+0.5
12985.29	8248.52	Integrated Oils	1.32	14.34	18665	11515.91	11303.95	11515.91	+197.59	+1.7
7453.57	4446.17	Oil & Gas Producers	0.25	14.60	51753	6387.86	6345.80	6351.63	+3.56	+0.1

YIELD is the dividend yield for the index or subindex (the weighted average dividend in relation to the weighted average price).

THE CLOSE is the index reading at the end of the trading day.

P/E is the price-to-earnings ratio for the index or sub-index (the weighted average earnings per share in relation to the weighted average price).

INTERNATIONAL INDEXES

— 52 week high	low		Close	Net chg	% chg
Japan					
20833.21	14464.56	Nikkei	14664.64	-323.90	-2.16
1754.78	1379.96	Topix	1395.71	-21.31	-1.50
Britain					
4156.80	3321.70	FT Ords	3557.60	-53.30	-1.48
6930.20	5994.60	FTSE 100	6274.80	-125.40	-1.96
3421.63	2979.73	FT 500	3001.60	-53.16	-1.74
3261.57	2852.60	FT All Shr	3014.18	-57.48	-1.87
3934.25	3270.08	FT EurTop	3653.31	-48.32	-1.31
Germany					
2502.47	1820.20	FAZ	2050.95	-57.63	-2.73
8064.97	5814.74	DAX	6742.10	-109.59	-1.60

NET CHANGE is in points and % change is that point move expressed as a percentage. For tables published during the week, the change is from the previous day's close. Tables in weekend editions have weekly summaries for the indexes with change from the previous week, a month ago and a year ago.

WHERE YOUR INFORMATION IS COMING FROM

Pssst! Wanna buy a hot stock?

Lots of people have advice on investing and one piece of good advice is to look carefully at the source of the information.

A famous stock market story is attributed to Joe Kennedy, patriarch of the U.S. political family, who made a fortune on Wall Street in the 1920s. Kennedy started selling after a shoeshine boy offered him a stock tip. He concluded the market was overextended if shoeshine boys were buying.

Stocks often are sold, not bought, and the selling usually is done by promoters. This is a recognized role in the securities business and, in the best light, a promoter raises money for a start-up venture that might otherwise not be able to find financing.

IT IS BUYER BEWARE WHEN SEARCHING STOCK TIPS ON THE INTERNET

Many of Canada's established mining houses started out as penny stock ventures under the guidance of a promoter and the early investors struck paydirt when the company found commercial grades of ore. But prospecting is a high risk business and over the years the majority of the juniors don't strike it rich.

There is a similar failure rate for fledgling high-tech firms. A modern forum for stock tips is the Internet. Chat lines are a regular source of investment tips and readers should be aware the format of the Net makes it easy for unscrupulous promoters to conceal their identities to casual readers.

WHO ARE THE BROKERS AND WHAT DO THEY DO?

Broker is a term that covers a lot of ground and investors need to be clear on whose interests are being represented by the various specialists in the investment industry. Traders, corporate finance specialists, fund managers and salespeople all fit into the general category of brokers and their roles in the business are much different.

As well, the roles of the firms can be different. Chartered banks now have a dominant position in the securities industry and some banks have more than one brokerage subsidiary to cover different roles.

TRADITIONALLY, A BROKER ACTS AS AN INTERMEDIARY BETWEEN BUYER AND SELLER

The traditional brokerage function is to serve as an intermediary between buyer and seller. This can be done by discount brokers, firms that simply execute a transaction when an investor makes his or her own decisions.

When research is added to the brokerage function, the investor pays higher commissions because advice is part of the service. Research departments provide recommendations on which stocks to buy or sell and on appropriate weighting in a portfolio among stocks, bonds and other types of investments.

CHINESE WALLS ARE INFORMATION BARRIERS THAT PROTECT CONFLICTS OF INTEREST

Large investment dealers also represent the issuers of securities, which leads to an industry concept called "Chinese walls" in Canada and "firewalls" in the U.S. These are information barriers within a firm that are designed to isolate potential conflicts of interest between, for instance, a firm's corporate finance department, which is representing a company issuing stock, and its investment advisers, who are selling the shares to clients.

PORTFOLIO MANAGERS TAILOR THE PORTFOLIO TO THE CLIENT

Big firms also trade for their own accounts. This is standard practice in bond trading, as trading by the large firms provides liquidity to the market and gives the firm an inventory of bonds from which to fill small orders. Most stock trading is done to fill client orders but specialist traders within a firm can hold inventories from day to day.

THE LOWDOWN | ON DIVIDENDS

Dividends are the returns on an equity stake. Dividend announcements may also affect stock prices if there is a change in a regular pattern, if a company that has not paid dividends begins paying, if a dividend-paying company omits a dividend or if there is a change in the rate.

Stock dividends will be announced by companies in advance of payment. **The pay date** indicates when the dividend will be paid. **The record column** indicates that investors who were on record as owners of the companies' shares on that date will receive the dividend.

Stocks will trade ex-dividend (without dividend) from the second business day before the record date. The ex-dividend date is significant if shares are bought or sold around dividend time because the share price normally drops when the dividend is paid (a market adjustment for the payout). The calculation of ex-dividend date has to do with the fact that a stock trade is settled on the third business day after the transaction. Thus, the issue of whether the dividend goes to the new owner or the old owner is based on when the money changes hands in a stock transaction.

D I V I D E N D S

Figures supplied by FP DataGroup

Details	Dividend amount	Pay date	Record date
Dividends declared			
Regular			
CAE	.05	Dec 29	Dec 15
Extndcare II	.125	Dec 15	Nov 30
Onex	.0275	Jan 31	Jan 10
Yield Mgmt	.16	Nov 30	Nov 30
Stocks ex-dividend			
Wednesday			
Algoma Ocntl	.15	Dec 1	Nov 17
BC Gas	.31	Nov 30	Nov 17
BP Amoco	u.35	Dec 11	Nov 17
British Air	e1.10817	Feb 7	Nov 17
Enbridge	.3225	Dec 1	Nov 17
Enbridge 5.5pf	.34375	Dec 1	Nov 17
Falconbrdg pf	.3672	Dec 1	Nov 17
Metalore Res	i.055	Dec 8	Nov 17
Nrth West Fund	.54	Dec 15	Nov 17
Quebecor A	.13	Dec 13	Nov 17

Investors who are not comfortable with making decisions themselves can turn to portfolio managers. For small investors, that means mutual funds. A large portfolio can be managed by an investment specialist who tailors the portfolio to the client. Portfolio managers charge fees for their services and their costs include trading fees. Typically, these fund managers are among those who negotiate cut-rate fees for stock trades.

When a client buys or sells a security directly, there is a commission on the transaction. A portion goes to the sales agent and the rest goes to the firm to cover its business costs, which includes salaries and commissions for traders who actually do the share deal for the client.

Fees vary from firm to firm, and clients who do a lot of business often can negotiate commissions. In Canada, brokers must complete the Canadian Securities Course – a comprehensive study course dealing with stocks, bonds, analysis of company financial statements and other securities-related matters.

FROM THE BIG FLOOR TO THE SMALL SCREEN

Many people think of stocks and big trading floors when they think of the word exchange, but these days the markets for securities mainly are interlinked networks of computers. Exchanges still exist as intermediaries in the trading of securities and some markets still have large floor operations. More and more, though, the big volume in different markets is being done by trading desks at investment firms and banks.

Computer screens carry offers to buy or sell and the deals are done directly on the screens. Payments are simply electronic transfers and credit lines are regulated by advance authorizations when traders are assigned passwords to sign on to the systems.

Stocks mainly trade through exchanges. Bond trading is mostly done over the counter (OTC), which means transactions are among dealers. But there's more to the securities universe than stock exchanges and dealer trading rooms.

DERIVATIVES ENCOMPASS A BROAD RANGE OF FINANCIAL PRODUCTS

Derivatives are a good way to look at the distinctions between public markets that characterize most trading in stocks and private markets that handle bond transactions. Specialized exchanges, such as the big futures and options markets in Chicago, have developed a broad array of derivatives. Trading is visible and volume is high for benchmark products such as the future on the U.S. government 10-year treasury bond. Those benchmarks tend to serve as pricing guides for their respective cash markets. Over-the-counter derivatives are specialized hedging arrangements. Consider an example where a European pension fund has a large holding of 10-year U.S. government bonds. And a round of downsizing is underway so this fund knows it will have extra pension payouts but can't be sure of how much until all the downsizing decisions are made. It may need to sell some of those bonds and is concerned about possible currency or interest rate fluctuations. The solution is a specialized hedge to lock in a price in case it needs to sell.

These products, tailored to a specific situation, are bought over the counter. Large financial institutions – generally banks and investment dealers – dominate the over-the-counter market because a large capital base is needed to operate at this level.

A STOCK EXCHANGE HAS REGULATORY POWERS OVER BROKERAGE FIRMS

Part of the value of a stock exchange to investment firms is that an exchange's reputation can give credibility to a broker's services because the exchange has regulatory powers over the conduct of brokerage firms.

Since the 1990s there has been a trend to establish a business model for stock exchanges. Owners have shares and share ownership may be open to the public. This trend has been led by private trading networks made possible by computers. In Canada, both the Toronto and Montreal exchanges have taken the privatization route. Each of these exchanges has converted itself from a co-operative structure, which is the historical model for a stock exchange. In a co-operative structure, each firm that trades on the exchange must be a member. Being part of the club is called owning a seat.

Regardless of the structure, investment dealers must adhere to exchange rules of financial strength, trading practices and business standards. A government oversight agency, such as the Ontario Securities Commission, will have veto power over rules of the exchange and will provide guidance in the creation of those rules. Typically, a large Canadian brokerage firm will be represented on the Canadian exchanges and the New York Stock Exchange. Some have a formal presence on other world exchanges.

EACH OF CANADA'S FIVE STOCK EXCHANGES SPECIALIZES IN DIFFERENT AREAS

The Toronto Stock Exchange, which first set up shop in 1852, is by far the largest stock exchange in Canada. It accounts for more than 90% of the value of all domestic trading. Bay Street is synonymous with the TSE, just as Wall Street means the New York Stock Exchange to most people. From 1937 to 1983 the TSE was located on Bay Street in Toronto's financial district. Now it's just around the corner on King Street and since the spring of 2000 has been known formally as The Toronto Stock Exchange Inc.

Ironically, the TSE moved because it needed more room for its trading floor. But the trading floor was closed in 1997 and has been replaced by a network of computer terminals that link the exchange with trading rooms in brokerage firms.

The Montreal stock exchange dates to 1874 and its stock trading operations are mainly in shares of Quebec-based companies. It has carved out a specialty in derivatives trading and became Bourse de Montreal Inc. following its 2000 demutualization. In English Canada, it's still known colloquially as the ME. Its futures contract on three-month bankers' acceptance notes has gained wide acceptance as a pricing guideline in the money market. Trading in derivatives has been done in pits on the trading floor but the floor operation was to move to a computer network in 2001.

Canada's history of rich mining discoveries has long been the basis for over-the-counter markets in speculative junior stocks. As the economy has matured, promoters that work this turf have expanded into technology stocks. The penny stock market has

QUARTERLY SNAPSHOT | TABLES

The Quarterly Snapshot is a series of 10 sets of tables usually published on the first Saturday or within the following week after the end of each quarterly period. These tables cover key financial and market developments for leading public companies in Canada.

Top TSE % winners

Rk	Stock	Ticker	Vol 00s	06.30 cls	09.29 cls	—52-wk— high	low	Net % chg
1	Salix Pharma	SLX	36898	2.30	10.85	11.00	0.175	+371.7
2	Magnifoam Tch	MTG	54432	1.25	4.05	4.60	0.90	+224.0
3	Janna Systems	JAN	206474	27.25	83.00	85.70	11.75	+204.6
4	MOSAID Tech	MSD	105348	20.00	53.70	67.50	11.10	+168.5

Top TSE net winners

Rk	Stock	Ticker	Vol 00s	06.30 cls	09.29 cls	—52-wk— high	low	Net chg
1	Resrch Motion	RIM	338269	66.70	149.00	260.00	35.00	+82.30
2	Janna Systems	JAN	206474	27.25	83.00	85.70	11.75	+55.75
3	NPS Allelix	NX	7959	37.60	85.00	85.00	12.30	+47.40
4	MOSAID Tech	MSD	105348	20.00	53.70	67.50	11.10	+33.70

Top TSE % losers

Rk	Stock	Ticker	Vol 00s	06.30 cls	09.29 cls	—52-wk— high	low	Net % chg
1	Hart Stores	HIS	22477	2.65	0.30	8.05	0.25	-88.7
2	Microforum	MCF	250707	7.80	1.68	15.00	1.50	-78.5
3	Pacific Rim	PFG	45383	4.55	1.50	5.65	1.06	-67.0
4	IDS Intellgnt	ISD	89377	2.15	0.73	11.00	0.55	-66.0

Top TSE net losers

Rk	Stock	Ticker	Vol 00s	06.30 cls	09.29 cls	—52-wk— high	low	Net chg
1	JDS Uniph Cda	JDU	421951	177.10	143.10	219.00	43.28	-34.00
2	E-L Finl	ELF	1106	205.00	175.00	220.00	110.00	-30.00
3	GSI Lumonics	LSI	98330	51.90	24.75	64.00	7.60	-27.15
4	Nurun	IFN	13066	42.25	17.60	89.00	8.25	-24.65

The first four sets of tables in the series are the winners and losers on the Toronto, Montreal and CDNX stock exchanges. This series is much like the daily gainers and losers tables, except that **the quarterly series** highlights the top 25 and the bottom 25 on a quarterly basis. **Quarterly winners and losers** are counted on a net basis and a percentage basis. **Net change** is simply the dollar amount and this list generally includes stocks that start from a price level that is higher than average. **The percentage change table** tends to pick up lower-priced stocks that are more speculative. But this list does provide a valuable guide to the changing fortunes of some industry sectors and companies whose fortunes are rising and falling. Investors should check the volume numbers in these lists because a large price move on small volume may not be significant.

Top 25 dividend yields on the TSE - common

Rk Stock	Ticker	Cls. 09.29.	Ann. div.	% yield	Freq.	Most recent rate chg.	Pymt @ curr. rate
1 Split Yld cap	YLD	10.55	1.80	17.1	q	July 31, 1998	s	9
2 Amisk A	AS.A	2.05	0.30	14.6	q	Jan. 15, 2000	s	4
3 Glendale Intl	GIN	2.00	0.25	12.5	s	Jan. 20, 2000	i	2
4 Fst Aust Prm xc	FAP	7.05	0.84	11.9	m	July 14, 2000	d	4
5 Le Chateau	CTU.A	3.45	0.40	11.6	q	May 15, 1998	i	11

Top 25 dividend yields on the TSE - preferred

Rk Stock	Ticker	Cls. 09.29	Ann. div.	% yield	Eligible for — redemption — $	date
1 B Split pf A	BST.PR.A	27.50	3.88	14.1	n.a.	Dec. 1, 2002
2 Ivaco pf sr5	IVA.PR.I	24.00	2.62	10.9	25.00	now
3 Ivaco pf srD	IVA.PR.D	24.00	2.50	10.4	25.00	now
4 Pac NthGas nf	PNG.PR.A	16.50	1.68	10.2	26	now

The next three sets of tables in this series concentrate on the blue chips listed on the Toronto Stock Exchange. The pair of tables on dividend yield highlight the common and preferred stock issues that paid the return. **Dividend yield** is simply the dividend stated as a percentage of the price. The table on **common share dividends** includes a column showing the date at which the current dividend rate was set. Companies with long-standing, stable dividend policies are prized by investors. **The preferred dividend table** Includes columns on redemption price and redemption date, which is the price at which the shares may be bought back by the company and the date on which the buyback rights become effective. (In this table, "now" means the issue can be redeemed at any time.)

Price/earning ratios on the TSE
Lowest   Highest

Stock	Ticker	09.29 cls.	EPS	P/E	Stock	Ticker	09.29 cls.	EPS	P/E
Metals & Minerals				13.3					
Sth Am Gold	SAG	0.085	u 0.04	1.4	Dynatec	DY	0.28	0.01	56.0
Inmet Mining	IMN	2.15	0.98	2.2	Western Garnet	WG	0.78	u 0.01	51.9
Denison Mines	DEN	0.10	0.03	3.3	Aur Res	AUR	3.15	0.08	39.4
Solitario Res	SLR	1.40	u 0.28	3.3	Highwood Res	HWD	0.55	0.03	22.0
Sherritt Intl	S	4.80	1.29	3.7	Cameco	CCO	19.50	1.19	16.4

The price earnings table shows the highest and lowest ratios among the industry sectors represented by subindexes in the Toronto Stock Exchange 300 index. The **ratio of price to earnings** is generally considered to be an indicator of whether a stock is over- or undervalued. **P/E** is current market price divided by annual earnings per share.

TSE lowest price/book value per share

Rk	Stock	Ticker	Cls 09.29	Book value per sh	$ per
1	Hart Stores	HIS	0.30	6.22	0.05
2	Tenke Mining	TNK	0.78	15.85	0.05
3	Loewen Grp	LWN	0.42	u 3.87	0.08
4	Agro Pac A	API	0.14	1.84	0.08
5	Laminco Res	LMR	0.04	0.47	0.09
6	Gldn Rule Res	GNU	0.065	0.53	0.12

TSE highest price/book value per share

Rk	Stock	Ticker	Cls 09.29	Book value per sh	$ per
1	Sun Life Finl	SLC	31.05	0.01	3105.00
2	Kasten Chase	KCA	5.55	0.07	79.29
3	Minacs Wrldwd	MXW	0.68	0.01	68.00
4	01 Communique	ONE	6.70	0.10	67.00
5	IMI Int Med	IMI	4.50	0.08	56.25
6	Genetronics	GEB	2.30	u 0.03	52.90
7	Infowave Soft	IW	10.50	u 0.15	48.54
8	Vasogen	VAS	13.20	0.29	45.52
9	Second Cup	SKL	8.00	0.18	44.44
10	Wi-LAN	WIN	36.80	0.85	43.29

Tables showing the highest and lowest price-to-book ratios measure companies on a break-up value basis. **Book value** is asset value on the balance sheet that is attributed to the owners, which means shareholders in the case of a public company. **Book value per share** simply divides the total for shareholder equity by the number of shares. **Price per book value** is the share price divided by the book value per share.

QUARTERLY SNAPSHOT

Figures supplied by FP DataGroup

Toronto 35 earnings estimates

Name	Symbol	Quarter end	Report expected	Yr. ago EPS $	No. of analysts	High $	Low $	Mean $
Barrick Gold	ABX	3/31	21/04	0.15	9	0.20	0.17	0.18
Alcan Aluminium	AL	3/31	16/04	0.46	14	0.52	0.32	0.48
Bombardier Cl.b	BBD	1/31	21/04	0.43	2	0.43	0.36	0.40

The final table in this quarterly series is a survey of forecasts by investment house analysts of corporate profits for the companies that make up the Toronto Stock Exchange index of 35 stocks. The "report expected" column shows the date on which the company is scheduled to issue financial results for the most recent quarter. Most Canadian companies have a fiscal year that coincides with the calendar year. The "quarter end" column shows the different dates. "Year ago EPS $" means earnings per share for the year ago quarterly period expressed in C$. "No. of analysts" refers to those who contributed to this report and the next three columns give the high, low and average (mean) for the forecasts by this group.

been a persistent headache for securities regulators because of the potential for abuse or fraud in OTC selling to unsophisticated investors.

The Vancouver Stock Exchange has been the main public market for shares of junior companies but there have been active markets in other regional exchanges as well. In November 1999, the VSE merged with the Alberta Stock Exchange, which dealt mainly with Alberta-based resources companies, to form the Canadian Venture Exchange (CDNX). Subsequently, CDNX acquired the Canadian Dealing Network and the Winnipeg Stock Exchange. Canadian Dealing Network had been a Toronto-based over-the-counter market run by the Toronto Stock Exchange. After the merger of those four separate entities, CDNX had listings for about 2,600 companies active in the technology, resource, industrial and manufacturing sectors.

BUILDING A CROWD AND MAKING A MARKET

The "crowd" is an important concept in securities trading. It means having a big enough group of buyers and sellers to ensure the best price is set when a trade is done.

Building a crowd for trading has a long history, from early trading in farm animals through the "curb" market in London, where stock trading was originally done on the street.

Brokerage firms have traders who buy or sell on behalf of their clients but the crowd can be small if a company's shares are not being traded actively.

When there is little trading, a market is illiquid and an investor risks not getting the best price.

Over the years, securities markets have adopted various practices to build liquidity.

The New York Stock Exchange has a group of traders called "$2 brokers." They are independent traders who trade for a fee on behalf of brokerage firms. Their fee used to be US$2 for a board lot (100 shares) and by spreading the business around, a firm could move a large stock order without disrupting the market.

Stock exchanges also have "locals" as traders. They trade for their own accounts and may be managers of pools of investment funds.

MARKET-MAKERS STEP IN TO BUY OR SELL AND MAINTAIN LIQUIDITY

Specialists are a key element in ensuring liquidity on Canadian exchanges. They're also known as registered traders or market-makers and their role is to stand ready to buy or sell up to a pre-set limit.

If an order can't be filled by a regular trader because there is an imbalance of orders, the specialist provides a bid or an offer.

Specialists are essentially independent traders who are bankrolled by securities firms and they earn their keep by trading for their own account or a share of the return on a firm's account.

QUARTERLY EARNINGS | SURVEY

The quarterly profit survey covers the key financial numbers for the major companies in the Toronto Stock Exchange 300 index. It usually runs the sixth Saturday after the calendar quarter end and eighth Saturday after the calendar yearend. The categories in the table correspond to the subindexes in the TSE 300. The figures are for the most recent quarter compared with a year ago.

Generally, year-to-year comparisons are made with quarter reports in order to account for any seasonal factors in a particular industry.

Revenue is money taken in from operations and does not include special items, such as a sale of assets.

Net income is operating profit after taxes, depreciation and amortization.

EPS is basic earnings per share, which is net income divided by the number of shares outstanding. This calculation does not include shares that may be issued at a future date on exercise of options or other share issue obligations that a company might have.

Cash flow from operations shows the cash kicked off from day-to-day operations of a company, before extraordinary items.

Figures in $millions		--- Q3 revenues ---			--- Q3 net income ---			--- Q3 EPS ---		cash flow ops	
	Ticker	1998	1997	% chg	1998	1997	% chg	1998	1997	1998	%chg
Metals & Minerals											
Alcan Aluminium Ltd.*	AL	2,950.4	2,697.4	+9%	161.9	110.7	+46%	0.70	0.47	443.3	+57%
Aur Resources Inc.	AUR	25.1	23.9	+5%	-0.8	1.3	n.m.	-0.01	0.02	6.9	+9%
Total		6,690.9	8,040.1	-17%	144.6	303.2	-52%	...	...	642.6	-52%
Gold & Precious Minerals											
Aber Resources Ltd. (Jul. 31)	ABZ	nil	nil	n.m.	0.2	-0.2	n.m.	0.01	-0.01	0.7	n.m.
Barrick Gold Corp.*	ABX	490.2	434.6	+13%	115.0	-436.0	n.m.	0.30	-1.16	220.9	+30%
Total		1,363.8	1,291.7	+6%	159.0	-399.2	n.m.	...	...	549.9	+41%

For example, an exchange may stipulate all orders for XYZ Ltd. stock up to 399 shares will be filled; this is known as the minimum guaranteed fill.

If an order is made to sell 300 shares at the market price, and only 200 shares are available, the specialist responsible for XYZ stock will immediately sell the remaining 100 shares.

COMPUTER PROGRAMS AID INVESTMENT DEALERS TO BUY AND SELL STOCK COMBINATIONS

Modern technology not only has made buying and selling stocks a faster, simpler process, but has had an effect on share prices. Some exchanges have stayed with the traditional open outcry on a trading floor, where traders shout their buy or sell orders. But computer-based trading systems are steadily replacing the trading floors.

One of the most pronounced effects of computerization is program trading. It's a complex strategy whereby investment dealers and their large corporate and institutional clients use computer programs to trigger buy and sell orders in many different securities. Depending on the levels of stock prices, stock market index options and stock market index futures, computers will automatically trigger these orders. If enough dealers follow the same route, stock prices may soar or plunge in a very short time.

Obviously, volatility is not good for markets. But computer trading has had a positive impact as well. Use of computers has been a major factor in narrowing the spread between bid and ask prices. When stock trading began in North America, $\frac{1}{8}$ of a dollar was adopted as the increment for changes in prices. So the difference between bid and ask would be $12\frac{1}{2}$ cents for an active stock and often more for those with lower trading volumes. Stock exchanges in Canada have adopted decimal trading and the spread between bid and ask can be as low as a penny. A narrow spread makes it easier for buyers and sellers to reach a market price and that makes for more efficient trading.

PROOF OF OWNERSHIP NOT NORMALLY REQUIRED

Just as credit cards have reduced demand for paper money, electronic record-keeping has diminished the importance of physical proof of ownership of securities. It's possible to get a certificate but fewer investors see the need to take physical possession of their shares. That's just fine with investment dealers because it's expensive to process and deliver a piece of paper.

The system of securities registration that has evolved has brought about considerable savings for the dealers. It works much like the system used by banks in moving money from one institution to another. It's called "netting" and anonymity of ownership is what makes it work.

ELECTRONIC RECORDS OF TRANSACTIONS ARE KEPT AT THE CDS

When ownership of a security is not registered to the buyer, it is said to be in "street name." That means the record of ownership is in a broker's files.

"The street" is a jargon term for the collection of brokerage houses that make up the dealer community.

Another component of the street is the Canadian Depository for Securities Ltd. (CDS), which is the organization that maintains electronic records for investment dealers, trust companies and banks.

Before there was central record-keeping, dealers would deliver certificates along the street to settle up for each day's trades.

BROKER, TRUST COMPANY AND BANK HOLDINGS ARE CALCULATED DAILY

Now, they simply report the trades to CDS and CDS adjusts the accounts of each firm. Instead of recording each trade in each security, CDS changes the net holdings at the end of each day.

Stocks held in brokerage house accounts by CDS mainly represent shares held in street name by the brokers. CDS files now hold dealer records for more than $1 trillion worth of stocks and bonds.

Those who actually take delivery of a certificate will find the following information printed on the document:

• **The name of the issuer,** either a company or a government.

• **Par value,** if applicable (otherwise it will say "no par value") and the number of shares (if it's a stock) or value (if it's a bond) represented by the certificate.

• **Conditions,** if any, attached to the security, such as how many votes each common share carries.

• **Details of transfer of ownership.**

• **Reproductions of the signatures of authorized signing officers.**

• **A CUSIP number.** CUSIP stands for Committee on Uniform Securities Identification Procedures and each security issue has a unique number.

EARNINGS SUMMARY | TABLE

Publicly traded companies report their earnings, or profits, four times a year. These earnings are the gauge of a company's success.

EARNINGS SUMMARY

Figures supplied by Canada NewsWire and other sources

COMPANY AND TICKER SYMBOL → · FISCAL YEAREND ←

CURRENT FIGURES → · YEAR AGO FIGURES ←

	Current	Yr.ago	%chg.
Brick Brewing Company (BRB/TSE) Oct. 31 - 3rd Q			
Revenue (000s)	5,245	5,458	-4
Net Income (000s)	(297)	(1,024)	71
EPS	(0.02)	(0.09)	
9 mos.			
Revenue (000s)	17,085	19,271	-11
Net Income (000s)	32	(574)	
EPS	n.a.	(0.05)	
Buhler Industries Inc (BUI/TSE) Sep. 30 - Year			
Revenue (000s)	116,700	79,961	46
Net Income (000s)	7,298	5,797	26

Earnings are what is left after payment of all expenses and are generally stated on the basis of continuing operations. For example, if a company sells a plant because it is dropping a particular line of business, the gain from the sale of the asset and any losses from the operation being sold would be reported separately in the earnings statement.

If a company has no earnings, another reliable measure of its financial record is cash flow, which is net income plus non-cash deductions such as depreciation. That means a company has enough funds to carry on day-to-day operations but is not bringing in enough money to cover future needs, such as buying replacement equipment.

Earnings reports should state the results for the last quarter and for the fiscal year to date. Comparisons are always with the prior year because most companies are affected by seasonal factors and a change from a year earlier will almost always be more significant than from a previous quarter.

CALCULATING THE TSE 300'S MOVES

The moves of the Toronto Stock Exchange index of 300 stocks are calculated by computer at the TSE and the computer program picks up every trade on a running basis during each trading session.

**The formula for calculating the TSE 300 index is
(aggregate float-quoted market value/divisor) X 1,000.**

It sounds complicated but it's actually a straightforward calculation. Aggregate float-quoted market value is a mouthful and it is easier to understand one bite at a time.
Aggregate simply means total.
Float-quoted means the number of free-trading shares listed on the exchange. That's the total number of shares issued minus the number of shares in the control block (when an individual or a group holds a controlling block of shares, that stock is not free-trading).
Market value means the price of the latest trade. Thus, the float-quoted market value is calculated for each listed company and these values are added together to get the aggregate.
The divisor is an invention that adjusts for changes in the composition of the index.

A common reason for change is when a company issues additional shares. Another reason the index changes is substitution, such as when a stock issue disappears because of a takeover and shares of another company are put into the index.

An easier example to follow is a stock split. When a stock is split two-for-one, the price drops in half when the split takes effect. A lower price would bring down the index value but in this case the number of shares in circulation is doubled.

The divisor adjusts for these changes in composition so that the index level is the same immediately before and after each change. The result of dividing market value by the divisor is then multiplied by 1,000 because the TSE 300 index was started at 1,000 in 1975 and this remains the base year for the index.

TRADING SECURITIES OVER THE COUNTER

Securities trading not done on exchanges is said to be done over the counter, a term that goes back to a time when shares could be bought over the counters of banks, investment dealers and even stores. Now, though, it means securities traded between dealers or sold directly by a financial institution to a client.

A general rule for OTC trading is that buyers should be more sophisticated about investing and they should have a keen understanding of risk.

WEEKLY UPCOMING EARNINGS | TABLE

UPCOMING EARNINGS

Figures supplied by First Call — firstcall@wsbi.com

Company	Ticker	Period	Consensus estimate $	Number of estimates	Earnings yr ago $
Monday					
Laurentian Bank of Canada	LB	4Q	0.78	2	0.51
Wednesday					
Bank of Nova Scotia	BNS	4Q	0.90	5	0.76
GTC Transcontinental Group	GRT	4Q	0.58	2	0.57
Thursday					
Cdn. Imperial Bank of Comm.	CM	4Q	0.93	6	0.68
Canadian Western Bank	CWB	4Q	0.67	3	0.47
Gildan Activewear (US$)	GIL	4Q	0.75	6	0.48

Profits are the most important numbers for mature companies and forecasts are published Mondays in this table. The predictions are the consensus view of investment analysts who follow the companies. The column to the right of the estimate gives the number of analysts who contributed. Usually, these are quarterly forecasts and the period column gives the fiscal period. The outlook for the current quarter is compared with the actual figure from a year earlier because year-to-year comparisons account for seasonal factors that might affect the business.

At one end of the OTC scale are custom-made hedges that banks and investment firms create for major clients. A large corporation with extensive foreign operations will need OTC contracts to cover the risks of currency fluctuations or interest rate changes. These OTC contracts are designed for a specific set of circumstances and many are unique to a specific situation.

At the other end are stocks bought by ordinary investors. Many people think of OTC trading as investing in speculative junior stocks. But some very big companies – Microsoft Corp. for example – have built their shareholder base through an over-the-counter market.

BONDS, CURRENCIES AND STOCKS TRADE OVER THE COUNTER

Bond and currency trading is done on interdealer markets and these transactions account for the biggest share of the dollar value of OTC trading. Rules are established by tradition and regulation. Pricing is efficient for actively traded issues and those heavy traders act as benchmarks for related securities.

In the U.S., the major OTC market is the National Association of Securities Dealers Automated Quotation system, or Nasdaq. This interdealer market has different levels of listing requirements and the Nasdaq senior board includes some of the largest U.S. corporations. Nasdaq listings do include many dividend-paying stocks and the dealer-run computer trading system operates like a stock exchange.

Overseas markets have followed the Nasdaq lead and the OTC market for stocks is no longer confined to shares sold by financing houses for high-risk startups. But those speculative issues, mainly in resource and technology sectors, still are a significant part of the OTC universe.

REASONS CAN VARY FOR AN OTC LISTING

Sometimes these companies trade over the counter because they are struggling ventures that cannot justify the expense of being listed on an exchange. But sometimes the reason is that the company cannot meet the exchange's listing requirements for capital adequacy. And sometimes the promoters of OTC stocks are less than forthright about the company's prospects.

Another reason for selling shares over the counter is that trading volume is too low to justify the cost of an exchange listing. Large multinational firms – for example, an overseas firm with a small number of shareholders in North America – might be in this category.

When investors look at shares in an OTC market they should look at the reason for that type of listing and assess the potential risk. A big issue in assessing OTC securities is liquidity. Low trading volume often is the reason a stock is sold on an OTC market, which means the shareholder might not be able to sell quickly. Lack of liquidity also means inefficient pricing.

UNDERSTANDING THE REGULATORY NETWORK

Regulation of Canadian financial intermediaries is divided between federal and provincial governments, so investors with a beef need to understand the distinctions when pursuing a complaint.

The basic distinction is that banking is regulated federally and securities trading is regulated provincially. But the reality of ownership of financial institutions makes the situation much more complex.

Chartered banks now own securities dealers so Ottawa has a role in overseeing these large financial conglomerates.

Large brokerage firms operate nationally and internationally, so the scope of their operations is beyond the jurisdiction of a single agency.

Credit unions can look much like banks but they are under provincial jurisdiction.

Insurance companies have expanded into certain investment areas and regulation of insurance is split between the two levels of government.

A further wrinkle in the regulatory network is that part of the industry is self-regulating under legislation authorizing "SROs" – self-regulating organizations.

Stock exchanges are SROs and they have rule-making power over the brokerage firms that are the owners of the exchanges. The Investment Dealers Association, which has an industry lobby role, also is an SRO with audit and enforcement authority over the brokerage firms and their employees.

The first question for anyone with a complaint about a securities industry practice or an action by a employee of a financial institution should be: Who is the principal regulator?

HERE IS A QUICK LIST OF REGULATORS

• The Office of the Superintendent of Financial Institutions is the federal regulator for banks, trusts, loan companies and federally registered pension plans.

• In broad terms, provincial securities commissions set policy. Subordinate regulators, such as the stock exchanges, do the policing. However, the commissions can pursue disciplinary matters (high-profile cases involving mutual fund managers is an example). Each province has a securities commission but the scope of their activities varies widely. The Ontario Securities Commission is the largest, a recognition of the fact that Toronto has the largest concentration of head offices of public corporations. The OSC often provides services to smaller commissions. The Quebec commission is a regional force and the commissions in British Columbia and Alberta have expertise in regulating resource companies. As a way of creating national standards, the provincial securities commissions have created an organization called Canadian Securities Administrators. This is an unofficial but effective way for commissions to co-ordinate their positions on major policy matters that cross provincial boundaries. The commissions oversee the SROs in their jurisdiction and act as an appeal body for challenges to decisions made by SROs.

• Stock exchanges used to have extensive audit responsibilities for brokerage firms but that relationship is changing and the primary responsibility of the exchanges is regulation of trading.

• The Investment Dealers Association has primary audit jurisdiction for most brokerage firms and it conducts disciplinary hearings in most cases where a broker is caught in allegations of misconduct.

• The Canadian Investor Protection Fund operates as an insurance fund to cover investor losses, up to a pre-set limit, in the event of a brokerage house failure. Its role is similar to that of the Canada Deposit Insurance Corp., which covers deposit losses in bank failures.

• The Investment Funds Institute of Canada (IFIC) represents the mutual fund industry. Its responsibilities include administering education courses as licensing requirements for those wishing to sell mutual funds. IFIC also acts as a lobby group for the industry on regulatory issues.

CHAPTER 2

UNDERSTANDING | EQUITIES

- The basics of buying and selling equities

- Block trades

- Bid and ask tables

- North American indexes

- Foreign market strategies

- Technical analysis

CANADA'S INVESTING MOSAIC

THE MARKETPLACE FOR STOCKS IS RELATIVELY SMALL BUT

GEMS CAN BE FOUND | BY PATRICK BLOOMFIELD

THE ART OF INVESTING IN STOCKS can be described as picking a reasonable spread of securities that promise to provide the best return at the lowest relative risk. In that respect, the Canadian marketplace can be a gold mine for a private investor with a talent for uncovering hitherto undiscovered stock values and a somewhat tougher place to dig for value for the money-laden investment professional. To understand the difference, keep in mind the Toronto Stock Exchange, which handles more than 90% of the business done on Canada's stock exchanges, is actually two markets. And one of those two can be divided in two sub-categories.

The senior market comprises 200 to 300 of the roughly 1,400 companies listed. Pension fund and mutual fund portfolio managers all tend to concentrate their holdings in this relatively narrow stock universe.

As a result, the prices of the stocks within it tend to respond more rapidly to any market rumor or news item and to be more tightly priced than others, particularly as Canadian rules stipulate 70% of the book value of a tax-deferred portfolio must be held in Canadian securities.

INVESTORS SHOULD DO SOME RESEARCH BEFORE ENTERING THE JUNIOR MARKET

The more junior market is made up of 1,000 or so TSE-listed companies and can prove a very happy hunting ground for private investors prepared to devote time and money to doing their own research. There's one caveat. The smaller the portion of a company's share capital that is available for public trading, the harder it can be to find ready and willing buyers when you want out.

This can be particularly the case when investing in one of companies specifically listed as "junior" stocks. This collection of smaller companies – roughly a quarter of the total listed – has less stringent listing qualifications but they are subject to special reporting requirements.

For the investor who is seeking a larger selection of smaller, more speculative, companies, there is ample additional choice, coupled with an ample degree of risk, in the stocks listed on the CDNX stock exchanges. For an investor who feels comfortable with political uncertainties, there is a selection of Quebec-based companies that are listed solely on the Bourse de Montreal.

A good starting point for an investor with an entrepreneurial bent is a look at the spate of new listings in the mid-1990s of entrepreneurially run public corporations. These emerging businesses represent a big change from 20 or 30 years ago when the TSE had half as many companies on its lists as it has today. In the 1970s and earlier, TSE listing boards were heavily larded with branch plant operations of U.S. majors and with Canadian companies under the control of a relatively small clique of family owners.

MANY JUNIOR STOCK COMPANIES ARE STILL RUN BY THOSE WHO STARTED THEM

Today, this "old" investment money is being replaced steadily with new money invested in younger companies, and the previous entrenchment of voting control of the more senior companies is gradually being eroded.

Trends in Canadian corporate governance have been tracked for many years by Fairvest Proxy Monitor Corp. When it was Fairvest Securities Corp. in the early 1980s, it surveyed the 300 stocks in the TSE composite index and found that almost half were stocks of closely controlled companies. More than 50% of the stock in these companies was held by a controlling shareholder or related group. By the late 1990s, less than one quarter of the TSE 300 companies had a control bloc that exercised majority control. The less happy side of this trend, however, is that 58 of the 300 listings in the index at the start of 2001 were from companies with "dual-class" capital. That means the voting power of outside shareholders is either restricted or nonexistent.

An assessment of the integrity and calibre of management, therefore, has to be an investment priority. One excellent yardstick is the extent to which employees are treated as partners in the company. Back in the late 1980s, Linamar Corp.'s majority owner, Frank Hasenfratz, insisted his underwriters restrain the price of the company's initial public offering – just to ensure his employee shareholders had a good ride.

Linamar subsequently posted outstanding investment returns, ranking as a top TSE performer.

THE CANADIAN MARKET CAN HOLD SOME REAL BARGAINS

There is another characteristic of Canadian markets that should also be kept in mind. They are better suited to those investors who hunt for stocks with a rifle rather than a shotgun. By and large, Canadian juniors tend to be more modestly valued than their U.S. counterparts, being followed by relatively few financial analysts and having a history that is often less well known. So, painstaking individual research can turn up bargains.

On the other hand, Canadian markets are not as well suited to investors who want to spread their holdings right across the economic spectrum. The TSE composite index is made up of only 39 business and industry subsector indexes. Its U.S. equivalent, the Standard & Poor's 500-stock composite, has more than 100 subsectors, reflecting a far greater diversity of listed stocks within a much bigger marketplace.

MECHANISMS THAT MAKE STOCK PRICES MOVE

"More buyers than sellers," or the reverse, is an old stock market cliche that has become a fallback explanation when there is no apparent reason for a price move. It's true prices for securities change when there is an imbalance in supply or demand and looking for reasons behind a price move is part of the process of making investment decisions.

General economic conditions are part of this mix, along with tax rates, political policies and how the domestic situation compares with other national economies.

Among the factors that affect the stock of a single company are assessments of management's competence, the extent to which the company has invested in maintaining its competitive position, the general outlook for its industry sector, the general economic climate and the number of shares outstanding.

Changes in fortune for an individual company occur with stock market cycles – a bull market on the way up and a bear on the way down. A rising tide lifts all boats and a bull market in stocks pulls up share prices for companies that have no news that would affect price. Similarly, a bear market will drag down the share values of companies that are prospering and paying dividends.

The term "bear" is thought to come from the expression "to sell the bear's skin before one has caught the bear," which refers to dealers who would sell bearskins before they caught bears. Eventually the term was applied to investors who were pessimistic about

HOW TO READ | THE STOCK TABLES

Equities on Canadian exchanges are shown in decimals. NYSE, Amex, Nasdaq and Unlisted stocks closing at less than $5 are shown in decimals. Those closing at more than $5 are shown in fractions.

Stocks in bold type closed at least 5% higher or lower than the previous board lot closing price. Stocks must close at a minimum $1 and trade at least 500 shares to qualify.

Underlined stocks traded Friday 500% or more above their 60-day average daily volume. Stocks both bold and underlined closed 5% higher on 500%-plus volumes.

	52W high	52W low	Stock	Ticker	Div	Yield %	P/E	Vol 00s	High	Low	Close	Net chg
	↑x29.25	21.15	MaxStocknaMAX	f0.50	1.96	7.4	210501	27.25	27.05	27.20	+0.10
	n 39.25	31.15	MaxStockna MAX	f1.00	2.83	10.3	210501	37.25	37.05	37.20	+0.10
	↓s49.25	41.15	MaxStocknaMAX	f1.50	3.30	13.2	210501	47.25	47.05	47.20	+0.10

1. Up/down arrows indicate a new 52-week high or low in the week's trading
2. 52-week high/low: Highest or lowest inter-day price reached in the previous 52 weeks
3. Stock names have been abbreviated
4. Ticker: Basic trading symbol for primary issues (usually common)
5. Dividend: Indicated annual rate. See footnotes
6. Yield %: Annual dividend rate or amount paid in past 12 months as a percentage of closing price in past 12 months
7. P/E: Price earnings ratio, closing price divided by earnings per share in past 12 months. Figures reported in US$ converted to C$

FRIDAY DATA
8. Volume: Number of shares traded in day in 00s;
nt – no trade;
z – odd lot;
e – exact number of shares
9. High: Highest inter-day trading price or last asking price if no trades. If no asking price . . . shown
10. Low: Lowest inter-day trading price or last bid price if no trades. If no bid price . . . shown
11. Dollar change: Change between board lot closing price and previous board lot closing price

EARNINGS DATA
12. Interim/fiscal: Earnings shown for latest interim or fiscal period, by month and reporting period
13. EPS: Earnings per share for latest reporting period
d – deficit; **u** – US$
14. 12 month EPS: Latest 12 month earnings per share. If earnings are negative, P/E not calculated

WEEK DATA
15. Volume: Number of shares traded in week in 00s
z – odd lot;
e – exact number of shares
16. High: Highest inter-day trading price during week
17. Low: Lowest inter-day trading price during week
18. Cls/last: Closing price or last board lot closing price in the last week
19. Dollar change: Change between board lot closing price and previous week's board lot closing price

If a Canadian listed stock has not traded during the week, its last bid and ask price can be found in the bid/ask table

FOOTNOTES
* – denotes Canadian listed stocks trading in $US
x – stock trades ex-dividend

n – stock is newly listed on exchange in past year
s – stock split in past year
c – stock consolidated in past year
a – spinoff company distributed as shares
♦ – shares carry unusual voting rights
ƒ – denotes companies covered by Financial Post Investor Reports, which may be purchased by calling (416) 350-6500

DIVIDEND/EARNINGS FOOTNOTES
★ – earnings announcement or change in annual dividend during week
r – dividend in arrears
u – US$
p – paid in the past 12 months including extras
y – dividend paid in stock, cash equivalent
f – floating rate, annualized
v – variable rate, annualized based on last payment

The earnings data columns provide the earnings per share for the latest interim period (usually the latest quarter) and the latest 12-month period. The date column in this series shows the month-end for the latest quarter and the stage in the fiscal year for that month.

the outlook for share prices and sold shares they didn't own, gambling the price would later drop so that they could buy them at a lower price.

The origin of "bull" is less certain. It may stem from bull baiting, a sport popular in Europe from the 12th to the 19th century, in which dogs were set loose on bulls chained to a stake. Because there was a similar sport of bear baiting, the stock market interpretation of "bull" may have arisen as a companion term.

Bull and bear markets are largely about expectations. If investors as a group think the economy will improve and corporate profits will grow quickly, they will bid up stock prices in advance. The rule of thumb is that the stock market runs at least six months ahead of the economy.

BULL MARKET OF 1980s AND 1990s WAS DRIVEN BY MICROCHIP REVOLUTION

While the business cycle is the traditional mover of investor expectations, the bull markets in the 1980s and '90s were driven by a supercycle event: the microchip revolution that has put portable computers into offices and homes around the world.

This bull market created a general aura around stock prices until the heady days ended in the spring of 2000, as no bull market lasts forever. Investors must be mindful of the other factors that affect stock prices.

There are two basic lists of reasons for movements in the prices of securities – ones that are specific to an issuer of securities and ones that are general.

For example, a gold mining company's stock price is likely to go up if it has a discovery but prices of all gold miners will appreciate if the price of gold is on the rise.

Or, consider what will happen to prices for bonds of a government-owned hydroelectric utility under two sets of circumstances: If it is downgraded by a credit rating agency, its bond prices will fall; but if interest rates fall in industrial economies because of generally easier credit conditions, prices for its bonds are likely to rise.

RESOURCE STOCKS ARE OFTEN FIRST TO PERFORM AS ECONOMY RECOVERS

One of the major influences on pricing of securities is change in returns from different classes of investments.

For example, a rise in interest rates makes bonds and treasury bills a more attractive alternative for investor funds. As money is diverted into fixed income securities, there is downward pressure on stocks. High interest rates also affect company profit, because companies must pay more to borrow for business expansion.

Within the broad flows of investor funds, there are a variety of factors that affect individual sectors. For example, high-tech stocks in the communications industries were star performers in bull markets of the 1980s and '90s.

But the business cycle remains the dominant influence on share prices and various sectors react differently as economic conditions change. When the economy is coming off a low point in the cycle, rising demand first hits the markets for basic industrial commodities. Thus the resource stocks generally are early performers when the economy is coming out of recession, but they tend to suffer badly in a slowdown when orders are cut back.

A recovery period usually means pent-up demand for housing and durable goods bought by consumers and stock prices will anticipate rising profits for companies supplying these markets.

After the economy peaks and a slowdown begins, interest rates will fall and a decline in the cost of money often means higher profits for companies that have high capital financing costs, such as pipeline or electric utilities.

WHERE TO FIND BASIC DISCLOSURE DOCUMENTS

Disclosure of information by an issuer of securities revolves around one basic definition – the meaning of a material fact. Securities laws define a material fact as information that significantly affects, or would reasonably be expected to have a significant effect on, the market price or value of a security.

Deciding what is material to investors and potential investors is mainly a matter of securities regulation and precedent. In most situations, it's obvious what is material and the definition can vary with the size of the company.

Details of a $10-million order for replacement equipment would not be a material fact for General Motors Corp. because the company's annual budget for capital spending would be many times that amount.

GM has ongoing capital costs, and the totals are disclosed in financial statements, but details would only be material if there were a significant change in the pattern or the amount of the capital budget.

However, details of a $10-million capital project would be material to a small mining exploration company that has a mineral discovery but no track record as a producer.

FOR COMPANIES, THE PERTINENT DETAILS USUALLY ARE FOUND IN CERTAIN DOCUMENTS

• Annual and quarterly reports and Annual Information Forms (AIFs).
• Prospectuses that go out with a new issue of securities.
• Annual information circulars that are sent out to shareholders with a notice for an annual or special meeting.
• Announcement of material corporate developments made through the financial press and professional analysts in the investment business.
• Insider trading reports and other material change reports that are made to securities regulators.

Governments also issue disclosure documents, such as budgets, and information in these documents is material to assessing their bonds.

Investment decisions about bonds, especially corporate bonds, often involve a review of ratings reports from credit rating agencies. These agencies also rate a broad array of corporate securities. The agencies that most widely follow the Canadian marketplace are Dominion Bond Rating Service, Moody's Investors Service and Standard & Poor's/ Canadian Bond Rating Service.

Basic disclosure documents often are available through large public libraries. Corporate information usually can be obtained from a company's transfer agent, which maintains an up-to-date list of shareholders and routinely sends these reports to shareholders. Securities commissions provide for reading rooms to view disclosure documents, but there may be a fee for this service. Some corporate information is available through Internet sites maintained by regulators and many companies also post material information on their Web sites.

HOW INVESTORS CAN USE THE ANNUAL REPORT, PROSPECTUS AND AIF

Annual reports of Canadian public companies contain financial statements for the year under review along with a section called "management discussion and analysis," which is a detailed review of the financial results.

Yearend financial statements must be audited and the annual report must include a note from the auditor. If anything in the statements does not conform to generally accepted accounting principles (GAAP), the auditor must flag the discrepancies.

NEW HIGHS & LOWS | TABLE

This table lists companies whose stock prices reach new 52-week highs and lows. The breakdown is for trades on the Toronto, Montreal and Canadian Venture stock exchanges.

Highs & lows 52-week

Toronto

High

Company	Symbol
AlimntCouch B	ATD.B
Burlington Res	BRX
CIBC pf sr 21	CM.PR.T
Caribbean Utl	CUP.U
Chieftain Int	CID
Denbury Res	DNR
iUnits iG5	XGV
Inco wt	N.WT
Labradr Ir un	LIF.UN
Lifeco Spl cs	LSC
Pembina Ppln	PIF.UN
Sun Life Finl	SLC
Suprior Propn	SPF.UN
TD Bank pf J	TD.PR.J
Trilon Fin A	TFC.A
Wall Fincl	WFC
Westcoast Enrg	W

Low

Company	Symbol
ATI Technlgys	ATY

Company	Symbol
Nu-Sky Energy	NUS

Low

Company	Symbol
Achieva Dev	AHE
ActFit.com	YAC.U
Admiral Bay	ADB
Aeon Vents	ANN
AfriOre Ltd	AFO
Airbomb.com	AIR
Aludra	YAD
Analyticl Soft	AYL
Appareo Soft	KNO
Armstrong	YRM
Aurogin Res	AUQ
Axion Communs	AXN
BGM Dvrsfd	BGD
Bard Ventures	CBS
Beaufld Cons	BFD
Birch Mtn Res	BMD
Blue Lightning	BLL
Book4Golf.com	BFG
Boulevard Cap	BVD
BrandEra.Com	YRN

Stock tables provide all the essential information on daily trading activity in markets where most Canadians invest. Weekend editions of The Financial Post carry an expanded summary with details for the previous week. The Canadian markets are the Toronto Stock Exchange, the Montreal Exchange, Canadian Venture Exchange (CDNX), and the over-the-counter market in Toronto called the Canadian Dealing Network (CDN is a subsidiary of the Toronto Stock Exchange).

The TSE is the main blue-chip market in Canada. The ME is mainly a regional stock market with a national base in trading in interest-sensitive derivatives. The CDNX and CDN listings are heavily weighted toward speculative junior issues. CDNX and CDN tables do not carry dividend and P/E information because companies on these lists are mainly juniors where the goal is to add value through the stock price.

In the U.S., the main market is the New York Stock Exchange, which lists virtually all of the big blue-chip U.S. companies. After the NYSE, the high-volume market is Nasdaq, which is the acronym from National Association of Securities Dealers Automated Quotation system. Nasdaq is an interdealer market that has different levels of over-the-counter listings. The senior Nasdaq board is heavily weighted toward technology stocks. The American Stock Exchange (Amex) carries listings of second-tier U.S. companies.

High and low prices in the left-hand columns indicate the trading range during the past 52 weeks.

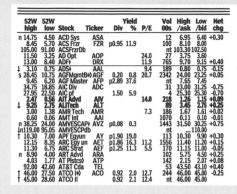

52W high	52W low	Stock	Ticker	Div	Yield %	P/E	Vol 00s	High /ask	Low /bid	Net chg
n 14.75	4.50	ACD Sys	ASA				12	6.95	6.40	+0.30
8.45	5.70	ACS Frzr	FZR	p0.95	11.9		100	8.10	8.00	
105.00	91.00	ACSFrzrDb					nt	103.30	102.50	
11.50	3.25	AD Opt	AOP			24.0	27	3.75	3.60	
13.00	8.40	ADF	DRX			11.9	765	9.70	9.15	+0.40
↓ 3.10	0.75	ADS	AAL			9.4	189	0.80	0.75	-0.15
s 28.45	10.75	AGFMgmtB	AGF	0.20	0.8	20.7	2342	24.00	23.25	+0.05
9.45	6.20	AGF Master	AFP	p2.89	37.6		nt	7.65	7.45	
34.75	18.85	AIC Div	ADC				31	33.00	31.25	-0.75
27.95	22.50	AIC pf		1.50	5.9		4	25.30	25.30	-0.70
7.47	0.56	AIT Advd	AIV			14.0	218	1.26	1.15	+0.09
↓ 9.25	2.75	ALI Tech	ALT				89	3.45	2.75	+0.25
3.00	1.38	AMR Tech	AMR			7.3	186	1.67	1.61	+0.02
0.60	0.06	AMT Int	AAI				1070	0.11	0.10	-0.01
n 38.25	24.00	AMVESCAP	AVZ	p0.08	0.3		1443	31.50	30.25	+0.75
↓n119.00	95.05	AMVESCPdb					nt	...110.00		
↑ 10.30	7.00	APF Egyun	AY	p1.90	19.0		113	10.30	9.90	+0.30
12.15	8.35	ARC Egy un	AET	p1.86	16.3	11.2	1556	11.40	11.20	+0.15
11.30	6.75	ARC Strat	AEF	p1.25	11.3	5.5	170	11.15	11.00	-0.05
n 8.90	4.00	ART Advd	ARA				102	5.75	4.50	+0.25
4.03	1.77	AT Plstcs	ATP				142	2.15	2.07	+0.08
92.00	42.60	AT&T Cda	TEL				53	43.50	43.10	+0.40
↑ 46.00	27.50	ATCO I	ACO	0.92	2.0	12.7	244	46.00	45.00	-0.25
↑ 45.00	28.60	ATCO II		0.92	2.1	12.4	nt	46.00	45.00	

Company names sometimes are abbreviated and are listed alphabetically.

Stocks are common shares unless identified as otherwise. For example, a **pf** after the company name refers to preferred shares.

Warrants are identified as **wts** and rights as **rts.** An **A** beside the name refers to class A shares. Restricted voting shares are identified by a diamond symbol before the company name.

The ticker is the symbol used by exchanges to identify a security.

Dividend rate refers to estimated annual dividends paid to shareholders, based on the dividend rate announced by the company. A **v** indicates variable rate dividends have been estimated at their annual value, based on the latest payment. An **r** means the company is in arrears on its dividend payments.

Yield is a calculation of a stock's dividend as a percentage of its current price. If no dividends are paid, a stock has no yield.

P/E is the price to earnings ratio. This is the price of a stock divided by its annual earnings per share for the latest 12-month period. (Earnings per share are the company's earnings, divided by the number of outstanding shares.)

High, low and close (or latest) indicate the highest and lowest prices for the trading period and the price at the close of trading. Prices of U.S. stocks of less than $5 are listed in cents. Canadian exchanges use decimal pricing for all stocks.

Net change shows the difference between the latest closing price and the price of the last traded board lot on the previous day. If the amount is preceded by a plus sign, the stock is up; if it's preceded by a minus sign, it's down.

Volume shows how many board lots have been traded (for the day in the daily list and for the week in the weekly summary). A board lot is 100 shares, which means actual volume is multiplied by 100. An **e** before the volume indicates exact number of shares; an **nt** means not traded; and a **z** refers to a an odd lot trade (an amount other than a board lot).

Net change is the change in price from the end of the previous week or the last time the stock traded during that week.

GAAP is a set of accounting standards. Those rules are set by the self-regulatory organization for accountants in consultation with securities regulators.

A prospectus should disclose all the corporate information an investor needs to assess a company's securities. However, a prospectus often will refer investors to other corporate documents for a complete picture of the securities.

The annual information form (AIF) covers information not provided in annual reports, such as details of insider shareholdings and executive compensation. These reports may not be sent to shareholders as a matter of routine but must be provided on request. Many companies distribute AIFs with the information circulars that go to shareholders with the notice of annual meetings.

THERE ARE DRAWBACKS TO INVESTING ABROAD

Returns from investments in foreign securities can be attractive, but investors looking beyond the border should consider two factors – taxes and risk. Domestic tax rules give Canadians a break on dividend-paying stocks when investing at home, and buying outside the country involves the prospect of currency fluctuations.

There are other reasons for weighing carefully the returns at home and abroad, but these two factors usually are at the top of the list. There is a solid reason why the tax rules favor investment at home by Canadians. Business needs money to invest in new plant and equipment, so capital formation is essential to the growth and development of the economy.

When Canadian governments were running up big debts, the economic priorities got mixed up and too much of the money invested at home went for the unproductive purpose of paying interest on government debts. But a rediscovered ethic for budgetary

INTERNATIONAL STOCKS | TABLE

INTERNATIONAL 12.15.00

Figures supplied by Reuters

Stock	Close	Chg	Stock	Close	Chg	Stock	Close	Chg	Stock	Close	Chg
London (in British pence)			Prudential	1061.19	-20.00	Sofina Opt	41		Femsa	18.50	-1.38
			RMC	548.00	7.50	Solvay	53	-2	Geo Corp	8.50	-0.68
			Rank	170.00	-3.00	UCB	40	1	ICA	1.90	-0.10
Abbey Natl	1179.15	-14.50	Reckitt Bencksr	884.00	2.50	Un Minier	39	-1	Kimberly A	23.80	-0.15
Allied Domc	439.87	8.00	Reed Intl	686.68	2.00				Maseca	2.15	-0.13
Anglo American	3529.95	-	Rentokil	200.00	2.00	**Frankfurt**			Modelo C	25.30	0.35
	145.00		Reuters Hld	1201.40	-30.00	(in euro)			Penoles	7.80	-0.10
Asc Br Food	489.76	24.00	Rexam	219.50	-1.50	Adidas	66.00	0.40	Sanluis	13.50	-0.16
AstraZeneca	3381.99	40.00	Rio Tinto	1108.73	-4.00	Allianz	372.00	-4.00	Soriana B	22.20	-1.75
BAA	577.33	-4.50	Rolls Royce	196.87	5.00				Televisa	22.65	-0.70

Listings of international stocks show prices in local currencies. See the foreign exchange and major currencies tables to convert C$s. **Close** is the closing price and the **change** is from the previous trading day.

STOCK ACTIVITY | TABLES

Most active stocks 12.19.00

Toronto		Vol. 00s	Cls.	Chg.	Montreal		Vol. 00s	Cls.	Chg.	CDNX		Vol. 00s	Cls.	Chg.
iUnits i60	XIU	145834	52.80	-0.95	Jitec	JIT	2211	1.20	+0.15	CalciTech	CLK	9090	0.28	unch
Nortel Networks	NT	121338	52.00	-3.60	Wesdome Gld	WDG	2000	0.26	+0.01	Krystal Bond	YKO	6703	0.25	+0.10
BCE Inc	BCE	36347	43.25	-1.35	Innovium Cap	IN	1420	0.32	unch	Manitex Cap	YMN	5120	0.40	unch
Bombard B	BBD.B	30147	22.50	+0.10	Limtech Techs	LTC	1327	0.55	-0.01	Galaxy OnLine	YGO	4557	0.33	-0.04
Manulife Finl	MFC	29242	44.60	-0.65	Genomics One	GNX	1153	1.25	-0.30	Wavve Telecom	WV	4474	0.43	-0.11
Mackenzie Fin	MKF	27260	26.00	-0.95	Photochannel	PNI	945	0.79	-0.11	UniqueBroadbnd	UBS	4309	1.16	-0.05
Abitibi-Cons	A	26241	12.40	-0.10	SouthMalartic	MSU	750	0.29	-0.01	Nuvo Network	NNM	3881	0.46	-0.09
T-D Bank	TD	26127	41.75	+0.45	Robex Res	RBX	682	0.45	+0.01	CGX Energy	OYLU	3616	u0.20	unch
Placer Dm	PDG	25184	15.15	+0.65	Arena Gold Rs	ARN	580	0.49	+0.01	TM Bioscience	TMC	3428	0.37	-0.03
Royal Bank	RY	25033	48.50	+1.20	nStein Tech	EIN	420	0.50	-0.09	Bridgetown	BRY	3370	0.55	-0.01

MOST ACTIVE STOCKS TABLES

The most active stocks table highlights stocks that have traded most heavily during the day (or the week, in the case of the weekly listing).

Volume is shares traded in board lots (blocks of 100). Most trading arenas count a buy and a sell as one trade, but Nasdaq counts each side of the transaction in reporting volume.

Closing price is the last trade of the day and change is from the previous day (or week in the case of the weekly column). Prices of U.S. stocks of less than US$5 are listed in cents. Canadian exchanges use decimal pricing for all stocks.

Top % gainers

Toronto		Vol. 00s	Cls.	Chg.	Montreal		Vol. 00s	Cls.	Chg.	CDNX		Vol. 00s	Cls.	Chg.
River Gold	RIV	343	1.35	+26.0	Global IIdga	GGII	16	0.30	+16.7	Discovery Aaq	DIC	16	0.70	+76.0
Badger Day	BAD	1336	1.10	+22.2	Jitec	JIT	2211	1.20	+14.3	Morgan Media	MRP	10	0.69	+72.5
MedcomSoft	MSF	710	2.95	+15.7	Calvalley A	CVI.A	176	0.62	+12.7	Krystal Bond	YKO	6703	0.25	+66.7
Lions Gate	LGF	1270	2.60	+15.6	NAR Resources	NRL	286	2.15	+8.6	Patent Enfrcmnt	PAL	95	0.30	+66.7
Mosaic Grp	MGX	9574	11.00	+14.0	Grilli Ppty A	GG.A	119	0.64	+6.7	Vanguard Aviatn	VAX	95	0.25	+66.7
Premdor	PDI	1331	6.00	+12.1	Prolab Tech A	PLT	13	0.85	+6.3	Regal Cons Vts	YRV	33	0.40	+60.0
Amtelecom Grp	ATM	398	1.40	+12.0	Wesdome Gld	WDG	2000	0.26	+4.0	Santoy Res	SAN	11	0.68	+54.5
SLMsoft.com A	ESP.A	207	2.35	+11.9	ArtQuest B	AQ.B	176	1.35	+3.8	Conquest Vents	CQX	35	0.75	+50.0
Microtec Entp	EMI	115	1.45	+11.5	LYRtech	LYT	356	0.70	+2.9	Pheromone Scn	PHS	909	0.75	+50.0
Wenzel Dwnhole	WZL	39	1.55	+10.7	Hornet Energy	HGY	193	0.83	+2.5	Techcana Cap	TCN	20	0.30	+50.0

TOP % GAINERS AND LOSERS TABLES

The top gainers and losers tables highlight those stocks with unusual price moves in the latest trading day. A caution in reading this table is that no adjustment is made for volume. An unusual trade of 100 shares can cause a stock to vault to the top of the list on one day if there is little day-to-day trading in that stock. In those situations, that unusual price is often reversed the next day. Prices of U.S. stocks of less than US$5 are listed in cents. Canadian exchanges use decimal pricing for all stocks.

- **Top % gainers** are stocks whose prices gained the most in percentage terms.
- **Top net gainers** are stocks whose shares appreciated most in dollar value.
- **Biggest % losers** indicates stocks with the largest price decline in percentage terms.
- **Biggest net losers** are the stocks that fell the most in dollar value.

DAILY MARKETS TABLE

The daily markets table in weekend editions tracks the day-by-day closing values for the main North American indexes and then compares the close for the week with the previous month and the previous year.

Weekly markets — day by day

	Monday	Tuesday	Wednesday	Thursday	Friday	Last Friday	Month ago	Year ago
TSE 300	8944.70	9279.04	9230.59	9166.80	9548.73	8941.17	9552.53	7820.06
TSE 200	470.25	478.17	478.64	477.49	489.95	468.15	500.99	430.86
TSE 100	555.67	577.85	574.40	570.11	594.95	555.73	593.61	482.37
S&P/TSE 60	531.71	552.25	548.67	544.13	567.70	531.16	561.19	464.18
Toronto 35	549.09	565.77	562.80	567.96	586.18	546.03	580.51	448.60
DJ Inds	10560.95	10898.72	10664.38	10617.36	10712.91	10373.54	10907.06	11068.12
DJ Trans	2767.77	2843.67	2815.71	2796.04	2879.95	2763.15	2777.07	2881.67
DJ Utils	388.05	385.64	383.72	385.36	385.82	385.38	390.20	273.70
S&P 500	1324.97	1376.54	1351.46	1343.55	1369.89	1315.23	1409.28	1403.88
Nasdaq 100	2554.40	2852.87	2743.70	2719.91	2895.39	2549.74	3059.09	3164.08

MARKET DIARIES TABLE

The market diaries table provides a view of the breadth of activity. For example, a sharp move in an index on a day of heavy trading is more significant that a similar change when there is light volume.

Volume is number of shares traded in board lots (blocks of 100). Most trading arenas count a buy and a sell as one trade but Nasdaq counts each side of the transaction in reporting volume. Advances and declines are the numbers of share issues that rose in price or fell.

Advance and decline volume refers to the total for shares that advanced or declined. Unchanged refers to the number of share issues that ended the day with the same price as the previous day. Issues traded is the total for advances, declines and unchanged.

New highs and lows refers to the number of issues that reached new high or low prices in the latest 52-week period.

Market diaries

	Volume 00s	Previous day 00s	Adv.	Adv. vol 00s	Dec.	Dec. vol 00s	Unch.	Issues traded	New highs	New lows
Toronto	1701647	1698147	468	666987	630	900988	265	1363	21	66
Montreal	29378	31582	25	13803	25	10966	18	68	nil	4
CDNX	409046	444156	355	127182	457	160149	435	1247	7	61
New York	15621505	10536676	1296	4460321	1618	10558134	413	3327	136	107
American	734382	537887	223	71716	388	615895	178	789	11	64
Nasdaq	15536719	17696078	1377	8380282	2514	18474761	709	4600	28	328

HOURLY MARKETS TABLE

Most people look at the closing level of an index for a read on the markets. But activity during the day can be an important indicator. Momentum in a particular direction may show up in the intraday trends. If there is a news development during trading hours that affects the stock price in general, the hourly markets table will provide a snapshot of how that event affected the market. Another measure of market health that can be extracted from this table is volatility, which means unusual swings from high to low. Volatile trading activity often occurs in turning points for markets and this table will show the swings. At one time, index levels were only reported hourly but computer power now allows indexes to be tracked with changes from each stock trade (tick by tick is the street jargon for this instant tracking).

Hourly markets

	Open	10:00	11:00	12:00	1:00	2:00	3:00	Close	Prev day	Wk ago	Mth ago	Yr ago
TSE 300	8942.99	8931.56	8922.71	8909.38	8904.11	8925.42	9036.72	9020.04	9069.38	9548.73	9187.05	7985.29
TSE 200	485.15	483.56	481.27	480.97	480.07	480.41	481.48	481.87	490.15	489.95	490.93	439.30
TSE 100	552.02	552.77	552.50	551.61	551.37	552.81	560.40	559.18	561.44	594.95	569.57	492.69
S&P/TSE 60	527.11	528.62	528.61	527.56	527.61	528.88	536.78	535.40	537.94	567.70	539.66	476.42
Toronto 35	543.88	544.87	545.63	545.10	547.08	548.92	553.58	550.51	552.93	586.18	561.16	469.26
DJ Inds	10647.98	10554.03	10504.36	10491.84	10473.26	10465.68	10514.97	10434.96	10674.99	10712.91	10707.60	11225.32
DJ Trans	2733.66	2732.30	2709.93	2710.72	2712.73	2717.05	2717.17	2698.68	2738.15	2879.95	2841.01	2919.54
DJ Utils	385.51	386.28	386.63	386.14	386.36	386.18	386.72	386.52	385.55	385.82	388.20	272.19
S&P 500	1340.93	1320.63	1315.83	1310.12	1307.64	1307.62	1317.92	1312.15	1340.93	1369.89	1390.04	1413.33
Nasdaq 100	2590.84	2550.53	2563.72	2532.44	2527.11	2514.27	2554.55	2549.48	2639.26	2895.39	3076.70	3239.18

TSE SECTORS WEEKLY WINNERS AND LOSERS TABLE

The TSE sectors table tracks the gains or losses for sub-indexes during the week and the top moves, up and down, within each sector. Volume is included as well as price because a big move on heavy volume is much more significant than a similar change on low volume. Instead of a dollar change, this table gives a percentage change, which allows for comparisons among stocks in different sectors.

Weekly TSE sectors — winners and losers

Sector	Cls	Wk % chg	Best performer		Vol 00s	Cls	Wk % chg	Worst performer		Vol 00s	Cls	Wk% chg
Industrial Products	9797.54	+11.8	Certicom	CIC	16661	34.00	+30.8	Geac Computer	GAC	26118	2.90	-17.1
Consumer Products	17001.62	+6.5	Theratechs	TH	1884	14.00	+40.0	TLC Laser Eye	TLC	5630	3.15	-21.3
Financial Services	10460.15	+6.1	AMVESCAP	AVZ	494	31.75	+23.3	Sceptre Inv A	SZ.A	406	15.05	-4.4
Gold & Precious Mnrl	4395.47	+5.8	Franco-Nevada	FN	40807	18.00	+15.0	Homestake Cda	HCX	179	7.00	-12.5
Conglomerates	11326.17	+5.5	Brascan A	BNN.A	17762	23.00	+10.0	Onex	OCX	17516	23.70	+3.3
Pipelines	5823.54	+5.1	TCPL	TRP	80507	15.95	+5.6	Westcoast Enrg	W	25280	34.00	+4.5
Oil & Gas	7993.98	+4.1	Paramount Res	POU	4640	17.50	+17.4	Baytex Engy	BTE	12695	10.35	-11.5
Paper & Forest Prods	4790.00	+3.5	Canfor	CFP	16006	9.90	+15.1	Bowater Cda	BWX	116	84.00	-2.3
Metals & Minerals	3659.82	+3.2	Aur Res	AUR	8356	2.01	+14.9	Boliden	BOL	5513	1.04	-3.7
Real Estate	2280.98	+1.7	Centrefd Rlty	CFE	948	10.25	+17.1	FirstService	FSV	358	21.00	-4.5
Utilities	15407.73	+1.6	Stratos Glbl	SGB	3905	11.00	+18.9	RogersWirlssB	RCM.B	3183	19.90	-14.2
Communs & Media	18743.57	+0.9	COGECO Inc	CGO	6393	30.90	+23.6	TVA Group B	TVA.B	2993	14.90	-5.4
Transn & Envrnmtl	5299.83	-0.4	Air Canada	AC	20268	16.20	+10.2	Laidlaw	LDM	96158	0.17	-19.5
Merchandising	5560.72	-0.8	Jean Coutu A	PJC.A	5499	25.00	+9.9	Bid.Com Intl	BII	7112	1.56	-12.8

restraint is starting to make more room for business in the allocation of investment funds. Dividends paid by Canadian corporations get preferential tax treatment in the hands of investors residing in Canada. Companies pay dividends out of after-tax income and this tax arrangement provides a big incentive for Canadians to pick a local company over a foreign one.

This situation tends to favor dividend-paying blue chip companies and the home advantage narrows for companies that do not pay dividends. Usually, a non-dividend paying company is in the development stage and the appeal to investors is the prospect of capital gains if the company is successful and grows. The tax issue takes on a new dimension when the investing is done through a registered retirement savings plan because dividends that accumulate within an RRSP are shielded from tax. There are limits on foreign investment by pension funds. The 2000 Budget increased the general foreign content limit to 25% from 20%, followed by a further increase to 30% in 2001.

FOREIGN SECURITIES IN MUTUAL FUNDS ARE NOT CONSIDERED DIRECT INVESTMENTS

With an RRSP, the foreign limit actually can be higher because the 30% applies to direct investment. If the RRSP holds mutual funds, each fund can hold foreign securities up to a 30% limit and those holdings are not counted as part of the limit on direct investment in foreign securities. With foreign holdings, there is the issue of exchange rate fluctuations. Currencies of the big industrial countries tend to move in long cycles against the currencies of their major trading partners. And those currencies tend not to have sharp adjustments when the trend changes. However, currencies of less developed countries have a history of sudden devaluations that come as a shock to investors.

Thus, the risk of currency surprises tends to be much less when investing in securities in the big industrial economies with large, established markets.

TIMING IS EVERYTHING WHEN SELLING

Often the most important investment decision is not when to buy but when to sell. A legion of investment advisers stands ready with advice on what to buy and when to buy but the decision on selling usually is a lonely one. Often, the reasons for selling are dictated by circumstance. Common reasons are that people need the money or that the securities are held in an estate being liquidated.

STOCKS BOUGHT FOR CAPITAL GAINS SHOULD BE SOLD WHEN TARGET PRICE IS REACHED

The plan for selling should be part of the decision to buy. When buying bonds, for example, a decision should be made on whether to hold to maturity.

Prices will fluctuate during the tradable life of a bond but it returns a fixed amount at maturity and this fact can have a bearing on what is a suitable interest rate for the individual shopping to buy a bond. A similar assessment may be part of the decision to buy a stock if the goal is to have dividend income. With a stock, of course, there is no fixed

FPX | TABLE

The Financial Post indexes (FPX) appear daily on the front of the Investing sections and Mondays in the same place in an expanded format (see below). They are divided into three basic portfolios: FPX Income index, FPX Balanced index and FPX Growth index. Each is broken down by asset mix, and none holds more than 11 securities. The FPX provides the investor a benchmark to compare how well his or her asset mix is performing.

FPX Growth: 1814.78 Weekly % change: -2.40

	Book* units	Book* price $	Book* value $	Book* % port.	Current units	Current price $	Current value $	Current Wk %chg.	Current % port.
Cash & equivalents			18,833.78	10.00			23,038.91	0.28	12.70
Cash	...	...	88.30	0.05	...	...	1,217.87	0.00	0.67
Accrued income	...	...	783.53	0.42	...	...	81.87	100.00	0.05
Gov't Cda 91-day T-bill	182	98.692	17,961.94	9.54	218	99.721	21,739.18	0.11	11.98
Fixed income			37,635.75	19.99			38,916.72	-0.09	21.44
Gov't Cda 5.5% June 1/09	387	97.250	37,635.75	19.99	387	100.560	38,916.72	-0.09	21.44
Equity			131,794.65	70.01			119,522.35	-3.62	65.86
iUnits i60	1,169	56.350	65,873.15	34.99	1,169	53.800	62,892.20	-5.36	34.66
S&P 500 Dep Rct	129	US151.188	28,291.38	15.03	129	US130.969	25,687.13	-2.03	14.15
iShares Germany	49	US26.563	1,888.07	1.00	49	US18.438	1,373.62	-2.77	0.76
iShares Japan	639	US16.250	15,062.51	8.00	639	US11.563	11,233.62	-1.93	6.19
iShares UK	256	US20.250	7,520.00	3.99	256	US17.500	6,811.39	-0.17	3.75
iShares Mexico	145	US17.875	3,759.71	2.00	145	US13.688	3,017.60	-3.76	1.66
iShares France	240	US27.000	9,399.84	4.99	240	US23.313	8,506.80	-0.08	4.69
Total value			188,264.18	100.00			181,477.98	-2.40	100.00

FPX Balanced: 1725.60 Weekly % change: -1.68

	Book* units	Book* price $	Book* value $	Book* % port.	Current units	Current price $	Current value $	Current Wk %chg.	Current % port.
Cash & equivalents			17,342.45	9.94			22,429.71	0.47	13.00
Cash	...	...	30.38	0.02	...	...	2,317.44	0.00	1.34
Accrued income	...	...	1,521.34	0.87	...	...	168.07	100.00	0.10
Gov't Cda 91-day T-bill	160	98.692	15,790.72	9.05	200	99.721	19,944.20	0.11	11.56
Fixed income			69,786.59	40.00			71,043.02	-0.13	41.17
Gov't Cda 7.25% June 1/03	225	103.400	23,265.00	13.34	225	104.060	23,413.50	-0.03	13.57
Gov't Cda 5.5% June 1/09	239	97.250	23,242.75	13.32	239	100.560	24,033.84	-0.09	13.93
Gov't Cda 8.0% June 1/27	178	130.780	23,218.84	13.34	178	132.560	23,595.68	-0.27	13.67
Equity			87,324.30	50.06			79,087.11	-3.62	45.83
iUnits i60	774	56.350	43,614.90	25.00	774	53.800	41,641.20	-5.36	24.13
S&P 500 Dep Rct	80	US151.188	17,545.04	10.06	80	US130.969	15,930.00	-2.03	9.23
iShares Germany	34	US26.563	1,310.09	0.75	34	US18.438	953.12	-2.77	0.55
iShares Japan	444	US16.250	10,465.97	6.00	444	US11.563	7,805.52	-1.93	4.52
iShares UK	178	US20.250	5,228.75	3.00	178	US17.500	4,736.05	-0.17	2.74
iShares Mexico	101	US17.875	2,618.83	1.50	101	US13.688	2,101.91	-3.76	1.22
iShares France	167	US27.000	6,540.72	3.75	167	US23.313	5,919.32	-0.08	3.43
Total value			174,453.33	100.00			172,559.84	-1.68	100.00

FPX Income: 1646.97 Weekly % change: -1.38

	Book* units	Book* price $	Book* value $	Book* % port.	Current units	Current price $	Current value $	Current Wk %chg.	Current % port.
Cash & equivalents			32,171.87	20.01			37,189.39	0.36	22.58
Cash	...	...	51.13	0.03	...	...	2,592.17	0.00	1.57
Accrued income	...	...	1,723.60	1.07	...	...	193.47	100.00	0.12
Gov't Cda 91-day T-bill	308	98.692	30,397.14	18.90	345	99.721	34,403.75	0.11	20.89
Fixed income			80,334.25	49.96			81,780.34	-0.13	49.66
Gov't Cda 7.25% June 1/03	259	103.400	26,780.60	16.65	259	104.060	26,951.54	-0.03	16.36
Gov't Cda 5.5% June 1/09	275	97.250	26,743.75	16.63	275	100.560	27,654.00	-0.09	16.79
Gov't Cda 8.0% June 1/27	205	130.780	26,809.90	16.67	205	132.560	27,174.80	-0.27	16.50
Equity			48,292.13	30.03			45,727.03	-4.84	27.76
iUnits i60	713	56.350	40,177.55	24.99	713	53.800	38,359.40	-5.36	23.29
S&P 500 Dep Rct	37	US151.188	8,114.58	5.05	37	US130.969	7,367.63	-2.03	4.47
Total value			160,798.25	100.00			164,696.75	-1.38	100.00

Index base value 1,000 on $100,000 invested April 1, 1996.   * at rebalancing April 3, 2000   Note: Totals may not add up due to rounding.

redemption date, but the timing on when to sell may be affected by the outlook for the business cycle.

In the case of a dividend-paying stock, the fundamental analysis that goes into the decision to buy should be kept handy for regular checks on whether the company's performance is living up to expectations. If it isn't, there should be guidelines in place on when to recognize facts and sell. If stocks are being bought on expectations of capital gains, part of the decision should be a target price. Once a stock reaches that target price, there should be fresh reasons for continuing to hold.

THE INSIDE STORY ON COMPANY INSIDERS

Timely information is essential to making investment decisions, and having a head start on that information means having an advantage in the market. That's why special rules apply to insiders – the people inside a company who have access to information that's not available to the general investing public.

One of the rules is that insiders are required to report their trading activity in a timely manner. These trades are reported in securities commission bulletins. News that insiders are buying or selling in big volume usually is an important signal to other investors about the prospects for the company. Insiders are defined in securities legislation and usually they are defined as senior management, the directors and those who hold a share of the voting stock.

INSIDERS HAVE ACCESS TO INFORMATION THAT CAN AFFECT STOCK PRICES

In Canada, the ownership threshold is 10%. The practical reason is that someone who represents 10% or more of the ownership can get through on the phone to the president or the treasurer and chat about the company's operations. But someone who holds a few hundred shares only gets the standard printed information sheets from the investor relations department.

Officers of a company are insiders because they see the financial results first and have the power to affect those results. Employees down the line may have insights not available to the general public, but they don't have the authority to act on those insights. Members of the board of directors are insiders because they get direct reports from management and the board sets the general policy direction for the company.

These definitions can extend to subsidiary companies or affiliated firms because information that is sensitive to the stock price usually is shared by these key people in a corporate structure. When insiders report their stockholdings, they give details on "beneficial" ownership. That extends to shares held by family members or held through personal holding companies.

PROMOTER'S ROLE NOT ALWAYS THE HEAVY

Promoter is a much-maligned term because most companies would never survive the development stage without the services of a promoter. They're the ones who tell the company's story and raise the money. As a group, though, they have a bad reputation because too many oversell the story and divert money away from legitimate corporate expenses.

Still, the securities industry needs promoters, and a working relationship has been established between those who hustle stocks and those who stand on guard against excesses in the investment business.

Securities acts define the role of promoters and this sets the ground rules for regulation of their activities.

THERE ARE TWO BASIC DEFINITIONS OF A PROMOTER

• Someone who "takes the initiative in founding, organizing or substantially reorganizing the business of an issuer [a company]."
• Someone who receives 10% or more of any class of securities issued by a company or who receives 10% or more of the proceeds from the sale of any class of securities.

Securities legislation doesn't distinguish between small and large companies but as a practical matter the role of promoter applies to speculative junior companies.

Typically, promoters are compensated with stock. They often get salaries as well but the big paydays come from getting founders' shares at next to nothing and selling into the market when the company strikes paydirt.

To protect outside investors, securities rules set minimum hold periods for stock held by promoters so as to ensure they cannot cash out while promoting sale of stock to the general public.

TICKERS REVEAL A LOT OF INFORMATION

The word "ticker" is rapidly becoming an archaic market term. In its original meaning, it referred to the ticker tape that transmitted stock trade prices from stock exchanges to brokerage firms. A specialized teletype machine, which made a constant ticking sound, used to print stock price information on long ribbons of paper. Ticker tape parades were possible in New York because Wall Street produced truckloads of ticker tape. They're confetti parades now.

These days, ticker usually means the unique symbol that identifies a stock. Those symbols are important to people who call up stock quotations from electronic databases.

But tickers also are important as a way of identifying the right securities where companies issue more than one class of security and trade on more than one exchange.

Many of the blue chip companies are in that category. For example, a search of Royal Bank of Canada in a securities database turns up about 40 different stock symbols.

There are between two and four components to the ticker. Look at "RY.PR.E-T" as an example. The first is the symbol for the company – RY for Royal Bank. If those two letters appear alone, it is a reference to Royal Bank common stock traded on the primary exchange – where the majority of trading takes place – which is the Toronto Stock Exchange in this case. The symbol "PR" tells us that this is an issue of preferred stock. The "E" means it is the bank's class E preferred stock. Finally, the "T" denotes the fact that these preferred shares are listed on the Toronto Stock Exchange.

Stock symbols are a feature of market columns in financial newspapers. Trading information for stocks on major Canadian and U.S. stock exchanges is published in the weekday editions of The Financial Post. The weekend edition also has a weekly trading summary.

All the basic information about trading in stocks is in these tables, including volume and earnings information as well as price activity.

Volume is important because a minimum volume is necessary to ensure liquidity, which means the stock can be bought or sold without a price distortion. A sudden change in volume compared with a longer term average usually means speculation about a corporate development.

Earnings show up in the stock tables as part of the ratio of price to earnings as well as the amount of earnings attributed to each share. Stock tables also show the latest dividend payout rate.

Price details include the high and low over the last 12 months, which provides a hint on how a current stock price fits into any cyclical pattern for that stock.

FUNDAMENTALS APPLY IN ANALYZING STOCKS

Stock picking is the primary job in managing most portfolios and the toolkit for this chore is called fundamental analysis. As the name implies, it involves getting down to basics. The approach is similar for both stocks and bonds. The underlying questions deal with the actual or expected profitability of the issuer.

Can it earn enough to sustain regular dividend payments or continue the flow of interest payments on bonds? And if the issuer is a company, can it expand its market share so that stockholders can share in the growth? As a general rule, there are two components to this line of inquiry – an analysis of different groups of issuers and then an assessment of which are the best performers in the best group. Sector analysis depends partly on broad economic trends. For example, the resource stocks usually lead the market when the economy is coming out of recession.

FUNDAMENTAL ANALYSIS INVOLVES TRENDS AND RATIOS

But the fundamental component of this exercise means looking at whether the resource sector is growing and how it is changing.

For example, what is the impact on mining companies of a trend in the auto industry to replace galvanized metal with plastic? Are the miners finding new customers as demand from the old ones declines?

If prospects for the sector look promising, the job then is to compare the players in that field. This rating often involves looking for the low-cost producers, but investors need to consider their own time horizons.

A company can be a low-cost producer by cutting back on research and development, a strategy that can give a quick boost to profits in the short term but ultimately put the company at a competitive disadvantage.

Fundamental analysis contains large doses of trends and ratios.

HERE ARE SOME OF THE THINGS TO WATCH FOR

• **Revenue, profit and cash flow:** Are these on a rising trend with no serious breaks in the pattern?

• **Profit margin:** Is the company getting a reasonable return on its revenue and invested capital?

• **Interest, asset and dividend coverage:** Is the earnings flow strong enough to ensure that interest and dividends can be paid with no strain and is the asset base big enough in relation to the current debt load.

• **Debt-to-equity ratio:** Is the size of the ownership stake big enough to provide a proper balance against bonds and bank debt? (An acceptable standard for the debt-to-equity ratio will vary from industry to industry.)

• **Product innovation:** Is the company keeping up with its peers in research, or, better, is it out in front?

• **Quality of management:** Is there depth on the bench in key areas – operations, marketing and financial?

THE GOLDEN ALLURE OF BLUE CHIP STOCKS

Perhaps unfortunately, the term blue chip comes from gambling – poker to be exact. Blue chips are the markers worth the most at the card table and in the stock market they refer to blue-blood companies. Another common term for the equity of these firms is widows and orphans stocks – shares that are bought for their income potential over the long haul. Historically, the shares of these senior companies have had earning power and have provided competition for bonds. Investors buy bonds for the interest income, and dividends paid by big companies have had to provide a competitive return.

More recently, rising stock prices have meant that investors have placed less emphasis on dividends. But big companies still retain their appeal because a steady income flow usually means their stock prices are less affected by cyclical turns in the market.

Tax treatment is an important consideration for those who buy dividend-paying stocks. Companies pay dividends with after-tax income. Since the money has already been taxed at the corporate level, shareholders get a tax break on dividend income from equities. Blue chips tend to be the biggest companies in a national economy and the 30 stocks in the Dow Jones industrial average often are seen as the bluest of blue chips. They all are large companies with international divisions and proven dividend records.

Most of the companies in the Toronto Stock Exchange 35-stock index have similar status in the Canadian economy, although some of those companies in the TSE 35 do not pay regular dividends.

PREFERRED SHARES PROMISE HIGH YIELDS

Investors who want the capital gains potential of common stocks but also want high dividends often look at preferred stock. However, the choice is not a simple one because preferred shares – known colloquially as "prefs" – come in several forms.

When research analysts look at a company's capital stock, some prefs are considered equity because they look more like common stock and some are considered debt because they look more like bonds.

GENERALLY, PREFERRED SHARES HAVE THESE COMMON CHARACTERISTICS
• **The dividend payment schedule** is fixed in advance and dividends must be paid. If a company is in financial difficulty, the terms of a preferred issue usually specify that dividends can only be postponed to a future date but back payments must be made when financial conditions improve.

BID/ASK | TABLE

The main stock table lists shares that have traded during the day. If a stock is in a bid/ask table, it means there was no trading activity during the day for which the table is dated. The bid is the best offer to buy and the ask is the best offer to sell. Brokers may have other bid or ask prices on their trading books but only the best prices are listed on lists seen by the public.

CDNX BID/ASK

Quotes for stocks traded in past three days

Stock	Ticker	Bid	Ask	Last	Stock	Ticker	Bid	Ask	Last	Stock	Ticker	Bid	Ask	Last
A&E A†	YAE	0.25	1.00	0.30	BardVentr	CBS	0.28	0.32	0.28	Conquest	YQR	0.10	0.11	0.11
A&E B†		0.25	1.00	0.30	Barramndi†	BAM	0.03	0.04	0.04	ConqstVen	CQX	1.16	1.34	1.30
A&B Geosci	ABG	0.26	0.32	0.20	Bay Eqty	BEQ	0.49	0.50	0.50	Conqstdr	CQQ	0.04	0.08	0.04
AC Enrgy	ACE	0.21	0.23	0.23	BeaumontA†	BMN	0.55	0.62	0.55	ConsTrnDr	CDT	0.16	0.22	0.16
ACGlblCap	ACG	0.23	0.34	0.23	BellCoast	BCP	0.19	0.20	0.19	Cons AMR	DCA	0.09	0.12	0.10
AHT	ASI	1.80	2.10	1.75	Bellevue	BVC	0.15	0.16	0.15	ConsEco	CES	0.48	0.50	0.51
AMT Fine	YAM	0.04	0.08	0.04	Belltech	BTV	0.18	0.22	0.20	ConsEpix*	JPG	0.30	0.35	0.31
AQM Auto	AQV	0.15	0.20	0.19	Berkshire	BKH	0.25	0.31	0.25	ConsExclr	CRR	0.35	0.50	0.35
ASC Avcan	ACN	0.33	0.40	0.44	BerkIntMng	BKR	0.05	0.07	0.06	ConGnDiam	GDA	0.04	0.06	0.04
ATIAirTst	AAT	0.38	0.50	0.40	Berwick	BWK	0.50	0.80	0.80	CnGlblMn	CTG	0.21	0.27	0.21
AVI Soft	AVF	0.47	0.90	0.53	BetterRs	BRZ	0.04	0.05	0.03	ConsGldbk	CVT	0.15	0.26	0.24
										ConGulfsd	CGL	0.07	0.10	0.07
										ConKaitone	CKT	0.20	0.28	0.24
										ConNorsmt	ILN	0.08	0.11	0.11
										ConPine	KPG	0.08	0.09	0.08
										ConsPinTch	CTT	0.04	0.07	0.06
										ConSilver†	CKS	0.16	0.19	0.19

CDN UNLISTED | TABLE

The CDN Unlisted table shows stocks that trade on a daily basis on the Canadian Dealing Network. CDN is operated by the TSE as an over-the-counter market in which securities transactions are conducted through a telephone or computer network connecting individual dealers, as opposed to the central auction system as operated by a stock exchange. Over-the-counter stocks are typically smaller cap and tend not to meet the more stringent listing requirements of stock exchanges.

CDN UNLISTED 09.15.00

Figures supplied by Star Data Systems Inc.

Stock	Ticker	Vol 00s	High	Low	Cls	Net chg	Stock	Ticker	Vol 00s	High	Low	Cls	Net chg
AVL Info	AVLL	240	0.30	0.29	0.29		Boreal	BSXC	30	6⅛	6½	6⅝	+⅛
ActFitcom*	ACTF	2400	0.30	0.30	0.30	+0.02	Braziln	BZIN	255	0.75	0.65	0.65	-0.15
Advntxcl*	AXCL	565	0.25	0.25	0.25		CME Tel	CMET	21	8½	8	8½	+½
Alive Int	ALIV	72	2.75	2.65	2.65	-0.05	Camberly	CAMB	203	0.25	0.25	0.25	+0.03
AllegEq	ALGN	10	0.22	0.22	0.22		Cdn1stFin	CFFG	20	0.55	0.55	0.55	+0.05
AllncFing	AFGI	345	2.00	1.75	2.00	+0.10	Canfibre	CFGL	15	0.75	0.75	0.75	+0.15
AlphaGrp	ALFG	290	1.05	1.05	1.05		CantexEn	CTXE	100	0.09	0.09	0.09	+0.02
Altaur	AAQE	3000	0.10	0.10	0.10	-0.03	CapturNet	CAPN	150	0.55	0.55	0.55	+0.05
Anatolia*	AMCD	90	0.18	0.18	0.18	-0.03	Carfinco	CAAR	170	0.30	0.30	0.30	+0.05
Armace	ARMC	20	1.75	1.75	1.75		CarmaFin	CARM	1430	1.00	0.85	1.00	+0.10
ArmstcRs	ACIG	500	0.025	0.025	0.025		CntrlCdn	CCFC	22	0.40	0.25	0.25	-0.10
AsstMgmtS	AMSS	600	0.95	0.85	0.85	-0.03	Chondrogn	CDGN	70	0.80	0.80	0.80	

- **Dividends** on most prefs are treated like common stock dividends for tax purposes in that the company pays out of after-tax income and the shareholder gets a tax break.
- **Preferred shareholders** rank ahead of common stockholders but behind bondholders in claims on the assets of a company in any bankruptcy proceeding.
- **Most preferreds** have a "par" or redemption value, which is the price a company pays for each share if it buys back a preferred stock issue.
- **Preferred stock** usually is non-voting stock.

Dividends on conventional preferreds are a fixed amount but some preferreds have variable rate dividends pegged to a benchmark, such as the prime loan rate. And some preferreds have provisions that allow a company to skip dividends under specified distress situations.

PREFERRED SHARES GENERALLY HAVE BUYBACK TERMS SET OUT AT ISSUE

A conventional, or straight, preferred share issue looks somewhat like a common stock, except that the prefs pay dividends and usually have a par value. But straight prefs usually are considered part of the permanent equity of a company. The distinction is that these preferred shares do not have a redemption date and the company is under no obligation to buy back the shares on a fixed future date.

Most preferred shares are callable (or redeemable), which means the company can buy back the stock at its convenience. The redemption price will be part of the terms of issue. If a pref share is retractable, the holder can force the company to buy back the stock. Again, the terms of a buyback will be set out in the terms of the issue, usually at a fixed price and on a certain future date or after a certain future date.

Convertible preferred shares can, as the name implies, be swapped for another class of security at a pre-set conversion rate. Usually, they're convertible to common stock and features will vary on when and how the conversion clauses are triggered.

Whether a preferred issue is more like a stock or a bond will affect the market price.

For example, a convertible preferred issue that can be exchanged for common shares will react to changes in the market price of the common. But a simple preferred issue with a fixed dividend amount, a par value and a pre-set redemption date looks much like a bond and the price of this preferred will react to changes in the general level of interest rates, just as bonds do.

A POUND OF ADVICE ON PENNY STOCKS

 Canadian markets have a long history of financing junior companies and some of these penny resource stocks have gone on to become blue chips. High-tech and biotechnology companies are a significant component of the penny stock universe and they share many of the features associated with stocks of junior mining exploration companies.

Like any small business, the failure rate is high among start-up companies with stock exchange listings. A further complication is that markets for these juniors have been a natural magnet for unethical operators and, in a few cases, outright crooks.

Dealing with shares of these companies means recognizing some of their inherent characteristics. They need promoters to raise money and the job is to sell a dream, whether it be a gold mine or the next breakthrough in medical science.

A concept driven by intellectual analysis always is at the core of an honest penny stock. With a resource exploration company, it is the geology of the area and likelihood of underground riches. With a technology company, it is a research project that the promoters believe can be turned into a commercial venture.

THUS, THERE ARE THREE COMPONENTS TO A PENNY STOCK

• **The concept:** Is it an idea that stands up to rigorous analysis? If it is an exploration project, have others found commercial grades in similar geology? If it is a technology concept, is it based on sound science? Obviously, research will be necessary to answer these questions – either direct research on the concept or a search for opinions from people who understand the concept.

• **The promoter:** Does the promoter have a track record for straightforward dealings and for backing winning projects?

- **The commercial application:** If a discovery or breakthrough is made, can it be brought to market? There are plenty of examples of exploration properties with real discoveries but grades that are too low or so far away from refining operations that transportation costs eat up the profits. With technology projects, there are plenty of examples where the breakthrough produces a product that no one needs or that too many others can imitate cheaply.

If a junior company does hit the jackpot, the historical lesson is that the company is not likely to survive as the operator. In most cases, the junior becomes a takeover target for two reasons. The first is that it will need development funds, which usually means a lot more money than is spent on the discovery process and it is the mature companies that have better access to big pools of capital. The second reason a successful junior is likely to be bought out is that the promotion skills in the junior are no longer needed and the junior is not likely to have the depth of management skills that are required to turn a concept into a profitable commercial venture.

When a junior company does strike it rich, the shareholders usually have two choices. They can sell into the market for cash when the company is shopping for a well-heeled partner to manage the project. If they wait, they likely will end up with stock in the senior company because most big companies prefer to pay with stock and not cash when taking over a junior with a valuable property.

NAVIGATING THE MUCH-CHARTED WATERS
By Roman Franko

Equity investors place their hard-earned savings in the market to make a return higher than they could earn in risk-free investments such as money market funds.

To profit successfully and consistently, they must identify stocks that offer favorable risk-reward odds. A close examination of a stock's past price and volume behavior over time can be a valuable, sometimes indispensable, form of analysis in ongoing efforts to reduce risk and maximize return. Here we will introduce the basic tools of technical analysis, as well as the mindset required to apply them successfully.

USING PRICE-BASED TECHNIQUES, ANALYSTS CAN IDENTIFY TRENDS

The technical analyst typically first examines price in its raw chart form to identify trends and patterns that have forecasting value and then uses a computer to calculate indicators to reveal price relationships not readily apparent. We'll examine price-based techniques and then apply them to one of the bluest of blue-chip Canadian stocks, Royal Bank.

Once a trend, either up or down, is established, it cannot be expected to proceed in an absolutely straight line. Rather, price typically moves higher in a two steps forward, one step back fashion. One technique of tracking whether a trend remains in place is seeing whether today's price remains above, or below, its average price over a selected period of time. Typically, two time frames are chosen: a shorter one such as 13 periods and a longer one such as 40 periods. In a chart covering a very long time frame, 80 periods will be used. The accompanying Royal Bank chart spans 20 years and is an analysis of very long-term trends. This chart uses monthly moving averages. When a shorter time frame is studied, weekly moving averages will be used.

In a strong trend, the price will remain above/below its shorter term **moving average** (MA). On occasion, it will move temporarily through its shorter MA but as long as the price does not penetrate the longer one, it remains in its trend. A penetration by the price and the short term MA of the longer one is a sign the trend is ending, and a sideways consolidation or reversal can be expected.

Many trading systems, which generate buy or sell signals to be mechanically taken without second guessing, are based on some variations of price and/or the shorter term MA crossing the longer one.

IINVESTORS KEEP AN EYE ON A STOCK'S UP AND DOWN TREND

The next step is to establish the boundaries of an up or down trend. Once a couple of **wave tops** or **bottoms** are established, one line can be drawn, with another initially unconfirmed line drawn parallel to it. These lines delineate the outer limits of the stock's value range. At

TECHNICAL ANALYSIS | BY ROMAN FRANKO

The **monthly MACD** has not confirmed the move by price since October 2000 to new highs by itself hitting a higher high. Should the MACD turn over and give a sell signal from a level lower than its May 1998 peak, this negative divergence between higher price and lower momentum highs would strongly suggest that the uptrend is over.

Moving averages (13-, 40- and 80-month periods) also provided rising support. It is notable that price did not fall through its 40-month moving average (the middle solid line) between July 1988 and December 1999. When price fell through that MA during January and February 2000, it did not lose contact with it and was able to rally back above it.

Volume surged to record highs during October and November 1996, powering price through the historical zone of selling. The move to new highs that began in April 2000 has been on lower volume than that witnessed between 1996 and 1998, and this also suggests that Royal Bank is in the final stages of a bull phase.

the upper line, bearish investors think price is overvalued and will sell and drive the price down. At the lower line, bullish investors feel the price is undervalued and will buy and bid it back into the range. A decisive break out of this range indicates the former consensus has broken down and a new one is being formed.

There are many price-derived indicators other than moving averages, some particularly helpful in trending markets, while others are of greater utility in markets that are trading sideways. **Moving Average Convergence Divergence**, or MACD, is a popular one, as it is useful in confirming trends in both kinds of markets. Its principal utility, however, is in signaling a change in trend by diverging, or not confirming, a price trend.

MONEY FLOW IS ONE INDICATOR OF A STOCK'S STRENGTH

Before we apply these techniques to Royal Bank, let's note that Royal Bank climbed cyclically from the $7 to $17 zones between mid-1980 and July 1996. A trend line drawn across the March 1981 and April 1983 peaks and extended to the right accurately identified a zone of rising selling resistance that stopped bi-annual cyclical uptrends during November 1989, November 1991 and December 1993. After price was able to break through that resistance, it soared to new highs.

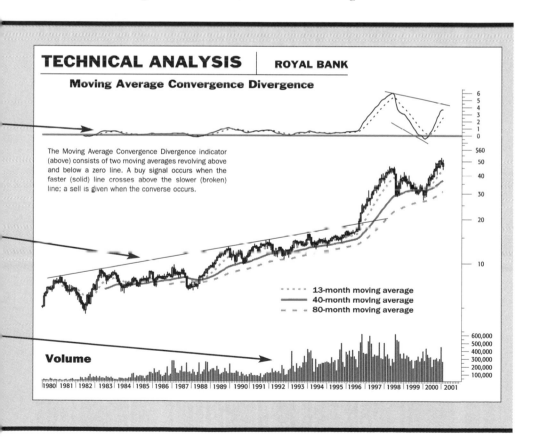

TECHNICAL ANALYSIS | **ROYAL BANK**

Moving Average Convergence Divergence

The Moving Average Convergence Divergence indicator (above) consists of two moving averages revolving above and below a zero line. A buy signal occurs when the faster (solid) line crosses above the slower (broken) line; a sell is given when the converse occurs.

· · · · · 13-month moving average
———— 40-month moving average
— — — 80-month moving average

Volume

BLOCK TRADES | TABLE

Block transactions – 100,000 shares or a value of more than $1 million – usually are trades for institutions, such as pension or mutual funds.

Ticker is the stock symbol; price is the trade price; volume is the number of shares. Buyer and seller are the brokerage firms on each side of the transaction.

A single name indicates it is a "cross," where the broker represents both sides.

A cross may mean that both buyer and seller are clients of the firm or that the brokerage house is buying or selling shares out of inventory in house accounts.

BLOCK TRADES

Stocks trading minimum 100,000 shares or $1-million

A single name for the buyer/seller indicates that the same brokerage is on either side of the transaction. Otherwise, the buyer appears on the first line and the seller on a second line.

Ticker	Price	Vol. 00s	Buyer/ Seller
Toronto			
AGF Mgmt cl B AGF.B	23.75	1385	TD Secs
ATI Technlgys ATY	11.00	1142	TD Secs
ATI Technlgys	11.00	1048	NatBkFC
			BMO
Nesbtt			
Abitibi-Cons A	11.65	2362	TD Secs
Abitibi-Cons	11.65	2067	NatBkFC
			BMO
Nesbtt			
Abitibi-Cons	12.00	1000	UBS
Bunt			
Abitibi-Cons	12.00	1000	RBCDS
Nesbtt			
Agrium Inc AGU	17.25	617	TD Secs
Agrium Inc	17.25	607	NatBkFC

Ticker	Price	Vol. 00s	Buyer/ Seller
Nesbtt			
BCE Inc	44.05	500	NatBkFC
BCE Inc	43.95	500	NatBkFC
BCE Inc	44.05	4026	NatBkFC
BCE Inc	44.05	500	NatBkFC
BCE Inc	44.15	286	UBS
Bunt			
BCE Inc	44.25	300	BMO
Nesbtt			
BCE Inc	44.40	250	BMO
Nesbtt			
BCE Inc	44.40	250	BMO
Nesbtt			
BCE Inc	44.55	250	BMO
Nesbtt			
BCE Inc	44.80	1100	BMO
Nesbtt			
BCE Inc	44.65	250	NatBkFC
BCE 1st pf YBCE.PR.Y	24.60	500	TD Secs

Ticker	Price	Vol. 00s	Buyer/ Seller
			Scotia
Bombard B	22.50	4777	NatBkFC
			BMO
Nesbtt			
Bombard B	22.50	1282	CIBC
			BMO
Nesbtt			
Bombard B	22.50	4156	CIBC
			RBCDS
Bombard B	22.50	502	CIBC
			TD Secs
Bombard B	22.50	769	Goldmn
			RBCDS
Bombard B	22.65	1000	RBCDS
Bombard B	22.65	528	RBCDS
Bombard B	22.75	1000	RBCDS
Bombard B	22.75	1000	RBCDS
Bombard B	22.70	498	TD Secs
Bombard B	22.60	1000	RBCDS

The subsequent correction during mid-1998 was sharp but in effect symmetrically consistent with the previous strong rise. Barring an unexpected breakdown, Royal Bank is well positioned to attain the $60 zone during the current uptrend.

Volume similarly provides a host of clues to the technical position of a stock. Very simply, rising volume provides a solid underpinning and confirms a price rise, while falling volume after a price rise has been in progress for some time is a sign of incipient weakness. In a bear market, the situation is somewhat different. A volume surge as a stock falls is a sign of urgent selling but the price can, and often does, fall on thin volume.

Volume-derived indicators have also been developed, all of which attempt to identify accumulation or distribution of stock. One helpful indicator is money flow, which measures the strength of money flowing in or out of a stock.

TIME PLAYS KEY ROLE IN THE RESOLUTION OF PATTERNS

The time factor can play an important role in at least two different ways. Most stocks cycle up and down with a greater or lesser regularity, generally in concert with others in their group. These cycles may be longer term and related to, for example, the often-cited four-year business cycle, or shorter term and dependent on, for example, seasonal fluctuations in supply and demand. Royal Bank's current bull market run is about at that four-year mark and thus the odds increasingly favor a correction.

Time also becomes important in the resolution of patterns. For example, Royal Bank formed a narrowing symmetrical triangle pattern between late mid-1998 and late in 1999. The rule of thumb is that if the price breaks out before it reaches two-thirds of the way to the apex of that triangle, the subsequent move will typically be strong. If, however, the breakout does not come in this time period, the price displays a strong tendency, even if it does breakout, to drift sideways to down.

TECHNICAL ANALYSTS DRAW ON YEARS OF EXPERIENCE

In short, technical analysis can minimize risk by identifying stocks that:
- Are at the lower edge of their price channels.
- Are at or above their moving averages.
- Have rising momentum.
- Are supported by favorable volume trends.
- And, are early on in their longer term cycles.

Conversely, these tools can identify stocks that are high risk if they:
- Are at an upper channel line.
- Are at or below their moving averages.
- Have falling momentum and unfavorable volume trends.
- And, are late in their longer term cycles.

To be done well, technical analysis has to be done thoroughly, looking at all relevant aspects of a stock's behavior in as objective a manner as possible. Like other forms of analysis, a partial or superficial treatment to justify an opinion previously arrived at, or seizing on one aspect while ignoring contradictory evidence, will undermine its utility.

Finally, the good technical analyst needs to strike a balance between taking a position and holding to it, and changing a position when the preponderance of evolving evidence requires it. At what point this change in evaluation takes place can only be decided in specific cases by drawing on years of intensive experience in assessing the many combinations and variations that arise.

CHAPTER 3

BEYOND | EQUITIES

- Understanding derivatives
- Investment strategies using options, warrants, shorts and REITs
- Commodities markets
- Futures and indexes

HOW THE TOP GUNS PICK

THEIR STOCK MARKET TARGETS | BY SONITA HORVITCH

THE HALLMARK OF PROFESSIONAL money managers is that they apply a consistent, disciplined approach to selecting stocks and constructing equity portfolios. The two principal styles employed by equity managers are value investing and growth investing. These two broad categories encompass a wide variety of practices as managers develop their own variations on the basic theme. In a nutshell, a value manager tries to identify stocks that are fundamentally cheap based on such standard valuation ratios as stock price to earnings, stock price to cash flow, stock price to book value and stock price to revenue. In a value portfolio, the standard valuations of stocks would typically be below those for the market as a whole.

Growth managers look for companies that are generating very high revenue, earnings and cash flow growth. They are hoping to find the next Microsoft Corp., Procter & Gamble Inc. or Coca-Cola Co. A growth manager's portfolio would typically trade at valuation ratios above those for the market as a whole.

Investing professionals say neither the value nor the growth style alone will result in peak performance at all times. Consultants who advise managers of large funds recommend a mix of styles in a portfolio to reduce fluctuations in returns over the long haul.

The concept of value investing is very much associated with Benjamin Graham who, in his magnum opus *Security Analysis*, published in 1934, said investors should be able to detect undervalued or bargain stocks by looking at financial ratios.

Graham had 10 key ratios on his list and he looked for stocks to fit into 7 of those 10 before deciding that they represented a value investment.

VALUE-ORIENTED INVESTORS LOOK AT TRACK RECORD TO PREDICT EARNINGS

Strict disciples of Graham's method assess a stock based on existing financials, not on potential. Often, companies in the portfolios of value-oriented fund managers become takeover targets of other companies because they meet Graham's conditions.

Proponents of value investing look at such historical benchmarks as price/earnings, price/cash flow and debt/equity. They estimate a company's likely earnings growth or asset growth over several years. The goal is to find stocks that they believe will be selling at the greatest discount to calculated value well into the future.

One test is to compare a company's market value (stock price multiplied by the number of common shares outstanding) against tangible book value (total assets minus liabilities minus any stock issues that stand ahead of common stock). If the market value is less than two-thirds the book value, it fits Graham's definition of good value.

VALUE MANAGERS TARGET BARGAIN STOCKS

Although value managers are essentially stock pickers, on occasion an entire industry or sector may present bargain opportunities. For example, the Canadian retail industry in the mid-1990s was seen to be under siege from foreign competition and was suffering from a general reluctance by consumers to spend. Stock prices of retailers were beaten down and canny value managers started to buy shares of some of Canada's largest listed retailers.

Generally, the value style of investing is viewed as conservative. Value managers say inexpensive stocks are likely to be less vulnerable to a market downturn. That's because they believe values are already depressed.

If the market as a whole is overvalued, and therefore vulnerable to correction, the value manager might have a tougher time identifying cheap candidates and is likely to have a high cash component that will serve as a cushion in a downturn.

GROWTH INVESTORS LOOK FOR STOCKS WITH OUTSTANDING POTENTIAL

The focus of a growth investor is decidedly on the future. This type of investor looks for companies or sectors able to produce the highest and most consistent growth in revenue, earnings or cash flow. A company may be generating earnings and cash flow growth both internally or through acquisition. Growth managers use such criteria as earnings momentum, return on equity growth and earnings estimate revisions when ranking stocks. The discipline in this approach is not to pay too much for growth.

Some sectors are viewed as traditional hunting ground for growth stocks. These include technology, both hardware and software, biotechnology, telecommunications, health care and consumer staples such as beverages, cigarettes and household products.

Because the prospects for these companies are generally seen to be excellent, the stocks trade at multiples that can be very high relative to market averages.

GROWTH STOCKS CAN WEATHER MARKET DOWNTURN

High price/earnings multiples make stocks vulnerable to any disappointing results. The stock of a company reporting earnings or cash flow below analysts' expectations can take a severe beating – even in a bull market. High technology companies are a prime example.

Nortel Networks Corp. fits into this category. In 2000, Nortel shares traded as high as $124.50. At that price, it was 107 times the consensus analyst forecast for earnings per share for the following 12 months. Nortel's P/E multiple was roughly four times the comparative price/earnings multiple of the TSE 300 index. This lofty valuation was quickly corrected as Nortel declined 60% within five months, closing at $49.30 at the end of 2000. In early 2001 the share price declined even further and the P/E dropped below 30. At that level, Nortel fell within the parameters of one of Benjamin Graham's ratios, which is that the P/E should be less than 40% of its peak in the previous five years.

In a market downturn, growth stocks may initially take a beating as investors take profits in their top performing stocks. But growth managers argue such stocks are likely to recover more quickly than the market as a whole – provided their growth potential is unscathed. This is because their earnings power will stand out relative to the rest of the market. As a general rule, though, true growth businesses are less sensitive to swings in the business cycle.

Growth managers will sell a stock when there has been a deterioration in the fundamentals or when the stock price is too high relative to its earnings prospects.

MANAGEMENT STYLES OFTEN ARE COMBINED

Many managers use a combination of styles in managing their portfolios. Professionals routinely compare relative earnings growth prospects with relative values of companies. That means checking the background and outlook for particular companies against those of their peers – Nortel against other telecom hardware companies, for example, or TD Bank against other banks, and so on. This is a "bottom up" approach in finding companies with favorable attributes.

Following broad industry trends is a "top down" approach. Often the reason for a move in a stock's price can be explained by industry factors. For example, the market price of any commodity, whether it be oil or memory chips, will have an impact on corporate sales and profit margins.

THE SAFE HARBOR THAT'S KNOWN AS DIVERSITY

Jay Gould, the 19th-century railroad baron, provides an insight into the potential perils of staking a portfolio on a single stock. Clifton Fadiman, in a book of anecdotes, tells a story of the rector at Gould's church who went to the financier for advice on how to invest his life savings. Buy Missouri Pacific, Gould said, but keep it confidential. The share price for Missouri Pacific did rise for a while, but then it plunged.

DIVERSIFYING IS KEY TO A BALANCED PORTFOLIO

The distraught minister complained to Gould, who promptly wrote a cheque to cover the loss.

This act of apparent generosity left the minister feeling guilty and he admitted to Gould that he had told several members of the congregation about the stock tip. "I know that," Gould said. "They were the ones I was after."

Diversification would have given the last laugh to Gould's enemies.

The goal in balancing a portfolio is to ensure that losses in a single security don't sink the investment fund.

Professional managers usually have limits imposed by their boards or investment committees. Typically, no more than 5% can go to one security and with a large fund the big holdings are in top quality investments.

For individual portfolios, a 10% limit usually is recommended for investment in a single stock.

A DIVERSIFIED PORTFOLIO HAS INVESTMENTS IN DIFFERENT ASSET CLASSES

In addition to limits on a single security, most portfolios also have guidelines on how much to invest in different asset classes – common stocks, preferred stocks, bonds, money market notes, cash, commodities and derivatives. For small portfolios, the mix usually is limited to the major categories of stocks, fixed income and cash. (The cash category generally includes term deposits.)

Diversification also can include a mix of types of securities within a class. For example, a portfolio can include foreign and domestic stocks and a collection of stocks from different industry sectors.

The mix of security classes and types in a portfolio will vary with the risk profile of an individual. Younger investors often will include more stocks that are considered speculative while seniors usually want a mix that emphasizes safety and a steady flow of interest and dividends.

All portfolios should be reviewed on a regular schedule to reassess the appropriate mix of investments.

HOW MUCH RISK ARE YOU WILLING TO TAKE?

Good fences make good neighbors and a financial hedge is aptly named – a proper hedge is designed to put a fence around risk.

Everyone wants a big return from their investments but too often the risk part of the equation doesn't get enough attention. In the jargon of the street, it's the reach for yield. Attitudes of many of today's investors were conditioned by the inflationary bubble of the late 1970s and early '80s. A high inflation rate brought with it a high return on term deposits at financial institutions. When those certificates came due, the holders looked around to reinvest at similar rates.

INVESTORS SHOULD FOLLOW BASIC TECHNIQUES WHEN DEALING WITH RISK

The stock market provided similar dazzling returns through the first two-thirds of the 1990s, with little inflation, and many investors began to see 20%-plus returns as normal, prior to the downturn in the spring of 2000.

But the lessons of history are that returns of 20% or more are extraordinary and high yields usually come with high risk.

The further lesson is that risk should be hedged.

Managers of large pools of funds use a variety of sophisticated hedging techniques but small investors also can follow basic techniques in dealing with risk.

A primary rule is to decide in advance the amount you can afford to lose. If the answer is zero, then stick to investments that will preserve the principle, such as good quality bonds that are held to maturity.

Once risk comes into the picture, some common-sense tools can be used. The basic approach is to assess the odds that something will go wrong.

The first thing to look at is "market" risk, the odds that prices in general will fall dramatically. This involves an assessment of the state of the business cycle and of the general level of prices in relation to long-term averages.

MEASURING VOLATILITY GIVES A GUIDE TO DEGREE OF RISK

In focusing on specific securities, a risk assessment can be done in relation to the market – is this particular security more or less volatile than the general market?

This measure of volatility is known as "beta" – which is a measure based on a scale that starts at one. A stock with a beta higher than 1.0 is more volatile than the general market and a beta below 1.0 means less volatility.

Betas are routinely calculated and brokers can provide this information on individual securities. Using betas can provide a rough guide to the degree of risk in a portfolio.

If there is high risk in a portfolio, derivative securities can hedge that risk. Stock options can fix a floor price for someone who owns the shares.

Options have a pre-set strike price and a put option can set a limit to loss. Options on market indexes can be used as a hedge against declines in the price of a basket of stocks. There is a cost to buying an option and that becomes a charge for protection against risk.

THERE ARE SOME BENEFITS TO BEING SHORT

Not everybody waits for a bull market to make money. Some people profit when stock prices fall. It's known as selling short, which is the reverse order from a normal stock purchase. Shorting a stock means selling first and buying later. If successful, the short seller buys back at a lower price in order to make a profit. A short seller is selling something he or she does not own. Doing so involves borrowing certificates from someone who does own the stock.

THE SHORT POSITIONS | TABLE

Short positions is a tally of shares sold by people who think the price will fall. Short sales are done with borrowed share certificates and the sellers hope to buy in later at cheaper prices to replace the borrowed certificates. Short sales are reported to the stock exchanges, which produce a twice-monthly summary of short sale activity that covers all trading on Canadian-listed issues.

The table reports the latest total for each stock sold short compared with the previous reporting period and the net change between the two. Average daily trading volume also is listed because trading activity is important in assessing the significance of a short position. The measure is how many days of buying would be required to buy back all the shares sold short. A large short position in relation to volume means a lot of people are betting the stock will take a big drop. If they are wrong, the stock price could rise sharply when they are forced to cover their short positions. This table usually appears on the second and fourth Saturday of each month.

SHORT POSITIONS 09.29.00-09.15.00

Figures supplied by TSE and FP DataGroup. Includes short interest positions for Canadian listed issues (except warrants and preferred shares), where current position is greater than 50,000 shares or the change is above 25,000 shares. Average volume excludes short sales.

Stock	Ticker	09.29.00	09.15.00	Net change	Avg. daily volume
AGF Mgmt cl B	AGF.B	31,300	76,242	-44,942	83,509
AIS Resources	AIS	25,000	...	25,000	13,100
AMI Resources	AMU	...	25,500	-25,500	17,694
AMVESCAP	AVZ	327,480	700,401	-372,921	398,950
ARC Enrg Tr un	AET.UN	31,968	...	31,968	133,756
ATCO I	ACO.X	221,300	222,000	-700	10,915
ATI Technlgys	ATY	390,444	482,897	-92,453	535,507
Abitibi-Cons	A	994,234	1,215,986	-221,752	1,409,353
Agrium Inc	AGU	290,530	242,037	48,493	258,991
AimGlobal	AGT	118,500	43,800	74,700	72,834
Air Canada	AC	1,764,945	2,036,008	-271,063	630,615
Alberta Enrg	AEC	671,898	1,312,480	-640,582	611,375
Alcan	AL	436,662	871,491	-434,829	1,145,044
Algo Group A	AO.A	209,309	108,944	100,365	523,127
AlgonqnPwr un	APF.UN	10,900	300,100	-289,200	45,963
Aliant	AIT	124,287	117,387	6,900	38,145
AlimntCouch A	ATD.A	100,000	...	100,000	100
AlimntCouch B	ATD.B	230,506	230,164	342	2,160
Allnce Atls B	AAC.B	148,550	79,000	69,550	253,186
AltaRex Corp	AXO	600	48,900	-48,300	183,471
Altrnatv Fuel	ATF	113,846	284,178	-170,332	248,939
Anderson Expl	AXL	615,081	575,757	39,324	752,247

Those who lend out certificates are known as short banks and usually it is a brokerage firm or a large institution that has a big inventory of stocks held for the long term. Short banks charge a fee for lending certificates and this is part of the cost of short selling. Typically, short selling is done on margin – in other words, with borrowed money. The need for cash arises if the stock price rises after a short sale. The margin account will cover that price difference up to a pre-set limit

Beyond that limit, the seller must cover, either by putting up cash to bring the margin account back into line or by buying the stock to replace the borrowed certificates.

PLACE YOUR BET ON FUTURE OF COMMODITIES

Businesses buy commodities in the cash market but the real action is in the futures market, which provides the pricing mechanism for raw materials from aluminum to zinc.

The cash market, also known as the spot market, doesn't exist in the formal sense. It's not a single formal trading arena. Instead, it's a broad trading network that includes specialized dealer firms, places like public stockyards where producers sell, and single-purpose agencies such as the Canadian Wheat Board.

Most futures trading takes place in organized exchanges and this is where commodity price trends are set.

The system is similar for futures in major currencies, bonds and stock market indexes. Futures markets for financial assets play a lead role in setting cash market values for underlying securities.

There is a fundamental reason for the importance of futures trading in commodities – producers are spending money long before they go to market and their products are subject to influences beyond their control.

When a farmer plants in the spring, the weather during the growing season is an unknown. When a mining company breaks ground for a new smelter, it can't be sure of industrial demand on the date that freshly minted ingots start rolling out the door.

COMMODITIES PRODUCERS FIND PROTECTION IN FUTURES

Producers can, and do, hedge against those uncertainties with futures – either with a contract for future delivery or with a forward sale. In the former technique, they are buying a specified amount of a commodity at a fixed price so they can cover delivery commitments if there is a production problem. In the latter, they are selling their product for future delivery and thus locking in an assured price.

With a contract for future delivery, the producer will deliver its goods if things work out as planned and the futures contract will simply expire with no action taken. The practical fact is that most futures contracts are not completed, which is what allows the system to work. The underwriter of futures contracts knows most contracts will expire unexercised and this allows the issue price of a single contract to be set at a price that is only a fraction of the value of the underlying commodity.

FINANCIAL FUTURES ARE AFFECTED BY BUSINESS CYCLE

Once a contract is issued, its price is affected by factors that will move the price of the underlying commodity. Wheat futures drop if there is a bumper crop. Copper futures rise if there is a labor dispute at a major producer. Natural gas futures fall if it is a mild winter. Oil futures spike higher if there is a threat of war in the Middle East, which still has the world's biggest, lowest-cost oilfields.

In each of these situations, the futures price is anticipating a change in the cash market when producers go to market with their products.

Financial futures work much the same way. Price moves for bond futures are reacting to the outlook for changes in interest rates. Swings in a stock index futures contract reflect expectations about general market trends. Currency futures respond to expected shifts in foreign exchange rates.

WHAT ARE CANADA'S COMMODITIES?

Chicago, London and New York are the world's major centers for trading in commodities and financial derivatives but markets in many other cities have staked out specialty roles in this business.

In Canada, the derivatives markets are in Montreal, for contracts on financial products, and in Winnipeg, for farm commodities.

CANADIAN EXCHANGES SPECIALIZE IN FUTURES MARKET NICHES

The Bourse de Montreal took the initiative in Canadian derivatives and focused first on interest-sensitive securities. At that time, stock options also were traded in Toronto and Vancouver. A restructuring of Canadian exchanges in 1999 and 2000 resulted in all non-farm derivatives going to Montreal. Toronto became the exclusive center for senior equities and the western exchanges banded together to form a unified market in junior stocks.

Derivative contracts in Montreal include futures and options on:
- Three-month bankers' acceptance (BA) notes and government of Canada bonds.
- The S&P/TSE 60 stock index.
- Individual stocks.

As well, the Bourse de Montreal is developing a series of futures on sectors in the S&P/TSE indexes. The most active market in Montreal is for BA futures and this contract is becoming an important pricing mechanism in the Canadian money market.

Winnipeg's position comes naturally from its historic role as a supply center for the Prairie farm industry. The Winnipeg Commodity Exchange has contracts on six Prairies crops – barley, canola, flax, peas, oats and wheat – but the big volume item is canola.

There are two reasons for Winnipeg's pre-eminence in trading futures and options on canola – it is a major crop for the region and canola is not a big contract in the huge commodity trading pits in Chicago.

In Montreal, the key contracts are in interest rate futures and options on three-month bankers' acceptance (BA) notes and government of Canada bonds. The most active market in Montreal is for BA futures and this contract is becoming an important pricing mechanism in the Canadian money market.

These exchanges have carved out market niches. A successful derivatives market needs a big volume of trading to be efficient and it can take years to build a dominant position. The C$ futures market provides an example of the significance of an established trading environment.

CASH PRICES | TABLE

Cash commodity prices are for wholesale volumes of common grades. While industrial use in any commodity may span dozens of grades, certain key grades provide benchmark pricing. Futures and options contracts will be based on those benchmark grades. The definition of benchmark may vary around the globe. In crude oil markets, for example, the main benchmark grade in North America is West Texas intermediate while in Europe it is Brent (from North Sea wells).

Delivery point is an issue that enters into the pricing of many commodities. Canadian grains, for example, usually are priced at shipping terminals in Thunder Bay, where grains are loaded on to ships. (Sea transport is the cheapest way to move bulk cargo.)

Cash prices
Supplied by Reuters

	Latest	Prev	Wk ago		Latest	Prev	Wk ago
Gold				**Canada grains (con't)**			
(US$ per troy oz)				(C$ per tonne at St.Lawrence)			
London a.m. fix	271.60	270.80	269.10	1 Amber durum	291.72	293.37	294.17
London p.m. fix	273.90	271.60	269.10	2 Amber durum	286.72	288.37	289.17
Zurich a.m. fix	273.00	273.35	268.75	3 Amber durum	281.72	283.37	284.17
Zurich p.m. fix	273.50	273.75	269.05	**U.S. grains**			
Silver				(US$ per bushel)			
(US$ per troy oz)				**Minneapolis**			
London a.m. fix	4.74	4.69	4.69	Wheat Durum (cnts)	502.00	502.00	522.00
N.Y. Handy&Har	4.76	4.75	4.68	Wheat 1 DNS 14%	3.66	3.70	3.78
Palladium (tr oz)	895.00	851.45	804.00	Malting barley	2.45	2.45	2.40
Platinum (tr oz)	610.66	603.40	602.00	Corn	1.78	1.82	1.82
Industrial metals (London fix)				Soybeans	4.81	4.75	4.73
(US$ per tonne)				**Kansas City**			

Chicago markets have active futures and options contracts on all the major currencies, including the C$. At one time the Toronto Stock Exchange, through its futures subsidiary, set up a competing market for C$ futures but the TSE never attracted enough volume and ultimately scrapped the contract.

COMPANIES TRADING IN FUTURES HAVE CONTRACTS IN KEY MARKET CITIES

Futures and options are bought and sold through investment dealers and specialized commodities brokers.

Large Canadian companies that rely on futures markets will have trading desks in those key market cities, the banks in Chicago and London for currencies and the big resource firms in London and New York.

The London Metal Exchange and the New York Mercantile Exchange perform key pricing functions for basic industrial commodities. Each commodity futures contract has a specific trading unit. For canola on the Winnipeg Commodity Exchange, it is 20 tonnes.

Prices are quoted in points and the size of a point can vary. For canola, it is 1/20th of the value of the contract, or, more simply, the price for one tonne.

Prices move up or down in ticks. A tick is the minimum amount by which a price can move, and varies, depending on the commodity.

SEVERAL FACTORS WILL AFFECT THE PRICE OF A CONTRACT

• **The price of the underlying commodity.** Seasonal and business cycles can influence the supply and demand of some commodities, thus influencing their prices.

• **Supply and demand for the contracts themselves,** created largely by speculators.

• **The time until the delivery date.** This reflects the carrying costs for the commodity.

Commodities exchanges often impose daily price limits to avoid panic selling and put a lid on frenzied buying. These limits govern price moves in a pre-set time period, often the trading day.

Futures contracts vary in length, depending on the commodity. Gold contracts, for example, can expire in anywhere from a few months to a number of years. Active grain contracts rarely go beyond a year.

OBLIGATION THE KEY TO HEDGING FUTURES RISK

A futures contract is a deal that won't actually take place for months – and sometimes years – down the road. It's an obligation to buy or sell a large amount of a commodity at a specific time in the future.

The price is set in advance, when the contract is made.

The key word here is obligation. Unlike options – where buyers have the right to not exercise their contracts – futures contracts are done deals.

That means the holder of a futures contract to buy 10 tonnes of cocoa must take delivery if the contract is held on the day it expires.

Similarly, the holder of a futures contract to sell 10 tonnes of cocoa must produce a truckload of cocoa on the delivery date.

COMMODITIES COMPANIES ARE MAJOR PLAYERS IN FUTURES MARKET

It may sound as though there's a whole lot of cocoa – or coffee, wheat, orange juice, lumber and other commodities – changing hands. But in reality, there isn't – only about 2% of all futures contracts involve physical delivery.

Most positions are closed out before the delivery date.

Closing out a contract is simply a matter of buying or selling an offsetting position.

For example, that holder of a contract to buy 10 tonnes of cocoa would buy a futures contract to sell the same amount and the two contracts would cancel each other.

Why don't holders of futures contracts take delivery instead of buying goods on the cash market?

Futures contracts are based on standard grades and most producers have highly specialized requirements. Substitutions of one grade for another may not be suitable. By buying on the cash market, producers get exactly what they need.

Major participants in futures markets are companies that deal in the commodities involved.

For example, growers of cacao and makers of chocolate bars are big players in the cocoa futures market.

Similarly, banks are big players in fixed income and currency futures because their product is money.

MOST FUTURES CONTRACTS ARE CLOSED OUT BEFORE DELIVERY

The traditional purpose of a futures market is to hedge risk. Commodity producers use futures to cover the risk of a price fall from oversupply and consumers cover the risk of high prices in cases of shortage.

Considering the amounts involved in commodities markets, the costs associated with buying futures contracts are negligible – mainly commissions paid to brokers.

Buyers and sellers of futures contracts must put up a margin deposit but this will be a fraction of the full cost of the contract, usually less than 5%.

The real cost of the contract for a buyer would be the money due upon delivery.

For the seller, it would be the commodity to be delivered. But, as has already been noted, delivery seldom takes place.

FUTURES MARKETS: HEDGER MEETS SPECULATOR

Futures markets are where you'll find an odd combination of players – from the high rollers of the investment world to conservative investors looking to hedge their bets.

It's easier to understand the ins and outs of these complicated securities by knowing something about the main players and how they use futures.

FUTURES PRICES | TABLE

The futures prices table lists futures under commodity groups: market indexes, currencies, interest-sensitive securities, grains, livestock and meat, foods, precious metals, industrial metals, petroleum and woods and fibres. The commodity is listed at the top of each series of prices. The abbreviations in brackets refer to the exchange where the futures are traded. For example, WPG refers to the Winnipeg Commodity Exchange. When contracts for the same commodity are traded on more than one exchange, separated listings are included for each exchange. Exchange specifications will list the size of the contract in relation to the underlying commodity.

Next to the contract size is the definition of a price tick. That is the unit of quotation stated in relation to the value of the contract. In the example of a gold contract traded on the Commodity Exchange, a US10¢ change in the price of the future represents a US$10 change in the value of the underlying contract for 100 troy ounces of gold.

The tables give price ranges between high and low for the latest trading day and for the life of the contract to date. **Month** is the month in which the contract expires, usually on the third Friday.

Open, in the price columns, refers to the price at which each contract opened when it began trading on the exchange. **Settle** is settlement price as determined by the closing range of prices. This is used to calculate trading gains and losses (setting an end-of-day market value for a portfolio). This notional settlement price also will be used for margin calls and is not necessarily the same as the closing trade price on the exchange

Previous open interest is the open interest – the total number of contracts that have not yet been offset by an opposite transaction or fulfilled by delivery – for the previous day. Previous open interest in the last column indicates the open interest for each contract on the previous day.

Estimated volume and previous volume are the trading volume estimates for the day of the listings and the previous day. Figures are the total for all the contracts on each commodity.

FUTURES PRICES 12.07.00

Figures supplied by Star Data Systems Inc.

High	Low	Mth	Open	High	Low	Settle	Chg	op.int
—Lifetime—			——Daily——					Prev

Currency

Australian Dollar (IMM)
A$100,000, US$ per A$; 0.0001 = $10 per contract

High	Low	Mth	Open	High	Low	Settle	Chg	op.int
0.6412	0.5075	Dec00	0.5481	0.5512	0.5459	0.5470	-0.0004	19,523
0.6390	0.5100	Mar01	0.5485	0.5510	0.5468	0.5476	-0.0005	8,702

Est. vol. 2,263   Prev. vol. 2,652   Prev. open int. 28,253

British Pound (IMM)
62,500 pounds, US$ per pound; 0.0002 = $12.50 per contract

High	Low	Mth	Open	High	Low	Settle	Chg	op.int
1.6500	1.3966	Dec00	1.4424	1.4498	1.4386	1.4432	+0.0008	32,010
1.6050	1.4010	Mar01	1.4462	1.4520	1.4418	1.4456	+0.0006	7,492

Est. vol. 5,974   Prev. vol. 6,629   Prev. open int. 39,506

Canadian Dollar (IMM)
C$100,000, US$ per C$; 0.0001 = $10 per contract

High	Low	Mth	Open	High	Low	Settle	Chg	op.int
0.7025	0.6403	Dec00	0.6545	0.6575	0.6531	0.6549	...	54,694
0.7040	0.6415	Mar01	0.6565	0.6586	0.6543	0.6562	...	9,276
0.6990	0.6425	June01	0.6573	0.6593	0.6557	0.6573	...	3,178
0.6905	0.6445	Sept01	0.6565	0.6604	0.6565	0.6583	...	1,170
0.6825	0.6452	Dec01				0.6593	...	513

Est. vol. 13,817   Prev. vol. 19,450   Prev. open int. 68,838

European Currency (CME)
125,000 ECUs, US$ per unit; 0.0001 = $12.50 per contract

High	Low	Mth	Open	High	Low	Settle	Chg	op.int
1.0655	0.8245	Dec00	0.8922	0.8980	0.8860	0.8892	-0.0021	80,007
0.9950	0.8284	Mar01	0.8953	0.9018	0.8900	0.8927	-0.0022	11,998

Est. vol. 23,999   Prev. vol. 21,231   Prev. open int. 92,526

French Franc (IMM)
500,000 francs, US$ per franc; 0.00002 = $10 per contract

Est. vol. 0   Prev. vol. 0   Prev. open int. 2

Cotton 2 (NYCE)
50,000 lbs., US cents per lb.; 0.01 cent = $5 per contract

High	Low	Mth	Open	High	Low	Settle	Chg	op.int
69.25	54.50	Mar01	67.06	67.50	66.80	67.25	-0.09	35,119
70.50	54.50	May01	68.55	69.05	68.40	68.83	-0.05	12,237
71.10	56.30	July01	69.55	69.90	69.45	69.85	-0.03	7,039
67.70	59.40	Dec01	65.90	66.05	65.80	65.95	-0.30	6,698

Prev. vol. 11,174   Prev. open int. 62,129

Flaxseed (WPG)
20 metric tons, C$ per metric ton; 10 cents = $2 per contract

High	Low	Mth	Open	High	Low	Settle	Chg	op.int
260.70	221.80	Jan01				250.30	+1.20	1,373
262.00	226.00	Mar01	251.80	252.20	250.60	251.00	...	2,140
256.50	244.00	May01	251.50	251.50	251.50	251.50	+0.50	1,055

Prev. vol. 297   Prev. open int. 4,773

Hogs (CME)
40,000 lbs., US cents per lb.; 2.5 cents per cwt. = $10 per contract

High	Low	Mth	Open	High	Low	Settle	Chg	op.int
59.700	48.700	Dec00	55.900	56.050	55.700	55.800	-0.225	8,522
59.850	50.050	Feb01	59.300	59.350	58.700	58.775	-0.525	27,388
58.800	48.650	Apr01	58.600	58.700	58.225	58.400	-0.300	5,961
65.300	55.200	June01	64.400	64.450	63.900	64.125	-0.375	3,900
62.550	54.775	July01	62.000	62.300	61.850	62.150	-0.150	1,109
51.900	46.400	Oct01	51.200	51.900	51.100	51.900	+0.400	1,004

Est. vol. 9,715   Prev. vol. 10,943   Prev. open int. 49,357

Lumber (CME)
80,000 bd. ft., US$ per 1,000 bd. ft.; 10 cents = $8 per contract

High	Low	Mth	Open	High	Low	Settle	Chg	op.int
335.50	220.70	Jan01	223.50	228.80	222.00	222.20	+0.80	2,293
304.80	233.10	Mar01	235.00	239.00	234.30	234.80	+1.50	1,294

Est. vol. 1,092   Prev. vol. 1,077   Prev. open int. 4,355

Oats (CBOT)

Speculators take on the risks that hedgers attempt to avoid. Their role in the market is not unlike that of an insurance underwriter, who assumes risk in exchange for a premium (in this case, the speculator's profit).

A hedger uses the futures market for insurance against fluctuating prices of commodities that are bought or sold. A hedger can be anyone, from a farmer selling grain to a big construction firm buying large amounts of lumber. Whoever they are, the goal of hedgers usually is not to make money, but to make sure they don't lose money.

Leverage is what makes futures so attractive to speculators. Using borrowed money magnifies profits far beyond what they would be if a speculator put up the full cost of the commodity. But it's also the reason a great deal of money can be lost on futures.

When futures just involved basic commodities, the market was easier to understand. Hedgers were mainly producers. Speculators were mainly investment houses that specialized in commodities.

With the creation of financial futures – on stock indexes, bonds and currencies – the mosaic of players in this market has changed.

HEDGE FUNDS REQUIRE LARGE MINIMUM INVESTMENTS

The basic division between speculators and hedgers remains, but it's no longer as easy to classify the participants. For example, any large financial institution will be a hedger when operating in a traditional banking role but also may have a division or subsidiary that takes a speculative position in these markets.

The investment community now includes a group called "hedge funds." This has become a catch-all name for a broad range of money managers, but the original meaning of hedge fund was a variation on the traditional hedger.

The original hedge fund technique was to structure offsetting investments so that the fund made money whether the price of a security went up or down. As the hedge fund category has grown, it has come to include funds that take speculative positions in the derivatives markets.

One thing these funds have in common is that they only deal with sophisticated investors, which means there are large minimum investments for single units in the funds.

A sophisticated investor is a term that has a special meaning in securities law. Anyone who spends a lot of money on a single security – generally more than $100,000 – is considered to be exempt from the usual rules that govern the issuance of securities. These are people who, in the view of regulators, can look after themselves financially.

However, many of the traditional participants in the futures markets are not heavy hitters. Farmers still constitute a core group and the farm example still is the best way of following the essential elements of the futures market.

THE FUTURES MARKET CAN BE EXPLAINED IN SIMPLE TERMS

Imagine a farmer who has planted his barley crop, but is worried that by the time it is harvested and ready to be sold, the going price for barley will have declined because of a bumper crop flooding the market.

To protect himself from that possibility, the farmer can enter a series of futures contracts to sell the amount of barley he expects to grow at a price that will cover his expenses. Those contracts become an insurance premium – if there is a bumper crop and prices drop, the farmer can deliver his own barley at the contract price.

But the contract will come into effect only if delivery takes place and most contracts are not completed.

For this example, assume the cash market price of barley is $100 a tonne and the farmer expects the crop to come in at 200 tonnes. To protect his crop, he sells futures contracts with a face value of $20,000, which the farmer calculates to be his break-even price on the crop.

By the time his barley is ready to take to market, the price has dropped to $90 a tonne. As expected, the farmer's crop totals 200 tonnes. He sells the barley to a brewery and gets $18,000 for his crop at current market prices – which is $2,000 under his break-even price. In other words, he's selling his crop at a loss.

During the same period, the price of barley futures on the commodities exchange has dropped proportionately – down to $90 a tonne. (The price of a commodity and the price of futures contracts usually move in the same direction, although the price differential may narrow or widen, owing to market forces.)

PROFITS BALANCE OUT LOSSES

So the farmer buys futures contracts that give him the right to $18,000 worth of barley. By doing this, he is closing out his position – buying as many contracts as he originally sold, so the offsetting contracts cancel each other. The difference between the earlier selling price of $20,000 and the buying price of $18,000 represents a profit of $2,000 – which covers the farmer's $2,000 loss from his barley crop. All without any barley changing hands on the futures market.

If the price moves in the other direction, the farmer will have extra profits from sale of the crop to cover a loss on the futures transactions.

THE GREEKS FIRST TO HAVE OPTIONS MARKET

Credit for inventing the options market goes to Thales, the earliest of the ancient Greek philosophers He made a fortune speculating in olive presses in a year when there was a bumper crop – sometime around 600 B.C. The story, as told by Aristotle, is that Thales became an investor after being stung by criticism that he was just an ivory tower theorist with no useful skills in the real world.

Thales was one of the first to predict an eclipse and he studied meteorology, which led to his forecast of a big harvest in the olive groves. Early in the season, Thales bought what amounted to options on all the olive presses in Miletus.

University of Toronto Greek scholar Lloyd Gerson says the translation from Aristotle's account suggests Thales leased the olive presses and then rented them to farmers at harvest time. "He made a killing," Gerson says.

Thales' strategy is essentially how the options market works. The leases tied up assets at a fixed price at a time when the future value was unknown. Then he collected a profit from the market rate when the value of the asset rose. An essential element in this strategy is that Thales' risk was limited to the cost of the leases. It's likely that the lease rate for one season was relatively low but the return soared when farmers needed every available press in the region.

FUTURE OPTIONS | TABLE

Options on futures are a high-leverage way of taking a position on the direction of a particular market. The advantage of options is that the potential loss is limited to the price of the option. Futures options on commodities, currencies, stock indexes and interest-sensitive securities are mainly based on exchange-traded futures. Contracts are listed under the names of the commodities exchanges on which they trade. The **strike price** is the price at which the underlying futures contract can be bought or sold when the option is exercised.

A call is an option to buy.

A put is an option to sell.

Options have a limited lifespan, often only three months. Usually the settlement date is the third Friday in the month. **Settle** in the column heading refers to the month in which the contract will be settled.

Volumes is the number of contracts traded and **open interest** is the number of outstanding contracts.

The price is the last trade price. An **s** in the price column means no options were offered for trading; an **r** means no trades took place.

FUTURES OPTIONS 12.07.00

Figures supplied by Star Data Systems Inc.

Currency
British Pound (CME)
62,500 pounds, US cents per pound

Strike	Dec	Jan	Feb	Dec	Jan	Feb
1320	s	s	s	r	0.03	0.07
1330	s	s	s	s	0.04	0.10
1340	s	s	s	r	0.05	0.14
1360	8.32	s	s	r	0.06	0.26
1380	6.32	s	s	r	0.12	s
1400	4.32	s	s	r	0.32	0.84
1410	3.32	s	s	r	0.44	r
1420	2.36	s	3.96	0.04	0.70	r
1430	1.42	2.60	s	0.10	1.04	r
1440	0.60	2.00	r	0.28	1.44	r
1450	0.18	1.54	2.30	0.86	1.98	r
1460	0.04	1.06	r	1.72	2.50	s
1470	0.02	0.72	r	s	s	s
1480	r	0.54	r	3.68	s	s
1490	r	0.36	0.96	4.68	s	s
1500	r	0.28	s	5.68	s	s
1520	r	0.12	0.46	7.68	s	s
1540	r	r	0.26	9.68	s	s
1560	r	0.02	0.16	11.68	s	s

Prev. open int. 9,339   Prev. open int. 4,349

Food and Fibre
Barley (WPG)
20 metric tons, C$ per metric ton

Strike	Mar	May	July	Mar	May	July
105	29.30	29.90	s	r	r	s
110	24.30	25.00	s	r	r	s
115	19.40	20.20	20.90	r	0.20	0.10
120	14.50	15.70	16.20	0.10	0.50	0.30
125	9.80	11.50	11.80	0.30	1.20	0.80
130	5.80	7.90	8.10	1.20	2.50	1.80
135	2.80	5.00	5.00	3.20	4.50	3.70
140	1.10	3.00	2.90	6.50	7.40	6.40
145	0.40	1.60	1.50	10.60	10.90	9.80
150	0.10	0.80	0.70	15.30	15.00	13.90

Prev. open int. 1,767   Prev. open int. 400

Canola (WPG)
20 metric tons, C$ per metric ton

Strike	Jan	Mar	May	Jan	Mar	May
230	38.40	44.50	s	r	r	s
240	28.50	34.70	39.70	r	0.20	0.50
250	18.50	25.40	30.80	r	0.80	1.40

Strike	Calls-Settle		Puts-Settle	
	Jan	Feb	Jan	Feb
280	0.01	0.01	0.03 209.25	209.25 209.25
290	0.01	0.01	0.02 219.25	219.25 219.25
300	0.01	0.01	0.01 229.25	229.25 229.25

Prev. open int. 38,829   Prev. open int. 11,814

Corn (CBOT)
5,000 bushels, US cents per bushel

Strike	Jan	Feb	Mar	Jan	Feb	Mar
150	57¼	s	64¾	s	s	s
170	s	s	44⅜	s	s	⅛
180	s	s	34⅜	s	s	⅛
190	s	s	25	⅛	s	⅜
200	7½	s	16⅝	⅜	s	1½
205	3⅝	s	s	1⅛	s	s
210	1¼	r	9	4	2⅞	4½
215	¼	s	8	5½	s	s
220	⅛	s	4½	12¾	7¾	9¼
230	⅛	1	2⅜	s	s	17⅜
240	⅛	s	1	s	s	26¼
250	⅛	s	½	s	s	35⅝
260	⅛	s	⅜	s	s	45½
270	⅛	s	¼	s	s	55⅝
280	s	s	⅛	s	s	65¼
300	s	s	⅛	s	s	85¼

Prev. open int. 197,046   Prev. open int. 110,189

OPTIONS | TABLE

Prices for options traded on Canadian stock exchanges can be found in the Options table. Canadian Derivatives Clearing Corp. (CDCC), formerly jointly owned by the Toronto and Montreal stock exchanges, is the clearing organization for Canadian stock, bond and stock index options. Since March 2000, all exchange-traded interest rate and equity derivative contracts in Canada have traded exclusively on the Montreal exchange, which then also became the CDCC's sole shareholder.

Equity options in Canada are American-style options, which means that they can be exercised at any time during their lifetime. European-style options, which includes many of the index options, can only be exercised at expiry.

The 10 most active options for the trading day are shown at the top of the table.

Each series is for options on a single security and the name of the issuer is at the top of the series. Names beginning with **Cda** are government of Canada bonds.

The name includes the expiry year and the coupon for the bond issue. After the name for each security is the symbol and an abbreviation for the exchange where options are traded.

The closing price for the underlying security is listed on the same line as the name.

EXP is the expiry month. Options expire on the third Friday of the expiry month.

P/C refers to whether the option is a call (an option to buy the underlying security) or a put (an option to sell).

VOL is the volume of option contracts traded and total volume for the series appears at the bottom on the section for each issue.

BID AND ASK PRICES are in C$s unless otherwise marked.

STK refers to strike price, which is the price at which the underlying security can be bought or sold when the option is exercised.

OPINT means open interest, which is the number of open positions at the end of trading. These are contracts that have not been exercised, closed out or allowed to expire.

OPTIONS 12.07.00

Figures from the Montreal Exchange supplied by Star Data Systems Inc.

10 most active options

Company	Vol	Op Int
Nortel Networks	2,880	112,703
TCPL	1,660	27,165
Rogers Comm B	1,510	4,492
Celestica	1,355	8,906
Barrick	1,316	24,619
Nexen	1,094	4,019
Placer Dm	707	22,342
Bombard B	643	41,501
Natl Bank	512	23,466
JDS Uniph Cda	476	9,105

CDCC Trades

	Vol	Op Int
Total	18,012	725,824

Stk	Exp	P/C	Vol	Bid	Ask	OpInt
ATI Technlgys (ATY)						11.60
11	Dec	C	5	0.70	0.95	11
12	July	C	6	2.30	2.55	13
Total option vol. 31				Total open int. 9,490		
Abitibi-Cons (A)						13.60
15	June	C	10	1.05	1.30	49
Total option vol. 10				Total open int. 2,791		
AEterna Labs (AEL)						9.75
10	Feb	P	50	1.05	1.30	90
11	Feb	C	60	1.50	1.75	148
11	Feb	P	20	1.80	2.05	20
Total option vol. 157				Total open int. 1,743		
Agnico-Eagle (AGE)						9.80
10	Jan	C	30	0.60	0.75	57

Stk	Exp	P/C	Vol	Bid	Ask	OpInt
74	Jan	P		7.50	8.50	
76	Jan	C		11.30	12.30	20
76	Jan	P		8.65	9.65	
78	Jan	C		10.35	11.35	
78	Jan	P		9.70	10.70	
Total option vol. 1				Total open int. 563		
Bank of NS (BNS)						39.65
40	Dec	C	10	0.50	0.70	1,838
35	Jan	C	10	4.90	5.15	1,704
40	Jan	C	45	1.35	1.60	4,560
42½	Jan	C	30	0.55	0.80	1,548
37¼	July	P	10	3.10	3.35	10
40	July	C	1	3.45	3.70	14
42½	July	C	6	2.40	2.65	34
Total option vol. 126				Total open int. 20,776		
Bank of NS LEAPS 2002 (WBN)						39.65
30	Jan	C		10.75	12.00	265
30	Jan	P		0.70	1.70	157
35	Jan	C		7.30	8.45	448
35	Jan	P		1.90	2.90	98
40	Jan	C	15	4.55	5.55	305
40	Jan	P		4.05	5.05	15
45	Jan	C		2.75	3.70	177
45	Jan	P		7.15	7.45	22
Total option vol. 15				Total open int. 2,037		
Bank of NS LEAPS 2003 (VBN)						39.65
35	Jan	C		9.45	9.85	215
35	Jan	P	6	2.85	3.10	38
40	Jan	C		7.00	7.40	161
40	Jan	P		5.10	5.50	64
45	Jan	C		5.05	5.45	83
45	Jan	P		7.95	8.35	10

Options often are seen as a sophisticated speculative strategy, and they sometimes are. But they can also be used as part of a conservative investment strategy.

The purchase of an option contract gives the holder the right to buy or sell a specific quantity of something at a stipulated price within a certain period of time.

Options can be bought on stocks, bonds, stock market indexes, commodities futures and other investments.

Options differ from futures in that the holder of an option contract isn't obligated to exercise the right to buy or sell the underlying security. That means option buyers will normally exercise their options only when it is to their financial advantage.

However, the underwriter of an option contract is obligated to carry out the other side of the transaction if an option is exercised.

Like stocks and bonds, options can be traded. Most options sold in North America can be exercised at any time. European-style options can be exercised on only one day.

The key to following the workings of modern options is understanding the strike price. An option gives the holder the right to buy or sell a security at a specific price.

For example, options can be used to limit losses if stock prices fall. If an investor holds stock with a current value of $100, an option could be purchased to sell at a strike price of $90. In that situation, the holder has a guaranteed price of $90 for the stock.

INDEX OPTIONS | TABLE

Index options represent a way of taking a position on the direction of a market. They are widely used by institutions as hedges against adverse moves in large stock holdings. The heading on each section is for the underlying index and the letters in brackets indicate the exchange where the options trade (for example, CBOE means Chicago Board Options Exchange).

The strike price is the price at which the underlying futures contract can be bought or sold when the option is exercised.

A call is an option to buy.

A put is an option to sell. Options have a limited lifespan, often only three months, and the month in the listings is the month in which the contract will be settled. Usually the settlement date is the third Friday in the month.

Volumes represent the number of contracts traded and **open interest** is the number of outstanding contracts.

The price is the last trade price.

An **s** in the price column means no options were offered for trading; an **r** means no trades took place.

INDEX OPTIONS 12.07.00

Figures supplied by Star Data Systems Inc.

DJ Inds Avg (CBOE) — Index close 10617.36

Strike	Calls Dec	Jan	Feb	Puts Dec	Jan	Feb
88	18.50	s	s	r	s	s
90	16.50	r	s	r	r	s
92	r	r	r	r	r	0.50
94	r	r	s	r	0.45	s
96	10.40	r	r	r	0.60	r
98	r	r	r	r	0.80	r
100	r	r	r	0.15	r	r
102	4.70	6.40	7.60	0.20	1.60	r
103	3.90	s	s	0.40	s	s
104	2.75	4.70	6.00	0.65	1.95	r

Russell 2000 (CBOE) — Index close 461.10

Strike	Calls Dec	Jan	Feb	Puts Dec	Jan	Feb
430	r	r	r	1.45	10.10	r
440	r	r	r	2.50	r	r
450	r	r	r	r	15.80	r
460	8.50	r	r	r	r	r
470	5.00	r	r	r	r	r
480	2.50	r	r	21.70	r	r
500	r	7.40	r	r	r	r

Total call vol. 77   Total put vol. 77
Prev. open int. 11,018   Prev. open int. 30,523
S&P/TSE 60 (ME)   Index close 544.13

VOLATILITY AND OVERALL MARKET TREND PLAY ROLES IN OPTIONS MARKET

The cost of an option rises as the strike price gets closer to the market price. If it is an option to sell, the option is cheaper as the strike price falls further and further below the current market price. With an option to buy, the pricing is reversed. The option gets cheaper as the strike price rises higher and higher above the current market price.

Options prices also vary according to the length of time to the expiry date. A short-dated option means less risk of price surprises.

But the price of the option rises as the term gets longer because there is a rising risk of price changes for the underlying security.

Two factors that come into play in the pricing of options are volatility and the trend of the overall market.

If the underlying security is volatile (fluctuates widely in price), the option price will be higher because of the increased possibility that investors will profit from their options.

If prices in general are rising, an option to buy will be more expensive because of the greater odds that market momentum will increase the price of the underlying security. Similarly, an option to sell will be costlier in a falling market.

INVESTING WITH OTHER PEOPLE'S MONEY

Buying on margin means using borrowed money.

Financial leverage is called gearing in Britain, which leads to a London variation on an old saying – "gear today, gone tomorrow." The meaning, of course, is that there is risk in leverage, as well as opportunity.

Margin simply involves getting a loan from a broker. In effect, it is a line of credit from an investment dealer that allows a portion of a securities purchase to be financed.

Returns to the investor can multiply when using someone else's money.

Typically, a purchase on margin involves putting up half the money. Rules on margin buying vary and speculative stocks often can be bought with less money down.

For an example of how margin works, assume there is a 50% limit. If a block of stock costs $2,000, buying on margin means borrowing $1,000. Thus, if the market value of the security goes up by 10% to $2,200, the investor's gain of $200 is a 20% return on the cash investment of $1,000. The fees associated with margin financing must be deducted from the return to the investor.

These calculations work the same way in reverse, so losses mount quickly if a stock price declines and the investor still must pay financing costs.

When the price declines, there will be a "margin call" requiring the investor to put up additional cash to maintain the 50% margin in the account.

This type of buying involves having a separate brokerage account called, logically, a margin account.

HAVING A MARGIN ACCOUNT MEANS GETTING A DOUBLE CLEARANCE FROM A BROKER

• The broker needs to ensure that the investor has sufficient tolerance for the risk involved in margin buying.

• And the broker will want to do a credit check to ensure that the investor has sufficient financial resources to cover potential losses.

INDEX CONTRACTS GIVE PIECE OF THE PIE

Basket trading, which means holding a bundle of related securities, is part of the standard strategy for managers of big pools of money, but new investment products have substantially broadened the possibilities of the technique.

Futures and options on indexes allow investors to take a position on the general direction of a particular market and now there are specialized funds that hold only indexes.

THERE ARE TWO BASIC REASONS FOR THIS APPROACH

• One is to go with the momentum of a particular market or market sector.

• The other is to improve the odds of picking the best performers with a bundle.

Large institutions can afford to buy baskets of stocks that mirror an index or an index category. But futures and options allow reasonably small investors to participate in this type of investing. High-volume markets for index derivatives are those based on the world's biggest stock markets – in New York, London and Tokyo. The spectrum of index futures is much broader but investors should check the liquidity of those products before plunging into smaller markets. Another choice for small investors is to purchase units of mutual funds that buy baskets of stocks in indexes.

INDEX FUTURES | TABLE

Index futures, allowing investors to hold a bundle of related securities, go with the momentum of a particular market or market sector and improve the odds of picking the best performers.

Index
Commodity Research Bureau (NYFE)
500 x index points; 0.05 pt. = $25 per contract

227.00	209.50	Aug00	220.00	220.80	220.00	220.00	+0.75	762
227.10	213.50	Nov00	221.75	221.75	221.40	221.25	+0.75	918
226.95	216.00	Jan01	222.60	222.60	222.60	222.25	+0.75	423
...	...	Feb01	...	...	...	221.40	+0.75	0

Est. vol. 0   Prev. vol. 52   Prev. open int. 2,103

Dow Jones Indl Avg Index (CBOT)
10 x index points; 1 pt. = $10 per contract

12126.00	9995.00	Sept00	10710.00	10720.00	10525.00	10585.00	-104.00	13,489
12180.00	8100.00	Dec00	10847.00	10847.00	10690.00	10730.00	-106.00	2,112
11285.00	10900.00	Mar01	...	...	...10878.00	-107.00		2
11093.00	11065.00	June01	...	...	...11034.00	-108.00		25
11217.00	10010.00	Dec01	...	...	...11372.00	-110.00		6

Prev. vol. 13,630   Prev. open int. 15,634

Goldman Sachs Cmmdty Index (CME)
250 x index points; 0.10 pt. = $25 per contract

233.00	192.50	Aug00	217.30	218.20	216.20	216.90	+0.90	35,868

Est. vol. 75   Prev. vol. 77   Prev. open int. 35,904

Municipal Bond Index (CBOT)

WARRANTS | TABLE

Warrants are, in effect, options to purchase shares. The difference is that warrants are issued by the company as a way of raising funds and warrants often are included as an incentive extra to a stock issue. They trade on stock exchanges just like common shares.

The WT attached to the stock symbol identifies the warrant and the table shows where the warrants are listed.

Generally, warrants are issued for periods of up to three years and the expiry date is listed in the table. **Years left** is the time to the expiry date in decimal format.

The exercise price is fixed at the time of issue, which means that prices for warrants can be volatile when the price of the underlying security changes. Intrinsic value is the market price of the share minus the exercise price of the warrant. This can be a negative number when the market price is below the exercise price.

Time value is the market price of the warrant minus the intrinsic value. In effect, time value represents the opportunity for a warrant to appreciate in value.

Leverage is the reason investors buy warrants because a small investment provides a call on the underlying security. In the table, leverage is a ratio derived from dividing the market price of the stock by the market price of the warrant.

WARRANTS 12.14.00

Figures supplied by TSE and FP DataGroup

Company	Stock close	Bid/ ask	Ticker	Stock exch.	Exercise price	Recent close	Warrant Bid/ ask	Warrant Intrinsic value	Warrant Time value	Lev'ge	Years left	Expiry date
ACD Systems Intl Inc	6.100		ASA.WT	CDNX	13.000	0.100	Bid	-6.900	0.100	61.00	0.7	Aug. 22, 2001
Akrokeri-Ashanti Gld	0.110		YAG.WT	CDNX	0.220	0.060	Ask	-0.110	0.060	1.83	2.0	Dec. 19, 2002
Alive Intl Inc	2.690		YAI.WT	CDNX	1.500	0.250		1.190	-0.940	10.76	0.1	Jan. 31, 2001
Annaren Software Inc	1.090		KNO.WT-A	CDNX	1.500	0.200		-0.410	0.200	5.45	1.5	June 11, 2002
Aqua-Pure Vents Inc	1.450	Bid	AQE.WT	CDNX	2.250	0.080 [2]	Bid	-0.800	0.080	18.13	0.3	June 11, 2001
Arcls Corp	2.000		RKS.WT	TSE	1.600	0.840 [2]		0.400	0.440	2.38	0.9	Nov. 7, 2001
Arius Research Inc	1.510		YAR.WT.A	CDNX	4.000	0.250	Bid	-2.490	0.250	6.04	1.9	Oct. 31, 2002
Arius Research Inc	1.510		YAR.WT.B	CDNX	7.500	0.100	Bid	-5.990	0.100	15.10	2.3	Mar. 31, 2003
Barton Bay Res Inc	0.100	Bid	YBT.WT	CDNX	1.100	0.100	Bid	1.000	0.100	1.00	1.5	June 1, 2002
CDA Intl Inc	2.200	Bid	YC.WT	CDNX	2.000	...		0.200	n.a.	n.a.	0.5	June 30, 2001
Cdn Gen Investments	10.200		CGI.WT	TSE	8.420	4.200 [2]	Bid	1.780	2.420	2.43	6.5	June 30, 2007
Cambolt Resce Corp	0.220		DNT.WT-A	CDNX	0.460	0.030 [2]	Bid	-0.230	0.030	11.00	0.2	Feb. 15, 2001
Citotech Systems Inc	0.350	Bid	CTE.WT	CDNX	0.350	0.120 [3]	Bid	0.000	0.120	2.92	0.9	Nov. 15, 2001
Command Drilling	1.200		CDZ.WT	TSE	2.500	0.120	Bid	-1.100	0.110	11.07	0.3	June 30, 2001
Copper Ridge Expls	0.150	Bid	KRX.WT.A	CDNX	0.400	0.040 [2]	Bid	-0.250	0.040	3.75	0.0	Dec. 15, 2000
Cubacan Expl Inc	0.020		CCX.WT.D	CDNX	0.250	0.020 [2]	Ask	-0.230	0.020	1.00	0.0	Dec. 31, 2000
Drillers Technology	1.200		DLR.WT	TSE	2.000	0.210	Bid	-0.800	0.210	5.71	1.0	Dec. 31, 2001
Dundee Precious	6.300		DPM.WT.A	TSE	25.000	0.300	Bid	-18.700	0.300	21.00	3.2	Feb. 20, 2004
Dundee Wealth Mgmt	8.100		DW.WT	TSE	10.000	1.100 [2]		-1.900	1.100	7.36	2.0	Dec. 9, 2002
Duran Vents Inc	0.240		DRN.WT	CDNX	0.460	0.020 [2]	Bid	-0.220	0.020	12.00	0.7	Aug. 13, 2001
ESI Envrnmtl Sensors	0.270		ENV.WT.A	CDNX	0.500	0.020 [2]	Bid	-0.230	0.020	13.50	0.0	Dec. 29, 2000
Electromed Inc	0.510		MED.WT.R	TSE	10.280	0.020	Bid	-9.770	0.020	25.50	1.8	Sept. 25, 2002
Ezenet Corp	2.600		EZE.WT	TSE	12.000	0.110	Bid	-9.400	0.110	23.64	0.7	Sept. 12, 2001
Frst Australia Prime	7.550 [1]		FAP.WT	TSE	10.200	0.035	Bid	-2.650	0.035	215.71	0.5	June 15, 2001
Franco-Nevada Mining	69.600 [1]		FN.WT	TSE	200.000	3.400		-130.400	3.400	20.47	2.8	Sept. 15, 2003
Franco-Nevada Mining	53.592 [1]		YFN.WT.B	CDNX	100.000	3.500		-46.408	3.500	15.31	2.9	Nov. 12, 2003
Future Beach Corp	2.050		FBC.WT	ME	2.500	0.300	Ask	-0.450	0.300	6.83	0.3	Mar. 17, 2001
Genomics One Corp	1.750		GNX.WT	ME	1.500	0.250		0.250	0.000	7.00	0.0	Dec. 29, 2000
Geomaque Expls Ltd	0.270		GEO.WT	TSE	0.900	0.075	Ask	-0.630	0.075	3.60	0.3	Apr. 14, 2001
Goldcorp Inc	3.500	Bid	G.WT	TSE	20.000	3.500	Bid	-16.500	3.500	1.00	8.4	May 13, 2009
Gldn Goliath Res Ltd	0.090		GNG.WT	CDNX	0.750	0.090		-0.660	0.090	1.00	1.8	Oct. 16, 2002
Haemacure Corp	1.500		HAE.WT	TSE	2.400	0.300		-0.900	0.300	5.00	1.0	Dec. 31, 2001
Heartlink Cda (1999)	0.350	Bid	HLC.WT	CDNX	0.600	0.010		-0.250	0.010	35.00	0.0 [3]	Dec. 31, 2000

CONVERTIBLE DEBENTURES | TABLE

Convertible debentures are bonds that may be converted to equity, usually common stock. Many of these are exchange trade securities, unlike conventional bonds.

The list of issuer names also shows the security symbol and the exchange. Those that do not trade on an exchange are shown as OTC (over the counter).

This listing has both bond and stock information for a conventional pricing of each security – maturity, coupon, bond price, yield to maturity and share price.

The conversion price is the pre-set price at which the bonds may be converted to stock. The conversion ratio states the conversion price in relation to a $100 unit of the bond. For example, a conversion ratio of 5 means the stock price is $20 (5 x $20 = $100).

The premium is a percentage and is the amount paid for the debenture in excess of the market value of the underlying share. The formula is the ((bond price – (share price x conversion ratio))/(share price x conversion ratio)) x 100.

Convertible debentures

*Supplied by RBC Dominion Securities Inc. Selected quotations on actively traded debentures. Premium is stated as a percentage and is the amount paid in excess of the market value of the bond's underlying shares. Yields are calculated to maturity. *US$*

Bond Issuer/listing	Maturity	% Coup.	price	Prem.	Yld	Share price	Conv. ratio	Conv. Price
Agnico* AEGGF	27-Jan-04	3.50	67.75	89.53	17.23	6.41	5.58	17.93
Bell Canada Int'l BI.DB	15-Feb-02	6.75	110.88	-28.44	0.00	29.05	5.33	18.75
Cdn Western CWB.DB.A	31-Mar-08	5.50	96.00	19.02	6.19	24.60	3.28	30.50
Centrefund CFE.DB.A	30-Nov-06	8.50	80.00	40.11	13.48	8.85	6.45	15.50
Centrefund CFE.DB.B	31-Jan-07	7.875	69.00	32.54	15.97	8.85	5.88	17.00

The Bourse de Montreal has futures and options on the S&P/TSE 60 stock index. These products are relatively new and it always takes time to build volume in a new financial product.

A more popular way of investing in a basket of Canadian stocks is through a product called "iUnits." The big-volume iUnit security is a basket of 60 stocks that mirrors the weightings in the S&P/TSE 60 index. This basket product was pioneered by the Toronto Stock Exchange, which first introduced a basket based on the TSE index of 35 senior stocks – called TIPS, for Toronto Index Participation Units. The TSE also had derivatives on the 35-stock index but those have been succeeded by the futures and options on the S&P/TSE 60 that trade on the Bourse de Montreal. As part of that restructuring, the basket units of stock were taken over by Barclays Global Investments Canada.

Index contracts, like all futures, can be used as part of a hedging strategy. An investor who holds a portfolio of Canadian stocks and feels the stock market is about to decline can sell an S&P/TSE 60 futures contract. That way, if the market declines, the investor's loss will be offset by the profits from buying back the contract at a lower price. Likewise, someone who believes the stock market is about to rise may buy an S&P/TSE 60 contract and resell it at a profit when the market rises.

A DEEPER POOL OF ASSET-BACKED SECURITIES

Asset-backed securities (ABS) represent a relatively new investment class in Canada and the field is still evolving. Mortgage pools in the U.S. were the first big market in this area and this has been the market to develop first in Canada. The U.S. now has a broad range of ABSs – including pools of credit card receivables and car loans – and Canadian financial institutions are heading in the same direction. A variation of the ABS market that has developed in Canada is the investment trust. Two sub-categories are real estate investment trusts (REITs) and royalty trusts. REITs, as the name implies, are pools of funds that invest in real estate assets. Royalty trust are pools that buy the cash flow from resource operations, natural gas wells and coal mines, for instance.

INVESTORS IN AN ABS HOLD UNITS THAT REPRESENT A PORTION OF THE POOL.
CHARACTERISTICS OF ABSs CAN BE DIVIDED INTO THREE BROAD CATEGORIES
• **Pass through:** Units represent a pro rata share of the pool. Income generated by the pooled funds is "passed through" to the investors after management fees are deducted.

THE MORTGAGE-BACKED SECURITIES | TABLE

Mortgage-backed securities are asset pools of mortgages insured under the National Housing Act (NHA). There are two basic types of pools – those that include mortgages that can be paid off early (prepayable) and those that do not.

Units in these pools return to investors portions of the interest and principal payments made each month by homeowners. If the pool receives extra funds from mortgage prepayments, the investors may get an additional distribution.

These pools act much like bonds. Coupon and maturity date are fixed. The yield varies with the general level of interest rates and that affects the price of a unit. The issuer will be a financial institution that has assembled the pool.

NHA Mortgage backed securities

Supplied by RBC Dominion Securities Inc. Bid side levels on minimum $1 million. Indicated yields assume no prepayments. All MBS are priced to their weighted average maturity date.

Non-prepayable

Pool #	Issuer	Coupon	Maturity	Price	Yield
99007239	TD Bank	6.375	Apr 01/01	99.91	5.93
99007478	TD Bank	5.375	Mar 01/02	99.30	5.84
99007635	TD Bank	4.750	Nov 01/02	97.91	5.84
99007452	Peoples Trst	5.750	May 01/03	99.63	5.82
99007932	Bank of Mntl	4.875	Feb 01/04	97.17	5.83
99008088	TD Bank	5.625	Sep 01/04	99.10	5.84
99008237	TD Bank	5.750	May 01/05	99.63	5.79
99008005	Bank of Mntl	5.375	Apr 01/09	96.34	5.95
99007981	TD Bank	5.500	Apr 01/24	90.64	6.46
97000038	Canada Trust	6.500	Jan 01/01	99.83	5.73

Prepayable

Pool #	Issuer	Coupon	Maturity	Price	Yield
97000004	Canada Trust	5.750	Sep 01/01	99.69	5.94
97000368	National Bnk	5.000	Jan 01/02	98.84	6.03
97000061	Canada Trust	4.875	Feb 01/02	98.66	6.03
97000269	Canada Trust	5.400	Aug 01/02	99.15	5.90

These pools will be set up by large financial institutions, often banks. Assets in the pool, such as mortgages or credit card receivables, are removed from the balance sheet of the institution that created the pool and put on the books of the pool itself.

• **Pay through:** These pools are, in effect, bonds that are backed by a pool of assets. Income from the assets is paid through to the investors but the assets remain on the books of the institution that created the pool.

• **Investment trusts:** These pools operate much like a pass-through pool, except that the trust nature provides certain tax advantages. The investor, who puts in money, also is a beneficiary of the trust (unlike a conventional trust, where the beneficiary is not a contributor). Creators of these trusts generally retain a hold on the assets in the trust. Many of these trust structures have the ability to borrow, which leverages the investors' funds. Borrowed funds will be put to work to buy additional assets and this gives investors the prospect of capital gain.

With pass-through and pay-through pools, the return generally is a combination of payments of principal and interest. A grey area with ABSs is the issue of liability to both issuers and investors in the event of financial problems in the pool. Issuers who move assets off their balance sheets may continue to have obligation for those assets. Investors in REITs that take on debts may have an obligation to cover those debts.

CURRENCY AND INTEREST RATE PROTECTION

Currency and interest rate risks are among the constants of modern investing and financial institutions have responded with a broad array of securities designed to hedge these risks.

Most of these financial instruments are aimed at big institutional investors, but some are accessible to small investors. For large institutions, these markets provide an opportunity to hedge. Generally, though, any retail investor would be a speculator because it takes a large portfolio to justify the costs of sophisticated hedge products.

Financial futures provide for hedging and work much the same way as conventional futures on commodities.

Futures or options on fixed-income securities such as government bonds, treasury bills and bankers' acceptances provide ways to hedge against unexpected shifts in interest rates.

For example, an insurance company may sell bond futures when it feels rising interest rates are threatening the value of its bond portfolio. If interest rates go up, the value of bonds will fall. So will the price of futures contracts on bonds. That means the company will have sold its bond futures contracts at higher prices and bought them back at lower prices.

The difference represents a profit that will offset the declining value of bonds in the insurance company's portfolio.

Currency futures operate in a similar way and corporations with large business dealings in foreign countries can lock in an exchange rate at a future date with a variety of hedge products.

As with commodities futures, the other side of a hedge is taken by speculators who are willing to assume the risk.

In Canada, futures contracts on government of Canada bonds and bankers' acceptances notes – short-term debt issued by bankers – trade on the Bourse de Montreal.

Contracts on 10-year government bonds can be used to hedge long-term interest rates, while bankers' acceptances can be used to hedge short-term rates.

The world's most actively traded futures contracts are U.S. treasury bond futures, which were introduced in 1977, and are traded on the Chicago Board of Trade.

U.S. and other commodities exchanges around the world offer a host of other financial futures, including treasury bills and bonds issued by the large industrial nations and all the major currencies.

THE REIT | TABLE

The REIT report is a monthly feature on real estate investment trusts and the accompanying table carries unit information on Canadian REITs, which are structured somewhat like a mutual fund.

Unit pricing is similar to the pricing for mutual funds, except that many of the REITs were issued as instalment receipts. With this type of financing, the investor gets a temporary security (the instalment receipt) with a downpayment and the underlying security is delivered when the final payment is made at a later date. The typical arrangement for REITs was $6 down and a further payment of $4 for each unit.

The distribution is estimated annual payment and the forward yield is the estimated distribution as a percentage of current market price. (In the case of instalment receipts, the forward yield includes a factor for the future payment.)

Market capitalization is number of units times current price on a fully paid basis, which means it includes the future payments on instalment receipts.

REIT REPORT 10.27.98

Figures supplied by CIBC Wood Gundy Securities Inc.

	10/30/98 close $	Monthly % chg.	YTD % chg.	52-wk. high $	52-wk. low $	1998E $ distr.	Current % yield	1999E $ distr.	Forward % yield	Units O/S (mil.)	Market cap ($mil.)
Avista REIT (AVS.UN)	7.85	12.1	(24.5)	8.95	6.00	0.89	11.4	0.97	12.3	20.0	157
CAP REIT (CAR.UN)	9.50	(1.0)	(9.5)	10.50	7.70	0.95	10.0	1.00	10.5	12.0	114
CHIP REIT (HOT.UN)	8.15	(10.4)	(40.1)	14.00	8.00	1.25	15.3	1.41	17.3	33.9	276
Cominar (CUF.IR)	9.50	4.4	(5.0)	10.35	8.10	0.77	8.1	1.03	10.8	14.5	138
CPL REIT (CPL.UN)	19.50	(4.4)	0.5	24.10	18.25	1.43	7.3	1.70	8.7	16.0	312
CREIT (REF.UN)	10.85	4.3	(14.6)	14.15	9.25	1.13	10.4	1.23	11.3	33.2	360
H&R REIT (HR.UN)	9.75	(2.0)	(10.1)	12.30	9.00	1.02	10.4	1.10	11.3	34.4	335
Legacy Hotels (LGY.UN)	6.40	12.3	(34.0)	10.15	5.00	0.76	11.9	0.90	14.1	28.7	184
Legacy Hotels (LGY.IR)	6.35	11.4	(36.5)	10.25	4.92	0.76	12.0	0.90	14.2	30.5	194
Morguard (MRT.UN)	8.20	3.8	(8.8)	8.25	7.00	0.86	10.5	0.94	11.4	25.2	207
RealFund (RFN.UN)	12.40	7.0	(20.5)	16.10	10.75	1.36	11.0	1.48	11.9	26.6	330
RESREIT (REE.IR)	8.95	1.1	(10.5)	10.75	7.85	0.83	9.3	0.90	10.1	21.6	193
RioCan (REI.UN)	9.65	7.2	(9.2)	11.35	7.25	0.95	9.8	1.08	11.2	70.5	680
Royal Host (RYL.IR)	6.85	5.4	(39.9)	11.50	5.75	1.06	15.5	1.19	17.4	20.4	140
Summit REIT (SMU.UN)	12.60	11.0	(19.5)	17.20	10.20	1.50	11.9	1.63	12.9	16.4	207
CIBC Wood Gundy Cdn. REIT Index	169.37	4.7	(14.2)	204.40	152.53						

Note: CIBC Wood Gundy REIT Index based 12/31/93 = 100. All REITs and corresponding calculations are represented on a fully paid basis. Distributions are I/B/E/S Inc. where CIBC Wood Gundy has no forecast.

The REIT Report appears the first Saturday of each month.

CHAPTER 4

CURRENCIES, | DEBT AND THE ECONOMY

- Short-term securities
- The attraction of bonds
- Foreign exchange investments
- Bank of Canada

WINDS OF ECONOMIC CHANGE

CAN BUFFET INVESTMENTS | BY DAVID THOMAS

THE VALUE OF ANY INVESTMENT you choose is influenced by broad economic trends. This is true whether you are taking a position in one currency versus another or buying Canada Savings Bonds, gold bullion or shares in a public company. The big economic picture is especially important to the bond market, whose value is about eight times larger than the stock market, and to the currency market, which is about five times the size of the bond market.

With rapid growth in global capital flows, events in other markets have a strong impact on local markets. National fiscal and monetary policies are more than ever influenced by global events.

Interest rate policy is especially important to fixed income markets. In Canada, the key cost of borrowing is the bank rate, which is the rate the Bank of Canada charges on short-term loans it makes to the big commercial banks. The banks build on that rate in their lending. The rate is also a base for calculating the interest on government treasury bills and corporate bonds.

Bonds are negotiated initially to pay a fixed amount of interest regularly over a set period. When that time is up, the principal is due to be repaid as well. Simply put, bonds are a tradable loan. The terms are negotiated based on rate conditions at the time. Then, when bonds begin to trade in the secondary market, their value varies in relation to prevailing interest rates, anticipated future rates and competing returns from other investments such as stocks.

CENTRAL BANKS USE INTEREST RATES TO CONTROL INFLATION

The direction of interest rates has a dramatic effect on bond markets. Central banks use interest rates as a tool to keep inflation in check. When inflation is rising, central banks will hike their key interest rates, which will increase the cost of borrowing throughout the economy, thereby cooling off economic expansion. When inflation is at a low level, rates can be lowered, which will encourage growth. Rate manipulation is a key part of monetary policy. Rising interest rates push bond prices down and vice versa. The reason for this inverse relationship is that when rates rise, investors will find new bonds, with higher interest payments, more desirable than existing bonds that were priced at lower interest rates.

ECONOMIC INDICATORS INFLUENCE BOND AND STOCK MARKETS

Bond and stock markets pay a lot of attention to the indicators that chart the economy's progress. The broadest economic measure is gross domestic product, or GDP, which is the value of all goods and services.

Monthly updates on GDP growth, adjusted for inflation, enable economists to take the pulse of the economy. Other indicators such as manufacturing shipments, retail sales, the rate of unemployment and housing starts offer pieces of a puzzle that put together point to the direction of the economy and how fast it is moving.

NO TWO BUSINESS CYCLES ARE THE SAME, BUT THEY ALL GO THROUGH SIMILAR STAGES

- Economic recovery facilitated by low interest rates.
- Rising momentum as new investment feeds growth.
- Overheating as the economy hits capacity, costs and inflation rise and interest rates are raised to cool things off.
- Contraction and rising unemployment.
- Recession, with falling interest rates.

Signs of steady growth may bode well for continued low interest rates, while signs of overheating and growing inflation signal interest rate rises are coming.

The consumer price index (CPI) charts the price of a fixed basket of goods, providing the best way of tracking inflation. Investors subtract inflation rates from the return on their investments to determine the real rate of return. Economists often try to predict the level of natural or full employment beyond which inflationary pressures begin to kick in and business cycles shift gear.

As technology continues to increase productivity, it has changed the labor market and altered conceptions of the business cycle. During the 1990s, North America experienced its longest post-war expansion. This heady period prompted some economists to argue that technology has altered the "natural" limits of healthy economic expansion. It's not clear that the basics of the business cycle have changed dramatically but it does seem evident that changes in communications and globalization of markets have brought about significant change in the investment landscape.

While economic pressures at home and abroad may sometimes limit its choices, the Bank of Canada has the ultimate word on interest rates. The central bank has a fine-tuning role in the economic cycle. Its job is to act to smooth out the bumps and to encourage or slow down growth as needed. The central bank monitors closely the amount of stimulus in the economy created by money supply, the value of the currency and interest rates. It has direct control over interest rates and money supply and can step in to intervene in currency markets during periods of volatility.

A CHANGE IN THE VALUE OF CURRENCY AFFECTS BONDS FOR FOREIGN INVESTORS

The value of a currency depends on a host of factors, including GDP, balance of trade and fiscal debt or deficits. Here, government spending and policies can have a major impact on fixed-income markets. The strength of the currency is especially important for bond markets because any change in the currency affects the value of bonds for foreign investors.

WHAT'S FOR SALE ON THE MONEY MARKET?

The money market is the part of the capital market in which short-term debt securities are bought and sold. Most of these securities mature in one year or less. In Canada, treasury bills are the main component of the money market. Like regular bonds, T-bills are tools used chiefly by governments for borrowing. They are short-term instruments, usually maturing in 91, 182 or 364 days. The federal government and several provinces issue T-bills. Instead of paying interest, T-bills are sold at a discount to their par value. The difference between the price paid and the maturity value represents the investor's return (which is then converted to a percentage figure). Federal government T-bills are auctioned biweekly by the Bank of Canada.

OTHER MONEY MARKET INSTRUMENTS

• Bankers' acceptances: Short-term debt securities issued by a corporation and guaranteed by its bank.

• Commercial paper: Short-term debt securities issued by companies. Their terms range from a few days to a year. Normally this paper is not secured by assets, although it may be backed by bank lines of credit.

• Finance company paper: Short-term debt issued by finance companies.

The money market now provides Canadians with the main alternative to bank or credit union savings accounts. Money market accounts are set up as a type of mutual fund but their investments include only top-quality short-term notes – T-bills or commercial paper from senior issuers.

PRESERVATION OF CAPITAL THROUGH BONDS

In times of high inflation, such as the late 1970s and early '80s, investors look for securities that will keep pace with price increases. These periods generate expectations that have come to be called "the reach for yield." Between 1978 and 1982, ordinary bank term deposits paid more than 10% and for a while these no-worry investments returned almost 20%. It took a long time to squeeze out the inflationary excesses of that period, with the result that double-digit returns seemed normal.

That high-rate period was followed until recently by an extraordinary bull market in stocks and, until the downturn in the spring of 2000, a continuation of expectations of double-digit returns on investing. But stock prices have great exposure to market forces – they can go down as well as up and there is no guarantee of principal at some future date. When a bull market for stocks ends and a bear market sets in, investors rediscover the merits of bonds. Simply stated, stocks start at one end of the risk spectrum and bonds at the other.

BENCHMARK YIELDS | TABLE

Benchmark treasury bills and bonds are those issues, mostly government, that provide a pricing point for other fixed income securities. The yield changes with market conditions and price is reached with a calculation that factors in the fixed interest payment and the variable market rate.

Latest % is the market close in North America. These issues can be traded on the interbank network around the world, so the close is a matter of convention based on local time zones.

Previous close is the prior trading session. Bond market close on weekends and bank holidays. Bond trades settle on a same-day basis, so banks must be open.

The spread is the difference in basis points (1/100ths of a percentage point) between one issue and a comparable Canadian issue.

BENCHMARK YIELDS

Bond or bill	Latest %	Prev. close %	Spd. off Can.
Canada 3-mo. T-bill	5.55	5.55	
U.S. 3-mo. T-bill	5.95	6.01	-40
Canada 2-yr bond	5.37	5.43	
U.S. 2-yr bond	5.33	5.40	4
Canada 10-yr bond	5.37	5.41	
U.S. 10-yr bond	5.17	5.18	20
Australia 10-yr bond	5.49	5.47	-12
Britain 10-yr bond	4.90	4.89	47
France 10-yr bond	4.96	4.97	41
Germany 10-yr bond	4.85	4.87	53
Japan 10-yr bond	1.68	1.64	369
Canada 30-yr bond	5.52	5.53	
U.S. 30-yr bond	5.45	5.42	7

BONDS | TABLE

Bond tables list prices and yields of federal, provincial and corporate issues. The provincial category includes bonds issued by provincial agencies such as utilities. The name of the issuer often is abbreviated. The key information in identifying a bond is the coupon (interest rate) and the maturity date. A dealer may refer to "Canada nines of 25," which means a government of Canada bond that pays a 9% interest rate and matures on June 1, 2025.

COUPON is the interest rate that is fixed as part of the terms of the issue.

YIELD usually refers to yield to maturity. But if the bond can be called in at an earlier date, the yield will be yield to the call date. A callable will have a three-character notation after the name – c06, for example. This example means that the bond may be called in 2006. Other special notations may be used. **CV** refers to convertible bonds, **EXT** is extendible, **RET** is retractable.

Bonds

Supplied by RBC Dominion Securities Inc. International from Reuters.

RBC DS Index	Index level	Total ret	Price ret	MTD tot.ret
Market	352.07	-0.11	-0.16	0.48
Short	299.23	-0.04	-0.09	0.43
Intermed	357.21	-0.12	-0.17	0.64
Long	433.61	-0.20	-0.25	0.39
Govts	350.94	-0.11	-0.16	0.51
Canadas	341.67	-0.11	-0.16	0.46
Provs	375.08	-0.10	-0.16	0.64
Munis	129.81	-0.18	-0.23	0.77
Corps	370.29	-0.09	-0.15	0.36

	Coupon	Mat. date	Bid $	Yld%
Canada	8.500	Apr 01/02	103.67	5.52
Canada	10.000	May 01/02	105.84	5.55
Canada	5.750	Jun 01/02	100.32	5.52
Canada	5.500	Sep 01/02	99.98	5.51
Canada	6.000	Dec 01/02	100.96	5.48
Canada	11.250	Dec 15/02	110.66	5.56
Canada	11.750	Feb 01/03	112.28	5.56
Canada	5.750	Jun 01/03	100.64	5.47
Canada	7.250	Jun 01/03	104.01	5.49
Canada	5.250	Sep 01/03	99.37	5.50
Canada	7.500	Dec 01/03	105.44	5.49
Canada	10.250	Feb 01/04	113.40	5.53
Canada	6.500	Jun 01/04	103.14	5.49
Canada	5.000	Sep 01/04	98.38	5.48
Canada	9.000	Dec 01/04	112.31	5.50
Canada	6.000	Sep 01/05	102.22	5.46
Canada	8.750	Dec 01/05	113.96	5.50
Canada	5.750	Sep 01/06	101.46	5.45
Canada	14.000	Oct 01/06	141.48	5.53
Canada	7.000	Dec 01/06	107.63	5.48

	Coupon	Mat. date	Bid $	Yld%
Quebec	7.500	Dec 01/03	104.86	5.69
Quebec	6.500	Dec 01/05	103.00	5.80
Quebec	6.500	Oct 01/07	103.45	5.87
Quebec	11.000	Apr 01/09	132.35	5.99
Quebec	5.500	Jun 01/09	96.90	5.97
Quebec	6.250	Dec 01/10	101.87	6.00
Quebec	8.500	Apr 01/26	126.95	6.35
Quebec	6.000	Oct 01/29	95.95	6.31
Quebec	6.250	Jun 01/32	99.25	6.30
Saskat	6.125	Oct 10/01	100.23	5.82
Saskat	5.500	Jun 02/08	97.99	5.84
Saskat	8.750	May 30/25	131.87	6.20
Toronto	6.100	Aug 15/07	101.34	5.85
Toronto	6.100	Dec 12/17	99.68	6.13

Corporate

	Coupon	Mat. date	Bid $	Yld%
AGT Lt	8.800	Sep 22/25	105.79	8.25
Air Ca	6.750	Feb 02/04	96.00	8.22
AssCap	5.400	Sep 04/01	99.58	6.00
Avco	5.750	Jun 02/03	99.13	6.14
Bell	6.500	May 09/05	100.75	6.30
BMO	7.000	Jan 28/10	105.05	6.26
BNS	5.400	Apr 01/03	98.98	5.88
BNS	6.250	Jul 16/07	100.01	6.25
CardTr	5.510	Jun 21/03	99.07	5.91
Cdn Pa	5.850	Mar 30/09	93.54	6.88
Clearn	0.000	May 15/08	81.75	9.69
CnCrTr	5.625	Mar 24/05	98.23	6.10
Coke	5.650	Mar 17/04	97.90	6.37
DlmrCCF	6.440	Apr 03/02	100.13	6.32

MATURITY DATE is when investors will be paid their principal. Only the last two digits of the year are used, so 05, for example, means 2005.

THE BID COLUMN lists the price at which investment dealers are willing to buy the bond. These prices are always quoted in relation to 100, no matter what the par value of the bond. Think of the bond price as a percentage. A price of 95 means that the bond traded at 95% of the face value, regardless of the size of the transaction. (Prices here are institutional prices, which usually means a minimum $100,000 trade.)

THERE ARE THREE ESSENTIAL ELEMENTS TO THIS EQUATION

• **Total return:** This is the combination of earned income and capital gains. Earned income is interest from bonds and dividends from stocks. A capital gain is the increase in value of the security itself. Interest payments are fixed for conventional bonds, which means the price will vary with changes in the general level of interest rates in the economy. The price of a bond is fixed if an investor buys when the bond is first issued and holds the bond until it matures. Anytime in between, the price will be subject to market forces and the investor has the prospect of a capital gain or loss but the bond buyer still is assured of getting the face value at maturity.

• **Relative return:** This is the question of whether a particular asset class is likely to pay better than another asset class – bonds versus stocks, or hard assets (such as real estate) versus financial assets (such as stocks).

• **The sleep factor:** As potential return rises, the potential risk rises and investors need to have a portfolio that allows them to rest comfortably at night. The big advantage of high-quality bonds is the investors can count on getting the principal back when the bond matures.

Risks associated with bonds vary from issuer to issuer. Few investors do the time-consuming research needed to ascertain that risk, so they rely on rating agencies. The likelihood of a bond investment turning sour generally can be divined from ratings established by agencies that measure the financial stability of businesses and governments.

In Canada, the major bond rating services are Dominion Bond Rating Service and Standard & Poor's/Canadian Bond Rating Service. The major U.S. rating services are Standard & Poor's Corp. and Moody's Investors Service. Bond ratings not only give investors an idea of how likely it is that their interest and principal will be paid, but also have an impact on the level of interest paid by new bond issues. High-risk borrowers have to pay higher interest to attract investors. Issuers with good credit ratings pay less.

THE ATTRACTION OF BONDS IS THEIR SAFETY

Bondholders are lenders, and therefore creditors, and part of the appeal of bonds is that creditors are second in line to get their money back if a company has problems. First in line is the tax collector. That potential claim on assets is why investment grade corporate bonds are considered safer investments than stocks. But government bonds are considered the safest of all because of the tax collector's preferred status.

Most Canadians probably think of Canada Savings Bonds when government bonds are mentioned, but CSBs are a tiny element in the fixed income universe. In fact, CSBs are not real bonds – instead they are term deposits issued by Ottawa with a feature that allows the holder to cash them in at any time. Bonds are tradable securities and the market in bonds is huge, much bigger than the stock market. Estimates of the value of average daily turnover in the bond market are about eight times the value of stocks traded on a typical day. The total of outstanding bond issues numbers in the thousands.

The anomaly in this situation is that most of the trading volume in bonds is confined to a small number of issues – perhaps 30 or 40 in the Canadian market. Federal government bonds are at the top of the active list and there is a good reason for having big volumes in a few issues. Bonds issued by the sovereign – in Canada, the federal government – carry the highest credit rating in any national market. Those bonds then become benchmarks for the pricing of other bonds, both when they are first issued and when they trade in the secondary market.

BONDS COME IN TWO BASIC FORMS: BEARER BONDS AND REGISTERED BONDS

The Bank of Canada, which is the fiscal agent for the national government, identifies key bond issues as benchmarks. These are bonds with at least $6 billion in circulation in maturities of two, three, five, 10 and 30 years. Investment dealers will pick certain other issues as benchmarks to fill out the range of maturities and to expand the benchmark category so that it includes some provincial issues and a few top-quality corporates. These benchmarks then become the standard when pricing other issues. For example, a lower quality 10-year corporate bond might be sold at 100 basis points over benchmark, which means the yield would be one percentage point higher than the yield on the 10-year Canada benchmark.

The price of a bond is set from the yield, which represents the prevailing rate of interest in wholesale markets for funds. Take the example of a 10-year bond that pays interest at 6.125%. But market conditions have changed slightly and on the issue day market yield has to be set at 6.176% to attract investors. In this example the price would be 99.624 instead of par at 100.

Bonds come in two basic forms – bearer bonds and registered bonds. Bearer bonds feature detachable coupons, which are clipped and cashed when scheduled interest payments are due. That's why the interest rate of a bond is referred to as its coupon rate. Bearer bonds are assumed to belong to whoever holds them. A registered bond shows the name of the owner and usually interest payments are sent to the registered owner by cheque from the borrower's trustee or paying agent. In Canada, a debenture is similar to a bond, but no assets or property are pledged as security for the loan. Instead, the debenture is backed by the general credit of the borrower and is an unsecured promise to repay the amount of the loan.

The line between bonds and debentures often is blurred. Technically, government bonds are debentures because no assets are pledged for the loan. But the power to tax means the government is highly unlikely to go broke. When bond traders and other investment professionals refer to yields, they are usually talking about the yield to maturity. But some bonds can be called in before the maturity date and the quoted yield on these issues usually will be based on the call date.

BONDS OFFER A PREDICTABLE RATE OF RETURN

When preparing to sell new bonds to the public, corporate issuers and some government issuers will consult with investment dealers and other distributors on the size of the bond issue, interest rate to be offered and any other attributes or conditions attached to the bond. This involves researching the current bond market carefully, including prevailing interest rates for other bonds and similar interest-bearing investments. Dealers will act either as principals – buying the issue and reselling it to investors – or as agents collecting commissions on sales. Large institutions, such as pension funds, represent the major market for bonds.

Pension funds like bonds because a predictable rate of return can be factored into the fund's actuarial requirements for future pension payments. Individuals can buy bonds in relatively small denominations and bond mutual funds are an important part of the buyer base for bonds. The popularity of bonds with institutions has led to the development of the "medium-term note" market. Essentially, these are bonds issued through a shelf prospectus, which means the issuer has all the required documents ready so that a bond can be sold on short notice, as short as a few hours.

If an investment dealer has a client with spare funds, the dealer will shop around for a corporate issuer with a need for funds and the two sides to the deal will be matched quickly. Actually, the name "medium-term note" is misleading. Originally, these bond issue programs were for shorter term securities but now they can be issued for long terms. The size of a note issue can be as little as $1 million – a small amount compared with a standard prospectus bond issue, which usually is at least $75 million.

THE DIFFERENCE BETWEEN THE BID PRICE AND THE ASK PRICE IS BOND DEALER'S PROFIT

Most federal government bonds are sold by auction with the Bank of Canada acting as the government's adviser on terms and conditions.

After new bond issues are sold to investors, they begin trading on the secondary market. As investors buy and sell bonds among themselves, the bonds begin trading at prices other than their face value. In Canada, most bonds are sold over the counter, although some fixed income securities are traded on stock exchanges. The bond trading network is an interdealer community made up of large financial intermediaries. On the secondary market, bond dealers act as principals. Instead of collecting commissions on sales, as they would in the stock market, they purchase bonds and resell them. They list prices at which they are willing to buy a specific bond – the bid price – and a price at which they are willing to sell – the ask price. The difference between the two prices is the dealer's profit.

CANADA SAVINGS BONDS STILL HOLD APPEAL

Victory Bonds proved popular during the Second World War. The government of the day in Ottawa, knowing a good thing when it saw it, followed up with Canada Savings Bonds (CSBs). At times, CSBs have been a mainstay of the federal government's financing program. But through the 1980s and much of the '90s Ottawa relied mainly on conventional bonds. Now the federal government has a renewed interest in these venerable securities. It has expanded the program with the creation of a separate agency to handle CSBs – Canada Investment and Savings.

Canada Savings Bonds differ from the rest of Ottawa's bonds in that they are not marketable. When cashed, the government buys them back and cancels the certificates.

The big change in the marketing plan is in the timing of sales. They used to be sold just in October but now the government has extended the sales period through the end of March. The reason, of course, is to have products available during that period when Canadians are shopping for investments to put into RRSPs at the end of the tax year. Ottawa has follow-through support with no-fee plans for tax-sheltered retirement savings and for a registered retirement income fund.

As well, there are changes to the product line. In addition to regular CSBs, Ottawa offers what it calls Canada Premium Bonds. These pay a slightly higher return than regular CSBs but can only be cashed once a year without an interest penalty.

Traditional CSBs can be cashed at any time. That feature has made them popular because interest is paid up to the latest month, unlike bank term deposits where purchasers may lose interest payments by cashing out early. There are two types of CSBs – regular interest bonds and compound interest. Regular interest bonds allow bondholders to collect annual interest by cheque or by direct deposit to a bank account. With compound interest bonds, a bondholder collects no annual interest. Instead, the interest accumulates (with interest on the interest) until the bond is cashed.

CSBs are sold through banks, investment dealers and other financial institutions. A core element in the government's distribution system is the payroll deduction plan and sales through this method are stable year after year.

CROSS RATES | TABLE

A cross is simply a trade between two currencies. Generally, currency values are set in relation to the reserve currency – C$ vs US$, German mark vs US$, and so on. Cross rates then recalculate those currency values to produce exchange rates for the C$ vs the mark and so on. This table shows the currencies on which there is an active C$ market. These also are currencies that can be hedged through the futures market. Gold is included in this list because of its historic role as an alternative currency. These rates are wholesale market rates, which means trades of at least $100,000.

Currency cross rates
Supplied by Royal Bank of Canada – indicative wholesale late afternoon rates

	C$	US$	euro	DM	Yen	£	Fr.fr.	Itl	Sw.fr.	A$
C$	–––	1.5241	1.3347	0.6824	0.0138	2.2186	0.2035	0.00069	0.8891	0.8232
US$	0.6561	–––	0.8757	0.4477	0.0090	1.4557	0.1335	0.00045	0.5833	0.5402
euro	0.7493	1.1419	–––	0.51129	0.0103	1.6623	0.15245	0.00052	0.6661	0.6168
DM	1.4654	2.2335	1.95583	–––	0.0202	3.2512	0.2982	0.00101	1.3028	1.2064
¥	72.72	110.83	97.05	49.62	–––	161.34	14.80	0.05012	64.65	59.86
£	0.4507	0.6870	0.6016	0.3076	0.0062	–––	0.0917	0.00031	0.4007	0.3711
Fr. fr.	4.9148	7.4907	6.55957	3.3539	0.0676	10.904	–––	0.00339	4.3695	4.0461
Itl	1450.8	2211.1	1936.3	990.0	19.951	3218.7	295.2	–––	1289.8	1194.3
Sw. fr.	1.1248	1.7143	1.5012	0.7676	0.0155	2.4955	0.2289	0.00078	–––	0.9260
A$	1.2147	1.8513	1.6212	0.8289	0.0167	2.6950	0.2472	0.00084	1.0799	–––

REAL RETURN BOND | TABLE

Real return bonds are government bonds that are indexed to inflation as measured by the consumer price index. They pay a base rate of 4.25% (the real return). Then there is an adjustment, called the index ratio, based on changes in CPI. The real yield is a combination of real return and the indexing for inflation. In addition to the inflation adjustment on the coupon, there is an inflation adjustment to the payment of principal at maturity. These bonds were first issued in 1991 with a 30-year maturity and the federal government now issues additional real return bonds on a quarterly schedule.

Real return bond
Supplied by RBC Dominion Securities Inc.
Bid side levels

Coupon	Maturity	Real price	Real yield	Index ratio
Issuer: Government of Canada				
4.250	Dec 01/21	108.98	3.64	1.14435
Issuer: Government of Canada				
4.250	Dec 01/26	110.81	3.61	1.08247
Issuer: Government of Canada				
4.000	Dec 01/31	107.60	3.59	1.04034

CAUGHT IN CURRENCY CROSS-CURRENTS

Currency risk and the opportunity to make gains from foreign exchange used to be issues that only concerned bankers and the treasurers of big companies in Canada. But the increasing globalization of markets means ordinary investors must pay much more attention to shifting rates for currencies. Individual portfolios may not contain direct investments in foreign securities, but almost every portfolio will have some exposure to currency risk.

THERE ARE TWO COMMON REASONS WHY FOREIGN CURRENCIES CAN AFFECT INVESTMENTS
• Investors who buy stocks indirectly through mutual funds are likely to have a foreign currency component because these institutions will have non-Canadian stocks within many of their portfolios.
• Canadian public companies are increasingly global and their foreign currency exposure in trade will have a bearing on their earnings outlook, which in turn affects stock prices and the ability to cover bond interest payments. A related factor is that many industries are global and prices charged by foreign competitors can have an impact on the pricing power and profitability of Canadian companies.

One way of looking at currency value is to think of it as the stock price for a country. A strong currency represents solid national earning power. A weak currency represents a weak economy and any signs of improvement will be reflected in a rise in the currency value. There are several reasons why a currency value fluctuates. When interest rates change more in one country than in others, foreign investors take notice. Higher rates in Canada compared with the U.S. represent a Canada premium to offshore investors looking to place money in North America. High rates attract money into the country, creating a demand for C$s.

That demand pushes up the value of the currency. Strength in the currency allows interest rates to fall, which means swings in currency values will be corrected by the market if there are no other factors in the equation. But there may be political risks that force interest rates higher and those risks can depress a currency value. The Quebec referendum on separation is one of the best examples of how political risk can drive down a currency.

TOO MUCH DEBT PUTS DOWNWARD PRESSURE ON CURRENCY

Inflation is another significant factor in the mix of influences on currency values. A rapid rise in prices represents an artificial increase in the value of assets within the domestic economy and the international marketplace will correct that situation by devaluing the currency. Too much debt within the domestic economy – either through government or private sector borrowing – can put downward pressure on the currency. In this situation, the borrowers must rely on foreign lenders and the currency will suffer if the economy is seen to be dangerously exposed to external creditors.

An important concept in the study of money is the reserve currency, which is the anchor of the international monetary system. The reserve currency is now the US$. As that name implies, the US$ is the unit of measure for official reserves held by central banks around the world. Those reserves are kept for the defence of the local currency

MAJOR CURRENCIES | TABLE

Trading desks at financial institutions measure currency values against the reserve currency, which is the US$. But the exchange rates that matter for Canadians are with the C$. The Major Currencies table gives both in relation to those currencies that represent Canada's major trading partners. Changes are given over the past four weeks and the % change columns allow comparisons of trends for different currencies.

Major currencies

Supplied by Royal Bank of Canada – indicative wholesale late afternoon rates. * inverted

Per US$	Latest	Prev day	Week ago	4 wks ago	% chg on day	% chg in wk	% chg 4 wk
Canada $	1.5013	1.4960	1.5025	1.4769	0.35	-0.08	1.65
euro*	0.8692	0.8693	0.8819	0.8698	-0.01	-1.44	-0.07
Japan yen	108.86	109.16	108.19	106.13	-0.27	0.62	2.57
UK pound*	1.4485	1.4462	1.4742	1.4201	0.16	-1.74	2.00
DMark	2.2503	2.2501	2.2179	2.2487	0.01	1.46	0.07
France franc	7.5471	7.5463	7.4384	7.5411	0.01	1.46	0.08
Swiss franc	1.7503	1.7501	1.7275	1.7787	0.01	1.32	-1.60
Italian lira	2228	2228	2196	2226	0.01	1.46	0.08
Australia $*	0.5337	0.5355	0.5432	0.5565	-0.34	-1.75	-4.11
Mexico peso	9.4710	9.4550	9.4370	9.3025	0.17	0.36	1.81
Hong Kong	7.7959	7.7962	7.7967	7.7985	0.00	-0.01	-0.03
Singapore $	1.7490	1.7489	1.7394	1.7357	0.01	0.55	0.77
China renminbi	8.2790	8.2790	8.2798	8.2794	0.00	-0.01	0.00
Per C$							
US $	0.6661	0.6684	0.6656	0.6771	-0.35	0.08	-1.63
euro*	1.3049	1.3004	1.3250	1.2845	0.34	-1.52	1.58
Japan yen	72.51	72.96	72.00	71.86	-0.62	0.70	0.91
UK pound*	2.1746	2.1635	2.2150	2.0973	0.51	-1.82	3.69

FOREIGN EXCHANGE | TABLE

This foreign exchange list is a handy guide for business travellers or vacationers. A cautionary note, though: These are wholesale market rates and foreign exchange dealers will add a commission when buying or selling. The tables gives exchange values in both C$s and US$s, and these two exchange rates can be valuable to investors. If a Canadian company in an investor's portfolio is expanding into a foreign country, the C$ exchange rate is a guide to the company's local costs in that country and the US$ exchange rate is a guide to costs for commodities that are priced in world markets.

Foreign exchange by country

Supplied by BMO Nesbitt Burns Capital Markets – indicative noon rates

Currency	in C$	in US$	Daily % chg	Currency	in C$	in US$	Daily % chg
Antigua, Gr. EC $	0.5839	0.3745	nil	Kuwait (Dinar)	5.0501	3.2446	0.10
Argentina (Peso)	1.55921	1.00020	-0.04	Lebanon (Pound)	0.001030	0.000661	-0.02
Austria (Schill)	0.09615	0.06168	-0.36	Luxemb. Franc	0.03280	0.02104	-0.36
Bahamas (Dollar)	1.5589	1.0000	nil	Malaysia (Ringgit)	0.4102	0.2632	nil
Bahrain (Dinar)	4.1361	2.6532	0.03	Malta (Lira)	3.3525	2.1505	-0.24
Barbados (Dollar)	0.7834	0.5025	nil	Netherlands Gulld.	0.6004	0.3851	-0.36
Belgium (Franc)	0.03280	0.02104	-0.36	Neth. Ant. Guilder	0.8758	0.5618	nil
Bermuda (Dollar)	1.5589	1.0000	nil	New Zealand $	0.6186	0.3968	-1.02
Brazil (Real)	0.8094	0.5192	2.08	Norway (Krone)	0.1654	0.1061	-0.42

during times of instability. For example, the Bank of Canada intervened in currency markets – selling US$s to buy C$s to support the C$'s price – when there were turbulent trading periods at the time of the last Quebec referendum.

EURO MAY RIVAL US$ AS MAJOR RESERVE CURRENCY

Another feature of the reserve currency is that it is the unit for pricing major commodities. It's also the currency used for the accounts of such international agencies as the World Bank and the International Monetary Fund. While the US$ is the world's most important currency, the euro, despite a rocky ride since its debut in January 1999, has already gained wide global acceptance by central banks and the investment community.

There is no comparable currency in Asia and until 1997 many Asian currencies were formally pegged to the US$. The notable exception has been the Japanese yen and financial reform in Asia may involve the emergence of the yen as a regional reserve currency. The relationships between the currencies of different countries are established on foreign exchange markets in much the same way as the values of other investments are determined – through supply and demand. Currencies are traded through a computer and telephone network, much as bonds are bought and sold. Banks and investment dealers that operate internationally form the core of this market and London is the main centre for trading. New York is also a large currency trading location and Chicago has the leading markets for currency futures.

Euro-deposit rates and London interbank offer rates (Libor) are the international equivalent of commercial paper. These are short-term rates in an interbank market that operates outside the regulatory environment of national economies. Participants in this market are mainly financial institutions and multinational corporations. These rates are financing costs in the major currencies when a borrower goes abroad. The euro and Libor markets provide benchmark pricing in the international marketplace for funds. The table shows changes over the past four weeks. These trends reflect shifts in credit conditions or in currency values, or both.

International

Supplied by Royal Bank of Canada.

Euro-deposit rates (bid)

		Latest	Prev day	Wk ago	4 wks ago
US$	Overnight	6.48	6.44	6.51	n.a.
	1-month	6.60	6.65	6.63	n.a.
	3-month	6.47	6.49	6.55	n.a.
	6-month	6.37	6.41	6.47	n.a.
C$	3-month	5.63	5.63	5.75	n.a.
euro	3-month	4.93	4.93	4.91	n.a.
DM	3-month	4.93	4.93	4.91	n.a.
•	3-month	0.69	0.67	0.48	n.a.
£	3-month	5.81	5.85	5.94	n.a.

London interbank offer rate US$

	Latest	Prev day	Wk ago	4 wks ago
1-month	6.72	6.71	6.75	n.a.
3-month	6.59	6.55	6.67	n.a.
6-month	6.49	6.47	6.59	n.a.

THE SHINE HAS GONE OFF INVESTING IN GOLD

In the span of a generation, gold has moved from the centre of the monetary system to become the ultimate contrarian symbol. Until 1971, gold had an official role as a reserve currency. In that year, the U.S. dropped the gold standard (by then, it was only a partial gold standard). Central banks still hold gold but the mystique is gone and in recent years there have been steady reductions in official holdings.

The Bank of Canada, at the direction of the minister of finance, has sold off most of its gold over time. At the end of 1979, the Bank of Canada's gold store was worth more than its holdings of US$s. By the end of 2000, the central bank held US$67 in US$ assets for every US$1 worth of gold. At the start of the 21st century, only the hardiest of gold bugs still believed in the traditional safe haven status of gold. The gold standard meant that governments backed their currencies with gold. In theory, someone could go to the central bank with paper money and swap it for gold at the official exchange rate.

Full convertibility to gold ended in Canada in the 1920s. Following the Second World War, a modified international gold standard, in which only national governments could convert their foreign currency holdings into gold, was instituted. But that system fell away in the 1970s. Now, gold trades like any other commodity and there are no official rates. Annual mine production has been less than market demand for several years, but central bank selling has steadily depressed the price. Gold is important as an industrial metal and the electronics industry is among the big consumers. Gold is a good conductor of electricity and it can be spun into fine wires – these features make it ideal for tiny computer chips. (Copper is far less useful for these miniature applications.)

GOLD MAY NEVER REGAIN ITS MONETARY APPEAL

Gold also retains its appeal for jewelry and this demand is consistent from year to year. But hoarding – the term used for buying gold as a currency – has gone out of style. The historical reason that people hoarded gold was its reputation as a store of value. It was an international currency that could be cashed anywhere during times of war. Gold also was seen as a protection against inflation. When paper money was devalued, gold held its purchasing power. The rule of thumb used to be that an ounce of gold was roughly equal to the price of a good men's suit.

Silver has had a role similar to gold's in many parts of the world, notably Latin America and Asia. Silver still has monetary appeal in parts of Asia and gold still has its fans, but the monetary power of gold has been weakened considerably. Central banking has

CANADIAN/U.S. YIELDS | TABLE

Yields in this table represent the basic financing costs in the domestic market for business. They are for large value transactions by those companies or institutions that have top credit ratings. Those with lesser credit ratings would pay a premium over these yields. The significance of this table is that it shows the trend over the latest four weeks for interest rates at different terms (from one month to 30 years).

Treasury bills and bonds are benchmark issues of federal government securities. Bankers' acceptance notes are the highest quality commercial paper. They are notes issued by a corporation and guaranteed as to principal and interest by a bank.

Forward rate agreements (FRAs) are contracts for delivery of a specific amount at a rate for a future term. In effect, an FRA is a forward contract for funds.

Canadian yields   U.S. yields

Supplied by Royal Bank of Canada. Indicative wholesale late afternoon rates. Ask price where applicaable.

	Latest	Prev day	Week ago	4 wks ago		Latest	Prev day	Week ago	4 wks ago
T-Bills									
1-month	5.39	5.41	5.37	n.a.	1-month	5.92	5.90	6.05	n.a.
3-month	5.53	5.52	5.59	n.a.	3-month	5.90	5.91	5.99	n.a.
6-month	5.58	5.60	5.68	n.a.	6-month	5.80	5.79	5.87	n.a.
1-year	5.60	5.62	5.69	n.a.	1-year	5.48	5.48	5.55	n.a.
Bonds					**Bonds**				
2-year	5.47	5.47	5.60	n.a.	2-year	5.52	5.50	5.59	n.a.
5-year	5.46	5.45	5.59	n.a.	5-year	5.32	5.30	5.44	n.a.
7-year	5.45	5.46	5.59	n.a.	7-year	5.30	5.27	5.56	n.a.
10-year	5.42	5.43	5.55	n.a.	10-year	5.35	5.34	5.52	n.a.
30-year	5.53	5.53	5.56	n.a.	30-year	5.54	5.54	5.66	n.a.
Banker's acceptances *(ask price)*					**Commercial paper**				
1-month	5.74	5.74	5.77	n.a.	1-month	6.54	6.51	6.51	n.a.
3-month	5.74	5.74	5.78	n.a.	3-month	6.35	6.40	6.50	n.a.
6-month	5.70	5.69	5.76	n.a.	6-month	6.42	6.47	6.57	n.a.
3-mth forward rate agreement					**3-mth forward rate agreement**				
3-month	5.64	5.62	5.71	n.a.	3-month	5.72	5.72	5.72	n.a.
6-month	5.50	5.48	5.65	n.a.	6-month	5.68	5.68	5.68	n.a.
9-month	5.44	5.42	5.63	n.a.	9-month	5.77	5.77	5.77	n.a.

FORWARD EXCHANGE RATES | TABLE

Currencies can be bought or sold for delivery at a future date at a current price. You buy a contract (a sort of down payment) to lock in the exchange rate. The spot price is the current price, stated as an exchange rate in relation to US$s (the reserve currency). The forward rates are the exchange rates that will apply in the future when the delivery takes place. The changes over time represent the present market sentiment on exchange rate trends, plus factors for the time value of money and the risk of surprises during that time. These rates are wholesale rates for large transactions and there will be fees or commissions to the bank or investment dealer that underwrites the transaction.

Forward exchange rates

*Supplied by Royal Bank of Canada. Indicative wholesale late afternoon rates. * inverted*

Per US$	Spot	1-mo	3-mo	6-mo	1-yr	2-yr	3-yr	4-yr	5-yr
Canada $	1.5241	1.5230	1.5211	1.5188	1.5152	1.5082	1.5027	1.4962	1.4893
euro*	0.8757	0.8771	0.8792	0.8822	0.8876	0.8981	0.9047	0.9131	0.9047
Japan yen	110.83	110.25	109.25	107.69	104.79	99.23	94.13	89.43	85.23
DMark	2.2335	2.2299	2.2248	2.2173	2.2039	NA	NA	NA	NA
UK pound*	1.4557	1.4568	1.4582	1.4601	1.4633	1.4444	NA	NA	NA
Per C$									
US $	0.6561	0.6566	0.6574	0.6584	0.6600	0.6630	0.6655	0.6684	0.6715
euro*	1.3347	1.3358	1.3373	1.3398	1.3449	1.3545	1.3595	1.3662	1.3474
Japan yen	72.72	72.39	71.83	70.91	69.16	65.79	62.64	59.77	57.23
DMark	1.4654	1.4642	1.4626	1.4599	1.4545	NA	NA	NA	NA
UK pound*	2.2186	2.2187	2.2180	2.2175	2.2172	2.1784	NA	NA	NA

changed the popular notion of gold's value. Now, faith is placed in the ability of central banks to protect the value of money. Many people question whether gold will ever regain its monetary appeal.

Gold can still be bought as bullion by those who have kept the faith. Wafers begin at an ounce and gold still can be bought in bars. Those who do buy often do not take physical delivery. Instead, they have a certificate from the seller, usually a bank, and they pay a storage fee. People who buy gold and hold it themselves usually go to coins. Several countries have gold coin series and the Canadian Maple Leaf program is among the most popular in the world. The most common way to invest in gold is through the common stocks of producers or promising exploration companies. As well, there are several mutual funds that specialize in precious metals and these funds may hold bullion as well as stocks. More adventurous investors can buy gold futures or options on gold. These options and futures are traded on major exchanges.

CENTRAL BANKS GUARD MONEY'S VALUE

A cornerstone of modern central banking is that the bank should be independent of political decisions made by the government of the day. In Canada, the finance minister holds all the shares of the central bank. The finance minister and the governor of the Bank of Canada meet regularly and there is broad agreement on policy.

As the owner of the bank, the finance minister appoints the deputy finance minister to represent the government on the board of the Bank of Canada. This is a non-voting position and by tradition the governmwent treads carefully when giving the Bank of Canada its views on monetary policy. The government has the power to issue a policy directive to the central bank, but this unusual step would only be taken in the event of a crisis of confidence in central bank management.

Successive finance ministers and bank governors have been mindful of the fact that the perception of independence is important. The German central bank, the Bundesbank, is widely considered to be the model for modern central banks. It came into being after a period of runaway inflation caused social breakdown in Germany during the 1920s. That experience instilled a deep faith in the need for a credible monetary authority to protect the value of money. Monetary unification in Europe has meant that the Bundesbank has ceded its major policy role to the European Central Bank. But the ECB is heavily influenced by the historical role of the Bundesbank and by the influence of German representation on councils of the ECB.

North American central banks have followed that pattern and in the U.S. the Federal Reserve Board has unequivocal power to set monetary policy. The Fed, as it is known, has not worried much about currency value because the US$ is the world's reserve currency. But that fact also means the Fed has a de facto influence on the monetary policy of other industrial countries. When the Fed changes monetary gears, the Bank of Canada usually has to make a shift as well.

INTERNATIONAL STANDARDS FOR BANKING ARE SET IN SWITZERLAND

Globalization of markets has brought with it a globalization of policy. It now is almost impossible for one country to maintain for long a policy stance that is at odds with general trends elsewhere in the world. The usual reason for one central bank being out of step is that the government of the day wants easier credit conditions to stimulate local business. But when interest rates are artificially depressed, the usual result is a devaluation of the currency and the local economy pays a bigger price in the end.

BANK RATES | TABLE

These are benchmark rates that are subject to change without notice. The prime rate is generally considered to be the rate charged the most creditworthy customers and adjustable rate commercial loans will be set at a rate pegged to prime but at a fixed number of basis points above prime.

Bank rates

Canada		U.S.	
Bank of Can.	6.00	Discount	6.00
O/N MM Fin Rate.	5.76	Prime	9.50
Prime	7.50	Fed Funds	6.50
Call Loan Ave.	5.75		

The Bank of Canada rate is the rate charged by the central bank in its role as lender of last resort to the financial system. In the U.S., the discount rate and the fed funds rate are like the bank rate.

The call loan rate is the market rate for overnight loans between financial institutions.

Within the industrial world, the monetary authorities are connected through the Bank for International Settlements (BIS), based in Basel, Switzerland. This is the central bankers' bank and its main role has been in the setting of international standards for commercial banking. BIS has a role complementary to that of the International Monetary Fund (IMF), which is the lender of last resort when national financial systems get into trouble. When the IMF provides funds for a bailout, the terms will include negotiated agreements to implement financial reforms. IMF funds come from the industrial countries and the workouts are done in less developed countries. The other major international financial institution is the World Bank, which provides development financing to poorer countries.

BANK OF CANADA EXERCISES ITS POWER

Ottawa's banker – the governor of the Bank of Canada – is the most powerful unelected official in the country. Looking after the federal government's finances is just part of the job. The bigger chore for the central bank is in finding the right balance for the C$ and the interest rate structure. As the name implies, the central bank is the banker to the financial system. It's the lender of last resort when a commercial bank is short of cash.

The Bank of Canada is the only bank in the country that can print paper money, although that was not always the case. After Confederation in 1867, the government allowed chartered banks to issue money. The stock market crash of 1929 and the depression that followed created a crisis for the world's banking system and governments looked for ways to prevent a recurrence of that devastating experience. Creation of the Bank of Canada in 1935 was part of the policy prescription. It was a public stock company at first but political pressure for more government control resulted in the federal government buying back all the shares by 1938. The bank's role has been revised and expanded over the years but the essential job is still managing monetary policy.

• Most of the day-to-day work at the Bank of Canada is in overseeing the smooth functioning of the financial system. It conducts a daily balancing of accounts for the banks as a group. This is called the payments settlement process, which means making sure that Bank A gets money owed from Bank B and so on.
• In its policy role, the bank controls the money supply and exercises a direct influence on the level of interest rates. These actions are carried out within the broader goal of sustaining non-inflationary growth in the economy. Price stability – which means low inflation – is the essential element in the bank's master plan.
• As fiscal agent for the government, the Bank of Canada advises the Finance Department on how best to manage taxpayers' money. It conducts the government's banking. When Ottawa needs extra cash, the bank is the underwriter for the sale of bonds, treasury bills, Canada Savings Bonds and other securities.

WHAT YOUR SAVINGS EARN | TABLE

Money in the bank is a loan to the bank and in a normal market the cost of money rises as the length of the loan increases. To a point, there is a premium as well for larger loans. For that reason, most financial institutions have minimum levels for posted rates on term deposits. This table gives those posted rates. In certain circumstances, lenders may be able to negotiate for a better return.

The lowest rates are for demand deposits, which means money in the bank can be withdrawn on demand. Rates may vary among institutions because of the situation of the borrower. Financial institutions try to balance their deposit and loan business and this can be a factor in setting rates. For example, if a financial institution has had a big demand for five-year mortgages, it may pay a premium to attract five-year term deposits.

Financial institutions listed in this table may vary from week to week.

Rates are "annualized" – the rate for a full year, not the return for the period specified. Institutions may offer variations on the certificates of deposit listed here and these rates provide benchmarks to assess the value of returns from other combinations.

Minimum amounts generally apply to deposits for fixed terms and these minimums are indicated in the various categories below – up to six months, one to five years, monthly interest and compound interest.

Most fixed-term deposits pay interest at the end of a term if less than a year and annually if more than a year.

The table also shows rates for five-year deposits that pay interest monthly and that pay compound interest. (Compounding means the payments are held by the financial institution and reinvested, so the lenders get a lump sum payment at the end of the term.)

WHAT YOUR SAVINGS EARN 11.30.00

Rates are quoted on Thursday and subject to change. Selection of financial institutions may vary weekly. Figures supplied by Fiscal Agents

Banks	Savings monthly	Accts daily	Term Deposits min inv	30-59 days	60-89 days	90-119 days	120-179 days	Certificates/Debentures interest paid annually min inv	1 yr	2 yr	3 yr	4 yr	5 yr	5 yr Term Int paid monthly min inv	%rate	Comp int	Cert aftr 5 yrs
Amex Bank of Canada	-	5.00	-	-	-	-	-	-	-	-	-	-	-	-	-	-	-
BCI Bank	0.75	0.50	5,000	3.65	3.75	3.95	3.95	1,000	4.85	5.10	5.15	5.20	5.30	5,000	4.70	5.300	1,294
Bank of Montreal	-	0.20	5,000	3.65	3.75	3.95	3.95	1,000	4.85	5.10	5.15	5.20	5.30	5,000	5.05	5.300	1,294
Bank of Nova Scotia	-	0.25	5,000	3.65	3.75	3.95	3.95	500	4.85	5.10	5.15	5.20	5.30	5,000	5.05	5.300	1,294
BIBO	0.il	6,000	3.6C	3.7C	3.0C	3.0C	1,000	4.9C	5.10	5.15	5.20	5.25	5,000	5.10	5.350	1,797	
Citibank Canada	-	0.20	5,000	3.65	3.75	3.95	3.95	5,000	4.85	5.10	5.15	5.20	5.30	5,000	5.05	5.300	1,294
Citizens Bank	-	0.50	5,000	4.50	4.50	5.00	5.00	500	5.50	5.50	5.50	5.50	5.50	500	5.00	5.500	1,306
HSBC Bank Canada	-	0.25	5,000	3.65	3.75	3.95	3.95	1,000	4.85	5.20	5.25	5.30	5.40	5,000	5.15	5.400	1,300
ING Direct	-	4.85	-	-	-	-	-	0	5.65	5.65	5.70	5.70	5.75	0	-	5.750	1,322
Laurentian Bank	-	0.05	5,000	3.65	3.75	3.95	3.95	1,000	4.85	5.10	5.15	5.20	5.30	10,000	4.92	5.300	1,294
Manulife Bank	-	5.25	25,000	5.35	5.40	5.45	5.45	5,000	5.65	5.65	5.90	6.00	6.00	10,000	5.75	6.000	1,338
National Bank	-	0.10	5,000	3.65	3.75	3.95	3.95	1,000	4.85	5.10	5.15	5.20	5.30	10,000	4.80	5.300	1,294
NBG Bank	0.75	1.00	5,000	3.65	3.75	3.95	3.95	1,000	4.85	5.10	5.15	5.20	5.30	5,000	5.30	5.050	1,279
Royal Bank	-	0.30	5,000	3.65	3.75	3.95	3.95	500	4.85	5.10	5.15	5.20	5.30	5,000	5.17	5.300	1,294
State Bank of India(Can)	1.50	1.50	5,000	4.75	4.75	5.00	5.00	5,000	5.50	5.75	5.75	5.75	6.00	-	-	-	-
Toronto Dominion Bank	-	0.20	5,000	4.15	4.25	4.50	4.60	1,000	4.85	5.10	5.15	5.20	5.30	5,000	5.05	5.300	1,294

• The bank is the designated crisis manager when there are problems in Canada's econo-my or when this country's financial system is exposed to problems elsewhere in the world. That can include intervention in the currency market or loans to financial institutions.

The central bank does not set a target rate for the foreign exchange value of the C$. When it does intervene in the currency market, the purpose is to smooth the trading patterns. However, the bank does influence the value of Canadian currency through its hold on the interest rate structure. The general policy stance is that by keeping a lid on inflation, the central bank provides a stable environment and that in turn allows the economy to give strength to the C$.

The Bank of Canada is governed by a board of directors, which is appointed by the finance minister. The board appoints the senior officers of the bank and sets broad cor-porate objectives. By tradition, there is a regional balance to the board. Monetary policy is formulated by a governing council that consists of the governor, senior deputy gov-ernor and four deputy governors. The governor is appointed for a seven-year term and senior officers usually are career employees at the bank.

The monetary tool that attracts the most public attention is the bank rate. This inter-est rate has two roles, as a policy signal and as a backstop to the banking system. The policy role is easier to understand by knowing the basics of the practical application of the bank rate. The Bank of Canada will lend overnight funds to a financial institution at the bank rate. The central bank will borrow from a financial institution at a rate that is 50 basis points lower. This 50-point spread – one half of a percentage point – is called the central bank's "operating band."

THE BANK OF CANADA SETS THE BANK RATE – THE BASIS FOR INTEREST RATE STRUCTURE

Commercial banks need overnight money to meet obligations when they settle accounts at the end of the day. Usually, another bank will have spare cash to lend and most of the time the overnight rate in commercial markets is close to the middle of the Bank of Canada's operating band. Only if there are distortions will a bank be forced to rely on the central bank.

But when the Bank of Canada sets the bank rate, it is fixing the starting point for the interest rate structure. When the bank rate goes up or down, commercial interest rates and bond yields generally follow. In this way, the bank has a direct influence on an eas-ing or tightening of credit conditions. It has two essential enforcement options to back up its view of the appropriate level for interest rates. In effect, this involves making the financial system an offer it can't refuse.

If the bank wants to push commercial rates down, it uses "special purchase and resale agreements," a financial tool known colloquially as "specials." These are overnight loans offered at a rate that is below the prevailing market rate. By making cheap money available, the bank takes the steam out of upward pressure on rates. The opposite tactic is a "sale and repurchase agreement," generally referred to as an SRA. With this instrument, the bank can nudge commercial rates higher by, in effect,

MORTGAGE RATES | TABLE

The Mortgage Rates table provides rates for standard terms at selected financial institutions. This is the largest class of consumer loans and the spread between mortgages and wholesale funds for similar terms is an indicator of credit conditions. When there is easy credit, the spread, or difference, will be narrow between wholesale and retail rates of the same term.

For shorter terms, lenders offer both closed and open mortgages. **Open** means the loan can be paid off early. Rates for open mortgages are indicated by the **op** symbol.

Variable rate mortgages are those with rates that fluctuate according to general interest rate trends. Often, these mortgages are pegged to the prime rate. If this type of mortgage is not offered, it is indicated by an **n.a.** in this column.

MORTGAGE RATES 12.01.00

Rates are subject to change. Selection of financial institutions may vary weekly. Figures supplied by Fiscal Agents.

	Variable rate	6 months	1 yr	2 yr	3 yr	4 yr	5 yr
Banks							
Effective December 1, 2000							
BCI Bank	n.a.	8.15-8.60op	7.90-8.70op	8.00	8.10	8.20	8.25
Bank of Montreal	7.50	8.15-8.60op	7.90-8.70op	8.00	8.10	8.20	8.25
Bank of Nova Scotia	7.50	8.15-8.60op	7.90-8.70op	8.00	8.10	8.20	8.25
CIBC	7.50	8.60op	7.90-8.70op	8.00	8.10	8.20	8.25
Citizens Bank	n.a.	7.65-8.10op	7.40-8.20op	7.00	7.10	7.20	7.25
HSBC Bank Canada	7.50	8.15-8.60op	7.90-8.70op	8.00	8.10	8.20	8.25
ING Direct	n.a.	-	6.95	-	-	-	7.10
Laurentian Bank	n.a.	8.15-8.60op	7.90-8.70op	8.00	8.10	8.20	8.25
Manulife Bank	n.a.	8.15	7.90-8.70op	8.00	8.10	8.20	8.25
National Bank	n.a.	8.15-8.60op	7.90-8.70op	8.00	8.10	8.20	8.25
NBG Bank	n.a.	8.15-8.60op	7.90-8.70op	8.00	8.10	8.20	8.25
Royal Bank	7.50	8.20-8.65op	7.95-8.75op	8.00	8.10	8.20	8.25
Toronto Dominion Bank	7.50	-	7.90-8.70op	8.00	8.10	8.20	8.25
Trust & Loan							
Canada Trust	7.50	8.15-8.60op	7.90	8.00	8.10	8.20	8.25
Canadian Western Trust	n.a.	8.15 8.60op	7.90	8.00	8.10	8.20	8.25
Desjardins Trust	n.a.	8.15-8.60op	7.90-8.70op	8.00	8.10	8.20	8.25

borrowing at a rate that is above the prevailing commercial rate. In this situation, the bank is paying a premium in the market.

INVESTMENTS DON'T EXIST IN A WORLD APART

Any portfolio strategy is incomplete without an assessment of how security values are affected by political policy, natural events and social trends. One of the most widely talked about examples is the impact of baby boom demographics on asset values. When the boomers started having children, there was a building boom and home prices

ECONOWATCH | TABLE

FP Econowatch appears in Monday editions and provides a snapshot of the Canadian economy. Key statistics on the U.S. economy also are included. These statistics on business activity, banking, prices and the labor market in Canada are the key numbers that define the state of the economy. Generally, these numbers are adjusted to account for seasonal factors and the table gives the latest figures compared with the previous period. The year-to-year % column provides percentage change and these figures are guides to annual growth rates in the economy.

The top numbers in the list are for gross domestic product, which is the total value of goods and services produced by the economy.

The quarter figures are all-inclusive counts of domestic activity. The monthly GDP figures are less inclusive in that they do not account for indirect taxes. But the monthly figures provide a valuable interim assessment of the pace of economic activity. **Business activity** statistics take stock of the economy at various stages, from new orders at factories through to retail sales. **Banking** statistics measure the base costs of money (treasury bill yields and bank rate) as well as volume (money supply and loan activity).

Price indexes (not shown below) are measures of inflation and also are commonly used in contracts to regulate price changes.

Labor market figures (not shown below) provide a rough measure of prosperity but they are also a guide to business activity. Month-to-month changes in employment are, essentially, a count of jobs created in the economy.

ECONOWATCH 12.01.00

Figures supplied by Bank of Canada,
Statistics Canada, Nesbitt Burns

Business activity

	Term	Latest period	Prev. period	% chg.
GDP, 1992 prices, $bil.	3Q00	930.25	919.50	1.2 (annual rate)
GDP at factor cost	Sept.	...	...	0.0 (mo.-over-mo.)
GDP at factor cost	Sept.	...	...	4.1 (yr.-over-yr.)
GDP price deflator 1992=100	3Q00	113.1	112.5	0.5 (annual rate)
Composite Leading Indicator 1992=100	Oct.	167.6	166.4	0.7 (mo.-over-mo.)
Manufacturers shipments $bil.	Sept.	44.85	45.30	-1.0 (mo.-over-mo.)
New orders $bil.	Sept.	44.43	45.15	-1.6 (mo.-over-mo.)
Retail sales $bil.	Sept.	23.55	23.46	0.4 (mo.-over-mo.)
Retail sales	Sept.	...	...	6.0 (yr.-over-yr.)
Housing starts 000s	Oct.	164.8	157.1	4.9 (mo.-over-mo.)
New Motor vehicle sales 000s	Sept.	142.548	139.962	1.8 (mo.-over-mo.)

Trade & investment

	Term	Latest period	Prev. period	% chg.
Merchandise trade balance $bil.	Sept.	4.30	4.06	n.a.
Current account balance $mil.	3Q00	6,962	3,282	n.a.
Exports $bil.	Sept.	34.95	34.92	0.1 (mo.-over-mo.)
Imports $bil.	Sept.	30.65	30.85	-0.7 (mo.-over-mo.)

Banking

	Term	Latest period	Prev. period	% chg.
Money supply, M1 $bil.	Oct.	105.809	104.632	15.6 (yr.-over-yr.)
Money supply, M2 $bil.	Oct.	491.638	488.663	5.8 (yr.-over-yr.)
Total household credit $mil.	Oct.	621.982	617.321	6.3 (yr.-over-yr.)

soared. Now, the boomers are looking ahead to retirement and their savings patterns have been credited with powering a bull market in stocks. The influence of that demographic bulge will continue as they sell down their equity portfolios to finance retirement.

A broad range of government actions affects securities values and the most common examples are tax measures. Tariff policies are another high profile valuation issue, but many other government regulations have an impact. Some of these rules, such as environmental standards, affect the cost section of corporate income statements. A government policy issue that is more significant to Canadian companies than to those in the U.S. is one that comes under the general heading of sovereignty.

Several domestic industries have been protected over the years by the Canadian government. Energy, financial services, transportation and cultural sectors are prominent examples of industries that have been protected because of the view that Canadian ownership was a national priority.

Almost by definition, those protected industries are less competitive than their foreign counterparts. Usually, the goal of protection is to give local firms time to develop to the stage where they can stand toe-to-toe against outside competition. Sometimes this works and sometimes it doesn't. A recent example is in the brewing industry, where Canadian beer companies have had difficulty adjusting as tariff and non-tariff barriers have tumbled.

THESE ARE KEY ISSUES FOR AN INVESTOR
• To what extent is the issuer of a security dependent on special circumstances?
• What is the likelihood that those circumstances will change?

These two questions can apply to governments, as well as corporations. For example, how would the ratings of Newfoundland bonds be affected by a prolonged ban on cod fishing that resulted in continued high social assistance costs? Many of these non-financial influences on securities values can be anticipated by a careful reading of the daily news. But sometimes there are genuine shocks – fires, train wrecks, chemical spills and so on.

The issue here for investors is to check on the extent to which an issuer of securities protects against the unexpected. Often, this involves relying on professional analysts who visit the companies and quiz financial managers about insurance coverage and disaster plans. But if the investment is in a company that has facilities open to the public, a visit will give an impression of how well the company is run. If the facilities are well maintained and the staff appears knowledgeable and courteous, it's likely that the same standards apply in back-office operations.

CHAPTER 5

MUTUAL | FUNDS

- Mutual funds defined
- What they are and how they work
- No loads versus loads
- Reading *FP*'s fund tables to track performance and risk

A TOOLKIT FOR TUNING UP

YOUR MUTUAL FUND INVESTMENTS | BY SUSAN HEINRICH

THIS INVESTMENT GUIDE IS DESIGNED to better acquaint mutual fund investors with the information available in the *Financial Post*'s various fund reports and show how it can help them understand their fund investments. The reports offer more than performance information. The statistics in the monthly and quarterly reports and the 15-year review, as well as the weekly packages, are designed to be a comprehensive and accessible resource for fund investors of all types. Whether for a quick glance at the latest returns or more in-depth analysis of holdings and asset allocation, they are organized to provide fast answers.

All investors would be wise, no matter how trustworthy their advisers, to try to understand their investments and follow their performance and costs. Although a mutual fund investment may be appropriate when it is made, markets and circumstances change. A fund's performance can lag, a portfolio manager departs, new products become available or the investor's objectives change. Monitoring is important and the *FP*'s mutual fund tables are monitoring tools.

MUTUAL FUNDS MONTHLY REPORT TRACKS PERFORMANCE OVER THE SHORT AND LONG TERM
Most experts agree longer terms of historical performance data provide a better indication of how a fund will perform in the future. *FP*'s *Mutual Funds Monthly Report*, for example, allows readers to look at a fund's performance over the short or long term. Returns are calculated based on the latest available data but extend as far back as 10 years (15 years in the case of the Mutual Funds 15 Year Review).

In using the tables to interpret performance, readers should remember that rates of return for periods of more than one year are expressed as "average annual compound returns." These figures do not show fund volatility – a particular fund may have achieved 16% in the first year, -3% in the second year and 5% in the third, but the table would show a 6% three-year return. The three-year standard deviation numbers provide an indication of fund volatility.

*Average figures for each mutual fund tell you whether
the performance is above or below average*

Not only will the numbers vary from fund to fund but there can be significant differences between classes of funds. As an example, one monthly report showed fixed income (bond) funds as having a three-year standard deviation of 1.2 for the bond group as a whole. Bonds are almost always less volatile than stocks and that same report had Canadian equity funds with an average three year deviation of 5.5. Equity funds that invest in emerging equity markets, such as Latin America, had a standard deviation of 8.1.

Average figures for each fund category can tell you whether a particular fund's performance is in line with the rest of the group or above or below average. *FP's* fund reports also include a list of benchmarks – stock and special indexes created and tracked by investment firms – such as the Scotia Capital Markets bond indexes.

MANAGEMENT EXPENSE FEES CAN IMPACT THE BOTTOM LINE

Many investors do not realize they pay management expense fees on every fund – known colloquially in the industry as MERs, for management expense ratios. Those fees can have a major impact on the bottom line.

Management expense should reflect the complexity of the work. Picking equities is a more difficult job than running a money market fund that invests mainly in treasury bills. In early 2001, the average MER for Canadian equity funds was 2.5% and the average MER on money market funds was 1.1%.

Return to the investor is a big factor in this equation. When investors were paying a 2.5% MER on Canadian equity funds, the overall return on the average Canadian equity fund was a negative 0.1%. During the same period, bond holders had a happier experience. Average MER for a Canadian bond fund was 1.7% and the six-month average return was 4.5%.

Obviously, general market conditions have a big impact on returns. And six months is too short a time period to make hard judgments on different types of funds. But the general point is that investors should look closely at the cost of managing their money.

Investment professionals don't mind paying for advice. They believe that good managers should be well compensated. In turn, those good managers should be generating above average returns on their portfolios. In that way, they earn their keep. But if there is no significant difference in the history of returns, pick the managers with lower MERs when choosing a fund.

MONTHLY AND QUARTERLY REPORTS LOOK AT WORLD PERFORMANCES

For those investors who are keen market watchers, both the monthly and quarterly reports analyze what has gone on in the markets around the world and how that has affected fund returns. The *Quarterly Report* is designed to help investors better understand how money managers react to changing market conditions by providing an in-depth analysis of portfolio holdings. An investor might learn, for example, that his or her balanced fund – which usually holds a combination of bonds and equities – is no longer balanced at all. Bullish on equity markets, the manager of the fund may have moved out of fixed income entirely and placed all bets on the stock market.

Some investors like this sort of strategy, but others buy balanced funds in the expectation they'll remain diversified. *FP*'s fund reports can help them make sure their investments are on the right course.

INVESTING IN MUTUAL FUNDS

A mutual fund is a pool of money contributed by many individuals and invested by professional investment managers. There are many types of mutual funds. Some invest in stocks, some in bonds, some in specialty investments such as real estate. Some are high-risk funds where investors hope to make big gains. Some are extremely conservative, investing in low-risk money market instruments that produce moderate returns.

Yet they all work on the same principle: a pool of capital contributed by mutual fund investors is used to buy and sell securities and other investments held by funds. Just what is bought and sold is controlled by investment managers who aim to do what every investor wants to do – make money. Most of the profits go back to the individuals who invested in the fund. There are a number of ways this can occur, depending on the nature of the fund and its investment.

MUTUAL FUNDS 12.07.00

Close or latest for DEC 07, 2000 supplied by Fundata Canada Inc. Prices reported are for information purposes only. Confirmation of price should be obtained from fund. Date following fund name denotes last valuation. The codes mean: X - ex-dividend; U - US$; ... - change less than 1¢; * - RRSP eligible (funds without * may generally be held in RRSPs as foreign property); Z - not available to the general public; N - No load fund; F - Front end acquisition fee (generally negotiable); D - deferred declining redemption fee based on original capital invested; R - deferred declining redemption fee based on market value; FD - F or D at buyer's option; FR - F or R at buyer's option; B - both front end and back end fee. (n) not a member of IFIC.

Fund	Specifics	NAVPS	$ chg
@rgentum Management C$			
Cdn Equity Pt	*FD	10.45	unch
Cdn L/S Equ	*FD	9.27	-.04
Cdn Perform Prt	*FD	14.05	-.09
Discovery Port	*FD	11.12	.06
Income Port	*FD	9.10	+.02
Intl Master Prt	FD	11.70	-.16

Fund	Specifics	NAVPS	$chg
Discovery RSP	*FD	4.54	-.13
Discovery U$	UFD	5.91	-.17
Enterprise	*FD	6.52	unch
Enterprise Sml	*FD	6.55	-.09
Europlus C$	FD	6.13	+.02
Europlus RSP	*FD	5.20	+.02
Europlus U$	UFD	4.01	+.01
Gl Balanced	FD	6.00	+.04
Gl Balanced RSP	*FD	5.79	+.03
Gl Balanced U$	UFD	3.93	+.02
Gl Hgh Yld BdU$	UFD	3.36	unch
Gl Hi Yd Bd RSP	*F	5.37	...
Gl High Yld Bd	FD	5.13	...
Government Inc	*FD	4.78	...
Income Gro DSC	*D	8.34	+.01
Income Gro SC	*F	8.34	+.01
Indo-Pac RSP	*FD	4.55	-.02
Indo-Pacific C$	FD	5.76	-.02
Indo-Pacific U$	UFD	3.77	-.01
Intl Co C$	FD	5.29	+.01
Intl Co RSP	*FD	4.92	+.01
Intl Co U$	UFD	3.47	+.01
RSP Equity	*FD	8.57	+.04
RSP Fund	*FD	5.77	
Sel Balanced	*FD	8.53	...
Sel Cdn Growth	*FD	9.19	unch
Sel Growth C$	FD	15.43	-.04
Sel Growth RSP	*FD	5.74	-.02
Sel Growth U$	UFD	10.11	-.03
The Amer RSP	*FD	5.05	.04

Fund	Specifics	NAVPS	$chg
Gbl Managers	FD	10.27	+.01
Global	FD	19.64	unch
Global Energy	FD	13.62	+.12
Global Tech	FD	29.03	-.36
Global Telecom	FD	43.25	-.05
Global Value	FD	12.16	-.05
Harbour Sector	FD	11.83	+.07
Intl Value	FD	11.27	-.04
Japanese	FD	13.50	-.12
Latin Amer	FD	7.66	+.08
Ldmk American	FD	14.01	unch
Ldmk Global	FD	8.67	-.01
Pacific	FD	9.47	-.06
Short-Term	FD	8.50	unch
Sig Am Sml Co	FD	7.79	-.02
Sig Explorer	FD	9.80	-.06
Sig Gl Sml Co	FD	8.20	-.06
Signature Cdn	FD	13.52	+.03
CI Sector Funds U$			
American MarsU$	UFD	6.88	-.01
American U$	UFD	9.16	unch
BPI Amer Equ U$	UFD	5.23	-.01
BPI Glo Equ U$	UFD	5.35	-.01
BPI Int Eq U$	UFD	5.37	-.02
Canadian U$	UFD	5.17	+.01
Emerg Mkts U$	UFD	5.54	-.01
European U$	UFD	5.45	-.02
Gbl B2B U$	UFD	4.79	-.08
Gbl Biotech U$	UFD	12.25	-.13

Daily listings permit constant monitoring of fund performance. For those mutual fund investors who like to stay on top of their investments, the *Financial Post* publishes daily mutual fund performance listings. Unlike the other listings, these are organized by fund management company rather than investment category. Separate listings are provided for segregated life insurance company funds venture capital funds, and a general "other" category. The first column after the fund name shows a number of fund specifics as follows:

X – ex-dividend

U – US$

••• – change is less than 1¢

* – fund is RRSP/RRIF eligible as 100% Canadian content

Z – unavailable to the general public

N – no load

F – front-end load

D – deferred declining back-end load (redemption fee) based on original acquisition cost

R – deferred declining redemption fee based on market value

FD – F or D at buyer's option

FR – F or R at buyer's option

B – both front-end and back-end loads

n – not a member of the Investment Funds Institute of Canada (IFIC)

Money Market

Fund	Specifics	Curr yield	Eff yield	%pt chg
@rgentum Management C$				
ST Asset Port	X*F	5.37	5.51	-.63
Acadia Investment Funds				
MMF 12/06	*N	5.26	5.40	unch
Acuity Mutual Funds				
MMF	X*FD	3.26	3.20	+.06
AGF Funds Inc.				
Money Market	X*F	4.33	4.42	.05
U$ MMarket	XUF	6.05	6.23	-.07
AIC Income Fund Series				
MMF	*FD	4.70	4.81	+.07
AIM Funds C$				
MMF	*FD	4.52	4.62	unch
AIM Funds(Trimark)				

The next column of the listings shows the fund's NAVPS (net asset value per share) as at the previous day's or latest closing, and the final column shows the dollar change from the previous day's/latest closing. The daily listings provide a separate section for money market funds (segregated as well as regular), with different performance figures than for other funds. In this case, after fund names and specifics, the tables show the fund's current annualized yield, the effective yield over the past 12 months and the dollar-change figure over the preceding day's/latest close. The daily listings also provide a table of dividend distributions made that day or recently, showing type, amount and distribution date.

OPEN-END FUNDS

Almost all Canadian mutual funds are known as open-end funds. That means you can invest money or cash in your investment at any time. When you invest in a fund, you buy units (also known as shares) of that fund. As with stocks, the value of these units fluctuates, so you pay the current price when you buy into the fund.

HOW UNITS ARE PRICED

Unlike stocks, mutual fund unit prices don't fluctuate because of supply and demand. They fluctuate according to the value of the investments and other assets held by the fund. The unit value is calculated by taking the total assets of the fund, subtracting the fund's liabilities, and dividing that amount by the number of units outstanding. For example, if the net value of assets is $100 million and there are 10 million units, each will be worth $10. This is known as the net asset value per share (NAVPS).

Let's say you buy 100 units for a total of $1,000. And thanks to some wise decisions on the part of the fund manager, the fund's investments double to $200 million over a few years while the number of shareholders remains the same. Each unit is then worth $20, and your investment has doubled to $2,000. At that point, any new investors in the fund have to pay $20 a unit. Of course, the number of unitholders isn't likely to remain the same. More units will be bought, and some will be cashed in. But if the fund is doing well, it is likely to attract more investors than it loses.

There is no set number of units. That's because every time new units are sold, the proceeds increase the fund's assets and the net asset value per share, or unit price, remains unchanged. To return to our example, if 10 million new units were added to the fund at $20 a unit, it would increase total assets by another $200 million. The fund would then be worth $400 million, and each of the units, now totalling 20 million, would be still worth $20.

The NAVPS remains the same when units are redeemed, or sold back, to the fund. If 10 million units were bought back by the fund, its assets would be reduced to $200 million, and the number of units would be back to 10 million. The NAVPS would still be $20.

Many funds calculate their net asset value daily. That's easy to do for an equity fund, for instance, because the value is based on the price of stocks. So you may see the price of your units change from day to day. Some funds calculate their assets weekly; real estate funds do so even less frequently, as they have to have properties appraised to determine their value.

WHO OPERATES MUTUAL FUNDS?

Many mutual funds are part of groups, or families, of funds operated under the auspices of a central company. They may be sold directly by the company's sales force or through investment dealers and other independent agencies. Some funds are managed and sold by banks, trust companies, credit unions, caisses populaires and life insurance companies.

WEEKLY MUTUAL FUNDS | TABLES

Weekly tables allow closer monitoring of investment performance. In addition to the monthly and quarterly mutual fund reports, the *Financial Post* publishes complete fund listings every weekend, providing detailed daily as well as historical weekly NAVPS (net asset value per share).

As with the weekday listings, the funds are grouped by fund company and, if applicable, fund family.

Money market funds, segregated funds and venture capital funds are listed separately from the mainstream mutual funds.

How to read the mutual fund tables

Mutual fund rate of return figures appear in the Financial Post Mutual Funds Monthly Report, which runs the third Saturday of each month.

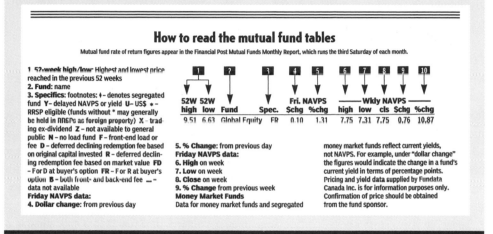

1. **52-week high/low:** Highest and lowest price reached in the previous 52 weeks
2. **Fund:** name
3. **Specifics:** footnotes: ✝ – denotes segregated fund **Y** – delayed NAVPS or yield **U** – US$ ✱ – RRSP eligible (funds without * may generally be held in RRSPs as foreign property) **X** – trading ex-dividend **Z** – not available to general public **N** – no load fund **F** – front-end load or fee **D** – deferred declining redemption fee based on original capital invested **R** – deferred declining redemption fee based on market value **FD** – F or D at buyer's option **FR** – F or R at buyer's option **B** – both front- and back-end fee ... – data not available
Friday NAVPS data:
4. **Dollar change:** from previous day

5. **% Change:** from previous day
Friday NAVPS data:
6. **High** on week
7. **Low** on week
8. **Close** on week
9. **% Change** from previous week
Money Market Funds
Data for money market funds and segregated

money market funds reflect current yields, not NAVPS. For example, under "dollar change" the figures would indicate the change in a fund's current yield in terms of percentage points. Pricing and yield data supplied by Fundata Canada Inc. is for information purposes only. Confirmation of price should be obtained from the fund sponsor.

WHY FUNDS CHARGE FEES

Mutual funds are in the business of making money for investors. But they also charge investors fees for managing their money. Those fees can take a number of forms.

• **Sales charges:** Some funds charge commissions when you buy units. These are known as front-end loads, and the charge once was as much as 9% of the purchase price. But now the percentage is considerably lower. And the rate may decline as the number of units purchased is increased. These fees aren't added to the cost of your investment. Instead, they are deducted from your total contribution to the fund, with the remainder used to buy units. So if you invest $10,000 with a fund that has a 5% front-end load, $500 will go toward commissions and $9,500 will be used to buy units.

Back-end loads, or deferred sales charges, are levied by some funds when you redeem units. These loads may be based on the initial cost of your units or on the redemption value. In most cases, the percentage declines over time, and typically will be reduced to zero after six or seven years.

No-load funds charge no fees when you buy or sell units. This practice, spearheaded by banks and trust companies that offer funds, is becoming more popular in the competitive mutual funds marketplace.

• **Management fees:** All mutual funds charge management fees. These are calculated as a percentage of assets managed by the fund and typically range up to 2% a year. Sometimes the percentage will decline as the value of assets under management grows. These fees are not levied directly on investors. Instead, they are charged to the fund. So if your fund's investments generate a 10% annual return, a 2% management fee would reduce the return to 8%. This is the return that is published in *The Financial Post*.

• **Other fees:** Some funds charge distribution fees, or sales administration fees. They are used to provide commissions paid to sales personnel and are also charged directly to the fund.

TYPES OF MUTUAL FUNDS AND WHAT THEY INVEST IN

Mutual funds cover a broad range of investments and can be divided into the major categories listed below. Many of the funds in each of these categories will be eligible for tax shelter status within an RRSP, where the requirement is that 70% of direct investment must be Canadian. As a practical matter the potential foreign content is higher when investors put mutual funds in their RRSP. That's because the rules apply to direct investment. So an investor can have direct holdings of up to 30% in foreign securities and then also hold RRSP-eligible Canadian mutual funds that also have foreign content in their portfolios.

• **Equity funds** invest in stocks. Within this category you will find funds that specialize in a management style – a growth or a value orientation. The most common distinction, though, is geographic. Canadian equity funds are in the majority because these investments will be RRSP-eligible. Investors who want to broaden their horizons can find funds that specialize in major markets, such as the U.S. and Europe, or emerging markets such as Latin America. Another distinction in the equity category is in the size of the company that issues the stocks. Some funds invest only in senior companies while others may specialize in shares of mid-size or junior companies. Another sub-set of equity funds are those that invest in market sectors, such as high technology or natural resources.

• **Fixed-income funds** invest in bonds. The question of RRSP eligibility also applies to bonds and the most common of this type are funds that qualify for RRSP status. Typically, the bond funds will have a mixture of government and the debt securities of large corporations. But there are bond funds that specialize in high-yield issues, commonly known as junk bonds.

• **Balanced funds** hold a mixture of stocks, bonds and money market securities. Typically, these funds will be run by a team of managers and not a single star manager. As the name suggests, the goal is to hold a mixture of securities in order to reduce risk. The rationale is that there often is a counter-cyclical dynamic between stock and bond markets. If stocks are weakening because the economy is slipping into recession, bond prices should be rising. And when the economy is steaming ahead in a recovery, bond prices usually fall. The goal of a balanced fund is to produce a steady return through the ups and downs of the business cycle. Typically, a balanced fund will hold a higher proportion of stocks – for example, 80% when the economy is booming and perhaps only 50% in slack times.

• **Money market funds** invest in short-term securities such as treasury bills and commercial paper. When a fund manager talks about holding cash in a portfolio, that usually means holding money market paper. These short-term securities are treated like cash because they can be easily converted to cash. Individual investors use them the same way. If they sell a stock or bond fund, they can hold the cash in a money market fund until that cash is reinvested. These days, many people use money market funds as savings accounts for reserve funds.

• **Specialty funds** cover the niche markets. Real estate is one of them. Precious metals is another. These funds may be primarily equity funds and can be slotted into the equity category. They may also have holdings that are not equities – direct investment in property as part of a real estate fund or gold bullion in a precious metals fund. Another group of funds in the specialty category are the so-called ethical funds, which restrict their investments for ideological reasons. For example, an ethical fund may avoid securities in certain countries because of human rights issues. Labor funds is another specialty category, although they are grouped in the equity classifications. They are sponsored by labor organizations, have certain tax benefits and invest only in Canadian job-creating enterprises. Yet another specialty category are hedge funds, so-called because the objective is to use derivatives to profit from offsetting hedge positions. Hedge funds are mainly for very sophisticated investors because typical minimum investments are high and the funds are dealing with high levels of leverage.

• **Segregated funds** are a unique type offered only by insurance companies. That's because there is a life insurance component to the funds. By law, these funds must pay at least 75% of the original investment after 10 years or upon the death of the investor. In other words, there is a guaranteed minimum on the investor's holdings.

CLOSED-END FUNDS

There are a handful of closed-end investment funds in Canada. These funds operate differently from conventional open-end funds. When they start out, closed-end funds offer shares to the public in much the same way as a new stock offering. They then use the money to make investments.

After the initial offering, shares of closed-end funds trade on stock exchanges or over the counter. Instead of redeeming your shares to the fund, you sell them on an exchange, just like stocks. New investors in the fund must buy shares on exchanges, not directly from the company.

The market price for shares in closed-end funds is generally less than their net asset value per share. This reflects the fact that it may be more difficult to sell closed-end shares, tax liabilities and other factors.

WEEKLY MUTUAL FUND | HIGHLIGHTS

Fund snapshot offers a package of information on a noteworthy fund. The weekly mutual fund highlights page is built around a Fund Snapshot package featuring a fund that has been chosen for its exceptional performance or for a recent development. The snapshot includes a brief statement of why the fund was chosen, then provides detailed information on the fund and its operations.

Fund information: The list of information includes fund category, legal status, fund managers, inception date, total net asset and NAVPS figures as at the indicated date, RRSP eligibility as Canadian content, loads, minimum investment requirements, MER and category average MER, valuation frequency, dividend distributions and their frequency.

Comparative performance: The second component of the snapshot is a series of tables depicting the annual percentage performance of the fund, the category average and related indexes and/or subindexes over each of the preceding five years. For example, a precious metals fund might be compared with the TSE 300 as well as the TSE gold and precious metals subindex. This shows at a glance how well the fund performed against the averages.

Asset allocation: This section of the snapshot includes two pie charts showing the asset allocation of the highlighted fund and the corresponding category average.

Top holdings: This listing shows the top holdings of the fund as a percentage of total assets (as at the specified date).

Fund comparison: The featured fund is included in a listing of several similar funds, ranked according to the percentage of their assets invested in the featured fund's primary area of focus. For example, a Far East fund specializing in Hong Kong would be compared, in terms of percentages invested in Hong Kong, with several other Far East or Pacific Rim funds.

P/E ratios or volatility: The snapshot also provides a chart of the featured fund's price-earnings ratio (in the case of Canadian equity funds) or three-year standard deviation (for other funds) compared with other similar funds and two market indexes.

Fund Snapshot: AIM Canadian Balanced

This $304-million fund is a solid long-term performer, with compound annual returns of 18.5% after three years, and third in its category over this period.

Fund category: Canadian Balanced
Legal status: unit trust
Managers: Clas Olsson, Bob Alley, Jason Holtzer, Brad Conger, Carolyn Gibbs, AIM Capital Management
Inception date: 07.15.00
Asset value: $304.3-million
RRSP eligibility: yes
Load: front-end or back
Min. investment: $500
Fund MER: 2.73%
Category average MER: 2.35%
Valuation frequency: daily

Data at 10.31.00

STANDARD DEVIATION
In per cent

- AIM Cdn. Balanced
- Category average
- Scotia Cap. Markets Universe
- Morningstar Balanced III

0 5 10 15 20

PERFORMANCE ANNUAL RETURN
In per cent

50

25

0

-25

1996   1997   1998   1999   2000*

- ■ AIM Canadian Balanced
- □ Category average
- ▨ Scotia Capital Markets Universe
- ▧ Morningstar Balanced III

*Year to date at 10.31.00

ASSET ALLOCATIONS

AIM Canadian Balanced
Cash 15.3%
TSE Financial Services 6.4%
Canadian Bonds 32.2%
TSE industrial products 17.8%
Other 28.3%

Category average
TSE consumer products 9.2%
TSE financial services 7.8%
Cash 9.6%
Other 42.0%
Canadian Bonds 31.4%

Top holdings at 10.31.00

Holding	% assets
Cash - Canadian Dollar	15.1
JDS Uniphase Cda Exch Non-Vtg Shs	2.2
Celestica Inc. Sub Vtg Shs	1.9
Nortel Networks Corp.	1.8
Canada Gov't 7.250 Jun 01.07	1.8
Canada Gov't 7.000 Dec 01.06	1.7
Canada Gov't 8.750 Dec 01.05	1.7
Four Seasons Hotels Ltd. Vtg Shs	1.6
Janna Systems	1.5
Onex Corp Sub Vt	1.5
AT&T Cda. Inc. 7.625 Mar 15.05	1.5
GMAC 6.650 Jun 16.05	1.3
Canada Gov't 6.500 Jun 01.04	1.2
BC Prov 5.375 Oct 29.08	1.2
C-MAC Industries Inc.	1.2

Funds with largest Canadian Bonds positions

Fund	% assets	as of
Astra 125	91.2	09.00
AGF Canadian High Income	73.2	10.00
Acadia Diversified Atlantic	70.6	09.00
LFC LLIM Income Plus	69.4	10.00
Great-West Life Income(G) A	65.5	09.00
Astra 110	63.5	09.00
TD Mg Index Income RSP Portfolio	63.1	10.00
CI Canadian Income	63.0	10.00
TD Mg Index Income Portfolio	62.9	10.00
Industrial Alliance Diversified Secu DS	61.9	10.00
Astra 110 - Series II	61.1	09.00
National Bank Moderate Diversified	59.7	09.00
CIBC IPRS Income RSP Portfolio	58.0	10.00
CIBC IPRS Income Non-RSP Portfolio	58.0	10.00
AIM Canadian Balanced	32.2	10.00

CHOOSING A FUND

Before you invest in a mutual fund, you should decide on your investment objectives. For example, do you want growth, income or low risk? Only then should you begin the task of finding suitable funds for your investment. Fortunately, there is plenty of information and advice available.

Stockbrokers, financial planners, bank mutual fund representatives and independent mutual funds salespeople are all excellent sources of advice. Keep in mind, however, that their advice is not always objective – some have a vested interest in selling you certain funds.

There are many sources of mutual funds. No-load funds – those that don't levy sales charges – are usually sold directly by the fund organization. No-load funds include those sold by banks, trust companies, credit unions and large mutual fund organizations.

Funds that charge loads usually are sold through sales representatives such as stockbrokers, financial planners and independent mutual fund brokers.

MONTHLY PERFORMANCE TABLES

The *Financial Post*'s monthly fund performance survey is the primary source of performance-related statistical information on more than 1,600 mutual funds available in Canada. It is published in the *Mutual Funds Monthly Report* on the third Saturday of each month and provides data covering various periods up to the end of the preceding month.

CLOSED-END FUND | PERFORMANCE FIGURES

As part of its weekly mutual fund performance listings, the *Financial Post* provides performance figures for "closed end" funds. Once a predetermined number of units/shares have been purchased, the fund is closed to further investment – although, like stocks, shares already issued can be traded on the open market. The fund cannot issue any more shares. The listings provide the fund name as well as its stock ticker identification. This is followed by:

NAVPS: the net asset value per share (see monthly listings for definition).

Market value per sh.: This is the closing market price of the shares as of the date specified at the bottom of the table. The price at which the shares would change hands.

Prem.(+) or disc.(-)%: The final column of this table indicates the premium (+) or discount (-)

Closed end funds
Figures supplied by Reuters

Fund	Ticker	NAVPS	Mkt.val. /sh.	% Prm.+ disc.-
ARC STRAT	AEF.UN	14.36	11.15	-22.35
BioCapital Investments	BCK.IR	16.43	15.60	-5.05
Cda Tr Incm (Nov)	CNN.UN	9.38	7.70	-17.91
Cdn General Inv	CGI	13.95	10.20	-26.88
Cdn World Fund	CWF	6.00	3.50	-41.67
Central Fd Cda	CEF.A	5.34	4.55	-14.79
Citadel Divrsfd	CTD.UN	8.31	8.40	1.08
Citadel S-1	SDL.UN	23.53	26.00	10.50
DDJ Cdn Hgh Yld	HYB.UN	22.25	19.15	-13.93
Dundee Prec Mtls	DPM.A	11.38	6.30	-44.64
Economic Inv Tr	EVT	159.29	94.00	-40.99
EnerVest	EIT.UN	6.24	6.15	-1.44
First Asia Incm	FAI.UN	7.05	6.30	-10.64
Fst Austria Prime	FAP	9.58	7.55	-21.19
Hlth Care&Biotch	HCB.UN	12.96	10.50	-18.98
NCE Diversified	NCD.UN	4.55	3.63	-20.22
Newcstl Mkt (Aug)	NMN.UN	19.52	15.60	-20.08
HeadlineMedia (Sept)	HMG	1.79	2.90	62.01
Polar Hedge Tr	PHT.UN	4.97	4.89	-1.61
Templeton Emrg	TEM.UN	12.97	7.65	-41.02
Third Cdn Gen Inv	THD	19.72	14.00	-29.01
United Corps	UNC	76.84	42.50	-44.69

All funds valued weekly on Dec 14 except as noted.

between NAVPS and market value, expressed as a percentage of NAVPS. When the market value is lower than NAVPS, it is said to be discounted, and vice versa.

MUTUAL FUND | AND OTHER INDEXES

Each weekly mutual fund report includes a brief summary of performance figures for mutual fund and other indexes.

This table provides each index's rate of return over one month and one year (simple rates of return), as well as three and five years (compounded average annual returns). For definitions of these indexes, refer to the "benchmark" information on page 131.

Index & benchmark rates of return

Month end figures at 08.31.00 converted to Canadian dollars. Figures supplied by Fundata.

	Rate of return			
	1mo.	1yr.	3yr.	5yr.
20001006				
100 Price Ind	...	...	...	...
30 Day T-Bill	0.4	4.8	4.5	4.3
91 Day	0.5	5.1	4.5	4.6
Amex Comp Index	3.1	20.0	15.5	...
Avg 1 year GIC	0.4	4.5	3.8	3.7
Avg 5 year GIC	0.4	5.4	4.8	5.1
Canadian CPI	0.00	2.7	1.9	1.8
Commodity Index	4.0	14.1	-2.1	-1.1
DJ30 Ind Avg C$	5.6	2.2	16.0	21.7
FPX Balanced	3.2	24.1	14.5	...

The monthly fund listings are divided into 33 categories, generally reflecting the nature of each fund's underlying investments. Some funds may hold those types of investments exclusively, while others may invest in other types of assets as well. For example, certain fixed-income funds might also invest in mortgages. Fund managers typically keep a small portion of assets in cash or equivalents such as treasury bills.

For the majority of Canadian investors, tax liability is a major issue in choosing investments. That's why the lion's share of Canadian mutual fund assets is invested in Canadian securities. When looking abroad, investors need to consider currency exposure and political risk. They should look at the track record of the fund managers to see how successful they have been in managing these risks.

Listed below are the categories in *FP*'s monthly fund listings. Where there is a geographical definition – in Canada, the U.S., Japan, and so on – the fund will invest a minimum of 50% of total assets and 75% of non-cash assets within that geographical definition. In some of the equity classifications, holdings of the funds may include index derivatives that allow the fund to have a proxy exposure to baskets of stocks.

EQUITY FUNDS

• **Canadian equity funds** invest in Canadian stocks. At least six of the Toronto Stock Exchange's 14 sub-indexes must be represented. Weightings of those six must be at least 50% of each sub-index weighting within the TSE 300 composite index.

• **Canadian large-cap equity funds** have a minimum of 50% of total assets and 75% of non-cash assets in companies in the TSE 100 stock index. At least 50% of equity weighting must represent at least two of the TSE 100s four major sub-indexes, which are industrials, resources, consumer products and interest-sensitive stocks.

WHAT FUNDS | HOLD

This section of the weekly mutual fund report involves the selection of a newsworthy stock that soared or plummeted during the week. The stock's weekly performance is charted, and a brief explanation is provided of why the stock performed as it did.

Finally, mutual funds are ranked according to their holdings of each stock; the eight biggest holders are listed beneath the chart and explanation. This top eight list shows the number of shares held by each fund, the percentage that this represents of the fund's total assets, and the date upon which the fund information is based.

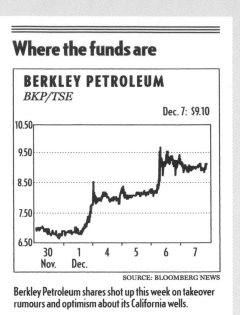

Where the funds are

BERKLEY PETROLEUM
BKP/TSE

Dec. 7: $9.10

SOURCE: BLOOMBERG NEWS

Berkley Petroleum shares shot up this week on takeover rumours and optimism about its California wells.

Top holders

Fund	No. shares	% total assets	as of date
Pacific Total Return	300	6.6	10.31.00
Montrusco Select Growth	549,672	5.1	10.31.00
Standard Life Natural Resources	30,000	4.2	10.31.00
TD Energy	452,700	3.1	10.31.00
Marathon Performance Nth Amer Lg-Short	2,400	3.0	10.31.00
TD Resource	325,000	2.6	10.31.00
CI Global Energy Sector	234,900	2.5	11.30.00
Global Strategy Canada Growth	564,300	2.2	09.30.00
Global Strategy Canadian Opportunities	293,000	2.2	09.30.00
GS Canadian Equity	505,500	2.0	10.31.00

• **Canadian small/mid-cap equity funds** have a minimum of 50% of total assets and 75% of non-cash assets, based on individual market value, in Canadian equities that have a median market capitalization that is less than 0.2% of the total market capitalization of the TSE 300 stocks. That median top limit for market capitalization of individual stocks was $2.9 billion at the end of 2000.

• **Canadian dividend funds** have a minimum of 50% of total assets and 75% of non-cash assets in dividend-paying securities of Canadian companies, in securities convertible to equity of dividend-paying Canadian companies or in royalty and income trusts. Investment in trusts is limited to 25% of the portfolio. The investment objective is to provide a steady stream of income and a tax advantage through the dividend tax credit. Equity investments may be in common or preferred stock. These funds distribute dividends and other income at least quarterly.

• **Labor-sponsored venture capital funds** invest in Canadian businesses that are start-ups or expanding. Investors get a federal tax credit and, in some provinces, a matching provincial credit.

- **U.S. equity funds** invest in companies located in the U.S. or in derivative-based exposure to the U.S. stock market. The latter means holdings in index products.
- **U.S. small/mid-cap equity funds** invest in equities of U.S. companies that have a market capitalization of less than US$6 billion.
- **North American equity funds** invest in equity or equity equivalents of companies located in Canada or the U.S., or have derivative-based exposure to these markets. The U.S. equity component must represent at least 25% of non-cash assets.
- **Global equity funds** invest in equities or equity-equivalents of companies in Asia, the Americas and Europe, or have derivative-based exposure to these markets. A portion of the funds may be placed in Canada.
- **International equity funds** invest in equities or equity-equivalents of companies outside Canada and the U.S., or have derivative-based exposure to those markets.
- **Asia-Pacific Rim equity funds** invest in equities or equity-equivalents of companies in Asia, Australia or New Zealand, or have derivative-based exposure to these markets.
- **Asia ex-Japan equity funds** invest in equities or equity-equivalents of companies in Australia, New Zealand and Asia, except for Japan, or have derivative-based exposure to these markets.

WEEKLY PERFORMANCE | THE BEST AND THE WORST

As part of the weekly fund report, all the funds in several broad categories (e.g. Canadian equities) are ranked according to their performance over the past one-week period. The eight best and eight worst-performing funds in terms of percentage growth (or decline) in NAVPS are then listed on this table. The listings show the fund name, its most recent Friday closing price and the dollar and percentage changes between this figure and the preceding Friday closing price. The listings also provide the weekly performance average for each fund category.

Weekly performance   *Data supplied by Fundata Canada Inc.*

Best %	Close	$ chg	% chg	Worst %	Close	$ chg	% chg
Cdn. divers. equity/large-cap eq. avg. +4.22							
C.I. Sector Canadian Uf	5.45	+.58	+11.91	IG/GWL Cdn Ent Seg Fund	10.79	-.36	-3.21
REA Inc Investiss IDEM	21.24	+2.17	+11.40	Westbury Cdn Life Equity	22.05	-.46	-2.06
Pacific Total Return Fund	6.5	+.65	+11.11	NW/Marathon Perf Cdn	5.74	-.12	-2.04
C.I. Canadian Growth	7.38	+.68	+10.15	Equitable Life Cdn Stock	18.72	-.37	-1.96
C.I. Canadian Sector	8.28	+.75	+9.96	Equit Life Seg Comm Stock	26.58	-.53	-1.96
Transamerica GS CdnEquity	16.13	+1.46	+9.95	Hartford Canadian Equity	14.57	-.23	-1.55
MTC Growth Fund - 1 Inc	16.24	+1.43	+9.68	IG/GWL Cdn Eq Seg Fund	11.81	-.18	-1.48
Altamira Capital Growth	28.71	+2.50	+9.54	NAL-Investor Equ Growth	23.78	-.34	-1.43
Cdn. small-cap equity average +3.27							
HSBC Future Grth Pooled	46.79	+6.86	+17.18	Hartford Aggress Growth	8.64	-1.03	-10.65
HSBC Can Growth Pooled	15.8	+1.61	+11.37	CTI Strategic Growth Fund	4.29	-.42	-8.94
Lotus Cdn Equity	17.1	+1.58	+10.16	Concordia Special Growth	24.51	-.64	-2.53
AGF Cdn Aggr All-Cap	5.48	+.49	+9.82	Cypress Small Cap Growth	13.48	-.33	-2.40
HSBC Sm Cap Grth	16.44	+1.41	+9.41	YMG Emerging Companies	20.1	-.39	-1.90
AGF Cdn Aggressive Equity	6.59	+.54	+8.93	University Ave Cdn Sm Cap	7.7	-.14	-1.78
CDA Special Equity (K)	27.7	+1.93	+7.50	GBC Canadian Growth	30.97	+.02	+.06
Investors Cdn Sml Cap II	12.95	+.84	+6.94	All-Canadian CapitalFund	8.51	+.02	+.24

- **Japanese equity funds** invest in equities or equity-equivalents of companies in Japan, or have derivative-based exposure to the Japanese market.
- **European equity funds** invest in equities or equity-equivalents of companies in Europe, or have derivative-based exposure to the European markets. More than one country must be represented at all times.
- **Latin American equity funds** invest in equities or equity-equivalents of companies in Latin America, or have derivative-based exposure to those markets.
- **Emerging markets equity funds** invest in equities or equity-equivalents of companies in emerging markets, or have derivative-based exposure to those markets. Those markets are mainly in southeast Asia, Latin America and the former Soviet bloc economies of central Europe.

BEST/WORST PERFORMERS | OVERALL

As part of the *Mutual Funds Monthly Report,* the *Financial Post* provides a table listing the best and worst-performing funds overall for the six periods used in the main listings – one month, six months, one year, three years, five years and 10 years – as of the end of the preceding month. The table ignores fund categories and simply looks at the bottom line. For the most part, the best performers tend to be equity funds, foreign or domestic, plus the occasional bond fund. The worst performers tend to be equities as well, particularly foreign or specialty funds. This table underscores the vast divergence in performance that these types of funds can generate.

WINNERS AND LOSERS
JULY

Best performers

One month	%
Caratax LP – 1997	15.97
Friedberg Tor Intl (US$)	14.13
AGF Mgd Futures Val	12.03
Navigator Asia Pac	10.91
Opt Strat R-Estate	10.25
Fidelity Focus Fin	8.36
Fidelity RSP FocusFS	8.19
AIC RSP Amer Adv	7.75
AIC Amer Advantage	7.73
AIC Am Adv Seg 75%	7.68

Six month	%
Caratax LP – 1997	77.50
Resolute Growth	54.53
Talvest Glo Hth-Care	50.57
Tera Capital Venture	47.78
Wealth Management Tr	45.67
CI International	41.89
Georgian Glo 24 A	40.34
Dynamic Inf Wlth Mgt	38.40
Guar Dyn Inf Wlt Mgt	38.19
CIBC Financial Cos	37.67

Worst performers

One month	%
Universal Japan	-16.26
AGF Aggr Japan Cl	-15.38
Strategic Value	-15.17
Excel India	-14.88
CIBC Japanese Equity	-13.41
Atlas Pac Basin Val	-13.37
Altamira Japan Opp	-13.32
Altamira RSP Jap Opp	-13.32
AGF India	-12.92
Dynamic Global Res	-12.45

Six month	%
AGF India	-44.08
Strategic Value	-33.43
Excel India	-33.12
Friedberg Divr (US$)	-33.08
Cambridge Amer Gth	-31.65
AIM Pacific Gth Cl	-30.76
DJ Internet Tr 99 Pt	-29.76
Cambridge Americas	-27.45
CTI Strategic Gth	-26.14
Cambridge Special Eq.	-25.44

- **Country-specific equity funds** invest in equities or equity-equivalents of companies in a specific country, or have derivative-based exposure to that market. The two common ones are China and India, which are too big to be considered part of the emerging market economies.
- **Science and technology funds** have a minimum of 50% of total assets and 75% of non-cash assets in equities or equity-equivalents of companies that operate mainly in science or technology fields. There are no geographic restrictions.
- **Natural resources funds** have a minimum of 50% of total assets and 75% of non-cash assets invested in companies in natural resource fields. There are no geographic restrictions.
- **Precious metals funds** have a minimum of 50% of total assets and 75% of non-cash assets invested in companies engaged in extraction, production and refining of precious metals. There are no geographic restrictions.

FIXED-INCOME FUNDS
- **Canadian bond funds** have a minimum of 75% of market value in Canadian-dollar denominated bonds, debentures or short-term notes issued by governments or corporations. The portfolio's average term to maturity, including short-term investments, must be greater than three years.
- **Canadian short-term bond funds** have a minimum of 75% of market value in short-term Canadian debt instruments with an average term to maturity of less than five years and more than one year. The portfolio may include bonds, mortgage-backed securities or term deposits. At least 50% of the fixed-income section must be in short-term instruments with an average term to maturity of less than three years.
- **High yield bond funds** have at least 75% of market value in Canadian-dollar denominated bonds, debentures or short-term notes. Average credit rating of the underlying bond positions is BBB or less. A bond rated BBB or less is not considered investment grade by a rating agency and higher yields come with this credit risk.
- **Foreign bond funds** have a minimum of 75% of market value in debt instruments denominated in a foreign currency and have a dollar-weighted term to maturity that is greater than one year.
- **Canadian mortgage funds** have a minimum of 75% of market value in Canadian industrial, commercial or residential mortgages or mortgage-backed securities. At least 50% of the fund's fixed-income section must be in mortgages or mortgage-backed securities.

BALANCED FUNDS
- **Canadian balanced funds** have a minimum of 75% of market value in Canadian equity and Canadian fixed-income securities. The total of fixed-income and cash must be at least 25% but not more than 75%.
- **Canadian asset allocation funds** have a minimum of 75% of market value in Canadian equities, Canadian fixed-income securities and cash. There are no restrictions on asset weightings and managers of these funds use a tactical asset allocation strategy.

The monthly performance tables provide a broad range of statistical information for investors, but the two monthly "snapshots" that accompany the tables provide some key data in a handy encapsulated format.

The first snapshot table shows the average one-year simple returns and average five-year compound returns for each of the 27 categories in the main listings, again as of the end of the preceding month. This enables investors to quickly determine how their own fund(s) fared against the category averages.

The second snapshot table provides the average one-year returns for the 20 largest mutual funds in terms of total assets. The first column shows the fund, the second column shows the fund's net assets in millions of dollars, and the third column shows each fund's one-year return as of the end of the preceding month.

PERFORMANCE SNAPSHOTS
NOVEMBER

Figures supplied by FP DataGroup

The asset groups

The following table lists the average one-year rates of return at 11.30.00 for the principal mutual fund categories.

Fund category	1-yr. % return	5-yr. % return
Labour–sponsored	18.82	8.28
Cdn. dividend	18.29	13.11
Cdn. large–cap eq.	17.57	13.27
Cdn. divers. eq.	16.09	12.51
Cdn. high income	15.51	8.51
Real estate	14.10	5.49
Cdn small–cap equity	11.45	7.89
U.S. small/mid–cap eq.	10.56	14.62
Cdn. balan.	10.54	9.64

The giant funds

Average one-year returns at 11.30.00 for the largest individual funds (in terms of total assets in $millions).

Fund	Assets $mil.	1-yr. % return
Templeton Growth	10,161.9	3.11
Fidelity Intl Port A	8,286.3	–3.10
Royal Balanced	7,349.3	11.23
Fidelity Cdn A–All A	6,818.7	11.45
Templeton Intl Stock	6,624.1	3.38
Trimark Select Gth	5,404.6	14.97
AGF Intl Value	5,295.9	30.56
TD Cdn Money Mkt	5,227.5	4.73
Investors Dividend	5,071.9	18.41

• **Canadian high income balanced funds** have a minimum of 25% of total assets, including cash, in interest-income-bearing securities and a minimum of 50% in securities that are not interest-bearing but produce income. That latter category would mainly be dividend-paying stocks.

• **Global balanced and asset allocation funds** hold a combination of equities, fixed-income securities and cash from a global securities base. At least 25% must be non-Canadian.

MONEY MARKET FUNDS

• **Canadian money market funds** invest in top-quality short-term securities, such as government treasury bills and commercial paper of senior corporations. Securities regulations set restrictions on type of securities that these funds can hold.

• **Foreign money market funds** invest in top-quality U.S. and foreign short-term securities, such as government treasury bills and commercial paper of senior corporations. Securities regulations set restrictions on type of securities that these funds can hold.

SPECIALTY FUNDS
- **Real estate funds** have a minimum of 50% of total assets in firms with a primary business relationship or a direct investment in commercial and residential real estate. There are no geographic restrictions.
- **Specialty and miscellaneous funds** have a minimum of 50% of total assets and 75% of non-cash assets in the sectoral or geographic specialty stated in the fund's prospectus.

SURVEY OF MANAGEMENT EXPENSE RATIOS

A fund's management expense ratio (MER) can have a significant impact on the yields investors end up receiving. Although loads tend to be higher in percentage terms, they're a one-shot cost. Management expenses are deducted annually and over several years they can far outstrip the dollar cost of any one-time load. The survey of MERs published in the *Mutual Funds Monthly Report* is calculated using PAL Trak software by Morningstar Canada. It shows these expenses can range from a fraction of a percentage point of fund assets up to 4% or even more in a few cases (excluding any sales loads or redemption charges).

The first part of the table provides the unweighted average MER figures for each of the 27 fund categories. The expense ratio figures are expressed as a percentage of assets. The listings also provide the one-year total returns for each fund category. The survey goes on to list those funds with the highest and lowest MERs in their respective general groupings (for example, all Canadian equities are treated as a single group in this table). Where available, the one-year total return for each fund is provided as well.

As can be seen from the category figures, MERs tend to be lowest with money market funds (which also tend to have the lowest yields). Equity funds generally tend to have the highest MERs and bond funds fall between these two categories. But the individual fund listings display many exceptions to this general rule – some equity fund MERs are lower than for many money market funds, and some bond funds have MERs higher than many equity funds. These listings enable investors to gauge how their own funds compare with other funds of the same type and with category averages.

MARKET BENCHMARKS MEASURE PERFORMANCE

The *Financial Post* monthly performance survey includes a list of market "benchmark" indexes that can be useful in evaluating the performance of mutual funds. These indexes are meant to reflect the performance of a particular market or markets during each of the years listed. Non-Canadian index figures have been adjusted to reflect exchange rate fluctuations during the period in question (as have returns for funds investing outside Canada). All indexes used by *FP* are total return indexes, meaning any dividends or

How to read the performance tables

Fund name	notes	R	fgn	% assets $mil.	Net per sh.$	NAV distr. $	YTD % simple rate of return				% avg annual compound return			Std dev	Exp rat	
							1 mo.	6 mo.	YTD	1 yr.	3 yr.	5 yr.	10 yr.	3 yr.	%	L
PerformFund	i	R	8	623.9	34.86		-0.3	-25.3	-18.0	-22.6	+8.7	+9.5	+8.7	5.1	1.09	N
PerformFund Plus		R	16	181.8	18.56	0.29	+0.5	-24.5	-15.9	-21.8	+8.5	+9.3	+9.1	5.0	1.18	F
PerformFund Eq Pen	e		16	1060.3	54.95		-0.6	-23.2	-14.8	-18.4	+11.6	+10.9	+9.6	5.0	0.54	C

This instalment of the Financial Post's monthly mutual funds report compares funds at 07.31.00. **Performance returns shown in boldface** type are those outperforming the group average in the given period. All footnotes are shown in the ⅝rst column after the fund name.

Here's a guide to each column:

1. Fund name provides the fund name (sometimes abbreviated). Some funds are split into series or classes, depending on when sales fees are levied. Refer to the Load column.

2. Notes a - fund entry is restricted to certain groups or professions, b - the minimum initial purchase is more than $5,000, c - sold by offering memorandum (not by prospectus), d - total assets and NAVPS are shown in US$, e - the fund is not available for direct purchase, f - the fund's portfolio may include some precious metals, leases, or other non-equity investments, g - unit values are stated before management fees, h - returns do not take into account performance fee charged to individual unitholders, i - insurance fund, j - there is a restricted redemption policy; see fund's prospectus for details, k - management fee includes life insurance costs, l - labor sponsored fund, m - management fee in lieu of an expense ratio, n - a new fund launched in the past year, o - offshore fund, p - fund is valued semi-annually, thus returns of less than one year are not shown. Other data as of the most recent calendar year semi-annual period end (Sept. 30 or Dec. 31), s - not a mutual fund (fund-company asset-allocation service), t - NAVPS are shown in US$, total assets shown in C$, u - NAVPS are shown in C$, total assets shown in US$ w - available only through the Internet.

3. RRSP and RRIF eligible 'R' indicates eligibility for registered retirement savings plans (RRSPs) and registered retirement income funds (RRIFs).

4. Percentage foreign ownership shows the amount each fund has invested outside Canada.

5. Net assets is total assets minus current liabilities—the fund's size at month end.

6. Net asset value per share is total assets minus current liabilities, divided by the number of shares outstanding. Investors buy at this value, plus sales charge (if any), and sell at this value, minus redemption charge (if any).

7. Year to date distribution indicates the total value of distributions (dividends paid in the form of interest, stock dividends, or capital gains) by the fund to its unitholders from Jan. 1 to the end of the month surveyed.

8. Simple rate of return over one month, six months, year-to-date, and one year is the change in net asset value over the period, including reinvestment of dividends and capital gains, and excluding sales or redemption charges. An ellipsis (...) indicates no data for this period. A zero value (**0.0**) indicates return is not meaningful, rounding to less than 0.1%.

9. Average annual compound rate of return three, ⅝ve and 10 years measures the average annual change in NAVPS, assuming all dividends and capital gains are reinvested on the date of distribution or realization. This measurement excludes any sales or redemption fees. An ellipsis (...) indicates no data for this period. A zero value (**0.0**) indicates return is not meaningful, rounding to less than 0.1%.

10. Three-year standard deviation shows variability in the fund's rate of return. It provides a measure of volatility, and therefore a measure of risk.

11. Expense ratio is total operating costs per $100 of assets (exclusive of any sales or redemption charge) as a percentage of the assets.

12. Load is sales fee charged to investors for purchasing fund. Five load methods are denoted: **N** - no load, **F** - front-end load, **D** - deferred sales charge (or back-end load), **C** - combination of front- and back-end loads, **O** - optional front- or back-end load. Some no-load funds may charge early redemption fees.

Data supplied by Financial Post DataGroup

interest payments made by the underlying securities are assumed to be re-invested. This is important since the same methodology is used in calculating the annual performance of mutual funds.

An important distinction must be made between indexes and mutual funds. Because they are not actively managed, indexes do not have to account for management expenses. Mutual funds do. For example, if a fund reports a one-year return of 8% and expense ratio (MER) of 2%, the manager actually had to achieve a 10% gross return, because performance is reported net of expenses. Managers of mutual funds are often evaluated by how much or how often they are able to outperform an appropriate index, often referred to as "beating the market." The key is to select the index(es) that most closely reflect the fund type. But keep in mind that comparing a fund's performance with an index is only one way to measure performance – one should compare other "like" funds as well.

Following are brief descriptions of the indexes used as benchmarks:

CANADIAN EQUITY

• **TSE 300:** A collection of 300 of Canada's largest, most liquid stocks, representing 14 broad industry groups. The TSE 300, like many indexes, is capitalization-based (or capitalization-weighted), meaning larger stocks are weighted more than smaller stocks. Size is measured by market float, or the number of shares outstanding times the current price of the stock. Price changes for larger companies therefore have a more dramatic effect on the overall index than do price changes for smaller companies.

• **TSE 100:** The top 100 (by capitalization) stocks found in the TSE 300. This index is useful for comparisons with funds that focus primarily on large-capitalization stocks.

• **TSE 200:** The bottom 200 stocks of the TSE 300. Used in evaluating small- to mid-cap Canadian equity funds.

• **TSE 35:** Stocks of 35 of the largest companies listed on the TSE. It was designed to include very liquid issues that closely track the performance of the TSE 300 index. Useful in evaluating diversified Canadian equity funds.

• **S&P/TSE 60:** Stocks of 60 of the most liquid TSE companies. The index is divided into 10 sectors and provides a more focused comparison of the economy than does the broader TSE 300 index, which includes many low-volume stocks.

• **Russell 300 Growth:** Includes TSE stocks that have a greater-than-average growth orientation. Stocks in this index tend to exhibit higher price-to-book and price-earnings ratios, lower dividend yields and higher forecast growth values. Because higher earnings levels have yet to be realized, these stocks typically have less earnings to distribute in the form of dividends and hence a typically lower dividend yield. Useful in evaluating growth-oriented Canadian equity funds.

• **Russell 300 Value:** Includes TSE 300 stocks with a lower-than-average growth orientation. Stocks in this index generally have low price-to-book and price-earnings ratios, higher dividend yields and lower forecast earnings growth. Useful for comparing Canadian equity funds oriented toward value investing.

- **Russell 100 Growth:** Contains those Russell 300 growth stocks that are also in the top tier of TSE stocks. Useful in comparing Canadian funds that invest in large-cap, growth-oriented stocks.
- **Russell 100 Value:** Contains those Russell 300 value stocks that are also in the top tier of TSE stocks. Useful for evaluating Canadian funds that invest in relatively large, value-oriented stocks.
- **Bmo Nesbit Canadian Small-Cap:** Composed of 400 stocks with a market capitalization of less than 0.1% of the TSE 300. Useful for evaluating Canadian small-cap mutual funds.

FINANCIAL POST PORTFOLIO INDEXES
- **FPX Income:** Each of the FPX indexes is composed of cash, fixed income and equity components. These correspond to the safety, income and growth nomenclature generally used in conventional investment planning asset allocation models. The income portfolio is the most conservative of the three and consists of 20% in 91-day treasury bills, 50% in federal government bonds and 30% in equities.
- **FPX Balanced:** This is a classic 50/50 portfolio consisting of 10% in 91-day treasury bills, 40% in federal government bonds and 50% in equities.
- **FPX Growth:** The growth portfolio is the most aggressive of the three and consists of 5% in 91-day treasury bills, 25% in federal government medium-term bonds and 70% in equities.

U.S. EQUITY
- **Standard & Poor's 500:** A basket of 500 U.S. stocks, selected primarily from the New York Stock Exchange, designed to reflect the broad U.S. equity market. Because the S&P 500 is constructed to reflect as many industry groups as possible, it does not take just the largest stocks, although it is normally representative of 75% to 80% of the total value of stocks traded on the NYSE. This is a useful index for evaluating diversified U.S. equity funds.
- **Dow Jones Industrials:** The oldest of the U.S. indexes and a basket of 30 of the largest and best-known U.S. stocks. The DJIA is price-weighted, meaning that higher-priced stocks affect index performance more than lower-priced ones. Although popular, the usefulness of this index has been criticized in recent years. Because it is price weighted, it does not properly reflect the relative size of the companies listed and it does not accurately reflect the more diverse (both by size and industry) nature of the broader U.S. equity market.
- **Nasdaq Composite:** The most broadly based U.S. equity index. It includes more than 5,000 stocks traded over-the-counter and many of the new high-octane technology start-ups. These stocks are not listed on the New York Stock Exchange.
- **Russell 2000 Small-Cap:** The bottom 2,000 U.S. securities in the Russell 3000 index, which consists of the 3,000 largest U.S. securities as determined by market capitalization. Representing roughly 1/10th of the Russell 3000's total market capitalization, the 2000 is a widely used small-cap index in evaluating funds that specialize in small U.S. companies.

WINNERS AND LOSERS | DURING THE MONTH

As part of the Mutual Funds Monthly Report, the *Financial Post* publishes a table of "winners and losers" from each of the 34 mutual fund categories in the main listings. At left in bold type is the fund category, accompanied by the unweighted average total percentage yield for the month for that category. Reading across, the middle column shows the fund with the best performance for the month in that category, along with its total return. The right-hand column shows the fund with the worst performance, along with its total monthly return. This table provides a frame of reference for evaluating the monthly performance of any fund(s) you may own: Is your fund's performance near the top or the bottom of these two extremes? The table also provides a snapshot of relative performance between different fund categories during the month.

PERFORMANCE BY CATEGORY
JULY

Category	Average return on month	Best performer	Return on month	Worst performer	Return on month
Real estate	+2.9	Opt Strat R-Estate	+10.3	Royal Lepage Comm RF	0.0
Cdn. high income	+1.5	Acuity High Income	+4.4	CIBC Balanced Port	–0.1
Cdn. dividend	+1.3	Empire Dividend Gth	+3.4	Valorem Dividends	–1.1
Cdn. large-cap eq.	+0.8	CLCG Trust 2000	+5.0	London L-Comp (MF)	–8.5
Cdn. mortgage	+0.7	Natl Bk Mortgage	+1.0	Industrial Mort Secs	–0.4
Cdn. money market	+0.4	Montrusco Sel T-Max	+0.5	Hartford Life M-Mkt	0.0
Cdn. short bond	+0.3	APEX Mortgage	+0.7	Altamira S-T Govt Bd	0.0
Foreign money market	+0.3	PH&N $US Money Mkt (US$)	+0.5	Altamira S-T Glo Inc	–1.4
High yield bond	+0.3	IRIS NA H-Yield Bond	+1.5	ODonnell US High Inc (US$)	–1.7
Cdn. divers. eq.	+0.3	Synergy Cdn Gth Cl	+7.3	University Ave Cdn	–8.6
Cdn bond	+0.2	Guardian Cdn HY Bd C	+2.3	Fallingbrook Gth B	–1.3
Cdn. tactical asset	+0.2	Acuity Pooled Con AA	+4.0	Trans-Canada Pension	–3.2
Cdn. balan.	0.0	CGO&V Balanced	+3.4	Cambridge Balanced	–6.4
Labor-sponsored	–0.2	Cdn Science&Tech Gth	+4.2	Dynamic Ven Oppor	–4.0
Country-specific	–0.2	Talvest China Plus	+5.1	Excel India	–14.9
European equity	–0.4	Investors Euro MC Gt	+6.8	All Points Euro Ind (US$)	–4.4

FOREIGN EQUITY

• **Morgan Stanley World:** All Morgan Stanley Capital International indexes are constructed to ensure that all industry groups are proportionally represented. They are capitalization-based. In each case they are designed to represent at least 60% of the market capitalization of each country, across all industry groups. The world index is made up of more than 2,700 stocks from 23 countries with developed markets. This is a useful index for evaluating global mutual funds.

• **Morgan Stanley EAFE:** Comprised of about 1,500 stocks (representative samplings of small, medium and large caps) from 20 developed European, Australasian and Far East countries. Useful for evaluating international equity funds.

• **Morgan Stanley Emerging Markets:** Includes 818 stocks from 28 emerging market economies.

• **Morgan Stanley Europe:** Comprised of stocks from European countries.

• **Morgan Stanley Far East:** Comprised of stocks from Asian countries.

- **Morgan Stanley Pacific ex-Japan:** Comprised of stocks from the Pacific Rim countries, excluding Japan.
- **FT London FT-SE 100:** The principal measure of the British equity market, the "footsie" includes 100 blue-chip stocks traded on the London Stock Exchange.
- **Tokyo Nikkei Average:** A simple price average of 225 of the largest stocks in terms of market capitalization listed on the Tokyo Stock Exchange.
- **Hang Seng:** An aggregate market capitalization index consisting of 33 stocks on the Hong Kong Stock Exchange. These stocks account for about 70% of the total market capitalization on the exchange.

BONDS
- **Scotia Capital Universe:** Represents a broad selection of hundreds of Canadian corporate and government bonds. These bonds cover the full range of maturities: short-term, up to five years; medium-term, five to 10 years; and long-term, more than 10 years. This index is meant to reflect the broader Canadian bond market, much like the TSE 300 is used to measure the broader Canadian equity market.
- **Scotia Capital Short-Term:** Represents a broad selection of Canadian corporate and government bonds with terms of one to five years.
- **Scotia Capital Mid-Term:** Represents a broad selection of Canadian corporate and government bonds with terms of five to 10 years.
- **Scotia Capital Long-Term:** Represents a broad selection of Canadian corporate and government bonds with terms greater than 10 years. Used in conjunction with the short- and mid-term indexes, this index can be used to illustrate the volatility of returns that often go with longer-term bonds.

MONEY MARKET
- **Three-month Canada Treasury Bills:** Issued by the Canadian government and widely used by fund managers to "park" cash balances. It is a valuable gauge for what is known as the "riskless" rate of investment.

MARKET BENCHMARKS | TABLE

MARKET BENCHMARKS 07.31.00

	Value	Simple rate of return %				Avg. ann. cpd. rate of ret. %			Std. dev
		1m.	6m.	YTD	1yr.	3yr.	5yr.	10yr.	3yr.
Canadian equity									
TSE 300 total return	22373.50	+2.1	+23.4	+24.5	+48.9	+16.5	+19.7	+14.0	5.8
TSE 100 total return	753.28	+2.9	+25.4	+26.5	+54.2	+18.2	+20.7	+14.3	5.9
TSE 200 total return	548.38	-4.2	+9.4	+10.1	+18.0	+7.2	+13.7	+12.0	6.1
TSE 35 total return	989.64	+4.6	+17.3	+16.1	+37.9	+17.0	+20.5	+14.1	5.8
S&P/TSE 60 total return	1116.86	+3.3	+28.9	+29.6	+56.0	+20.9	+23.8	+16.4	6.1

- **Six-month Canada Treasury Bills:** Longer-term federal treasury bills. Not as popular as three-month bills but still useful as a measure of the short-term cost of money.

SEARCHING FOR TRUE MUTUAL FUND RETURNS

"How did I do?" The average mutual fund investor cares only about that seemingly simple question. But in their quarterly performance statements, fund companies are only beginning to work on the answer. Putting aside the consideration that some brokers and financial planners don't really want people to know how poorly their recommendations are doing, it's true that calculating individual, or "customized," rates of returns is no trivial exercise.

For the typical investor buying new fund units monthly and making occasional switches, redemptions and one-time lump sum additions, calculating personal rates of return can entail the sort of mathematics not seen since he or she struggled with Calculus 101 in school. Add to that yearly, quarterly or monthly distributions of dividends from the fund companies and other tax-related phenomena and what appears to be a simple little calculation becomes a major undertaking.

PERFORMANCE FIGURES DON'T ALWAYS REFLECT FUND'S RETURNS

Furthermore, unless an investor buys each fund at the beginning of the month and sells at the end without paying sales charges, the total returns shown in newspaper performance roundups are unlikely to reflect actual performance. And, needless to say, the advertisements showing spectacular performance numbers won't necessarily reflect your returns either. That doesn't mean those numbers are exaggerated. Sometimes an investor can do better than those numbers, sometimes not – it all depends on when they're bought or sold and how markets perform over time. Little wonder, then, that a survey by Toronto-based Marketing Solutions found that 42% of fund investors do not always believe the performance figures provided by their fund companies.

TIME-WEIGHTED RATES OF RETURN SHOW INVESTORS' PERSONAL GAINS OR LOSSES

The standard in the pension and private-client investment industry is "time-weighted" rates of return for clients' segregated portfolios or pooled funds. That calculation is not influenced by the amount of money invested, and the guidelines are set by the Association for Investment Management & Research (AIMR), based in Charlottesville, Va. Pension managers typically have only hundreds of clients, while fund companies must deal with hundreds of thousands of customers, and very few compute unitholders' personal returns.

However, there is steady pressure on the industry to provide more details to small investors. The U.S. Securities & Exchange Commission has asked U.S. fund companies to personalize performance data. Glorianne Stromberg of the Ontario Securities

MONTHLY DIVIDEND | TABLE

Almost all mutual funds have "dividend" distributions on a regular basis – monthly, quarterly or sometimes yearly. These payments reflect the proceeds of trading activities by fund management, as well as income earned by the fund. While they're called dividends, they actually can comprise interest income and/or capital gains and/or regular dividends, depending on the nature of the fund and its earnings.

In many cases these distributions are automatically reinvested to buy more fund units on behalf of the investor. But even if they are, you may receive a slip at tax time and have to pay tax on the income. The slip you receive from the fund company should separate the different types of income for tax purposes.

The table that accompanies the monthly mutual fund performance tables lists all dividends issued by Canadian mutual funds during the previous month. Here is a brief explanation of the information in these listings:

Type: This column shows the nature of the distribution. **I** represents income in the form of stock dividends and interest, **C** represents capital gains, and **X** represents a non-taxable return of capital and income distributions during the month.

Amt.: This is the amount of the distribution, expressed as dollars per mutual fund unit.

Pay date: The date the distribution became payable.

MUTUAL FUND DIVIDENDS

Figures supplied by FP DataGroup

Fund	Type	Amt.	Pay date	Fund	Type	Amt.	Pay date
@rgentum Income Port	I	0.0537	Jul. 31	Altamira S-T Cdn Inc	I	0.0400	Jul. 31
@rgentum S-T Asset	I	0.0408	Jul. 31	Altamira T-Bill	I	0.0455	Jul. 31
AGF Canadian Bond	I	0.0274	Jul. 31	Atlas American M-Mkt	I	0.0418	Jul. 31
AGF Cdn High Income	I	0.0494	Jul. 31	Atlas Canadian Bond	I	0.0450	Jul. 31
AGF Cdn Money Market	I	0.0358	Jul. 31	Atlas Cdn H-Yield Bd	I	0.0627	Jul. 31
AGF Global Govt Bond	I	0.0360	Jul. 31	Atlas Cdn Inc & Gth	I	0.0307	Jul. 31
AGF RSP Global Bond	I	0.0168	Jul. 31	Atlas Cdn Income Tr	I	0.0625	Jul. 31
AGF US Income	I	0.0393	Jul. 31	Atlas Cdn Money Mkt	I	0.0366	Jul. 31
AGF US$ Mny Mkt Acc	I	0.0478	Jul. 31	Atlas Cdn T-Bill	I	0.0334	Jul. 31
AGF US S-T H-Yield	I	0.0191	Jul. 31	Atlas World Bond	I	0.0245	Jul. 31
AIC American Inc Eq	I	0.0250	Jul. 31	Avix Bond	I	0.0380	Jul. 31
AIC Income Equity	I	0.0250	Jul. 31	Avix Money Market	I	0.0388	Jul. 31

Commission, who has done detailed work on mutual fund industry practices, is a proponent of the time-weighted approach. Canadian fund managers are responding to demands for more details and have been upgrading statements to clients.

STANDARDIZED CALCULATION OF INDIVIDUAL RATES OF RETURN MAY BE ON THE HORIZON

Time-weighted returns show investors how their assets performed without distortions caused by investor cash flows. There are several variations on time-weighted return. The most accurate is a daily valuation method. A simpler approach is to weight cash flow by the amount of time it is held in the portfolio. This method is slightly less accurate than the daily valuation time-weighted rate of return, according to AIMR. A third method links monthly returns with a geometric averaging formula for the time-weighted return. It takes into consideration the exact timing of each cash flow.

The Investment Funds Institute of Canada has recommended to its members that they use a time-weighted rate of return calculation for reporting individual rates of return to clients. Fund companies have all the necessary information. The main question is in determining the format that consumers really want.

Rates of return and other information about mutual funds can be found in reports published four times a year by the *Financial Post*. Tables and charts on pages 140 to 145 give you details on how to read this report.

MUTUAL FUNDS | QUARTERLY REPORT

Four times a year, the *Financial Post* publishes the Mutual Funds Quarterly Report, an extensive package of information intended to help investors make decisions on their fund portfolios. These quarterly reports appear the third week in February, May, August and November each year. The largest single element in this supplemental quarterly information is the exclusive portfolio analysis survey conducted by Portfolio Analytics Ltd., using its PAL Trak databases. The survey provides detailed statistics on numerous Canadian and foreign equity funds, Canadian bond funds and Canadian balanced funds. The statistics include portfolio composition, as well as other key measurements such as interest rate sensitivity, relative yields, price/earnings ratios and capitalization. This information is generally calculated as at the end of the preceding quarter and can be very useful for ensuring that a fund is in good financial shape and conforms to unitholders' investment objectives and portfolio requirements.

Here is a guide to reading this table:

CANADIAN EQUITY PORTFOLIOS

Cash/short term: This column represents the percentage of a fund's total assets invested in cash and cash "equivalents" – various types of short-term (less than one year) notes and bonds, at the end of the preceding quarter.

Common equity as % of total: These two columns show what percentages of the fund's total assets were invested in (a) Canadian equities and (b) foreign equities at the end of the preceding quarter. Note that these figures represent common equity only and exclude dividend-generating preferred shares.

Equity sectoral asset allocation: The five columns under this heading show the percentages of each fund's common equity content invested in the following sectoral groups:

- Resource (includes oil and gas, paper and forest products, metals and minerals).
- Precious metals.
- Consumer (includes consumer products, merchandising, communications and media).
- Industrials (includes industrial products, transportation, environment and conglomerates).
- Interest sensitive (includes financial services, utilities, pipelines, real estate and construction).

TSE similarity: This column indicates how closely the sector weightings of each fund correspond to those of the TSE 300. For example, an index fund would have a "high" similarity, while resource or precious metals funds would have a "low" rating. In general, the higher the rating, the closer the yield should be to the TSE 300.

Fundamental analysis: This table provides fund ratings in terms of three key measurements of corporate size and performance – dividend yield, price/earnings ratio and capitalization. These ratings reflect unweighted averages for all the companies held by each fund and are relative to each other.

For example, capitalization represents the average size of companies in the fund and is calculated by multiplying the price by the shares outstanding of each underlying stock. The values are then compared across all of the equity funds and a relative ranking is set. "High" means the fund invests primarily in relatively large-cap companies. "Low" reflects small-cap portfolio holdings.

Similar relative rankings are done for the dividend yield and P/E columns. A fund that invests in small-cap growth companies would typically show a "high" P/E ratio, a "low" capitalization ranking and a "low" dividend yield ranking.

Weighted averages: The Canadian equity statistics are summarized at the bottom of the listings, as weighted overall averages for all funds in the category. Where space permits, these averages are followed by corresponding figures for various stock indexes to provide a means of comparison with overall markets.

Canadian Equity
Fund Holdings 06.30.00

Figures supplied by Morningstar Canada

Fund	Cash/ short term[1]	Common equity % of total		Equity asset allocation		Prec.		Int sen	TSE sim.	Fundmental analysis[3]		
		Cdn[2]	fgn[2]	Res	met	Cons	Indus			Yld	P/E	Cap
Sun Life Spectrum Cdn Investment 75%	9.8	74.1	13.2	19.2	2.7	14.3	31.4	30.8	M	H	L	M
Sun Life Spectrum Cdn Max Gth P¾ 100%	17.7	50.4	30.1	18.2	2.2	13.0	41.1	24.6	M+	M+	M-	M
Sun Life Spectrum Cdn Max. Gth Pl 75%	17.7	50.4	30.1	18.2	2.2	13.0	41.1	24.6	M+	M+	M-	M
Sun Life Trimark Select Cdn Growth 100%	11.6	72.2	15.6	22.2	6.0	11.7	26.5	33.6	M-	H	L	M-
Sun Life Trimark Select Cdn Growth 75%	11.6	72.2	15.6	22.2	6.0	11.7	26.5	33.6	M-	H	L	M-
Synergy Cdn. Growth Class	8.3	74.2	17.4	15.6	0.0	25.6	51.1	7.7	M	L	H	M-
Synergy Cdn. Momentum Class	7.0	74.6	18.1	19.9	2.0	16.0	43.3	18.8	M+	M-	M	
MSynergy Cdn. Small Cap Class	2.3	78.8	18.3	29.7	0.3	16.9	49.1	3.5	M-	L	H	L
Synergy Cdn. Style Management	13.6	68.1	17.3	21.8	1.9	16.6	41.9	17.7	M+	M-	M-	M-

Canadian Bond
Fund Holdings 06.30.00

Figures supplied by Morningstar Canada

Fund	Cash & short-term % of total[1]	Bonds % of total	% invested by maturity			Avg matur. yrs[2]	% invested by issuer			% fgn exp
			1-5	5-10	10+		fed govt	other govt	Corp	
Empire Bond	1.3	97.3	37.4	39.3	23.2	9.2	47.3	24.2	28.5	0.0
Empire Foreign Currency Canadian Bond	9.8	89.8	100.0	0.0	0.0	3.6	100.0	0.0	0.0	0.0
Equitable Life Canada Accum. Income	11.3	88.7	50.5	31.1	18.4	7.2	58.2	16.5	25.3	3.5
Equitable Life Canada Canadian Bond	3.4	96.6	47.3	31.9	20.8	8.6	56.8	17.6	25.6	0.0
Ethical Income	20.4	78.5	26.5	43.8	29.7	9.2	53.8	24.7	21.6	1.2
Ficadre Obligations	0.0	98.2	50.6	27.3	22.1	9.5	31.6	40.7	27.8	0.0
Fortress Inv Canadian Bond	6.6	84.8	28.1	44.2	27.7	10.0	42.8	13.0	44.2	0.0
Global Strategy Rothschild Bond	1.8	52.7	100.0	0.0	0.0	3.5	46.1	53.9	0.0	0.0
Great-West Life Bond(S) A	4.8	95.2	47.9	26.5	25.6	8.9	45.5	21.9	32.7	1.8

Canadian Balanced
Fund Holdings 06.30.00

Figures supplied by Morningstar Canada

Fund	Cash/ short term[1]	Cdn bond	Fgn bonds	Convert bonds	Pref. sh.	Total fixed income	Cdn[2]	Equity U.S.	Int'l	Total	% fgn cont[3]
Acadia Bal.	1.9	40.9	0.0	0.0	0.0	40.9	50.1	7.1	0.0	57.2	7.1
Acadia Diversi¾ed Atlantic	29.0	71.0	0.0	0.0	0.0	71.0	0.0	0.0	0.0	0.0	0
Acuity Cdn. Bal.	9.9	30.1	0.0	0.0	0.0	30.1	42.8	12.8	4.4	60.0	17.2
Acuity Pooled Cdn. Bal.	8.6	30.4	0.0	0.0	0.0	30.4	41.7	13.9	4.8	60.4	18.7
Acuity Pooled Conserv. Asset Alloc	1.5	28.1	0.0	5.2	0.6	33.9	59.8	5.5	0.0	65.3	5.5
AGF Cdn. Bal.	15.6	24.4	0.0	0.0	0.0	24.4	45.4	12.2	1.2	58.8	17.5
AGF Cdn. High Income	4.2	54.7	0.0	1.0	31.5	87.2	2.9	0.0	0.0	2.9	0
AGF Cdn. Tactical Asset Allocation	31.7	11.3	0.0	0.0	0.0	11.3	56.4	0.0	0.0	56.4	0
AIC Income Equity	2.3	23.4	0.0	0.0	0.0	23.4	61.0	13.2	0.0	74.2	13.2
AIC Income Equity Seg 100% (Transam)	2.3	23.4	0.0	0.0	0.0	23.4	61.0	13.2	0.0	74.2	13.2

Foreign Equity
Fund Holdings 06.30.00

Figures supplied by Morningstar Canada

Fund	Cash	Cdn.	U.S.	U.K.	Ger.	Other Fra.	Eur.	Jap.	Asia/Paci¾c H-K	↓	Other Latin Mex.	Amer.	Other
@rgentum Int'l Master Portfolio	1.0	2.4	37.2	11.2	4.8	9.7	19.1	12.5	-	-	-	-	2.0
Acuity Global Equity	1.7	5.3	58.9	-	-	12.8	12.6	6.3	-	2.5	-	-	-
Acuity Pooled Global Equity	5.3	5.2	55.9	-	-	12.5	12.5	6.1	-	2.5	-	-	-
AGF Aggressive Global Stock	4.5	3.2	22.2	10.3	7.1	7.0	12.0	11.1	6.2	8.8	0.9	2.6	4.1
AGF Int'l Value	-0.1	1.7	51.8	15.1	0.8	3.8	5.3	8.4	1.8	1.4	4.1	5.0	1.0
AGF Intl Stock Class - Intl Group	0.1	4.4	-	30.6	7.1	6.4	15.6	14.3	5.8	4.0	2.6	8.2	0.9
AGF Multi-Manager Class	11.9	21.5	44.5	4.1	3.4	2.7	5.6	1.3	0.6	0.6	1.5	1.5	0.7
AGF RSP Int'l Equity Allocation	0.9	5.3	45.9	3.3	2.6	7.2	18.9	5.8	5.0	5.2	-	-	-
AGF World Equity Class - Intl Group	8.2	1.4	44.9	3.3	0.4	0.7	5.9	8.8	-	5.1	0.9	6.0	14.3

CANADIAN BOND PORTFOLIOS

Cash/short term: This column is the same as the corresponding column for Canadian equities – cash and equivalents with terms of less than one year.

Bonds: This column shows the percentage of assets invested in bonds (with terms of one year or more).

% invested by maturity: These three columns show the percentages of each fund's bond holdings allocated to short-term (one to five years), medium-term (five to 10 years) and long-term (10-plus years) bond maturities.

Average maturity yrs: This column shows the average maturity of the fund's entire portfolio, including cash/short-term holdings. Cash is assumed to have a zero maturity and short-term notes are pegged at 90 days.

% invested by issuer type: These three columns show what percentages of the bond portfolio are federal government, other government and corporate issues. This information, along with maturity figures, gives some indication of how aggressive or conservative a particular bond fund is.

% foreign expos.: This column shows the percentage of bond holdings that are exposed to foreign-exchange fluctuations (excluding currency hedging instruments unless otherwise noted).

Weighted average: As with the Canadian equity listings, the Canadian bond fund listings conclude with weighted averages for the entire category and comparable index figures where space permits.

CANADIAN BALANCED PORTFOLIOS

Cash/short term: same as above.

Canadian straight bonds: This column shows the percentage of fund assets invested in Canadian straight bonds.

Foreign bonds: Percentage of fund assets invested in bonds issued by foreign countries.

Convertible bonds: Percentage of fund assets invested in corporate convertible bonds that can be traded for equity holdings subject to the conditions set by the bond issuer.

Preferred shares: Percentage of fund assets invested in preferred shares.

Total fixed income: This column provides a total for the preceding four columns (excluding cash and equivalents). It reflects the total fixed-income component in each balanced fund's portfolio.

Equity: These four columns show the percentage of total fund assets invested in Canadian, U.S. and foreign equities respectively, followed by a total figure for the equity component in each balanced fund's portfolio.

% foreign content: This column shows the percentage of fund assets issued by non-Canadian corporations or governments (excluding currency hedging instruments unless otherwise noted).

Weighted average: As with the preceding categories, weighted averages are provided for all funds in the Canadian balanced fund listings.

FOREIGN EQUITY PORTFOLIOS

These listings provide the total percentage of each fund's assets that are invested in cash and equivalents of less than one-year maturities, along with percentages invested in equities from various geographic regions around the world. These figures enable investors to ensure a fund's geographical diversification is in keeping with their own objectives and preferences. As with other categories, weighted averages are provided at the bottom of each column.

The weighted average holdings of funds in the four broad categories surveyed are presented in four pie charts that accompany the Portfolio Analysis survey's introductory article.

The average percentages are adjusted to give more weight to funds with greater assets under management.

This TSE subindex chart compares total returns during the quarter for each of the Toronto Stock Exchange's 14 subindexes, plus the TSE 300, 100 and 200 broad indexes.

The bond indexes chart compares total returns during the quarter for Scotia Capital Markets' benchmark Canadian bond indexes.

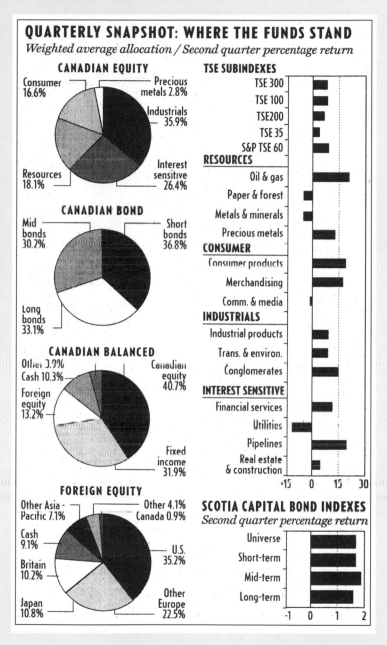

QUARTERLY SNAPSHOT: WHERE THE FUNDS STAND
Weighted average allocation / Second quarter percentage return

CANADIAN EQUITY
- Consumer 16.6%
- Precious metals 2.8%
- Industrials 35.9%
- Interest sensitive 26.4%
- Resources 18.1%

CANADIAN BOND
- Mid bonds 30.2%
- Short bonds 36.8%
- Long bonds 33.1%

CANADIAN BALANCED
- Other 3.9%
- Cash 10.3%
- Foreign equity 13.2%
- Canadian equity 40.7%
- Fixed income 31.9%

FOREIGN EQUITY
- Other Asia-Pacific 7.1%
- Other 4.1%
- Canada 0.9%
- Cash 9.1%
- Britain 10.2%
- U.S. 35.2%
- Japan 10.8%
- Other Europe 22.5%

TSE SUBINDEXES
- TSE 300
- TSE 100
- TSE200
- TSE 35
- S&P TSE 60

RESOURCES
- Oil & gas
- Paper & forest
- Metals & minerals
- Precious metals

CONSUMER
- Consumer products
- Merchandising
- Comm. & media

INDUSTRIALS
- Industrial products
- Trans. & environ.
- Conglomerates

INTEREST SENSITIVE
- Financial services
- Utilities
- Pipelines
- Real estate & construction

(scale: -15, 0, 15, 30)

SCOTIA CAPITAL BOND INDEXES
Second quarter percentage return
- Universe
- Short-term
- Mid-term
- Long-term

(scale: -1, 0, 1, 2)

MOST POPULAR STOCKS | BEST AND WORST PERFORMERS

Each quarterly mutual fund report provides two tables listing the most popular stocks held by top and bottom performing mutual funds at the end of the most recent quarter. The top performing funds are identified as those ranked in the top performance quartile during the two most recent quarters combined. In other words, these were the most popular stocks held by the top performing funds during the quarter. The first table lists the stocks held by funds in the top performance quartile. The second table lists the stocks held by funds in the bottom performance quartile.

Rank: The two columns at the extreme left show each stock's popularity ranking, in terms of total value of that stock held by top and bottom quartile funds at the end of the quarter. The first column shows the current ranking, and the second column shows the stock's ranking at the end of the preceding quarter.

Issuer: The corporation issuing the stock.

Issue: The type of stock being held, such as common, voting or subordinate or non-voting.

 # funds holding security: The number of top-quartile funds holding each security at the end of the quarter.

Value of holdings ($000s): This column provides the total dollar value of holdings by top-quartile funds of each stock, expressed in thousands of dollars. This figure constitutes the basis for each stock's popularity ranking in the first column of the table.

Chg in value ($000s): This column shows the amount by which fund ownership of each stock in the tables grew or declined between the ends of the most recent and the preceding quarters, again in thousands of dollars. A negative figure reflects net sales of the stock by the top-quartile funds during the period.

Chg in # funds vs. 03/00: This column shows the number of additional (or fewer) top-quartile funds holding the stock compared with the number of holders at the end of the preceding quarter.

Best fund performers

Stocks held at 06.30.00 by Canadian equity funds ranked in top performance quartile during the nine-month period ended that date.

Rank Jun. 00	Mar. 00	Issuer	Issue	# funds holding security	Value of holdings $000s	Chg in value $000s	Chg in #funds vs03/00
1	1	Nortel Networks	common	74	4,754,730	4,754,730	173
2	3	Toronto-Dominion Bank	common	67	796,030	(131,894)	2
3	5	Royal Bank of Canada	common	58	706,044	150,036	12
4	7	Bombardier	class B sub vtg	67	546,351	61,979	9
5	4	JDS Uniphase Cda	exch non-vtg shs	55	534,136	(310,152)	0
6	18	Bank of Montreal	common	54	508,898	273,379	18
7	13	Bank of Nova Scotia	common	57	496,283	172,313	19
8	2	BCE	common	59	486,871	(1,931,249)	(3)
9	6	Seagram	common	49	446,169	(38,864)	5
10	11	CIBC	common	55	423,222	50,723	11
11	10	C-MAC Industries	common	60	331,783	(72,776)	7

Worst fund performers

Stocks held at 06.30.00 by Canadian equity funds ranked in bottom performance quartile during the nine-month period ended that date.

Rank Jun. 00	Mar. 00	Issuer	Issue	# funds holding security	Value of holdings $000s	Chg in value $000s	Chg in #funds vs03/00
1	10	Nortel Networks	common	31	182,326	(479,583)	21
2	3	Royal Bank of Canada	common	34	640,126	(427,453)	0
3	1	Toronto-Dominion Bank	common	35	1,130,017	1,130,017	134
4	4	Bank of Montreal	common	36	585,492	(86,134)	(4)
5	39	Bombardier	class B sub vtg	21	206,073	206,073	120
6	2	BCE	common	24	709,704	16,192	(9)
7	17	Nova Chemicals	common	22	312,416	29,212	3
8	139	Celestica	sub vtg shs	16	183,810	6,147	0
9	14	Bank of Nova Scotia	common	21	327,839	56,400	16
10	7	Thomson Corp.	common	19	430,518	64,428	4
11	26	Hitachi	jpy50	5	270,723	(92,441)	(12)

TOP AND BOTTOM | QUARTERLEY PERFORMERS

The quarterly mutual fund portfolio analysis contrast funds' holdings against the fund performance for the preceding three-month period. Tables show the top 10 and bottom 10 funds in terms of three-month simple return in each of the four broad categories surveyed (Canadian equity funds, Canadian bond funds, Canadian balanced funds and foreign equity funds). Each table also provides the overall average return for each table's fund category.

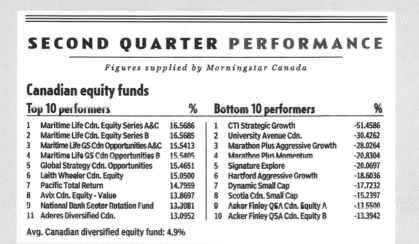

SECOND QUARTER PERFORMANCE

Figures supplied by Morningstar Canada

Canadian equity funds

Top 10 performers	%	Bottom 10 performers	%
1 Maritime Life Cdn. Equity Series A&C	16.5686	1 CTI Strategic Growth	-51.4586
2 Maritime Life Cdn. Equity Series B	16.5685	2 University Avenue Cdn.	-30.4262
3 Maritime Life GS Cdn Opportunities A&C	15.5413	3 Marathon Plus Aggressive Growth	-28.0264
4 Maritime Life GS Cdn Opportunities B	15.5405	4 Marathon Plus Momentum	-20.8304
5 Global Strategy Cdn. Opportunities	15.4651	5 Signature Explore	-20.0697
6 Leith Wheeler Cdn. Equity	15.0500	6 Hartford Aggressive Growth	-18.6036
7 Pacific Total Return	14.7959	7 Dynamic Small Cap	-17.7232
8 Avix Cdn. Equity - Value	13.8697	8 Scotia Cdn. Small Cap	-15.2397
9 National Bank Sector Rotation Fund	13.3081	9 Acker Finley QSA Cdn. Equity A	-13.5500
11 Aderes Diversified Cdn.	13.0952	10 Acker Finley QSA Cdn. Equity B	-13.3942

Avg. Canadian diversified equity fund: 4.9%

MUTUAL FUNDS | 15 YEAR REVIEW

The Mutual Funds 15 Year Review is published twice a year and provides tables showing one-year returns for each of the past 15 years. Funds are sorted in the same asset categories as the monthly performance tables. This year-over-year review of one-year returns gives investors an indication of the performance volatility for individual categories and funds.

CANADIAN EQUITY 06.30.00

Fund name	15 yr. cmpd	2000	1999	1998	1997	1996	1995	1994	1993	1992	1991	1990	1989	1988	1987	1986
							rate of return %									
Overall Cdn. equity avg:	10.0	25.2	-3.9	10.6	25.9	16.1	11.5	2.9	27.2	4.2	3.7	-1.1	12.0	-5.2	18.0	22.5
Overall Cdn. equity med:	10.4	23.0	-3.8	11.0	26.7	13.4	12.0	1.9	20.9	3.9	3.3	-1.0	12.4	-4.6	16.9	21.4

Canadian large-cap equity

Minimum of 50% of total assets and 75% of non-cash assets must be invested in companies of the TSE 100 index. At least 50% of equity weighting must represent at least two of the TSE 100's four major subindexes.

Fund name	15 yr. cmpd	2000	1999	1998	1997	1996	1995	1994	1993	1992	1991	1990	1989	1988	1987	1986
Cdn. large-cap eq. avg:	10.4	28.8	-4.0	12.2	25.7	12.5	12.4	1.4	23.2	2.9	4.2	-2.4	13.2	-6.9	18.0	17.6
Cdn. large-cap eq. med:	10.5	30.1	-3.8	12.8	27.1	12.8	12.7	1.3	20.6	2.3	3.4	-1.9	13.3	-4.8	20.0	16.6
@rgentum Cdn Eq Port	---	14.2	-7.3													
APEX Cdn Gth (AGF)	9.3	37.4	0.8	3.1	15.0	13.4	9.3	10.5	9.8	-0.8	3.6	-0.1	13.2	-2.3	13.2	19.1
ASTRA Indice Cdn	---	22.2														
Altamira Capital Gth	12.5	61.2	8.8	15.6	14.0	4.0	14.8	6.6	20.8	19.7	3.1	6.3	12.0	-14.3	19.6	10.0
Altamira Pre Cdn Ind	---	46.2														
Atlas Cdn L-Cap Gth	---	16.7	-7.4	20.2	34.2	15.9	13.8	1.9	6.9	-1.5	3.6	-0.8	13.5	-9.2	13.3	---
Atlas Cdn L-Cap Val	---	39.9	-0.4	14.4	21.7	5.9										
Avix Cdn. Eq L-Cap	---	38.0														
BMO Equity	---	30.8	0.7	15.9	32.8	13.2	14.5									
Batirente Sect Act	---	35.2	-4.1	8.9	10.2	10.2										
BNP Paribas CdaCdnEq	---	41.1	-5.2	14.5	30.5	13.4	14.1	-2.8	19.5							

CHAPTER 6

INVESTMENT | PLANNING

- The basics of investment strategies and styles
- Bonds
- Building a balanced portfolio
- GICs
- Asset allocation and diversification
- Equities

JUST HOW MANY BLACK MONDAYS

CAN YOU HANDLE? | BY JONATHAN CHEVREAU

E'RE ALL LONG-TERM INVESTORS in a bull market it seems. It's easy to get carried away by the big themes – demographics, globalization and the information revolution, for instance – and end up going overboard on stocks in a portfolio. In good times, it's understandable that investors gravitate to stocks. As the famous charts of Chicago-based Ibbotson Associates show, $1 invested in the U.S. markets in 1926 would have grown to $2,000 by the early 1990s if invested in small-cap stocks and to $700 in large-cap stocks, but only to $11 in government bonds and $10 in treasury bills. Roger Ibbotson, a Yale School of Management professor, is among the best-known stock market bulls in the U.S. In 1974 he made a 25-year call on the Dow Jones industrials average, predicting it would top 10,000 by the end of the 1990s. That forecast did come true and he now is calling for the Dow to surpass 120,000 by 2025.

Stocks for the long run (that happens to be the title of a fine book on the subject by Jeremy Siegel) is a fine credo for those who have the stomach for it. But in the long run we are also dead. Investors have to live day by day and their capacity to absorb the highs and lows of the roller-coaster varies greatly. The danger in believing we're in a new era where stocks go only up is that investors throw caution to the wind and throw out such traditional safety measures as diversification and maintaining an appropriate balance among the various asset classes – stocks, bonds and cash.

Investors who bought into Asian or gold mutual funds learned this lesson the hard way during the mini-crash of Oct. 27, 1997. When the Asian flu spread to stock markets around the world, many investors found out just how long-term their time horizons really were. That decline tested the resolve of believers in the buy-and-hold philosophy. The stomach-churning one-day drop in October of '97 was followed by one of history's greatest rallies. But that rally came to an end in 2000 and the Nasdaq stock index went into a steep reversal. There is a beneficial, yet perverse, side-effect to these market downdrafts. They re-acquaint equity investors, some of whom have never experienced such declines, with the risk side of the risk/return equation.

INVESTORS SHOULDN'T IGNORE THE BASIC PRINCIPLES OF DIVERSIFICATION

The flip side of glorious 40% and 50% single-year returns achieved on individual technology stocks or through specialized equity funds has always been the sharp drops of the type experienced in the 1997 instalment of Black Monday. If you really believe the prevailing axioms of baby boom demographics, stocks for the long run and buying on dips, then you'd take the view of Nathan Mechanic, a broker with RBC Dominion Securities Inc., that whenever such drops occur, "we're having a sale" on stocks and equity funds. If, however, the thought of wading in and scooping up bargains in the next market swoon makes you queasy, you've probably flunked what one financial planner calls the tummy test.

If there is panic when markets take a big one-day dive, it's likely felt by people who ignored the basic principles of diversification. A hefty drop in market indexes serves as a much-needed wake up call for investors with 100% of their portfolio in aggressive stocks or equity funds – doubly so for those who borrowed money to maximize returns in a market they thought could only go up. Remember that stocks or equity funds constitute only one of three major classes of financial assets. The other two, cash and fixed-income investments, also should be represented in the portfolios of most investors. For larger portfolios, 5% or 10% positions are sometimes added in real estate, gold and derivatives.

A BALANCED PORTFOLIO IS SPREAD OUT OVER DIFFERENT ASSET CLASSES

What constitutes a balanced portfolio varies with the risk tolerance and growth objectives of individual investors. A standard way of looking at this situation is through what's called the financial planning pyramid. At the base are items everyone should have for basic security – insurance and a will. Next are the independence items – a cash fund for emergencies, a debt-management plan, home-ownership and a pension plan. Then come the investments, starting with conservative securities that pay regular income, like bonds and dividend-paying stocks. Next are growth stocks, then derivatives and, at the top, speculative investments. As you go up the pyramid, the width narrows. That means risk rises and you should narrow your exposure the higher you go up the pyramid.

Another basic way of looking at your investments is through what's known as the life cycle theory. Early in your working career, your savings should go into investments that pay off well into the future. You can have a relatively high proportion of your investments in growth stocks that don't pay dividends because your objective will be to broaden the base of that financial pyramid through capital gains. As you approach retirement you will want a greater and greater proportion of your investments in securities that produce regular income. At age 45, you may have 75% of your portfolio in equities. By age 65, the proportion likely will drop below 50% and perhaps much lower than that. The mix of equities will change as well, from more growth stocks at a young age to mainly dividend-paying stocks at retirement.

Traditionally, the advice of investment counselors has been to hold fixed income investments inside an RRSP and equity investments outside. That's because fixed income investments are highly taxed outside an RRSP, while capital gains and dividend income get slightly more favorable tax treatment. Many middle class investors have only nominal non-registered investment portfolios. For these investors, it makes sense to have some equity exposure inside an RRSP. But aggressive equity funds may not be wise choices for RRSPs. If they go down in value, you've lost precious RRSP room that cannot be regained. At least outside an RRSP, capital losses can be used to offset capital gains.

Most of the big mutual fund companies and banks try to advocate a "portfolio" approach to investments. Investment counselors will ask investors to fill out a short questionnaire to determine their risk tolerance and objectives. They usually have computer programs that use the personal information to produce a range of suggested asset classes and appropriate products. A long-term plan that changes the mix in a portfolio is called strategic asset allocation. Often this objective can be achieved with something as simple as a balanced fund, which typically offers a 60% equity to 40% bond mix.

MARKET TIMERS TRY TO PREDICT HIGHS AND LOWS TO SAVE INVESTOR FROM LOSSES

In opposition to the tried and true "buy and hold" approach involved in strategic asset allocation is the market timing approach. Market timers believe they can predict market highs and lows, thereby saving investors from the gut-wrenching crashes. Of course, many investment professionals believe this is impossible and that market timing also leads to "missing" the market for the powerful one-day ascents that make up most market gains. So-called "tactical asset allocation" consists of short-term attempts to pick the asset class that will outperform and then giving that class more weight. This approach is taken by tactical asset allocation funds but, historically, their performance has been no better than traditional balanced funds.

INVESTORS SHOULD MAINTAIN A STRATEGIC ASSET ALLOCATION MIX

For most investors, occasional (once a year, perhaps) rebalancing of a strategically allocated asset mix is probably preferable to market timing. A market timer is either 100% in the market or 100% in cash. If you're willing to take the risks, by all means engage the services of market timers. But such drastic calls usually are beyond the abilities of the average investor. Taking partial profits on the way up is another matter. Suppose, for example, that you have a portfolio that is 60% stocks, 30% bonds and 10% cash. This asset mix is a common balance in portfolios, so let's assume it meets your current needs. And suppose that there is a strong surge in prices of stocks in that portfolio. After a while, your portfolio has been transformed into a 75% stock weighting, 18% in bonds and 7% in cash. An asset allocation strategy suggested selling 20% of those equities, thereby reducing the 75% stock weighting to the 60% level. You'd reinvest the proceeds back into bonds and cash.

Such an approach makes eminent sense. Having a strategic plan forces you to sell your most overvalued assets. But investment advisors will tell that a correction is not the time for rebalancing a portfolio. You should have developed a balanced strategy before the correction. Once a correction has occurred, the damage has been done. Ideally, investors should take partial profits on stock funds on the way up and not have a rebalancing problem. When there is a correction it's the hot stocks that take the big hits. Investors who have already taken profits in the hot stocks are not likely to have as much volatility in their portfolios.

THE PROSPECTUS IS A COMPLEX TOOL

Prospectuses are required reading for anyone buying mutual funds, but how helpful are these long, complex legal documents for the average investor? And what should the investor be looking for when reading them? Here are some pointers from Riley Moynes, author of *The Money Coach*, co-author of *Top Funds 2001*, and senior financial adviser and principal of the Equion Group in Toronto.

INVESTMENT OBJECTIVES

This key element of the prospectus is intended to help you ensure the fund's goals are in keeping with your portfolio needs. In general, this section will list any restrictions on permissible investments, and discuss the nature of the risks facing buyers. "This is intended to help investors, but when you read, for example, that every equity fund's stated objective is to provide long-term growth along with security of capital, how much help is that?" asks Moynes. "Prospectuses are not always the best place to get the distinguishing features of different funds."

PORTFOLIO HOLDINGS

A listing of assets, usually presented as of the fund's latest fiscal yearend, is another key element of the prospectus. Do these holdings reflect the fund's stated aims regarding growth versus security? Are some holdings more conservative or aggressive than expected? Is the balance right? Says Moynes: "Assuming you are capable of drawing informed conclusions from this information, holdings can give you a pretty good idea of the fund's style, for example, whether they're small or large cap, growth or value-oriented, and so on. But are you equipped to make sufficiently informed decisions?"

FUND MANAGEMENT

Individual fund managers can have a big bearing on portfolio contents as well as performance since they're the ones who actually make the buying decisions. The prospectus should provide a brief history of the management team along with any recent changes. If there are new people at the helm, how have they performed in the past, and what tendencies did they display? What management style or styles do they employ? What can you expect from them?

FEES AND CHARGES

All funds charge management and expense fees, and sometimes these can have a significant impact on growth statistics. Some funds also charge one-time sales fees ("front-end" or "back-end" loads), complicating the profit equation. The prospectus should detail all these fees, and you should keep them in mind in comparing performance figures with other funds. "Many people are still unaware that funds charge any fees at all," says Moynes. "And I would hope people don't make decisions based only on management expense ratios. As anywhere, you generally get what you pay for. With smaller accounts, no-load can mean no help. This may be fine for those who can make their own decisions, but you should consider what added value those fees provide."

FINANCIAL STATEMENTS

Funds are required to provide complete financial statements, accompanied by an auditor's statement, in the prospectus. "This is essential information, for those who can understand it," Moynes says. A couple of further points: How are transactions performed? Are there restrictions or lead time requirements, as is often the case with real estate funds, that can limit your ability to act quickly? What about transfer fees? How liquid is your capital? What are the dividend distribution policies of the fund? Are dividends automatically reinvested? Also, the timing of distributions in relation to purchases can affect your after-tax results (for instance, if you buy just before the distribution, you might end up with little profit and a year's worth of tax liability).

"One of the other things I would like to see in a fund prospectus is annual performance figures from the date of inception," Moynes adds. "Average annual yields can be very seductive, but they can mask several losing years. Returns for each calendar year would be very helpful in revealing fund performance patterns."

MANAGEMENT STYLE IS IMPORTANT TO WATCH

Diversification is a fundamental tenet of investing, but many investors overlook management style when spreading their money around mutual funds. Yet style can have a substantial impact on the content and trading patterns of a particular fund, not to mention its bottom line. Growth and value are the two basic styles. GT Global Canada, now part of AIM funds, did a two-year study on these styles and used market information over a 17-year period. Over that time, the Toronto Stock Exchange 300 index averaged an annual return of about about 10%. Growth investing would have yielded 20%, and value investing would have yielded 15% but with lower volatility.

Value investors seek underpriced stocks – high-quality sleepers that offer good prospects of long-term capital appreciation. Growth investing is more volatile but average returns are higher. Value investors buy at the bottom of a cycle and may have to wait a while to make money. Growth investors buy when a business is already firing on all cylinders and poised for very strong results. The two styles generally do well in different years, making them complementary elements in an equity portfolio.

FUND MANAGERS RESEARCH COMPANIES LOOKING FOR STRONG MANAGEMENT TEAMS

Another basic style difference relates to company size – "small cap" versus "large cap." Some managers prefer smaller, and therefore generally more volatile, companies for their greater growth potential. Others stick to blue chips. Some fund groups try to get the best of both worlds with separate funds for each.

Yet another style variant is "bottom up" versus "top down." In the bottom-up approach, managers look throughout the corporate universe for promising stocks based on intrinsic indicators such as price earnings ratios and earnings growth rates. This style of assessing companies involves a thorough analysis of the strength of management. The theory is that a good management team will make the best decisions under any economic conditions. The top-down style looks at the macro-economic picture. When these fund managers identify the most promising industries, they focus on the best companies within them.

AN INDUSTRIAL SECTOR WEIGHTING DEPENDS ON STAGE OF THE ECONOMIC CYCLE

Sectoral rotation is a variant of the top-down style, one in which different weightings are given to industrial sectors during different parts of economic cycles. For example, companies not affected by economic cycles – such as pharmaceuticals and food producers –

get emphasis during economic downturns. During periods of economic growth, the retail sector, for instance, will be back in favor.

Both the bottom-up and top-down styles use fundamental analysis, which means assessing the details of each company that is a prospective investment for a portfolio. Fundamental analysts look at intrinsic corporate performance measures, along with macro-economic considerations.

There also is an investment style that doesn't really care much about the fundamentals. This is known as technical analysis, an approach that looks at patterns for a stock or group of stocks. Price momentum is the key to this style. This means buying stocks that have a popular following because the momentum of the herd will carry them along. Technical analysis also tries to identify price support levels. If a stock falls through a key support point, it's time to sell.

MARKET TIMERS REJECT BUY-AND-HOLD STRATEGY

Bragging about your mutual fund picks is supposedly acceptable cocktail party chatter. But the next time there's a lull in the conversation, try the following experiment: Suggest that everyone who believes in market timing with mutual funds step into one corner, and those who believe in buying and holding funds over the long term occupy another part of the room. At a Bay Street party, just about everyone would be crowded into the buy-and-hold corner.

Generally, the fund companies eschew market timing. Some, such as no-load firm Altamira Investment Services Inc., limit switches to just 10 a year, on the grounds that frequent switches increase costs for unitholders and make life more difficult for the managers. "The academic studies we've seen tend to prove over time that you can't add value through market timing," says Altamira president Philip Armstrong. "Funds were designed and are best used for long-term holders."

Writing in *The FundLetter*, CIBC Wood Gundy Inc. vice-president Jon Kanitz lumped market timers in with sector rotators, asset allocators and momentum investors, concluding that "these techniques are so prone to error that they make fortune tellers look good by comparison." Kanitz, a dedicated stock picker

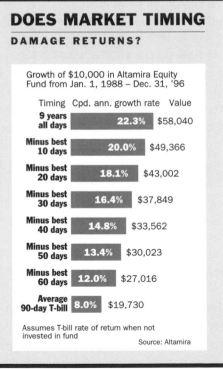

DOES MARKET TIMING

DAMAGE RETURNS?

Growth of $10,000 in Altamira Equity Fund from Jan. 1, 1988 – Dec. 31, '96

Timing	Cpd. ann. growth rate	Value
9 years all days	22.3%	$58,040
Minus best 10 days	20.0%	$49,366
Minus best 20 days	18.1%	$43,002
Minus best 30 days	16.4%	$37,849
Minus best 40 days	14.8%	$33,562
Minus best 50 days	13.4%	$30,023
Minus best 60 days	12.0%	$27,016
Average 90-day T-bill	8.0%	$19,730

Assumes T-bill rate of return when not invested in fund

Source: Altamira

who believes in staying fully invested at all times, adds that some combination of a value or growth approach to stock picking will outperform other styles over the long haul.

Market timers, on the other hand, swear they can beat the buy-and-hold camp and can trot out their own statistics showing the gains to be made by being out of the market during its worst times. Most market timers apply technical analysis to trade stocks or futures directly, and sometimes indexes. Harland Hendrickson, who has a PhD in biochemistry and publishes an insightful newsletter, *Market Trend Follower*, takes a similar tack but switches between mutual funds rather than stocks.

MARKET-TIMING MODELS CAN BE APPLIED TO MUTUAL FUND INVESTMENTS

Hendrickson believes funds are better that direct investments as market-timing vehicles. Funds provide instant diversification and there is little or no cost to switching from fund to fund. Picking multiple fund managers reduces risk and the broad base of mutual funds provides exposure to the full range of market sectors. Hendrickson uses a momentum strategy to move in and out of major sectors. The premise is that a trend in motion will continue in the same direction until it reverses or until you can find a trend that is doing better. The approach is decidedly short term.

Kenneth Norquay of Gorinsen Capital Inc. in Toronto, a long-time market timer, agrees that the same timing principles that work for stocks or futures can also be applied to mutual funds. But Norquay disagrees that funds are the optimal vehicle for market timers: "Mutual funds are the dull thud of investing. They hardly move at all. If you're going to time why not do it with something that makes money?" He suggests individual stocks and even bonds or groups of stocks.

FUND MANAGERS CAN BE TRUSTED TO MAKE DAILY TACTICAL DECISIONS

There is an irony in so much energy and science being applied to analyzing mutual funds. After all, isn't the whole idea of funds to delegate the decision-making to professionals? A happy middle ground might be to trust your fund manager with the daily tactical shifts of the markets and to rebalance your fund portfolio once or twice a year when major sea changes occur.

THERE IS MORE TO REAL ESTATE THAN BRICKS

It took Oscar Belaiche a year to sell $456 million worth of real estate in his old job. After a career change, he could move that much in a week. Belaiche was the real estate executive in charge of selling a Canadian portfolio of office, industrial and retail buildings accumulated by Prudential Insurance Co. of America. After that job was done, he moved over to the investment business to manage real estate mutual funds for Goodman & Co. His job continued to be buying and selling real estate. But instead of bricks and mortar, he was trading stocks. He was one of the first real estate operators to move over to the securities side of the business. Others have followed because real estate in Canada is becoming securitized. Property ownership is increasingly held through the stock market. A vehicle for much of this shift has been real estate investment trusts (REITs).

NEW CAPITAL ENTERING REAL ESTATE MARKET DRIVES INVESTMENT MARKET FORWARD

Owners of private fortunes used to be the big landlords of office buildings. REITs and the big pension funds are changing real estate from a privately owned to a publicly owned industry. The transformation began in the U.S. in the mid-1990s and the trend is being picked up in Canada. People in the industry expect that it will be a long-term trend, notwithstanding any short-term market volatility.

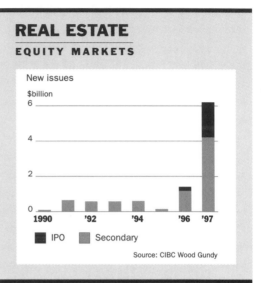

REAL ESTATE

EQUITY MARKETS

New issues

$billion

POPULARITY OF REAL ESTATE MUTUAL FUNDS IS GROWING IN CANADA

Real estate is an emerging industry in the stock market. The appeal of converting property into financial securities is liquidity. Selling a 50-storey office tower is a daunting job. The pool of potential buyers is limited. Fixing a market price is not easy because big buildings don't sell every day, so the going rate isn't evident. When real estate is securitized, the methods of evaluation change. "We're merging the portfolio management theories of the stock side with the portfolio management theories on the real estate side," Belaiche says. "It's a merging of the skills of the traditional CFA [chartered financial analyst] working with an operating person. Before, I was directly buying and selling real estate. Now, I'm buying the companies that are buying and selling real estate."

THE RIP VAN WINKLE STRATEGY MIGHT WORK

There are now almost 2,000 mutual funds available in Canada, not to mention hundreds more closed-end funds, offshore funds and other products. Little wonder investors are confused. An entire industry has sprung up to help them pick funds. The securities firms who are members of the Investment Dealers Association employ close to 40,000 people. Outside that circle is a network of financial planners, a large contingent of related specialists who speak at seminars, a slew of newsletters and a gaggle of book authors all claiming expertise in the field. This army of experts makes the topic of fund selection far more complicated than necessary. A vast library of esoteric information has sprung up, involving asset allocation, performance and style analysis, comparisons of volatility, relative expenses and risk/reward tradeoffs.

A TWO-FUND PORTFOLIO CAN BE AS GOOD AS A 20-FUND PORTFOLIO

Much of this is geared to fund switching, which usually means investors sell funds just when they should be buying and vice versa. Some investors emulate their financial planners by spending hundreds of dollars a year for monthly computer disk performance updates. Investors can now spend as much time analyzing mutual funds as they used to spend analyzing individual stocks. Wasn't the whole idea of mutual funds to delegate security selection to the professionals? Investors were supposed to be able to choose a fund or two, pay the 2% or so annual management fee and forget about it, spending their lives on more congenial pursuits.

Not now, however. Everyone is chasing the latest hot fund, frantically switching between regional equity funds and, lately, different industry sectors. If you're not worrying about bailing out of Europe and jumping into Asia, you have to decide between the computer industry, health sciences, financial services and consumer products sectors.

Anyone with more than eight mutual funds is probably overdiversified. Enter the Rip Van Winkle two-fund portfolio. At the risk of scuttling sales of the *Financial Post*'s annual *Smart Funds* guide, the idea that all you really need is two funds is an idea that has been floated at seminars and bounced off a few advisers. No one has refuted its logic. The two funds should be from proven, credible fund families and have below-average management fees. The idea is to buy these two funds and hang on for the next 40 years. No need for rebalancing, switching or even paying close attention to daily market changes. Anyone who adopts this approach has a good chance of matching the performance of the complex 20-fund portfolios of the gurus and pundits.

RIP VAN WINKLE
PORTFOLIO

Allocation

Fund	Original investment at 9/87 $	Monthly contrib. $	Value at 5/97 $
Templeton Growth	2,000	200	60,121
Trimark Income Growth	8,000	800	200,914

Performance

Simple rate	Rip Van Winkle portfolio	Canada Savings Bonds	Inflation	5-year GIC
Last month %	3.64	0.25	0.00	0.40
Last quarter %	3.36	0.74	0.22	1.20
Last year %	17.24	3.93	1.70	5.25

Annualized rate				
2 years %	16.27	4.69	1.45	5.78
3 years %	13.71	4.83	1.94	6.51
5 years %	14.67	5.22	1.49	6.57

Source: company reports

THE RIP VAN WINKLE | TWO-FUND PORTFOLIO

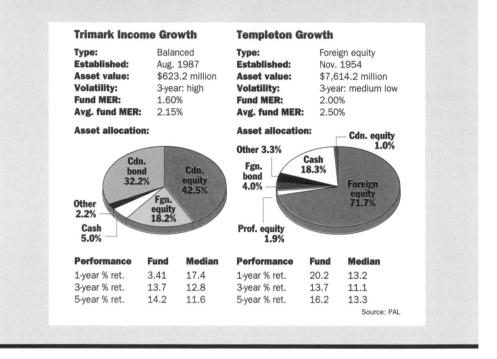

Trimark Income Growth

Type:	Balanced
Established:	Aug. 1987
Asset value:	$623.2 million
Volatility:	3-year: high
Fund MER:	1.60%
Avg. fund MER:	2.15%

Asset allocation:

- Cdn. bond 32.2%
- Cdn. equity 42.5%
- Other 2.2%
- Fgn. equity 18.2%
- Cash 5.0%

Performance	Fund	Median
1-year % ret.	3.41	17.4
3-year % ret.	13.7	12.8
5-year % ret.	14.2	11.6

Templeton Growth

Type:	Foreign equity
Established:	Nov. 1954
Asset value:	$7,614.2 million
Volatility:	3-year: medium low
Fund MER:	2.00%
Avg. fund MER:	2.50%

Asset allocation:

- Other 3.3%
- Fgn. bond 4.0%
- Cash 18.3%
- Cdn. equity 1.0%
- Foreign equity 71.7%
- Prof. equity 1.9%

Performance	Fund	Median
1-year % ret.	20.2	13.2
3-year % ret.	13.7	11.1
5-year % ret.	16.2	13.3

Source: PAL

PORTFOLIO HAS BALANCE OF STOCKS, BONDS, CASH AND FOREIGN INVESTMENTS

Rip Van Winkle is, of course, the fictional bearded character who falls asleep one day and awakes decades later to a very different world. The idea of the portfolio is to pick two funds that run on automatic pilot. If you leave the country for 30 years, or fall into a long coma, you should awaken to an investment portfolio that has grown considerably. You do nothing, nor does your financial planner. That doesn't mean the portfolio is static. At least two fund managers are continually engaged in stock picking, moving in and out of geographical regions and modifying asset allocation on your behalf.

This approach assumes an average RRSP/RRIF investor who wants a balance of stocks, bonds and cash and maximum foreign content. Growth and a little income.

SO WITHOUT FURTHER ADO THE ENVELOPES PLEASE

• Fund No. 1 is a basic low-fee Canadian balanced growth fund with a management expense ratio that is significantly below the Canadian average. It comes from the fund family of an established fund management firm, a blue-chip member of the mutual fund industry. This fund constitutes 70% of the Rip Van Winkle portfolio. It has a good cross-section of mid- to large-capitalization Canadian stocks, some bonds, cash and mortgage securities. The asset mix is the classic 60% equity to 40% fixed income. The fund maximizes its permitted 30% foreign content with mostly U.S. and some European and Japanese stocks.

• Fund No. 2 is a global equity growth fund with a long track record. Like Fund No. 1, it comes from blue-chip lineage. And it shares the characteristics of Fund No. 1, such as a management expense ratio that is well below the average of its peers. Its performance track record comes from having a good value-oriented geographical mix and it buys bargains around the world at times of maximum pessimism.

Fund No. 2 is your 30% foreign content in a registered plan. Coupled with the 30% of the 70% from Fund No. 1, you have maximized your exposure to world markets.

The combined asset allocation of these funds is skewed slightly to equities. That should be fine for any young investor. Older people could bring the total portfolio into a traditional asset mix by substituting with a global balanced fund that has similar attributes to those listed above.

RIP VAN WINKLE STRATEGY SUITS BEGINNING INVESTORS

This two-fund portfolio takes the fun out of the fund tracking and switching game, but it's doubtful all the energy spent on these pursuits would add to performance. If you add to your portfolio on a monthly or quarterly basis, you are "dollar-cost averaging" and this method evens out the impact of market corrections. The table on pages 157 and 158, prepared with Morningstar Canada's PAL Trak software, shows that Rip would have done very well with an initial $10,000 investment made in two well-known mutual funds. This example uses an 80/20 asset-allocation ratio because 20% was the limit on foreign investment until 1999.

Reaction to the Rip Van Winkle strategy is mixed among financial planners and mutual fund representatives. Joy Wolfson, a planner with Manulife Securities International Ltd., questions the one-size-fits-all advice, but concedes the Rip strategy is "appropriate for beginning investors with modest portfolios. I agree that overdiversification is a common and expensive mistake made by many novices."

Christopher Horan of Equion Group, a financial planning firm, agrees that constant fund switching is pointless and that "people's investment failures usually result from such big mistakes as overweighting asset classes that have gone up or underweighting assets that have gone down. An experienced adviser is needed to keep their clients on course."

Toronto-based planner Glenn Neuman likes the Rip portfolio, and notes that "one of the major hurdles I encountered was the clients' will to diversify into several different funds. They have ascribed to the 'don't put all your eggs in one basket' theory and simply see a mutual fund as only one egg. Some clients get very suspicious if you try to concentrate their assets into two or three funds."

WHEN CHOOSING A FUND, LOOK AT THE MANAGEMENT EXPENSE RATIO (MER)

Fees-only planner Warren Baldwin, of T. E. Financial Consultants Ltd., says the Rip portfolio "makes sense" for portfolios between $30,000 and $50,000. Beyond that, he'd like to see more diversification of management. With $75,000 or more, Baldwin says he "would use a couple more funds immediately." Baldwin puts even more stress on low

MERs and calculates the difference a half-percentage-point in MER makes. "Assume we are starting with zero in the RRSP portfolio and adding $12,000 per year over the next 25 years. Assume also that the portfolio grows at a compound rate of 10% per year. Assuming that an alternative average fund portfolio only grows at an annual rate of 9.46% [reduced due to the additional MER costs], the difference in accumulation after 25 years is almost $100,000." Baldwin adds that if going the broker-sold route, "we would negotiate the front-end load as low as possible."

Ted Cadsby, president of CIBC Securities Inc., believes that high net worth investors should strive to lower fees further by moving to "discretionary or pooled management, which can be cheaper and more tailored."

LABOR-SPONSORED FUNDS' POTENTIAL OVERLOOKED

After years of holding patiently, Canadian labor funds started to pay off in 2000–2001. Many outperformed regular funds that were hit badly by the sharp decline in the Nasdaq composite index. But comparisons to regular mutual funds are odious, says Denzil Doyle, chairman of the Capital Alliance Ventures Inc., an Ottawa-based technology labor fund. Doyle says a labor fund should start to outperform a regular equity mutual fund after four or five years. But he would prefer investors pay more heed to the growth in employment rates and revenues of the underlying investments. He says that despite a slow start for the unit value of his fund, there has been double-digit growth in employment and revenue among the companies in Capital Alliance's portfolio. Doyle believes those gains will pay off in time for investors in venture capital funds.

Attributes of labor-sponsored funds mean they are long-term instruments unlikely to show any significant appreciation in the first five years. That's consistent with Ottawa's treatment of these funds: generous tax credits of 30% (half federal, half provincial) are proffered in return for a commitment by the investor not to redeem for at least eight years. Investors who put these funds into an RRSP get a bonus. They can boost foreign content from 30% to 45%. Each $1 invested in a labor-sponsored fund gets you $3 in additional foreign content, to the US$ maximum.

CASH LEVELS IN LABOR FUNDS NEVER DROP BELOW 20%

These funds look like mutual funds and for that reason they must calculate unit values that reflect the values of the underlying companies. Those values don't change much in the short term – the way publicly traded stocks do – because most companies held by labor funds are not publicly traded. Their values only change if there is a new round of investment, an initial public offering, a sale of the company to a third party, or a termination or bankruptcy, Doyle says. All labor funds start out with capital invested in government treasury bills or bonds, and they are compelled by legislation never to

HOW LABOR FUNDS COMPARE

Fund No.	Fund Name	Total Asset $ Mill	1 Mth Ret	6 Mth Ret	1 Yr Ret
1	B.E.S.T. Discoveries	59.6	−1.2	−3.9	48.1
2	CI Covington	223.2	−11.1	−16.7	14.7
3	CI Covington II Inc. (LSVCC)	60.8	0.0	0.0	0.0
4	Canadian Medical Discoveries	323.1	−2.6	4.3	33.1
5	Capital Alliance Ventures	83.6	−6.7	7.7	67.6
6	Cdn Science & Technology Growth Fund Inc	59.0	−1.5	7.1	34.8
7	Centrefire Growth Fund Inc.	8.8	−0.9	−5.8	22.8
8	Crocus Investment Fund	163.1	−1.4	−0.7	−1.9
9	DGC Entertainment Ventures	6.2	−1.1	1.4	4.0
10	Dynamic Venture Opportunities	35.5	0.5	−3.0	14.0
11	ENSIS Growth Fund Inc. (LSVCC)	34.4	−0.9	0.9	2.4
12	First Ontario	58.8	1.0	−3.2	0.5
13	First Ontario LSIF Ltd. (Growth)	5.4	−0.1	−8.0	
14	Golden Opportunities	8.6	−5.6	−4.8	13.0
15	Retrocom Growth	75.1	0.0	1.4	2.8
16	Triax Growth	306.7	−18.1	−12.1	−3.1
17	Triax New Millenium Internet Balanced	23.5	0.3	0.9	
18	Triax New Millenium Internet Ventures	67.9	2.4	1.5	
19	VenGrowth Fund	736.7	−4.0	−0.7	34.2
20	VenGrowth II Investment Inc. (LSVCC)	157.2	−1.0	1.3	
21	Workers Investment	4.1	0.0	0.0	0.0
22	Working Opportunity Balanced	434.1	−5.3	12.0	31.3
23	Working Opportunity Growth	77.5	−7.5	10.6	
24	Working Ventures Canadian	750.5	−0.7	9.8	18.6

Source: Morningstar Canada

drop their cash levels below 20%. This provides liquidity for redemptions but also acts as a significant drag on performance, says Ron Begg, president of Working Ventures Canadian Fund.

As capital is invested, cash flow dries up and the value of the fund may drop. The only short-term prospect for appreciation is a second round of financing by another investor at a much higher price. Sometimes a venture capital firm may experience an IPO in one of its investee companies within months of the investment, but this is unlikely for labor funds because they are required to place much of their investments in early-stage firms. Another difference is the way investments are made and managed. Mutual fund managers rely on current and past financial information, while venture capital managers rely on business plans and operational scenarios.

CASHING IN LABOR FUNDS BEFORE MATURITY CAN RESULT IN LOSSES

"Testing the validity of those plans can be a complex task," Doyle says. To pick a labor fund, investors should analyze the potential of each of the companies in which the fund invests, he says. They should show incremental sales or rising market share and preferably "gaining market share in a growing market." Labor funds may also invest in firms with no sales at all, but which are still in research mode. Here the labor fund manager has to assess the capabilities of the entrepreneurs and technical staff behind the firms.

A well-managed labor fund will invest in companies that will survive what Doyle terms the "death valley" period of its first three or four years. He expects that of 10 investments, three will be losers, four will be so-so survivors and three will be exceptional performers. While investors may expect little more than the generous tax credits, many industry watchers believe that investors will get a pleasant surprise when they see the growth of these funds.

BROKERAGE WRAP PROGRAMS ARE BOOMING

In what may be an admission that their constant tinkering and switching may be hurting the returns of their clients, Canada's major brokerage firms are making an aggressive push into wrap accounts. These accounts provide investment management, brokerage and custodial services, all "wrapped" together for one set fee, typically between 1.5% and 2.75% annually on the total value of your holdings. They appeal to clients who want custom-tailored managed products, full service and one-stop shopping. During the latter half of the 1990s, wraps grew by roughly 50% to account for about $100 billion in investment dollars by the end of the decade.

WRAP ACCOUNT FEE STRUCTURE FEATURES A DIFFERENT WAY TO PAY FOR SERVICE

The fee-based approach of wrap programs eliminates the potential conflicts of interest that exist in a transaction- or commission-based model. Of course, as high net worth consultant Kelly Rodgers points out, "you pay a premium to have that transaction bias removed." The popularity of wrap programs also begs the question of what exactly brokers and financial planners have been doing all along to justify the generous commissions and trailer fees they get from stock and mutual fund transactions.

Rodgers points out that roughly two-thirds of the mutual and segregated funds in Canada are broker-sold load funds. Choosing among them, setting overall asset allocation and matching funds to investor temperament and objectives have presumably been the job of investment advisers all along, she suggests. "Clients don't like the commission aspect of traditional brokerages," she says. "[The wrap account] is a different way of paying for the advice and service brokers say they've been giving us for the past 20 years."

HIGH NET WORTH INVESTORS WILL BENEFIT THE MOST FROM WRAP ACCOUNTS

At the top end of the market, wrap programs are often offered as a segregated service – they select individual securities. Research by Investor Economics Inc. shows that the big growth is in this area – custom programs for high net worth investors. Lower on the scale of portfolio size, wrap accounts use mutual funds or pooled funds as the underlying product. A wrap account can be set up for a few thousand dollars. But the fees will be relatively high and the programs only make sense for much larger amounts. Wrap programs will have minimum investment amounts. The range of minimums is roughly between $10,000 and $250,000. Up to about $50,000, there may be additional fees as well as the basic wrap account fee. Investors need to be in the range of $500,000 or more to get personalized service.

Rodgers describes some wrap accounts as "private-label" mutual funds. "They have been structured to resemble pooled funds, with fees charged outside, but are offered by prospectus to allow investments of less than $150,000," Rodgers says. Pooled funds, which are sold by offering memorandum, require a minimum $150,000 investment in Ontario.

WRAPPED FUNDS MAY NOT CONTAIN TOP PERFORMERS BUT VOLATILITY IS LESS

Allen Clarke, a pioneer of the wrap industry in Canada and founder of Internet-based OPUS 2 Direct.com, says brokers stand to make less money initially with wrap accounts than through transactions. The break-even point is four or five years, which benefits the client because "they don't switch around, so they get much better performance and no up-front fees. The client is better off, but so is the broker as the assets grow and he retains the business." For this reason, beginning brokers may shy away from wrap accounts. "It takes a mature broker with a big enough base" for wraps to pay off for the broker, Clarke says.

Investors also need to be aware that, by design, the mutual funds in these programs will never be top-performing funds – generally not in the top quarter of fund performance rankings, although usually in the top half. "But the volatility will be a lot less. That's the thing to watch," Clarke says.

LEVERAGE GENERATES BIG GAINS – OR LOSSES

Leverage is the strategy of trying to magnify your investment gains by borrowing money. Say you buy $1,000 worth of a stock and borrow from the bank to buy another $4,000 worth, and the stock value rises 20%. You end up with $6,000 in shares which, after the bank loan is repaid, means you have doubled your money (excluding carrying costs and broker's fees) rather than earning just $200.

That's great when stock markets are rising and money is relatively cheap. But you'd better be confident that your stock prices will appreciate and you're not near the beginning of a bear market. As anyone who has borrowed in the past and been hit with a correction knows, the downside can be scary. "Never forget you have a fixed liability against a variable asset," says Warren Baldwin, regional vice-president at T.E. Financial Consultants Ltd., a fees-only financial planning firm.

INTEREST CHARGED ON LEVERAGE FUNDS IS TAX DEDUCTIBLE

Still, government tax policy encourages the practice of leverage, since the interest charges are tax-deductible (although you can no longer write off RRSP loan interest). If you invested the tax refunds from investment interest charges, you could go even further in magnifying the potential gains, or any losses, as illustrated by the accompanying tables prepared for *The Financial Post* by financial author and speaker Talbot Stevens.

AFTER TAX VALUES

AND COMPOUND RETURNS AFTER ONE YEAR

Investment of $50,000, with 70% margin borrowed at 7.5% interest rate

Before-tax return %	From	After-tax value after 1 year $		After-tax compound annual returns %	
		Unleveraged	Leveraged	Unleveraged	Leveraged
12.0	A good stock gain	53,750	57,031	7.5	14.1
10.0	A good equity fund	53,125	54,948	6.3	9.9
7.5	Current 5-year money	52,344	52,344	4.7	4.7
0.0	A mediocre investment	50,000	44,531	0.0	-10.9
-10.0	Recent gold funds	48,875	34,115	-6.3	-31.8
-43.0	Bre-X collapse	36,562	0	-26.9	-100.0
-85.0	Bre-X collapse	23,437	(44,010)	-53.0	-188.0

Losses would be greater if capital losses can't offset capital gains.

After-tax values and compound returns after 10 years

Before-tax return %	Unleveraged	After-tax value after 10 years $		Unleveraged	After-tax compound annual returns %	
		Leveraged, R0%	Leveraged, R100%		Leveraged, R0%	Leveraged, R100%
12.0	115,808	191,992	247,160	8.8	14.4	17.3
10.0	99,804	138,648	190,545	7.2	10.7	14.3
7.5	83,157	83,157	131,363	5.2	5.2	10.1
3.9	64,565	21,182	64,767	2.6	-8.2	2.6
2.4	58,364	0	42,388	1.6	-36.7	-1.6
0.0	50,000	game over	12,019	0.0	game over	-13.3
10.0	29,646	game over	game over	-5.1	game over	game over

R0% means refund from interest expense deduction is not reinvested; R100% means refund reinvested.
Game over means leverage loan would be terminated; therefore can't have negative balances
Source: Talbot Stevens for *The Financial Post*

The table's top section shows what happens after one year to an investment of $50,000, to which you add $117,000 on margin. This represents a 70% margin: your $50,000 represents 30% of the total investment of $167,000. The other 70% is borrowed from your broker at 7.5% interest. The table factors in taxation, assuming a 50% marginal tax rate, and assumes all the investment comes in the form of capital gains, half of which are now taxable. It also assumes capital losses are used to offset capital gains.

PERCENTAGE OF LEVERAGE AVAILABLE IS DETERMINED BY STOCK VALUE

You'd be ahead if the stocks or equity funds you bought returned more than 7.5%, which is the typical current rate for an investment loan. If the stock fell by 10%, though, your losses would be much greater than the gains from a 10% increase in the stock price. Margin rates on stocks vary with their price. According to Greg Clarke, vice-president of the Investment Dealers Association of Canada, dealers are not supposed to lend any money at all for illiquid securities or stocks selling for less than $1.50. For stocks between $1.50 and $1.75, brokers will lend you 20% and you have to put up 80%. Between $1.75 and $2, they can lend 40%. Above $2, it's 50%.

Finally, there is a list of about 300 highly liquid stocks on which dealers will lend you 70%. This group of stocks has to meet the criteria for listing of options under the Canadian Derivatives Clearing Corp., Clarke says. Many firms set their own margin rates, and may be even more (or less) selective. Mutual fund investors generally can get 50% margin from their broker, but Stevens said they can often leverage 100% of the purchase by arranging their own financing. And because of their inherent diversification, mutual funds are less exposed to downside risk than single stocks. "[The downside is why] I educate and only endorse conservative leverage that is long-term [minimum 10 years] and diversified, and where the margin call is eliminated, with a trusted adviser," Stevens says.

THE BREAK-EVEN POINT ON LEVERAGED INVESTMENT IS LOWER AND DECREASES OVER TIME
He defines conservative leverage as the type in which long-term annual cash flow is able to finance at least the interest expense and possibly repay some principal, too. That way, the interest expense does not compound and risk is reduced. The break-even point is lower and decreases over time. Given the variety of personal situations, Stevens calculated the average annual compound return a leveraged investor needs to break even – that is, to cover the interest on the loan as well as the capital gains tax due when the investment is sold. Using present value math, he adjusted for inflation ($1 of interest paid today is inherently worth more than $1 of earnings realized 10 years from now). As can be seen from the table on the previous page, the longer a leveraged investor holds on, the lower the break-even rate of return.

RETIREMENT-ORIENTED INVESTORS SHOULD CONSIDER 10- OR 20-YEAR HORIZON
Thane Stenner, a B.C.-based financial adviser, doesn't go so far as some planners who suggest that houses be remortgaged to provide investment capital. He recommends a home be paid off first and maximum RRSP contributions be made each year. Stenner then suggests high income earners borrow one year's worth of discretionary income against their home – say, $22,500 on an annual income of $100,000 – and invest that money in a conservative global equity fund. The second part of the table shows Stevens' leveraging analysis over the 10-year horizon that most retirement-oriented investors should be considering. (Twenty years would be better.) It does not track the downside of the poor investments shown in the top chart because no rational investor would keep reinvesting in such money-losing investments.

LOWER INTEREST RATES MEAN LOWER ADVANTAGE TO LEVERAGING
The table entries labelled "game over" do not show negative balances because the leveraged loan would be quickly terminated by the broker. The table also shows how further gains (or losses) would arise by reinvesting the tax refund generated by the interest-expense deduction. "Leveraging may not have been as effective a way of generating

financial wealth in the 1990s" as it was in the 1980s, concludes Jim Rogers, chairman of Vancouver-based Rogers Group Financial Advisors Ltd. "Though we are now experiencing relatively low interest rates, the spread between the cost of borrowed money and the rate of return is often much lower too, reducing the potential advantage of leveraging."

POOLED FUNDS OFFER EASY DIVERSIFICATION

Pooled funds do not receive nearly so much ink as mutual funds but, at certain levels of wealth, the "pooleds" have several advantages. Think of pooled funds as mutual funds sold wholesale by big banks, trust companies, pension managers and independent investment counsellors. Typical pooled funds will cost 1% or 1.5% a year in management fees, or about half the retail cost of 2% to 3% that goes with most equity mutual funds.

You do not see pooled funds advertised on television, nor are they accompanied by road shows or direct-mail blitzes. All that costs money. With pooled funds, about 1% a year stays in your pocket instead of going to brokers, ad agencies and other middlemen. However, pooled funds carry a higher than normal minimum investment. In Ontario, under "sophisticated investor" rules, the pooled fund minimum is $150,000, which puts them out of reach of many Canadians. Unlike mutual funds, pooled funds are not sold with a prospectus. Instead, they are accompanied by an offering memorandum. Conceptually, though, pooled funds are similar to mutual funds. As the name implies, assets of many clients are combined, or pooled, into one account and the investors receive units of the account proportional to their investment.

A FUND CAN BE MARKETED AS A POOLED OR A MUTUAL FUND BY THE SAME FIRM

The distinction between pooleds and mutual funds is particularly fine at certain firms. For instance, Vancouver-based Phillips Hager & North Ltd. has pooled funds for its pension clients, but almost identical no-load mutual funds for its individual investors. Usually, the mutual funds have more securities. Investment adviser Patrick McKeough suggests pooled-fund managers typically buy and hold stock. They are under less pressure than their mutual fund counterparts to show short-term performance gains. Internal trading costs, therefore, may be lower than with aggressively run mutual funds. Affluent investors seeking to hand over their nest eggs to a discretionary investment manager usually have the choice of pooled funds or separately managed accounts. The difference is that a manager is picking and holding stocks for the investor in a segregated or "separately managed" account. That means it can be tailored to individual preferences.

On the other hand, the distinctiveness of segregated portfolios may be overstated. Paul Starita, former chairman of CIBC Securities Inc., says "the reality is almost all the private managers pool their funds, no matter how they report them to you. It is efficient and consistent with good management."

POOLED FUNDS ARE A GOOD INVESTMENT IF YOU COME INTO A LARGE INFUSION OF CASH

Kelly Rodgers, author of *The Insider's Guide to Selecting the Best Money Manager,* says discretionary managers who offer both segregated and pooleds often "try to push people into pools." That is because it's easier for the firm, with the administrative and other efficiencies that pooling makes possible. Pooled funds can offer quick and easy diversification, particularly for investors who come into a large one-time infusion of cash. "But they're not so good if you have existing holdings because to go into pooled funds you have to sell your holdings," Rodgers says. "That can create a tax event, which is not advantageous for some people." Buying pooled funds late in the calendar year also makes you liable to tax on distribution of capital gains at the end of the year, even though you did not benefit from them most of the year. That is the same problem faced by mutual fund investors.

Over the past 10 years, information technology has developed to the point that cost-effective management can be made available to smaller asset pools. That same technology also makes it possible to run segregated portfolios for about the same cost as pooleds.

Pooleds may appeal to investors who are seeking a particular management style – for example, an actively traded bond portfolio for an RRSP.

DISCONTENT SPURS GIC ALTERNATIVES

These are desperate times for people living on a fixed income. When term deposits roll over at lower rates, the siren call of the stock market or equity mutual funds gets louder. But moving out of fixed-income products into volatile stock markets is a scary proposition for those who can't afford to lose their precious capital. Senior citizens in particular are facing a triple-barreled dilemma.

In addition to what appear to be chronically low interest rates, the average person's life expectancy is rising. Meanwhile, the federal government is slashing universal benefits and, by moving up the RRSP maturity deadline to age 69 from 71, has reduced the retirement-savings period.

NEW GICS LET YOU PLAY THE STOCK MARKET WHILE PROTECTING INVESTMENT CAPITAL

Seniors whose RRSPs have been converted to registered retirement income funds (RRIFs) are facing a yearly erosion of their capital if their plan is invested solely in traditional GICs. That's because the average yield on standard GICs is lower than the 7.38% minimum annual RRIF payout. As a result, several financial institutions have introduced what at first blush appears to be an ideal solution to the GIC dilemma – varieties of GICs that promise some participation in the stock market but also protect invested capital from the market's downside. Typically, these products will be linked to a stock market index.

These hybrids are called index-linked GICs. They're not perfect, but should markets crash you get back your principal (but no interest). If stocks continue to rise, they offer

HOW INDEXED-LINKED INVESTMENTS | COMPARE

Name	Underlying equity index	Cap on return	Term	How interest computed
Scotia two-year Stock Index GIC	TSE 35	20% (formerly 30%)	2 years	index level at maturity
Scotia G7 Stock Indexed GIC	7 global indexes	30% over 3 yrs.	3 years	index level at maturity
Scotia McLeod TSE 35 Bull Note	TSE 35	90% over 4 yrs.	4 years	index level at maturity
TD GIC Plus	TSE 100	no	3/5 years	based on averages
CIBC Stock Market Advantage	TSE 35	no	3/5 years	averaging over term
Sun Life Trust Global Index GIC	MSCI world index	no	5 years	averaging
Credit-union index-linked term deposit	TSE 35	no	3/5 years	monthly averaging
London Life	TSE 35	no	3 years	averaging formula

potentially higher interest payouts, although some issuers limit the gains by capping the payout at a predetermined level.

INDEX-LINKED GICS LOCK UP MONEY FOR TWO, THREE OR FIVE YEARS

Hybrid GICs don't pay dividends. You are participating only in the capital gains of the underlying stocks. Most are eligible for RRSPs but few, if any, can be held inside a RRIF. You also are locking up your money for two, three or five years. And, unlike cashable GICs, Canada Savings Bonds or the new Canada RRSP bonds, index-linked GICs are not redeemable. Finally, if held outside an RRSP, you pay tax on interest income, not the more favorably treated capital gains. There are also significant differences in how the interest is paid out. Most payouts are based on some averaging formula, but some are based on the final level of the index when the GIC matures. There are advantages and disadvantages to both.

Financial institutions are reluctant to describe what they're doing behind the scenes to make these GICs tick. Essentially, they lock in most of the principal (say, 70% to 90%) with a zero-coupon bond. Equity participation is achieved through derivatives, typically call options, that provide a gain if the underlying index rises.

Critics of index-linked GICs say you can do all this on your own and cut out the middleman's mark-up, an amount that banks are reluctant to divulge. But it's believed to be comparable with mutual funds' annual management expense ratios of 2% to 3%.

"My one-liner on these is they're all junk," says Moshe Milevsky, a professor of finance at York University's Schulich School of Business. Milevsky offers a compelling argument as to why investors would be better off cooking up their own combinations, such as putting 70% of their capital in a regular GIC and investing the balance in equity mutual funds.

FOR THE RISK-AVERSE INVESTOR, INDEX-LINKED GICS MAY BE THE WAY TO GO

But some financial planners say the new hybrid GICs may be appropriate for extremely risk-averse investors or those who do not want to create their own capital-protection scheme. Equity or balanced funds may be better investments for younger investors. But if forced to choose between basic GICs and index-linked GICs, even Milevsky concedes the latter might be the better choice. "What may be intellectually the thing to do is less important than what will sit well in the oldsters' tummies," says Jim Rogers, chairman of Rogers Group Financial Advisors Ltd., a Vancouver-based financial planning firm. "The banks know their market and the ultimate test of whether an investment is appropriate is the tummy test."

STRIP BONDS ARE FIXED-INCOME ALTERNATIVES

After the bloom came off the stock market in 2000, more than a few investors took a fresh look at the fixed-income portion of their portfolios. For Canadian RRSP investors, strip bonds, "strips" for short, have long been a favorite fixed-income alternative to the popular GIC. Understanding the concept of strips requires some knowledge about normal government or corporate bonds. Basically, bonds are debt instruments used by corporations or governments to borrow money. They "bond" or promise to repay the lender (you) the money at some point in the future (the maturity date), along with an agreed-upon interest rate paid periodically, also called the "coupon."

However, an investment dealer can "strip" this coupon from the bond, leaving a "residual." Both portions can be sold separately to investors. The coupons are normally sold to individual retail investors. Because they come in maturities of up to 30 years, they are ideal investments for RRSPs or RRIFs. Institutions tend to use the residuals because they can take advantage of time horizons that are often longer than those that apply to coupons. The "coupon" is a promise to pay interest. The bond residual, also called a "zero-coupon" bond, is a promise to pay the principal amount when due, along with any interest coupons that were not stripped away.

Both the coupons and the residual generate interest income because they are sold at a hefty discount to their face value. For this reason, Nate Mechanic, broker with RBC Dominion Securities, compares a strip with "a long-term treasury bill. Instead of maturing in three months, it matures 10 or 20 years later." While some brokers charge a $5,000 minimum to buy strips, there are some who will put through a trade for as little as $1,000. When you buy a strip, you specify the face value – what it will be worth on maturity. The further out that is, the less it will cost per $100 of face value.

THE MARKET PRICE FOR STRIPPED COUPONS RISES AND FALLS WITH INTEREST RATES

For example, the cost is $14.61 to purchase a $100 coupon maturing in 30 years and the yield would be 6.58% annually, says Mechanic. The price includes brokerage commissions. A good explanation of strip bonds is contained in the book *Investing for Income* by Hugh Anderson (Penguin Books, 1996). Like regular bonds, the market price of coupons and residuals "varies as interest rates rise and fall but usually in much bigger swings," Anderson writes. "Their price will, however, gradually rise toward their face value as the time for payment of the face amount approaches."

IF YOU HOLD YOUR STRIPS TO MATURITY, YOU KNOW HOW MUCH THEY ARE WORTH

One advantage of strips is they eliminate re-investment risk. With regular bonds, fluctuations in interest rates can change your return assumptions when it comes time to re-invest – something investors facing rollovers of GICs have found to their dismay. With a strip, there are no interest payments to re-invest. As long as you hold it till maturity, you know exactly how much it will be worth.

The disadvantage may arise if you wish to sell strips before maturity. As Anderson notes, the absence of regular interest payments makes their market prices very volatile. When interest rates rise, strip prices fall further and faster than regular bonds. On the other hand, when interest rates drop, strip prices rise more than regular bonds.

TO AVOID TAXES, KEEP YOUR STRIPS IN AN RRSP

Even though you don't actually receive income from a strip bond every year, Canada Customs and Revenue Agency takes the position that you have received the imputed interest for the year. Therefore, strips are best held inside registered plans rather than outside. Most financial advisers suggest creating a laddered series of strips maturing at different times in your projected retirement.

For RRSP clients, Warren Baldwin, vice-president at no-fee planner T.E. Financial Ltd., prefers strips to most fixed-income alternatives and particularly to bond mutual funds with their hefty management expense ratios. Mechanic likes strips for the fixed-income component of a 45-year-old's portfolio. But he also sees a place for bond funds in RRIFs or for elderly clients who aren't equipped to keep on top of interest rate and bond market shifts.

SEEKING PROFESSIONALLY MANAGED MONEY

It's probably safe to say most Canadian investors end up with a stock broker or financial planner more or less by default. At some point you decided to buy 100 shares of IBM or Bell Canada. Odds are you got a name from a friend or colleague or finally consented to give a shot to a cold-calling new broker. Alternatively, you may have stumbled on a mutual-fund-dispensing "financial planner" at a free "educational" seminar. Either way, you were sold on the services offered. In contrast, discretionary investment management or managed money is bought, says Kelly Rodgers, president of Toronto-based Rodgers Investment Consulting.

Just as people progress through a life cycle that includes adolescence, youth, marriage, parenthood and on up to retirement, there is also an investing life cycle. What Rodgers calls the "life cycle of the high net worth investor" starts with high income, moves to affluence (net worth of between $250,000 and $2 million) and finally to true wealth ($2 million plus). Somewhere along this upward trajectory, the objective changes from "aggressive growth" to "capital preservation."

IF YOUR ASSETS ARE AT LEAST $500,000, YOU NEED AN INVESTMENT COUNSELLOR

Beginning investors tend to start with stockbrokers or mutual funds, in part because they haven't accumulated enough wealth to hire a professional investment counsellor. True discretionary management tends not to be available until you have at least $500,000 in assets, although broker-sold mutual fund "wrap" accounts are available to those with $50,000. The role of investment counsellors is "to meet the unique needs of each client," Rodgers says. Since individual objectives for income and growth vary widely, the first step is for the client and counsellor to determine objectives and develop a portfolio that will meet them.

This process is documented by creating an investment policy statement. The portfolio manager may work with a client's accountants, lawyers, financial planner or other consultants to devise the final investment plan. Responsibility for security selection rests solely with the portfolio manager. This "discretionary" nature of investment counselling is a distinguishing feature of the industry. "For some clients, relinquishing control is initially difficult to accept," Rodgers writes, "but given the education and experience required to qualify as a portfolio manager and the high standards of professionalism that govern the industry, it is more readily accepted over time."

A FINANCIAL COUNSELLOR EARNS PERCENTAGE OF MARKET VALUE OF PORTFOLIO

Counsellors do not receive any compensation or commission for buying and selling stocks, bonds or other securities. "Being free from this potential conflict of interest means that the investment counsellor is rewarded only for managing the portfolio in accordance with the clients' objectives," Rodgers says. This freedom from transaction bias may be the most appealing feature for many investors.

Fees are calculated as a percentage of the market value of the portfolio being managed. Most counsellors have a set fee schedule that tapers down as a portfolio size grows. These charges are considerably lower than those of retail mutual funds or full-service stockbrokers, Rodgers says. Funds invested by investment counsellors are held by an independent custodian, usually a trust company. Custodial service fees may be billed separately or be included in the investment counselling fee. Investment counsellors are regulated by provincial securities commissions and must have distinct educational and work qualifications to become registered.

AN INVESTMENT COUNSELLOR FOLLOWS STRICT ETHICAL AND PROFESSIONAL STANDARDS

Most investment counselling firms are members of the Association of Investment Management & Research. This Virginia-based organization supervises strict ethical and professional standards and awards the chartered financial analyst (CFA) designation carried by many portfolio managers. This does not mean affluent investors do not or should not patronize stockbrokers. The decision to make your own stock picks, with some input from a broker, or to recognize your incompetence or lack of interest and delegate investment decisions to a professional counsellor will obviously vary with your temperament, ability and the time available to spend on your investments.

If you had perfect information, it's true a concentrated portfolio of a few well-chosen stocks may outperform highly diversified managed products. At one point, superinvestor Warren Buffett had US$2 billion spread among just three stocks. But most of us are not Warren Buffetts and neither are our brokers. The brokerage channel accounts for 20% of the $1.2 trillion of Canadian financial assets. Only the deposit-taking branch networks of the banks hold more of our savings, according to Earl Bederman of Toronto-based Investor Economics Inc. Brokerage firms continue to grow. The traditional transaction-based portion of the business (where brokers charge commissions for buying or selling investments) is expanding at 15% a year. Significantly, the fee-based portion is growing at 44%, Bederman says.

EXPECT PERFORMANCE FROM YOUR INVESTMENT COUNSELLOR IN A BEAR MARKET

Many an investor has fled to professionally managed money after experiencing losses on ill-considered stock trades. Such losses may be minimal in a bull market. Investment counsellors have more trouble finding clients when all is going well. It's during a bear market that counsellors really earn their keep, Rodgers says. The hazards of amateur stock-picking have been depicted in such books as Fred Schwed Jr.'s *Where are the Customers' Yachts?* (written in 1940 and republished in 1995 by Wiley Investment Classics). With commissions ranging from 8.5% on small trades to 1.5% on large trades, there's always the temptation for a broker to "churn" your account, contributing to a down payment on a yacht for him, not you.

Some investors who have got to the high net worth stage may opt to keep some of their "fun money" with a broker, the better to bet on junior golds like Bre-X Minerals Ltd. or obscure technology stocks that promise to be "the next Microsoft." But many opt to place the bulk of their assets – their "serious money" – with a discretionary manager. The hard part is to convince yourself you are an amateur investor and that you may have been expecting too much from your broker. You must realize that you and your broker are sharing responsibility for your investment health. "Brokers advise and make recommendations, they do not manage," Rodgers says. "Some people with serious money continue to deal with brokers because they think they're getting management, but they're not."

STOCKBROKERS DON'T HAVE TIME TO EFFECTIVELY MANAGE A HIGH NET WORTH PORTFOLIO

Investors have to be aware of what a broker is licensed and qualified to do and where the final responsibility lies. "If you're the type of client that does what your broker says, then you're abdicating responsibility and should be in a managed product or with a manager," Rodgers says. One investment adviser who works in a brokerage and caters to the high net worth market agrees and recommends using consultants such as Rodgers to pick an investment counsellor. "There are all kinds of strong reasons to go to a fee-based manager over a commission-based broker and probably over a fee-based broker," says the adviser, who asked not to be identified.

A typical broker tracks hundreds of stocks for hundreds of clients. Either they spend so much time on service they can't keep on top of the market or the reverse. More experienced brokers may have fewer, more affluent clients and be better able to juggle those twin demands. For the average investor, "it's a mug's game picking stocks," says the adviser. "Trading stocks on your own is reckless. The only time it may be appropriate is if you buy them for dividends and you hold them for decades."

WHAT ARE STOCKBROKERS' COMMISSIONS?

Do you know how much commission you're paying when you buy stocks through your full-service broker? Odds are you don't. Brokerage houses used to operate on a schedule of fixed commissions, but following deregulation in 1986, they were free to set their own rates. Now, most investors have to wait until they get a confirmation slip to find out how much they've paid the broker.

Shopping around is difficult because many brokerages refuse to provide commission schedules, even to existing clients. This appears to be the way Canada's mostly bank-owned brokerages like it. While the discount brokerage subsidiaries of the banks freely give out their commission schedules, their full-service arms usually decline to provide them when asked. "The firms are sensitive" about commission rates, says one broker. "The discrepancies can be enormous."

Nor does the Investment Dealers Association of Canada centralize this information for investors. Thomas Dalzell, IDAC's former vice-president of government and member relations, says there's wide variation among firms. In an informal survey, he found average commissions worked out to a fairly stiff 3.75% to 4.25% for trades of $2,000 or less. Because of minimum commissions, many investors unwittingly pay 8% or more on trades of $1,000 or less. Most brokers use some variation on a commission grid in which different rates kick in at certain break points. Dalzell found the key break points are at trade values of $2,500, $5,000, $10,000, $25,000, $50,000 and $100,000. The biggest discrepancies are at the lower levels. For a $10,000 trade, most commissions were between 1.36% and 1.8%. They fell to 0.7% to 1.1% at $50,000.

INVESTORS CAN AND SHOULD NEGOTIATE COMMISSION FEES

Based on calls to brokers, the average commission on a Canadian stock trade seems to hover around 2% plus a small per share charge. One RBC Dominion Securities Inc. broker says he charges 2% on all stocks, similar to the average mutual fund commission. If you're a particularly valuable client, a commission of 0.5% to 1% would be considered normal. In fact, at some point the full-service commission may actually be lower than at a discount brokerage. Firms don't like setting rates in stone because investors can and should negotiate better ones. "There's really no such thing as normal commission rates," says TD Evergreen Investment Services vice-president Ana Escubedo. "We allow our investment advisers to be flexible."

Some brokers will give discounts of 20% to 50% or more from the house grid; others won't budge. Commissions also drop rapidly on U.S. trades. If the principal exceeds US$2,500, Wood Gundy's commission on a U.S. trade is 0.9% of the principal value plus $22. Commission on US$20,000 worth of U.S. stock (priced above US$1 a share) is 0.6% plus $82. Beyond US$30,000, it drops to just 0.4% plus $142. Some brokers make a distinction between "unsolicited" trades initiated by the client and those that originate with the brokerage. In the first case, a discount would be appropriate since the broker did little more than execute a trade that any discount brokerage could have done. Beware of the minimum commission of $75 to $85. On a $1,000 trade, that's a hefty 8.5%, or 17% on a round trip (a buy followed by a sell). The minimum charge reflects about half an hour of administrative work.

COMMISSION DISCOUNTS ARE RARELY AVAILABLE ON SMALL TRANSACTIONS

A similar situation crops up in the case of parents or grandparents buying a few shares for their children or grandchildren. The trade doesn't make sense on the numbers alone, although some firms will put them through with a discount for customer goodwill purposes. Commissions on small trades can be three times lower at the discount brokers. But as the full-service firms' grid kicks in at bigger trades, the difference becomes less dramatic. Responsible full-service brokers advise waiting until you have $5,000 to buy a stock. The alternative for smaller amounts is to use a discount brokerage or to buy additional units of a mutual fund.

If you value the services of your full-service broker but don't want to get dinged on small trades, you may get the best of both worlds by maintaining both a full-service and discount brokerage account.

Such a hybrid strategy is now feasible since the discount brokerages have waived their fees on self-directed RRSP accounts of more than $25,000. An alternative is to use DRIPS and SPPs (dividend reinvestment and share purchase plans). This strategy is described in the book *Commission-Free Investing* by Cemil Otar (Uphill Publishing), which focuses on three dozen Canadian blue chips, including BCE Inc. and most of the banks, that allow you to make regular commission-free investments.

CHAPTER 7

TAX | PLANNING

- Tax basics
- Measuring after-tax investment returns
- Income splitting
- Drawing up a strategy
- Trusts

FIVE STEPS TO SIMPLIFYING

TAX-PLANNING UNCERTAINTIES

THE CANADIAN INCOME TAX SYSTEM UNDERWENT momentous change as the new millennium began, but much of this was not apparent to the general public. Previously, all of the provinces except Quebec used Ottawa's definitions of taxable income and piggybacked onto the federal system. Your provincial income tax was simply a certain percentage of your federal income tax. That was called a "tax on tax" structure. Now, each province is setting its own rules and rates. This is called a "tax on income" structure, or TONI. The immediate impact on you may not be that great because TONI is still in transition, but over time you may see major differences as each province seeks to meet its own needs. Fortunately, those outside Quebec will still be able to file just one tax return because the provinces with new TONI systems have hired the Canada Customs and Revenue Agency (formerly Revenue Canada) to administer their tax rules.

Another huge change that was generally overlooked came in 2000 when the federal government restored full inflation-indexing for the income tax system. Since 1986, the system was adjusted annually only for inflation above 3%. That meant tax credits automatically lost value each year and cost of living raises pushed many people into higher tax brackets even though their purchasing power was unchanged.

One big change that has received considerable attention occurred in 2000 when Finance Minister Paul Martin announced two reductions in the taxable portion of a capital gain. Together, they mean that only half of a capital gain now faces tax, the level that was in effect before 1988. That is down substantially from the 75% "inclusion rate" that applied in recent years.

Yet another change affects gays and lesbians. On Jan. 1, 2001 the income tax system recognized them as common-law couples providing they have lived together in a conjugal relationship for at least 12 months. If both partners agree, they can retroactively apply that status to tax returns from 1998 on.

Still, even amid significant changes, the basic concepts of tax planning remain the same. Those concepts can be divided into five categories:

- Tax deferral.
- Income splitting
- Conversion of income.
- Offshore planning.
- Maximizing credits.

Here, then, is a brief description of those five strategies.

TAX DEFERRALS

There is little doubt one of the most significant planning techniques revolves around the deferral of tax payable. There are two potential benefits from deferral: the fact that marginal tax rates may be lower in the future (much retirement planning, such as the use of RRSPs, is based in part on this premise) and the fact that deferring taxes in effect discounts the final bill. Lately, with interest rates low, the discounting effect is less significant than it was. But the value of deferring taxes cannot be underestimated, whether we are looking at short-term deferral or longer-term deferral through the use of companies, tax-sheltered investments or the holding of appreciated assets for later sale.

INCOME SPLITTING

As long as we have a progressive tax system and individuals within the family are separately taxed, there will be major tax benefits in shifting income from the higher income taxpayer to the lower-income individual. Most often, this is done between spouses or between parents and children. In some cases, the tax system itself allows such splitting (for example, through spousal RRSPs) but more often, splitting can be arranged only through careful and sophisticated tax planning. There is little doubt that for the most part, a major trend in amendments to the income tax system in Canada over the past 20 years has been an attack by the government (both through statute amendments and court challenges) on income splitting, which in itself is testimony to the effectiveness of this approach.

CONVERSION OF INCOME

Because different types of income are taxed in different ways, a significant amount of planning revolves around setting the stage to characterize income receipts. For example, Canadian corporate dividends are taxed at lower rates than ordinary employment income. As a result, self-employed people who are incorporated can reap substantial savings by taking part of their remuneration as dividends. The reduction of the capital gains inclusion rate means that for many investors, though not all, capital gains face less tax than dividends. This reverses a previous pattern and suggests that people who count on investment income should review their mix of interest, dividends and capital gains. Also, older Canadians should annuitize some funds to get pension income eligible for the pension income tax credit.

OFFSHORE PLANNING

This technique includes all forms of tax planning involving the use of offshore business plans and residence. As with most forms of tax planning, the laws have been changed so often that planning has become much more difficult and sophisticated than in the past. But greater international mobility means a greater segment of the population is in a position to consider offshore planning, up to and including giving up Canadian residence.

MAXIMIZING CREDITS

One of the major changes in the tax system since its landmark 1978 overhaul has been the replacement of many deductions with tax credits, including refundable credits. Dealing with this system has become a key element of sophisticated tax planning, one which barely existed 20 years ago. This strategy is especially important for people on lower incomes, who should plan to maximize everything from child benefit credits to provincial low-income credits, not to mention avoiding clawbacks on tax credits and transfer payments. Related to this is the avoidance of other levies, such as high probate fees (in Ontario especially) as part of estate planning.

Also linked to this technique is the need to ensure maximum use of allowable deductions, such as for child-care costs, moving expenses and relocation reimbursement, all of which may require sophisticated planning. The tax system has become ever more sophisticated and complicated over the past 25 years. Almost all the changes – even the massive rate cuts in 1981-82, 1987-88 and cuts slated for 2000-2004 – have carried a price added complexity and a system designed to limit the use of basic planning techniques.

Even socially progressive changes, such as the recognition of common-law relationships, were prompted not by a desire to bring the tax system into line with reality but to protect government revenue against "undue" claims for tax credits associated with children born to couples who have chosen not to get married. There is no doubt that tax planning is significantly harder now than it was in 1978, but the basics remain the same. There are only a handful of true tax-planning techniques. All the rest simply represent an attempt to maximize the use of these basic rules. To borrow from an ancient story: "This is the law. All else is commentary."

MAKE TAX RULES WORK TO THE ADVANTAGE

For most people, tax planning is much the same as flossing your teeth. You can't argue with the benefits, but the process is less than toothsome. And while it doesn't make you any extra money, it can help you keep more of what you have already earned. So to help you beat the taxman, here are 10 suggestions for tax planning.

1. A BIG REFUND MAY SEEM LIKE A WINDFALL, BUT IT MEANS POOR TAX PLANNING.

If you have large tax deductions (such as alimony or maintenance, high RRSP contributions, tax shelter investments, business losses, etc.), tell the source deductions department at your local federal tax office. Request permission to have your employer withhold less tax from your paycheque so you can take home more.

2. AVOIDING MORTGAGE INTEREST IS IMPOSSIBLE, BUT IT CAN BE MADE TAX DEDUCTIBLE.

Interest incurred to finance investments or a business is generally tax deductible. Your goal should be to convert all, or at least part, of your mortgage debt into an investment or business loan. For example, you may have a $125,000 mortgage and a $125,000 investment portfolio. Sell the portfolio and use the funds to pay off the mortgage. Immediately borrow the funds again, using the house as security, and repurchase the portfolio. As the purpose of the loan is to buy the investment portfolio (as opposed to a house), the interest is tax deductible.

However, don't forget about the income tax that may arise on the sale of the portfolio, the selling and buying commissions and early mortgage repayment fees. If you don't have an investment portfolio equal to your mortgage, perhaps you have a portfolio that could be liquidated to take advantage of the prepayment privilege that lets you pay down your mortgage by 10% or 15% each year without penalty. The result: part of your mortgage interest becomes tax deductible. If you're self-employed and work out of your home, a portion of your mortgage interest can be deductible, too.

3. CAN YOU EXCHANGE SOME TAXABLE BENEFITS FOR NON-TAXABLE BENEFITS?

How about giving up a little salary in return for employer-funded pension and/or profit-sharing plans? How about club fees where your membership helps further your employer's business opportunities? Changing jobs? This is the best time to negotiate. How about stock options? Do you have to move? Ensure moving expenses and related matters are designed to be tax-free. How about a no- or low-interest home purchase loan? These are not completely tax-free, but less costly than regular mortgages.

4. FOR THE MOST PART, LEAVING CANADA LETS YOU LEAVE OUR TAX SYSTEM BEHIND.

There is, however, a "departure tax." It's an income tax calculated on the assumption you sold all your assets. This "sale" will trigger taxes on accrued capital gains. However, there are many exceptions that you will want to fall into and you should talk to a tax adviser before leaving the country. Don't forget about the tax system of your adopted country. It will want a piece of you, too. Knowledge of your new country's tax system is a must.

5. IS THERE ANYTHING ELSE YOU CAN DO TO BEAT THE TAXMAN?

If your only income is from your job and you are already making your maximum RRSP contributions, is there anything else you can do? Maybe. And you only have to look as far as Mom and Dad. Parents can have significant income tax liabilities when they die. The "death" tax is based on the capital gain calculated under the assumption that the parent's assets are sold at the time of death for a price equal to the current value. The capital gains are taxed in the deceased's final return. Tax is owed but no cash has been received as the sale occurred for income tax purposes only. This tax reduces the value of the estate available to be passed on to the heir. You say your parents have no assets with accruing capital gains?

Don't forget the full value of RRSPs and RRIFs goes into the final return to be taxed. Ouch! Also, if your parents have U.S. assets, there is another tax system to worry about. The U.S. has both income and estate taxes. Ensure your parents' taxes on death are minimized as well as their exposure to U.S. estate tax and provincial probate fees. It's called estate planning – making sure your parents' affairs are organized to the benefit of their heirs and not to the benefit of Canada Customs and Revenue Agency (CCRA).

6. OUR TAX RULES PERMIT MOST OF US TO SELL OUR HOMES ON A TAX-FREE BASIS.

This is true where a home is designated as a principal residence. However, a principal residence does not have to be a city home. It can be the cottage, vacation condo, ski chalet or trailer.

Also, it is not necessary to designate which place is the "principal residence" until one is sold or considered sold (as in the case of death). The general rule is to select the property that has (or will likely have) the greatest capital gain per year of ownership, but remember, this is not always the city place. Until 1982, a husband and wife were both permitted to have their own principal residences and could be eligible for two exemptions. Tax planning in the '70s suggested one spouse own the city home and one spouse own the cottage no joint ownership of either. This sweet deal ended in 1981 but the current rules still allow a partial principal residence exemption on a second family property basically equal to the gain accrued before 1982.

Even better, you can adjust your ownership retroactively to take advantage of these rules. Do it now as the death of one spouse before the ownership change will void the advantage.

7. AFTER TAKING CARE OF YOUR PARENTS, TAKE CARE OF YOUR SPOUSE AND CHILDREN.

Exact tax-planning strategies depend on your income tax rate versus your spouse's and whether your children are older than 18. Your focus should be on family income splitting. You'll have to go through a few hoops to retain the constant level of family income (remember tax planning doesn't increase your income), but have the income spread among family members who are taxed at a lower rate than yourself.

What can you do?

• The spouse with the lower income-tax rate (spouse A) should do all the family's investing. The spouse with the higher rate (spouse B) should pay all living expenses (mortgage, groceries) including spouse A's income tax bill and RRSP contribution. All family investment income is taxed in spouse A's hands.

• Loan spouse A funds to invest, but make sure that the terms of repayment and interest charged are similar to those in the marketplace. The investment return must beat the interest rate on the loan to make this effective. This is your investment adviser's role – not your tax planner's.

• Invest in equity-based mutual funds in the names of your minor children. As the accounts are "in trust" you have control to ensure your children don't blow the money travelling around North America following the latest pop sensation. Capital gain allocations from these funds will be taxed in the children's hands – not yours. (What tax rate is your 11-year-old at?)

The end result: You have control of the funds and you can take advantage of your children's lower tax rates. Warning: Equity funds may also allocate dividend and interest distributions. These will be taxed in your hands. This is not a cost to you as it would be taxed in your hands anyway. The win here is the shifting of the capital gain tax to your children. This is a great way to help with a child's education costs. Don't forget you are the trustee of your children's money. Your role is to ensure the funds are used for the benefit of the children, not yourself.

Children over 18? It gets easier. Give funds (hey, an early inheritance!) to adult children. Even if they're in the same tax bracket as yourself, you may be ahead as your estate has been reduced for probate fee purposes and your lower income may minimize or remove the Old Age Security clawback. If you are the adult child, explain this to Mom and Dad. Make sure they realize you have their best interests at heart. Also, there is no problem in giving a financial gift or loaning funds to children to start a business.

8. WHY NOT HAVE YOUR CHILDREN OWN PART OF YOUR INCORPORATED BUSINESS?

Tax rules permit young children to be shareholders of non-investment businesses in Canada. The children's shares are owned on their behalf by a family trust. Through 1999 it was common for the incorporated business to pay dividends to the trust, which were then used to pay the child's tuition, music lessons, sporting activities, etc. This produced substantial tax savings – so much so that, starting in 2000, the government has a special levy that undermines this strategy by effectively taxing those dividends at top-bracket rates. This measure does not, however, prevent you from doing an "estate freeze" which would hold your children, not you, taxable on future appreciation of your company's shares. As well, each child can qualify for the $500,000 tax-free capital gains allowance for qualified small business shares. In setting up a trust situation, professional advice is essential to make sure you stay within the law.

9. SORRY THIS ONE'S NEITHER SEXY NOR FUN.

Don't miss out on the RRSP because it's an easy way to save taxes and prepare for your retirement. It's easier to sell the idea of an RRSP tax break than to persuade people to focus on the investment yield. Talking to a bank teller on Feb. 28 may not be the smartest move. Take a chance – talk to someone who has the ability to advise you on a variety of RRSP investment alternatives. You can make your RRSP contributions less painfully with automatic monthly payment plans. Take full advantage of the spousal RRSP rules to split retirement income. Don't forget the Home Buyer's Plan and the Lifelong Learning Plan. First-time home buyers can borrow up to $20,000 from their RRSP. The loan is repayable over the next 15 years. If you already have a home, why not give or lend your adult child funds to maximize his or her RRSP tax-deductible contribution, which can then be turned into a Home Buyer's Plan loan? The Lifelong Learning Plan is similar, but provides access to RRSPs in order to finance full-time study. The maximum withdrawal is $20,000 over four years, with no more than $10,000 taken in any one year. Repayments must be made over no more than 10 years, and the first repayment is not due until after you complete the course.

10. THE BEST WAY TO BEAT THE TAXMAN IS TO BE ACTIVE.

None of us, on our own, can influence tax rates or tax rules. So "kwityerbitchin" and start taking advantage of the tax rules (they are not loopholes) now to minimize the tax you and your family pay.

TAX EFFICIENCY THE NEW STANDARD FOR FUNDS

Tax efficiency has recently become one of the buzzwords of mutual fund analysis, and for good reason. Expectations of high investment returns have continued to fall amid low inflation, shrunken yields from fixed-income investments and, more recently, turbulence in equity markets. In this investment climate, putting together a portfolio that shields your returns as much as possible from the ravages of taxation has become all the more desirable. Mutual funds, because of their flow-through characteristics and the various types of income that they generate, present numerous opportunities to reduce taxes. Many tax-saving techniques have to do with funds' underlying assets and the different types of pay-outs they make.

By understanding tax efficiency, an investor is better equipped to choose an optimal mix of assets and decide which funds are best held inside or outside an RRSP or RRIF. Other tax-saving opportunities arise from the timing of an investor's purchase or sale of fund units and when the fund pays out its capital gains. To complement the analysis of the pretax returns and risks of funds, there is now an emerging body of knowledge on tax efficiency. One such initiative has come from Morningstar Canada, formerly Portfolio Analytics Ltd. of Toronto. It has developed a tax-efficiency ratio published monthly on its PAL Trak software, which is sold mainly to financial advisers. A common way to measure tax efficiency – and the approach used by Morningstar Canada – is to do a breakdown of how a fund's total returns after fees and expenses were achieved.

For mutual funds structured as trusts (which include the vast majority), distributions to unitholders are made in one of four ways capital gains, dividends originating from Canadian common or preferred shares, interest from Canadian sources or foreign income from either dividends or interest. These various sources have different implications for taxpayers, depending on individual situations.

Buying in to a fund late in the year may incur unwanted capital gains taxes. This is because mutual funds – mostly those in the equity category – commonly flow through their distributions to unitholders at the end of the calendar year.

The biggest pitfall to avoid is making a purchase late in the year of a mutual fund that has had substantial trading profits during the year and is about to declare a fat year-end capital gains distribution. After the distribution, the fund's net asset value falls by a corresponding amount. As a result, the unitholder who bought before the distribution is stuck paying capital gains tax on profits that he or she didn't really make.

The common solution is to buy into the fund early in the new year so that, if it makes a lot of capital gains during the year, you'll be in on the action. But, depending on the market climate and the individual's situation, some investors might benefit from buying late in the year and accepting a capital gain.

HIGH-TURNOVER PORTFOLIOS ARE BEST HELD IN AN RRSP

Individuals who have started a business this year or those who are expecting a big inheritance next year would have tax rates lower this year than next. They might be better off earning capital gains this year at a lower marginal tax rate. One of the most controversial aspects of tax efficiency is the debate over whether funds with high portfolio turnovers are less tax efficient than those whose managers practice a long-term buy-and-hold style. Turnover matters because there are two ways to earn capital gains on a mutual fund investment.

One source of gains results from the fund manager's trading profits, which are paid out annually to unitholders. The other is entirely up to the individual investor and occurs when fund units are redeemed at a profit, after sales fees. The greater a fund's portfolio turnover, the more likely capital gains will be distributed annually, instead of being built up over time and reflected in the fund's net asset value. The conventional wisdom is that funds with high portfolio turnover should be held inside RRSPs, where

HOW TO USE | TAX-EFFICIENCY DATA EFFECTIVELY

The PAL Trak tax-efficiency ratio is a measure of the percentage of a mutual fund's total return retained after tax by an investor holding the fund in a taxable account. The ratio is calculated over three-year or five-year periods. The highest possible score is 100%, which is achieved by funds that have paid no distributions and whose returns are reflected entirely in an increase in their net asset value.

The tax-efficiency ratio is based on assumptions that, while having the advantage of standardizing the calculations, do not purport to represent the actual tax situation of individual investors. It also assumes the investor is in the top tax bracket.

Interest income is assumed to be taxed at a marginal tax rate of 50%. As a result, almost all money market funds have a tax-efficiency ratio of 50% since their distributions are in the form of interest.

The most favorable treatment by PAL Trak is given to capital gains. This type of distribution is assumed to be taxed at a marginal tax rate of 37.5%. The greater the proportion of a fund's distributions that is generated by capital gains, the more tax efficient it is presumed to be.

An oversimplification in PAL Trak's methodology is the 50% marginal tax rate attributed to distributions of dividends from Canadian corporations.

Although PAL Trak's creator, Portfolio Analytics Ltd., now Morningstar Canada, acknowledges that dividends are taxed at a more favorable rate than interest income, the company says it lacks "comprehensive data" on dividend distributions.

"One can assume, therefore, that funds distributing dividends from Canadian corporations will have an understated tax efficiency," Morningstar Canada cautions its users.

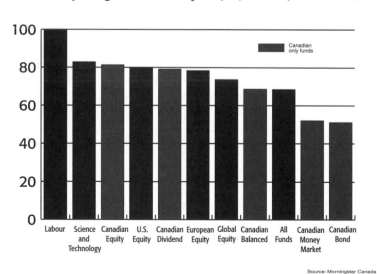

Comparing tax efficiency average 5-year efficiency at December 31, 2000

Source: Morningstar Canada

Most tax-efficient Canadian equity funds

Fund Name	Tax Efficiency 5 Yr	Total Assets $Mill	$ Distrib Dec 31/00	1 Year % Return	5 Year Return*
Optima Strategy Cdn Equity Value Pool	100.00	684.8	0.00	31.2	15.6
AIC Advantage	100.00	2847.0	0.00	26.2	21.9
Integra Equity	100.00	94.3	0.00	7.2	8.4
Investors Retirement Mutual	100.00	1895.3	0.00	17.3	7.1
AIC Diversified Canada	100.00	3693.0	0.00	18.4	23.2
Mac Sentinel Canada Equity	100.00	7.1	0.00	24.5	8.2
Trans-Canada Value	100.00	2.5	0.00	-26.4	3.6
Mac Universal Future	99.75	1878.9	0.00	-0.8	16.7
Scudder Canadian Equity	99.10	320.0	0.16	6.7	15.8
BMO Equity Index	98.88	496.1	0.01	8.2	14.1
TD Canadian Index	98.63	778.9	0.08	7.7	14.4
Bissett Canadian Equity CL F	98.38	689.2	0.99	19.7	17.4
TD Canadian Value	98.25	377.3	0.20	6.3	13.7
AIM Canadian Premier	97.59	905.1	0.00	3.4	18.1
APEX Canadian Growth (AGF)	97.10	48.3	0.00	16.5	11.1
Clean Environment Equity	96.34	254.1	0.00	6.0	11.7
AIM Canada Growth	95.84	1324.6	0.05	-11.3	15.9
Scotia Canadian Growth	95.50	799.1	0.00	9.7	11.8
Mac Ivy Canadian	95.36	5133.4	0.00	20.4	12.6
AGF Canadian Stock	94.60	1582.0	1.00	20.2	15.5
Leith Wheeler Canadian Equity	94.45	55.8	0.00	17.1	14.0
IG AGF Canadian Growth	93.47	784.2	0.00	15.5	7.1
Desjardins Environment	91.84	128.4	0.51	6.3	11.3

Least tax-efficient Canadian equity funds**

Fund Name	Tax Efficiency 5 Yr	Total Assets $Mill	$ Distrib Dec 31/00	1 Year % Return	5 Year Return*
OTGIF Diversified	78.50	77.5	0.24	6.1	14.4
PH & N Canadian Equity Plus Pension Trust	77.96	828.2	12.04	15.4	15.8
Saxon Stock	77.35	14.6	0.92	17.8	11.8
CI Canadian Sector	76.68	49.5	0.00	-6.9	8.8
Optimum Actions	76.57	9.9	2.44	18.4	16.8
Azura Canadian Growth	76.40	18.8	2.77	5.1	10.0
Beutel Goodman Canadian Equity	73.13	11.8	0.09	21.3	10.0
StrategicNova Canadian Large Cap Value	72.72	361.2	0.70	19.8	14.0
Jones Heward Fund Limited	72.50	64.1	2.60	15.5	15.0
Mac Universal Canadian Growth	71.77	1827.9	3.09	19.8	14.0
Trimark Select Canadian Growth	70.05	3838.3	0.49	15.2	9.7
Talvest Canadian Equity Leaders	66.78	140.0	2.21	15.0	12.5
Tradex Equity	66.74	118.6	0.17	11.9	17.0
Chou RRSP	66.02	4.8	1.10	16.5	18.9
Cdn Anaesthetists' Mutual Accumulating	65.57	39.8	0.00	8.3	13.8
Clarica Equifund	62.57	88.5	0.00	-11.3	7.8
Trimark RSP Equity	61.77	1525.4	0.27	17.6	8.9
ABC Fundamental-Value	58.46	155.0	0.16	7.5	11.4
PH & N Vintage	58.07	156.5	5.60	10.5	15.9
National Bank Canadian Equity	57.60	326.2	2.56	14.2	12.0
Trimark Canadian	57.46	2007.7	2.48	16.9	11.3
Altamira Equity	56.33	1574.3	7.51	5.2	10.8
ICM Equity	44.75	129.1	0.51	7.3	8.6
Global Strategy Canada Growth	36.66	189.4	1.27	5.8	5.9
CI Canadian Growth	35.80	819.5	0.80	-6.0	10.2
IMS CDN Growth	13.02	44.1	1.59	-12.8	8.5

* Compound annual return   ** Of those with 5-year records   Source: Morningstar Canada

tax efficiency doesn't matter as much, and that low-turnover funds are more suitable candidates to be held outside RRSPs.

BUY-AND-HOLD INVESTING MAY RESULT IN HEFTY DEFERRED TAX LIABILITY

Some contend that buy-and-hold investing is the surest path to wealth, and portfolio turnover triggers taxes that eat into the investor's returns. But unless a fund does no trading at all, it's untrue to suggest it can avoid tax liability. A fund that has a buy-and-hold policy can generate tax consequences each year if it sells some of its holdings each year.

Furthermore, independent fund analyst Duff Young suggests low-turnover funds may build up hefty deferred tax liabilities. A heavy tax load, as he calls it, might deter a fund manager from selling a security in a portfolio that has become overpriced. By comparison, he says, a high-turnover fund has "almost no tax liability" embedded in its net asset value. It's difficult to reconcile the radically divergent views on the impact of portfolio turnover. But it is safe to say the tax efficiency of a fund will vary. Market conditions, a portfolio manager's investment style or changes in a fund's objectives or managers all can have a significant impact.

TAX EFFICIENCY OF A PORTFOLIO IS DIFFICULT TO PREDICT

A value style and a growth-momentum style could have very different impacts on the after-tax returns of a fund. But both could be volatile year after year, depending on the level of the market and the trading patterns of the manager. Nor, should investors base their expectations of year-to-year distributions on what happened in previous years, unless the fund is a fixed-income fund with low volatility and a low rate of portfolio turnover. Since the degree of consistency associated with yearly equity returns isn't high, neither is its measure of tax efficiency.

Scott Mackenzie, vice-president of Morningstar Canada, agrees tax-efficiency ratios can vary. In addition, he cautions against attaching any significance to precise percentage measures, recommending instead that investors or advisers look at tax efficiency in terms of which funds fall into various ranges. Mackenzie shares the consensus that the most valid measure of tax efficiency is how it affects the individual investor.

"Tax efficiency is not a good or bad thing," he says. "It simply is a factor you should consider when constructing your portfolio."

DIVIDEND SHIFT CAN PROVIDE SAVINGS

Most tax-planning techniques are carried out well in advance of the actual day you sit down to complete your tax return. Exceptions include a decision on which spouse is to claim charitable donations. Another is deciding who claims the family medical expenses.

A third, which can be very useful to those who qualify, is the ability to shift dividend income from one spouse to another. This can be a significant tax saver in some circumstances. The basic rule is found in Subsection 82(3) of the Income Tax Act and applies only if the receipt of dividends by one spouse will reduce the other spouse's claim for a dependent spousal tax credit. Thus, this option is available only to couples in which one spouse is taxable and the other is not and in which the non-taxable spouse receives Canadian source dividends.

In effect, the rules allow the supporting spouse to remove dividend income from the dependent spouse's income and add it to that of the supporting spouse, who can also claim the associated dividend tax credits. For 2001, the federal tax credit on a dependent spouse is reduced when the dependent spouse's income exceeds $629. Thus, shifting the dividends only applies if the dependent spouse's income, including the grossed-up dividends, exceeds $629.

Unfortunately, there is no rule of thumb to quickly determine whether an election is beneficial, since it will depend on the amount of the dependant's income, whether there is income other than dividends, and the marginal tax rate of the supporting spouse. CCRA's Interpretation Bulletin IT-295R4 offers more information.

DIVIDEND TAX CREDIT HAS BENEFITS

Under the Income Tax Act, individuals who receive dividends from taxable Canadian corporations must report 125% of the cash dividends received. The extra 25% is known as the "gross-up" and the full amount is reported on line 120 of the income tax return. The theory behind this gross-up is that when a corporation pays taxes, some part of the tax burden is paid on behalf of shareholders. Today, that figure is arbitrarily set at 25% of the dividends received. In the past it has been as high as 33⅓%. To offset this gross-up, the taxpayer also gets a dividend tax credit. Thus, if a $100 cash dividend is grossed up to $125, there should be a $25 tax credit.

THE GROSS-UP AND BENEFITS SYSTEM WORKS TO TAXPAYERS ADVANTAGE

If you look at the individual tax return, you will find that the federal portion of the credit is 13.33% of the taxable dividends reported – that is, 13.33% of the grossed-up dividend on line 120 of the return. Thus, if you had a $100 dividend and grossed it up to $125, the federal dividend tax credit is ($125 x 13.33%) $16.67. On the other hand, most tax planners calculate the credit using a formula from the act itself, which indicates the dividend tax credit is two-thirds of the rate of the gross-up. Since the rate of the gross-up is 25%, two-thirds of this amount is 16.67% – which is applied to the dividend before it is grossed-up. In other words, it is 16.67% of $100, or $16.67, the same as using the other formula. In both cases, assuming a provincial tax rate of 50%, the dollar value of the tax credit for combined federal/provincial purposes rises to about $25, the amount of the gross-up itself. So when many tax planners offer examples of how the dividend tax credit works, they simply show a combined credit equal to the amount of the gross-up.

The gross-up and credit system benefits taxpayers. It adds $25 to income, meaning a tax increase of perhaps $13 or $14 at the top end of the income range. But the value of the credit is $25, so the system reduces the tax bite overall. The higher the gross-up and credit rate, the better off the taxpayer is.

TOTING UP | THE GROSS-UP

Dividend	$100
Gross-up amount	$25
Taxable dividend	$125
Combined fed/prov tax (at 44%)*	$55
Combined dividend tax credit	$25
Net tax	$30

*Assumes provincial tax equals 50% of federal tax. Calculation is subject to change as provinces implement tax on income system.

A final note on this topic: Figures used here are all approximations, because of variations in provincial tax rates and use of surtaxes. The move to provincial "tax on income" systems makes generalizations even less useful. But for quick calculation purposes, the rules of thumb as set out above are accurate enough to determine the approximate impact of taxation on dividends.

SOME BASIC RULES OF INCOME SPLITTING

Income splitting is the art of transferring income from a person in a high tax bracket to someone in the same family with a low tax bracket. Done legally, the family ends up with more after-tax cash. However, there are rules to keep you from simply shifting assets to your spouse or children. They're called "attribution rules" because they attribute the income from those assets back to you and tax it in your hands. Here's a quick walk through those rules.

SPOUSES

If you simply give your spouse investment money, you face tax on the proceeds. But not if you "sell" assets to your spouse at fair market value, in exchange for other property (or cash). So, maybe you hold an asset that's likely to soar and your spouse will be in a low- or no-tax bracket when it's sold for real. By selling or trading to your spouse, you'd pay tax now on appreciation to date, but all future growth would be taxable for your spouse.

If your spouse doesn't have enough property or cash to do the deal, you can grant a loan, but attribution will apply unless you charge interest. The same goes if you want to lend your spouse money to make an investment.

The rate you charge must be no less than CCRA's quarterly "prescribed rate," which is adjusted every quarter, based on 90-day treasury bill rates in the first month of the preceding quarter. Any fraction is rounded upward to the nearest full percentage point.

But once the loan is established, the rate can be locked in indefinitely, no matter where future prescribed interest rates go. The loan must be fully documented, including proof of funds moving from one bank account to another. The lower tax bracket spouse has to make real interest payments to the high tax bracket spouse within 30 days of each calendar yearend. Like all income, that interest must be declared on the annual tax form of the high earner. But the low-bracket spouse normally gains a tax deduction on the interest paid.

Brian Quinlan, a chartered accountant, uses the example of a couple named Richard and Fiona to show the results of this strategy. Richard is taxed at the top bracket. He lends Fiona $50,000 to invest. As she earns much less, she is taxed at just 26%. The couple documents the loan with a promissory note prepared by a lawyer, stating interest is 4% and is payable no later than Jan. 30 following each calendar year. Richard would pay tax on the first 4%, since that is the interest he receives from Fiona.

At the same time Fiona would claim a deduction based on the same 4% charge. The investment income beyond the initial 4% is taxed in Fiona's name at her lower marginal tax rate. For example, if the investment yielded 9% a year, Fiona would pay tax on 5%.

This same strategy could be applied to children. The easiest way to take advantage of the tactic is to make a loan, but if you do not have ready cash, it is possible to transfer investments owned outside an RRSP to low-bracket family members. The family member would pay you by giving you a promissory note. The transferred investment must be treated as if it had been sold at its current value.

A similar opportunity is also available if your employer lends you money to acquire a home. The prescribed rate would be deemed a taxable benefit, but can be locked up for five years. And if you receive a qualifying home relocation loan, you could gain an additional tax break.

There are two alternatives to the loan route. One involves "second-generation income." Say you give – not lend – your spouse $10,000 to buy a GIC that compounds at 5%. Each year you face tax on the first-generation income – the $500 of interest on $10,000 of capital. But all interest subsequently earned by that $500 belongs to your spouse without attribution. Attribution rules also do not apply to income from an active business. So you can lend or give money to an entrepreneurial spouse. But it must be a true business.

MINOR CHILDREN

The attribution rules also apply to children under 18 as well as grandchildren, great-grandchildren, nieces and nephews, with two exceptions. There is no attribution on capital gains earned by a minor. So you could give your child money for an equity mutual fund. But attribution is supposed to apply to interest and dividends on the capital. Also, with gifts – as opposed to loans – a minor's attribution stops at the end of the year in which the child turns 18.

ADULT CHILDREN AND OTHER FAMILY MEMBERS

Attribution applies to loans – but not gifts – to family members such as parents, siblings, grandparents and grandchildren. But that's if it's an investment loan aimed at reducing your taxes. The rules do not prevent Mom and Dad from funding a child's home mortgage. This attribution does not apply to nieces or nephews. Nor does it apply if you charge interest on the same terms as the spousal loan discussed above. Be careful about getting clever, though. There are anti-avoidance rules aimed at preventing you from funneling money through a third party to your spouse or child.

There are also rules to keep you from avoiding attribution by replacing initial assets or loans with new ones.

FAMILY EXPENSES

Each spouse has a separate bank account. The higher-taxed one pays all family expenses, leaving the other's full income for investment. If the lower-taxed spouse owes tax when the yearly return is due, the other can foot that bill so the low-taxed money stays invested.

GIFTS AND INHERITANCES

The same as above. Say you earn far less than your mate and receive money from your parents. Invest that in your own name so its earnings are taxed at your lower rate. Many people have relatives outside Canada. There is no attribution on money from someone who's not a Canadian tax resident. Say your parents send your newborn $10,000. That can be invested in trust for the child.

SPOUSAL RRSP

This is usually a long-term plan aimed at balancing a couple's retirement income. But spousal RRSP contributions can work in the short term, too, if one spouse plans to stop work in a few years.

TESTAMENTARY TRUST

This trust is created on the death of the person providing the money. Say you'll leave a pile of cash to your spouse to support the family. The investment income would all be taxable in his or her hands. Instead, your will could create a trust for each family member so his or her share of the income gets taxed at his or her progressive rates.

CHILD TAX BENEFIT

This cheque can be invested in your child's name without attribution. Save it for post-secondary education.

REGISTERED EDUCATION SAVINGS PLANS

Investment earnings are tax-deferred until withdrawn and then get taxed in the student's hands. RESPs became very popular after 1998 when the federal government introduced a subsidy. The Canada Education Savings Grant tops up the plan by 20% of each year's contributions, subject to a yearly maximum of $400 per child. In other words, if you contribute $2,000, Ottawa will add $400. That $400 annual entitlement starts in the year of birth and runs through the year in which the child turns 17. If the child does not pursue post-secondary education, the RSEP must repay the grants but gets to keep all of the earnings on that money. RESPs have also become popular because there are more flexible rules for what happens if the child does not continue past high school.

Previously, subscribers – the adults who fund the plan – got back their capital but sacrificed all earnings. Now, they still get back their contributions but also have access to the earnings. If they have RRSP room available, they can use up to $50,000 of RESP earnings as tax-deductible RRSP contributions. This does not increase their RRSP limits; it just provides a source of funds. RESP earnings that can't go into an RRSP can be taken as income. In that case, the money is fully taxed plus there's an additional 20% tax to keep people from using the plans simply as tax shelters. In the past, parents were advised not to use child tax benefit money for RESPs because the child tax benefit carried the same tax breaks even if invested separately. That's still advisable now if parents can otherwise afford RESP contributions. If they can't, the 20% federal grant can justify putting the child tax benefit into the plan.

CHILD'S ALLOWANCE
Pay all your teenager's expenses so he or she can save all part-time and summer job money for college or university. Children who file tax returns will be able to make RRSP contributions. So part of the savings could be tax-sheltered until withdrawal for school.

CPP/QPP SPLITTING
Retirees can have up to half their Canada or Quebec Pension Plan payments made to their spouses if both are at least 60. The split depends on a formula that factors in the contribution periods and marriage duration.

SELF-EMPLOYMENT OPPORTUNITIES
You can pay your spouse and child reasonable salaries for bona fide services.

FIVE CREDITS CAN BE TRANSFERRED TO SPOUSE

If one spouse's income is so low that he or she does not pay any taxes, then the other spouse can claim his or her unused non-refundable credits to reduce taxes further. There are actually five tax credits that can be transferred from one spouse's tax return to the other. They are the amounts for:
• Tuition fees.
• Education.

- Age (65 or older).
- Pension.
- Disability credits.

You are entitled to claim only the unused portion of these credits, meaning your spouse must use as much of them as required – along with credits for the basic amount, Canada Pension Plan contributions and employment insurance premiums – to reduce income taxes to zero first. These credits are transferred using Schedule 2 of the income tax return.

SPOUSE CAN CLAIM UP TO $5,000 OF EDUCATION EXPENSE

The tuition fee credit may be claimed if course fees during the year are greater than $100, in which case the actual amount of tuition can be claimed. The education credit is available only to full-time students, although the rules on what constitutes full time have been liberalized in recent years. Up to $5,000 in combined tuition fees and education amount may be transferred to your return from your spouse's. Receipts and forms to support claims for the tuition and education credits need not be submitted to CCRA when a tax return is filed. But they must be retained by the taxpayer, since the tax department may ask you to submit them later.

VARIOUS OTHER CREDITS CAN ALSO BE CLAIMED BY SPOUSE

You can claim the age 65 or older credit but bear in mind that it will be reduced 15% for each dollar of income above the maximum, set around $27,000. The credit disappears entirely if the taxpayer's net income exceeds about $51,000.

Amounts eligible for the pension credit include annuity payments from pension plans, RRIFs and other pension-related sources. It may be worthwhile to arrange your affairs so that your spouse receives at least $1,000 of eligible income annually to take advantage of this tax break.

Finally, the disability credit is available to taxpayers who have a severe and prolonged mental or physical impairment. To qualify for the credit, a physician must certify on CCRA form T2201 that the individual suffers from an ailment that significantly restricts his or her daily activities. The impairment must be expected to last for a continuous period of at least 12 months.

CALCULATING OTTAWA'S CUT CAN BE TAXING

Investors with stocks, mutual funds or other non-RRSP investments that generate capital gains face complications when filing their income tax returns. If you have sold securities outside your RRSP or RRIF, you're obliged to report the transactions on your tax return and pay capital gains tax if you made a profit. While your broker's statement should provide details of such transactions, there is no tax information slip to attach to your return when reporting capital gains, as there is for dividends and interest. But don't assume that because no one sent you a tax slip on the transaction that CCRA will not be aware of it. All capital gains realized during a taxation year must be reported on Schedule 3 of that year's tax return.

ONUS OF CLAIMING CAPITAL GAINS IS ON THE INVESTOR

The tax department used to rely on the honor system for reporting capital gains, and that's still the case for real estate transactions and interest payments under $50. However, investment dealers are required to file a Statement of Securities Transaction – form T5008 with CCRA, which reports sales of securities held directly by investors. Most fund companies have permission to file the T5008 electronically, so no form is sent to the unitholder. However, the information to make computations is provided to unitholders in the annual statements. Stocks not sold through an investment dealer, such as through employee stock purchase plans, may escape this net, which puts the onus on the taxpayer to report gains.

Unfortunately, it's no simple matter to calculate your resulting tax bill. The biggest problem involves calculating an investment's adjusted cost base (ACB). ACB typically must be computed by a mutual fund investor who buys units of a fund on a monthly basis, or engages in frequent switching, buying and selling of units. Obviously, you cannot compute a capital gain without first calculating your original cost. What's worse is that your fund company can't always do this for you because you may have purchased the same fund from more than one broker. And your broker can't do it for you because you may have bought through more than one broker.

DISTRIBUTIONS FROM FUNDS MUST BE CLAIMED BY TAXPAYER

CCRA is in no better position, which puts the onus squarely on the taxpayer, or on a competent tax preparer or other independent adviser working on your behalf. This is an area that confuses many brokers and financial planners, so it's worth figuring it out on your own. The effort is worth it because you might otherwise end up paying too much capital gains tax. An excellent source of information on this subject is found in AIM Funds Management Inc.'s four-part Taxation & Estate Bulletins.

Capital gains realized when mutual fund units are sold should not be confused with those on T3 slips that itemize distributions, which are capital gains, dividends and interest flowed through to investors by a fund. Funds distribute this income because Canada Customs and Revenue Agency (CCRA) classifies funds as flow-through entities. As a result, investors generally must pay some tax on a fund investment each year, even if you do not sell any units of the fund. Distributions usually occur once a year, but sometimes more frequently. Instead of a fund paying capital gains tax or being taxed on dividends or interest at the top marginal income tax rate, unitholders are taxed on these amounts, possibly at lower marginal rates. Distributions are deemed for tax purposes to have been received by the investor in cash, even if they are automatically reinvested in additional fund units.

CALCULATING | ADJUSTED COST BASE

Adjusted cost base sample calculations

Mutual fund investment		Cost	No. of units	Adjusted cost base per unit (ACB)
		A	B	A ÷ B
January 2, 1999	Opening balance	$ 80,000.00	5,000.000	$ 16.00
December 31, 1999	Reinvested distribution (@ $20.50)	2,050.00	100.000	20.50
		82,050.00	5,100.000	16.09
December 31, 2000	Reinvested distribution (@ $21.35)	2,180.00	102.108	21.35
		84,230.00	5,202.108	16.19
March 15, 2001	Purchase (@ $22.00)	11,000.00	500.000	22.00
		95,230.00	5,702.108	16.70
November 17, 2001	Partial redemption (@ $25.00*)	(16,700.00)	(1,000.000)	16.70
		78,530.00	4,702.108	16.70
December 10, 2001	Reinvested distribution (@ $24.60)	2,500.00	101.626	24.60
ACB – December 31, 2000		**$ 81,030.00**	**4,803.734**	**$ 16.87**

* Ignored for ACB calculation – see below.

Calculation of capital gain

In the above example, a partial redemption of 1,000 units at $25.00 per unit was made on November 17, 2001.

THE CAPITAL GAIN WOULD BE CALCULATED AS FOLLOWS:	
Proceeds at $25.00 per unit ($25.00 X 1,000)	$ 25,000.00
Adjusted cost base at $16.70 per unit ($16.70 X 1,000)	(16,700.00)
Redemption fees (deferred sales charge) – assumed	(125.00)
Capital gain	**$ 8,175.00**

Source: AIM Funds Management Inc.

PAYING TAXES ANNUALLY REDUCES TAXABLE CAPITAL GAINS AT REDEMPTION

This is where considerable confusion arises over a fund investment's adjusted cost base. The cost of the new units increases the ACB of your total investments, says Nathan Mechanic, a broker with RBC Dominion Securities Inc. The result is good news designed to prevent double taxation – a reduced taxable capital gain when you redeem your total holdings some time in the future. "Failure to note this increase in ACB could result in subsequently overpaying your capital gains tax over time, especially in a situation where an estate is filing returns and proper records haven't been kept," Mechanic says.

UMBRELLA STRUCTURES ALLOW SWITCHES, WHICH AVOID CLAIMING CAPITAL GAINS

When you do redeem fund units, calculate your capital gain by subtracting the ACB and expenses from the sale price of your units in the fund. Expenses can include commissions, redemption fees and transfer fees. Keep in mind that the "average unit cost calculation" provided in annual account statements is not necessarily the same as the ACB, nor will the statement take into account deemed redemptions, which can occur when beneficiaries change upon death, for example. Note, too, that transferring between funds is considered a redemption for tax purposes; hence the popularity of "umbrella" mutual fund structures that shield such switches. Under these structures you can switch, for example, between a fund family's European equity fund and its U.S. fund or between an equity fund and a bond or money market fund, without creating a disposition and realizing a capital gain.

IT IS THE INVESTOR'S RESPONSIBILITY TO CALCULATE ACB ON INCOME TAX FORMS

If you deal with just one broker and a few fund companies, you can ask the broker to get the companies to calculate the ACB for you. If you simply take a stab at guessing the ACB, don't assume CCRA's computers are going to recalculate and rule in your favor. The AIM Mutual Funds Taxation & Estate Bulletins cited above notes that dispositions for tax purposes don't normally appear on client statements as specific redemptions or transfers, nor does the company have to report them to CCRA.

The onus is on the taxpayer to report them. Failure to do so is considered tax evasion. Another situation to be wary of is a financial institution mistakenly issuing a tax information slip for income that is meant to be sheltered within an RRSP or RRIF. If you own the same fund inside and outside an RRSP, make sure you're being taxed only on the one held outside.

TAX RULES HAVE MAJOR IMPACT ON RETURNS

Investors should always be guided by two rules. First, investment decisions should be made on the basis of investment data, not tax issues alone. Second, tax issues must be taken into account in determining your final return from an investment – a key element in deciding whether to make dividend-paying or interest-bearing investments. The issue is often joined when it comes to deciding whether to sell or hold an investment. The timing of a sale, which triggers a capital gain or a loss, may best be determined by an impending year-end.

CAPITAL LOSSES CAN ONLY BE USED TO OFFSET CAPITAL GAINS

Generally, if you want to realize a gain, a delay until after year-end postpones tax liability. If you want to trigger a loss, the sale should be made before year end. However, since capital losses can only be offset against capital gains, not against ordinary income, some matching makes sense. Consider a not-uncommon situation. You rode the stock market wave and held your stocks and bonds when the market fell. Common sense may have told you to lock in those gains (or what you had left) by selling. But on the other hand, some of those stocks may have been good long-term holds. And to complicate matters, if you locked in the gains, you locked in the potential tax liability. Ironically, those who jumped on the bandwagon late and undoubtedly suffered, may have had the easiest way out. The financial pain associated with the sale of shares at a considerable loss could at least be mitigated in the long run by using the losses to offset gains on other investments.

INVESTORS SHOULD PLAN TO SELL LOSERS IN SAME CALENDAR YEAR AS WINNERS

While this sort of planning will never recoup dollar for dollar what has been lost on a stock, it can ease the overall tax bite. The general rule of thumb many investors follow when liquidating winners is to try to sell losers in the same calendar year to ease the tax bite. If you have winners you want to stick with, you have two options. You can simply hold them until you feel it is right to sell them or you can sell them now, take the gain and repurchase them. Realizing the gain should be done with a recognition that either you have offsetting losses or a tax bill will be forthcoming.

CAPITAL LOSSES CAN BE CARRIED FORWARD INDEFINITELY

If your losers in a year are in excess of your winners or if you want to dump losers while retaining winners, bear in mind that capital losses can be carried forward indefinitely and set off against future capital gains. Repurchasing winners after a sale to realize the gain is easy. But in the case of losers, the issue is more complicated from a tax perspective. Suppose you have a loss on a stock in which you still have confidence over the longer haul. If you just hold on, no loss is recognized. But you may choose to sell to offset gains realized on winners. If you do this, you have to understand the superficial loss rules.

In a nutshell, if you or a person "affiliated" with you sells a stock at a loss and acquires the same stock within 30 days of the sale (either before or after), the loss will not be recognized for tax purposes. ("Affiliation" basically means your spouse or a corporation with which you do not deal at arm's length.) The amount of the loss will simply be added to the cost base of the repurchased shares. Having a good understanding of the basic rules relating to when gains and losses are realized for tax purposes, how losses can be used against gains and the pitfalls of the superficial-loss rules will help minimize the tax bite associated with having stocks that have made a large move. You can, however, sell a losing position in a non-registered plan and simultaneously repurchase it inside an RRSP without the CCRA considering it a superficial loss.

A LOOK AT SOME KEY TAX NUMBERS

Here are some tax numbers that may prove to be handy in your financial planning. They reflect federal and provincial budget changes during 2000.

• The capital gains inclusion rate dropped from 75% to 50% as of Oct. 18, 2000.

• Canada Pension Plan contribution rates have been raised to 8.6% of pensionable earnings up to $38,300 for 2001. No contributions are due on the first $3,500 of income.

• When you turn 69, you must "mature" your RRSP by the end of the same year. To prolong the tax-sheltering effect, your options are to convert to a RRIF and/or an annuity. If converting to a RRIF, your first withdrawal does not have to be made until the end of the following year. You can also prolong your tax shelter by basing the RRIF withdrawals on the age of your spouse, if younger.

• The maximum Canadian Child Tax Benefit for a family's first child is scheduled to rise to $2,365 in mid-2001, and is slated to increase further to more than $2,500 for a family with one child.

• Payments under child support agreements signed or changed after May 1, 1997 are no longer taxable for the recipient parent nor deductible for the payor.

• A new reporting requirement for assets over $100,000 held outside Canada was introduced in 1999.

• In 2001, the threshold for Old Age Security recipients is $55,309 of net income. Recipients lose benefits based on whichever is less, the amount received or 15% of net income over the threshold. The seniors' $3,619 age credit is reduced by net income over $26,941 and is lost entirely when income passes $51,068 (separate rules apply to the Quebec seniors' benefit).

• As of 2001, the government has established four, rather than three, federal tax brackets: A 16% tax rate on income above a minimum threshold up to $30,754; a 22% tax rate is applied on income between $30,755 and $61,509; a 26% rate on income between $61,510 and $100,000; and the newly-introduced "upper middle tax bracket" of 29% on further income exceeding $100,000.

• The maximum RRSP contribution limit has been frozen at 18% of earned income to a maximum of $13,500 per year until 2004, after which it is slated to increase by $1,000 a year until it reaches $15,500; thereafter, it will be indexed to growth in the average industrial wage.

• The foreign content limit on RRSPs was increased from 20% to 25% for the 2000 tax year and rose to 30% in 2001.

• Self-employed individuals may deduct one-half of their CPP/QPP contributions after Jan. 1, 2001, while the rest remains eligible as a tax credit.

• The basic personal amount is now $7,412.

• The disability amount is now $6,000.

• The medical expense threshold is now $1,678.

• The married amount is $6,294 if a spouse's net income is up to $629. Partial credit may be available if spousal income is above that level.

• Charitable donation credit: The federal credit is now 16% on the first $200 of donations and 29% on the excess. The maximum annual claim was increased to 75% of annual net income in the 1997 federal budget, and this limit now applies to gifts to the Crown as well. The limit is 100% of net income in the year of death. (Special rules apply in Quebec.)

• RESPs: The maximum contribution to a Registered Education Savings Fund has been increased from $2,000 to $4,000 a year per beneficiary, although the cumulative lifetime limit remains at $42,000 per beneficiary. Also, the rules regarding forfeiture of earnings have been relaxed.

• Deductible leasing costs for newly acquired vehicles are capped at $800 a month plus taxes.

DEBT REDUCTION IS A GOOD INVESTMENT

Having a tough time with your investments? Would you like to earn 15% to 20% or more, risk-free? Just pay down your debts – and don't add to them. The accompanying tables show why accountants and financial planners nag clients to pay off debts that are not tax-deductible. Few investments pay anywhere near as well. That's mainly because of taxation. Now that the $100,000 capital gains exemption is dead, nearly all personal investment income is earned in pretax dollars. Meanwhile, payments on consumer loans are made in after-tax dollars.

PAYING DOWN DEBT CAN PUT PRETAX DOLLARS IN YOUR POCKET

The key is your marginal tax rate – the tax on your last dollar of income. Say you have taxable income this year of about $50,000. Your marginal rate on fully taxed income is about 40% (depending on province). So you must earn $1.67 to be able to pay $1 of interest on a loan. Since capital gains are taxed more lightly, the break-even point for earning that after-tax dollar would be $1.25. Now, suppose you have $5,000 parked in a money-market fund, waiting for a clear sign that the stock market is turning up

MARGINAL | TAX RATES

2001 combined federal-provincial marginal tax rates

for top-bracket taxpayers, including surtaxes and provincial flat taxes, based on budgets brought down in 2000 and subject to change after provincial budgets are brought down in 2001.

	Dividends %	Capital Gains %	Other Income %
British Columbia	36.0	24.4	48.7
Alberta	24.7	19.8	39.5
Saskatchewan	29.6	22.5	45.0
Manitoba	34.0	23.3	46.5
Ontario	31.3	23.2	46.4
Quebec	34.1	24.6	49.2
New Brunswick	31.6	23.4	46.8
Nova Scotia	32.0	23.7	47.3
Prince Edward Island	32.0	23.7	47.3
Newfoundland	34.2	24.3	48.6
Yukon	28.6	21.2	42.3
Northwest Territories	28.4	21.0	42.1
Nunavut	28.4	21.0	42.1

Source: PriceWaterhouseCoopers

again. Suppose you also have a 9% car loan. Look at the tables on the following page. Use the column for a 40% marginal tax rate and read down to the row for a 9% loan. Using that $5,000 to reduce the car loan is about the same as earning 15% in pretax interest or 11.3% in capital gains.

CASHING IN INVESTMENT FUNDS TO PAY OFF DEBT CAN EARN YOU MORE

Here's the logic. At 9%, a $5,000 loan costs $450 in interest payments for the year. For simplicity, these examples ignore compounding or whether the loan payment consists of a blend of principal and interest. Earning 15% in fully taxed interest brings you $750, but – at a 40% marginal rate – the tax collector takes $300. That leaves you with $450 to pay the interest on the loan. Earning an 11.3% capital gain brings you $565. Half of that – or $282.50 – will be taxed. At a 40% marginal rate, that costs you $113. Subtract that tax from the $565 gross gain and you net just about $450 – the amount due on the loan. The last row on the tables – 28.8% – is the rate for some charge cards issued by retail stores. Rates on Visa and MasterCard credit cards from financial institutions have ranged to 18.9%. But the gap between charge cards and credit cards is actually even greater. Charge cards typically compound interest monthly, so the posted 28.8% rate really works out to 32.9% if the balance is outstanding for a full year. Credit cards, however, don't compound interest.

Curiously, an Angus Reid poll done for Ernst & Young found that 58% of respondents with outstanding balances said they'd prefer to pay down their bank cards before their charge cards. In the above example, debt reduction means you'll lose use of that $5,000. But you'll free up cash flow that can then be invested. Why not calculate your monthly interest savings from the loan pay-down and invest that amount each month in an equity mutual fund? You'll build wealth over time and sleep a lot easier as you average out the market's ups and downs.

YOU'RE NEVER TOO YOUNG TO FILE A TAX RETURN

When the annual blizzard of tax returns hits homes across Canada, there may well be some people – including a great many young people – who should consider filing even though they haven't received forms from CCRA. The Income Tax Act says that if tax is payable, an individual must file a return. But these days, about one-third of the more than 20 million tax returns are filed by individuals who do not owe any tax. This is because in the past 10 or 15 years there has been a steady blending of the federal transfer system with the tax system so that many payments, ranging from Old Age Security to Family Benefits, are in fact linked to the tax system. The net result is that anybody eligible for federal or provincial transfer payments or refundable tax credits must file a return to ensure they receive those benefits.

MANY TAX CREDITS ARE CALCULATED BASED ON YOUR TAX RETURN

For many years, low-income parents have effectively been forced to file a return to get benefits associated with having children. When the goods and services tax came into

DEBT REDUCTION | VERSUS INVESTMENT

Debt reduction versus fully-taxed investment

Loan rate %	25%	30%	35%	40%	50%
		Equivalent pre-tax investment return %			
5.0%	6.7	7.1	7.7	8.3	10.0
6.0%	8.0	8.6	9.2	10.0	12.0
7.0%	9.3	10.0	10.8	11.7	14.0
8.0%	10.7	11.4	12.3	13.3	16.0
9.0%	12.0	12.9	13.8	15.0	18.0
10.0%	13.3	14.3	15.4	16.7	20.0
12.0%	16.0	17.1	18.5	20.0	24.0
14.0%	18.7	20.0	21.5	23.3	28.0
16.0%	21.3	22.9	24.6	26.7	32.0
18.0%	24.0	25.7	27.7	30.0	36.0
20.0%	26.7	28.6	30.8	33.3	40.0
22.0%	29.3	31.4	33.8	36.7	44.0
28.8%	38.4	41.1	44.3	48.0	57.6

Approximate marginal tax rate

Debt reduction versus capital gains investment

Loan rate %	25%	30%	35%	40%	50%
		Equivalent pre-tax investment return %			
5.0%	5.7	5.9	6.1	6.3	6.7
6.0%	6.9	7.1	7.3	7.5	8.0
7.0%	8.0	8.2	8.5	8.8	9.3
8.0%	9.1	9.4	9.7	10.0	10.7
9.0%	10.3	10.6	10.9	11.3	12.0
10.0%	11.4	11.8	12.1	12.5	13.3
12.0%	13.7	14.1	14.5	15.0	16.0
14.0%	16.0	16.5	17.0	17.5	18.7
16.0%	18.3	18.8	19.4	20.0	21.3
18.0%	20.6	21.2	21.8	22.5	24.0
20.0%	22.9	23.5	24.2	25.0	26.7
22.0%	25.1	25.9	26.7	27.5	29.3
28.8%	32.9	33.9	34.9	36.0	38.4

Approximate marginal tax rate

force, the associated tax credit required a tax return to be filed even if the person has no income. When the tax system started to recognize common-law marriages, it meant many young people were deemed to be married and thus had to file to be eligible for the GST credit. Almost all students at post-secondary schools should file tax returns, not only for the GST credit but because they may, depending upon the province, be eligible for a range of provincial tax credits that are linked to the tax system and require filing to make a claim. (Experience indicates many students fail to file unless prodded by parents and thus lose benefits, including the GST refund and credits linked to rent paid while away at school.)

INCOME CLAIMED BY YOUNG PEOPLE CAN BE CARRIED FORWARD FOR RRSP PURPOSES
The 1996 federal budget contained a provision that should have had the effect of increasing tax filings by young people. The seven-year limitation for the carry-forward of RRSP contribution eligibility was eliminated, meaning all earned income will qualify for RRSP contributions indefinitely. But that's only if CCRA is aware of the earned income. Suppose a young person living at home with parents gets a summer job and earns $1,200. In the past, he or she probably wouldn't file a tax return since no tax would be payable and the person was too young to be eligible for any of the other credits available. Furthermore, if the child were planning on attending a post-secondary school, the likelihood of having an RRSP within seven years was slight.

But with an unlimited carry-forward, things have changed. If the youth earns $1,200 a year from age 15 to 18, say a total of $4,800, he or she can contribute 18% of this amount, or $864, to an RRSP any time in the future. The key is that a return would have to be filed so CCRA knows the income was earned. (If there had been withholding tax, the filing of the return might also produce a modest refund.) Most individuals would normally start filing at age 19 in any event, to be eligible for the GST credit, but voluntary early filings might offer a deferred tax opportunity in the form of extra RRSP room when they do go to work.

Actually, if a financial organization agrees, a youngster can open an RRSP and make a contribution based on his or her allowable room. That gets the money growing on a tax-sheltered basis. There is, however, no point in the youngster claiming the associated tax deduction for the year in which the contribution is made. That's because a deduction is worthless for someone who doesn't earn enough to owe tax. The youngster can, however, indicate on Schedule 7 that he or she wishes to carry forward that deduction for use in a future year.

HELPING TEENAGERS FILE THEIR OWN RETURNS IS A FIRST LESSON IN TAX PLANNING
If a young person has never filed a return before, forms can be obtained from many sources. Once filing has occurred, the appropriate return will be sent automatically in future years. We also suggest that the youth, with parental help, do the return personally so the significance of filing is brought home at an early age. Obviously, one wouldn't want to pay a fee for having this sort of non-taxable return prepared. Since few

youngsters truly understand the nature of the income tax system and the obligations and opportunities it offers, this can be a very useful exercise. The benefits are long term, not immediate, but that too is a lesson in tax planning that is worth imparting.

BE CAREFUL SETTING UP "IN-TRUST" ACCOUNTS

Parents and other relatives often put child tax benefit cheques and other cash into bank accounts in a child's name, usually as an "in-trust-for" account so they can make deposits and withdrawals on the child's behalf. Interest from savings stemming from child tax benefit payments is taxed in the child's hands. Interest from other deposits is attributed back to a parent or other relative. Mutual funds and even stocks or bonds also are frequently held in an in-trust investment account, the assumption being any interest or dividend distributions will be reported on the contributor's tax return but capital gains will be taxed in the child's hands.

However, Lorn Kutner, a tax partner with Toronto-based chartered accountants Mintz & Partners, warns capital gains from these informal accounts may well be attributed back to the contributor.

THE PERSON WHO SETS UP AN "IN-TRUST" ACCOUNT MUST CLAIM ANY CAPITAL GAINS

For a trust to be a valid entity, Kutner says the settlor – the person who sets up (and usually funds) the trust – must formally transfer the property to the trust's trustees. "CCRA's published opinion is that an in-trust-for account is an informal trust arrangement which permits the transferor to withdraw the investment for their personal benefit. Therefore a true transfer of the funds has not taken place and any income, or capital gains, will remain the client's."

Even if there is a formal trust, you must ensure it is set up properly so that attribution of capital gains will not occur. Kutner cites Subsection 75(2) of the Income Tax Act, which says clearly that any income or loss from property, as well as any taxable capital gain or allowable capital loss from the disposition of property, is attributed to the person from whom the property was directly or indirectly received, if the trust states that the assets may revert to that person or that other beneficiaries may later be named by that individual. There also may be attribution if distribution from the trust requires the consent of the source of the assets. "Many in-trust-for arrangements seem to fit these criteria since [the person who contributed the assets] will have the power to withdraw funds or must consent to any sale," Kutner says.

BEFORE ENTERING A TRUST AGREEMENT, DETERMINE WHO PAYS TAX ON INCOME GENERATED

There is another potential problem, says Kutner, which often lurks in some brokers' off-the-shelf trust agreements that define the person setting up and funding the trust as the account's beneficial owner, not the trustee. "This will be fatal from CCRA's perspective and attribution of income will occur," he warns. He adds that if Subsection

75(2) is applicable to a trust, the assets cannot be distributed to the beneficiaries at their tax cost. "The property is distributed at fair market value so that, if it had gone up in value, a capital gain – and a tax liability – is created." These concerns might seem extreme for many taxpayers, but it appears CCRA has the right to tax capital gains in the hands of many parents, grandparents, aunts and uncles who are either too casual about how they transfer money to children or who concoct elaborate trust arrangements with too many strings attached.

DISABILITY CREDIT SCRUTINIZED BY TAXMAN

A generation or so ago, it seemed the vast majority of tax appeals had to do with capital gains, driven in part by the favorable treatment given this form of income. Nowadays, a large percentage of cases have to do with the disability tax credit. This credit is worth a maximum of $960 at the federal level, or about $1,400 for combined federal-provincial purposes in most provinces.

Consider the situation where an individual has a severe and prolonged mental or physical impairment. The effects of the impairment are such the individual's ability to perform a basic activity of daily living is affected. A medical doctor, or where the impairment is an impairment of sight, a medical doctor or an optometrist, has certified in prescribed form that the individual has a severe and prolonged mental or physical impairment the effects of which are such the individual's ability to perform a basic activity of daily living is markedly restricted.

The individual has filed the appropriate government forms for a taxation year. No amount in respect of remuneration for an attendant or care in a nursing home, in respect of the individual, is included in calculating a deduction under Section 118.2 of the Income Tax Act for the year by the individual or by any other person. If an individual does not have enough income to claim the credit, a supporting family member can make the claim.

DISABILITY APPEALS ON THE RISE

The number of cases being heard on appeal has increased, probably because of the use of the informal appeal system, which allows individuals to argue their own cases. An illustrative case was one heard by Tax Court Judge Donald Bowman in Cornerbrook, Nfld. Bowman rejected a claim that was being argued by the wife of a disabled taxpayer, but the latter was not called as a witness.

In such cases, Bowman said, it is useful for the court to see the person to help in making a judgment about physical capacity. In this particular case, the physician's certificate did not check the long-term disability box on the claim form. Bowman was forced to wonder whether this was intentional or inadvertent. The problem is deciding whether, to use the Tax Act's words, "the individual's ability to perform a basic activity of daily living is markedly restricted" is, in the end, a subjective call by the judge.

Disability cases generally end up being based on the particular facts of each case and it is difficult to find a common thread. As Bowman noted, the decision often depends upon how the person "looks" to the judge.

We suspect that in most cases, judges are faced with emotional situations in which personal sympathy vies with the protection of the public purse. But there is a conundrum here. On the one hand, the legislation itself is sound and tax relief is appropriate. However, the statutory tests are appropriate, and it is difficult to dispute the right to appeal when CCRA denies a claim. Having said all that, there is an enormous cost associated with these appeals, not only of money but in terms of the court's time. In the end, though, there appears to be no alternative process that offers tax justice to the individuals who are affected while at the same time producing a reasonable, cost-efficient method of providing that justice. Meanwhile, those who feel they are entitled to the credit should claim it – and hope for the best in court if the claim is rejected.

CHAPTER 8

RETIREMENT | PLANNING

- Estate planning
- Calculate the costs of your retirement
- RRSPs
- Maximizing foreign content
- Carry-forward options

RETIREMENT COULD COST YOU

A LOT MORE THAN YOU THINK

BY BRUCE COHEN AND
JONATHAN CHEVREAU

HOW MUCH MONEY DO YOU NEED to be able to retire? That depends largely on how much you spend each year and how many years you'll live. The first is fairly easy to determine. The second depends on your lifestyle and the genes you inherited. However, calculating your retirement costs can be a sobering experience and may bring you to the scary conclusion you'll have to become an RRSP millionaire two or three times over if you are to retire in style. If so, most Canadians are in for a rude awakening. Even a more modest retirement nest egg of $1 million is likely to be reached by only 6% of Canadians, according to a Gallup poll released by Deloitte & Touche chartered accountants. Of 1,002 adults surveyed, 12% expect to save between $500,000 and $1 million, 18% between $250,000 and $500,000 and fully a quarter of them less than $100,000.

MOST CANADIANS UNDERESTIMATE WHAT THEY WILL NEED FOR RETIREMENT

Of course, even $1 million isn't quite what it used to be, and will buy even less 20 years from now than it does today. Investing $1 million in a 5% guaranteed investment certificate (GIC) would yield just $50,000 a year before tax – hardly a fortune. A survey conducted by Toronto-based Marketing Solutions suggests that 60% of Canadians have not even tried to calculate how much they'll need to retire. As the old saying goes, if you don't know where you're going, you'll likely end up somewhere else. The survey found that many people "grossly overestimate how early they can retire," says president Dan Richards. On average, 45-year-olds think they can retire at 58. The younger the investor, the earlier they expect to retire.

RETIREMENT INCOME PROJECTIONS MUST CONSIDER INFLATION AND INVESTMENT RETURNS

Most financial planners use complex planning software like RRIFmetic to come up with scenarios appropriate for their clients' needs. But there are plenty of simpler software programs you can play with on a home computer. Most allow you to make multiple projections by changing variables such as inflation or investment returns. Just bear in mind that any projections are very sensitive to rates of return and assumed rates of inflation. Say you're 45, would like to retire in 10 years and figure you'll need $30,000 a year in today's money to top up whatever you get from the government and your employer. That's $30,000 before tax.

If we assume annual inflation will average 3% over the next 10 years, you'll need $40,320 for your first year of retirement. That's $30,000 times the 10-year factor of 1.344. Assuming 3% inflation and 8% growth, you'll need $17,489 of capital at 55 to fund a fully-indexed $1,000 payment each year for 35 years, until you're 90. For $30,000 a year in today's money, use the inflated 10-year figure of $40,320. You'll need a nest egg of $705,156 – that's 40.32 times $17,489. Depending on what you've already saved, and what it's earning, that may be achievable.

HERE ARE SOME POINTS TO PONDER

• The sooner you retire, the longer your money must last. Put another way, each additional year of work is one less in which you'll have to tap your savings. A 40-year-old man has just over a 10% chance of living into his 90s, according to Statistics Canada's general life expectancy tables. A 40-year-old woman has a 26% chance of passing 90 and a 10% chance of passing 95. At 8% growth and 3% inflation indexing, a 30-year income stream requires about 24% more capital than a 20-year stream. A 40-year stream requires about 39% more than a 20-year stream and about 12% more than a 30-year one.

• Generally, early retirement cuts off your build-up in savings and investments just when you can afford to set aside the most money. The qualifier "generally" is used because this assumes your children are on their own, your mortgage is paid off and you're not supporting your parents – three big assumptions.

• People generally hit their peak earnings in their 50s – again, watch that qualifier. Whether you fit that profile will depend on the extent of restructuring in your employment field.

• The longer your retirement, the more threat you face from inflation. Even if inflation is held at 2%, today's $1 would lose one-third of its purchasing power over the next 20 years. Goods and services that now cost $1 would run about $1.49.

• How much will you spend in retirement? Many people believe their expenses will fall but later find they don't. That's especially true for those who are healthy and active – big consumers of travel and expensive hobbies.

• Are you counting on your employer's defined-benefit pension plan? Actuarial reductions for early retirement mean a smaller monthly cheque because the pension will have to be paid over a longer period. That could be a major concern unless your plan provides for unreduced early retirement.

• Your Canada or Quebec Pension Plan cheque may also be lower than you expect. That's because of a feature called the "dropout." C/QPP computers automatically exclude low- or no-income months for up to 15% of your credited years dating back to Jan. 1, 1966, when the plans began. That's meant to cover career interruptions such as unemployment, illness and schooling. But it can hurt early retirees if the zero-credit years before age 60 total more than 15% of their records. Say you'll turn 60 on Jan. 1, 2006. Your C/QPP "career" will have spanned 40 years. The 15% dropout will cover six years. If you already have four low- or no-income years, full retirement at 55 would reduce your C/QPP entitlement.

• What employment benefits – such as a company car – would you give up? What about employer-subsidized drug, dental and medical insurance? How much would it cost to replace them?

• What will you do with your time? About half the affluent boomers in a Royal Trust poll said they work more than 50 hours a week. Research has found healthy retirees usually maintain the lifestyles developed during their working years. Do you have a fulfilling hobby or are you totally devoted to your job?

• Will close friends be retiring about the same time as you? If not, what would happen to your social life?

• Where will you live? Often retirees move to havens in British Columbia or the U.S. Sunbelt only to find they miss their friends and families. Even if you've vacationed in your prospective retirement haven for years, you may find it unsuitable as a permanent residence. Try living there a while before selling your current home

In the end, how much you need to save for retirement boils down to common sense. Because of the power of compounding, the earlier you start the better. If you're behind, you'll have to save more now and/or increase the return on your investments. If you're unwilling to do that, you'll have to face the fact that you'll either have to lower your expected retirement lifestyle or delay your retirement.

LACK OF PLANNING BODES POORLY FOR MANY

Half of Canadian adults claim to have a financial adviser but two-thirds do not have a financial plan for retirement, according to a survey done by A.C. Nielsen for Canadian Imperial Bank of Commerce. The CIBC Financial Health Poll of 1,000 people aged 18 or over found that younger Canadians are even less well prepared – four out of five people aged 18 to 35 have no retirement plan. While many Canadians seem appallingly ignorant about financial matters, the CIBC survey also can be interpreted as showing a significant number of financial planners are not doing their jobs properly. The poll data suggest that many financial planners have not put retirement plans in place for their clients.

YOUR FINANCIAL ADVISER CAN HELP WITH A RETIREMENT PLAN

A.C. Nielsen did a further analysis for the *Financial Post* on work done by financial planners. Roughly half of those polled used the services of a financial planner. Among those people, 52% had a plan and 48% did not. Of the other half who did not use an adviser, 15% had a plan and 85% did not.

Linda Hohol, CIBC executive vice-president, concedes some financial planners are transaction-oriented and more interested in commissions from selling mutual funds or stocks than in long-term financial planning. The term "financial adviser" is fairly loose, she said, and providers of financial advice, as opposed to products, are not regulated. "I wouldn't necessarily conclude they are not doing their jobs," said Terry Taylor, executive director of the Canadian Association of Financial Planners. "Someone [people in those surveys] may not have accepted their recommendations or not have enough dough to start the plan." Clients may agree a financial plan is a great idea but delay implementing it, Taylor added.

MARKET VOLATILITY FORCES PEOPLE TO SECURE A FINANCIAL PLAN

The end of a long bull market run in stocks seems to have sparked renewed interest in seeking proper advice now, not later. A typical reaction is from Joanna Mackie, one of the CIBC interview subjects who did not have a financial plan. "Recent volatility in the market has made me a little more uncomfortable about my current investments and certainly has reinforced to me the importance of securing a firm financial plan." Not surprisingly, higher income Canadians are more likely to have a plan: 59% of those with more than $75,000 in annual income have a plan. Because of the failure to plan, fewer than two in five Canadians know how much money they will need to retire comfortably. One in five fears not having enough money at retirement age. Yet the average Canadian expects to retire at 59.

RRSPS ARE THE MOST IMPORTANT EXPECTED SOURCE OF RETIREMENT FUNDING

Those saving for retirement began doing so on average at 28, though they feel they should have begun at 25. One in four has yet to put aside a single dollar for retirement; of this segment, 41% cited "lack of money" for their slow start. Registered retirement savings plans are by far the most important expected source of retirement funding. The 57% expecting to rely on RRSPs is almost double the number counting on the Canada Pension Plan or company pension plans. Despite saturation media coverage of mutual funds, 25% still rate themselves "not knowledgeable" about funds. While 43% are unsure of how to invest their money, 54% would place their money in mutual funds or stocks, 35% in fixed-income products like bonds or GICs, and 11% in other investments.

FOREIGN CONTENT OF AN RRSP OFTEN OVERLOOKED

CIBC's survey also developed a profile of mutual fund holdings. Canadian equity funds top the list and 69% of those who had funds held this type. Next came foreign bond or equity funds at 45%. Close behind were balanced funds at 43%, money market funds 40% and U.S. equity funds 39%. Bond funds were held by 29% of respondents. Two-thirds of those surveyed did not know that 30% of an RRSP can be invested in foreign securities. More than half did not know the current return on term deposits. Among that 50% who did not have a financial adviser, 32% said they would turn first to a bank or trust company employee for advice. Another 28% would use spouses, family or friends and 12% would rely on their own instincts. Only 9% would seek out an independent financial planner and only 7% would turn to a stock broker or investment adviser.

RRSPS TOP THE RETIREMENT-SAVINGS HEAP

Everyone should try to take advantage of tax-assisted ways to save for retirement. But many people fall short of the mark when it comes to investing in registered retirement savings plans, financial industry experts say. People shy away from setting up an RRSP for many reasons. "I know there are lots of excuses all across the board as to why people don't do it," says Gena Katz, senior principal at Ernst & Young's national tax group. "For those who are young, they don't do it because they have 40 years to retirement. And, once you get into a stage of life where you find you've got a lot of financial burdens, you've got other things you have to spend your money on, like mortgages. So you just can't see your way clear to saving for retirement."

RRSPS NOT ONLY SAVE TAXES, THEY ARE AN INVESTMENT FOR YOUR RETIREMENT

But, financial experts say, people have to come to terms with their need for income in retirement. The reasons for being concerned are manifest. People are living longer than ever, company pensions are often not overly generous – in some cases, not even available – and there are concerns about the viability of the public pension system. Even those with modest incomes should be setting aside sums for retirement, and the RRSP is the best vehicle for doing so. "I don't think anybody – from the upper to the lower-income tax brackets – can afford to ignore the RRSP. It's a tax-saving measure, and it's an investment, and it's your retirement planning," says Michele Wood-Tweel, a chartered accountant and principal in personal advisory services at KPMG in Halifax. "The plans have become more accommodating over the years. Even somebody who can afford to put away $25 a month from their spending can benefit."

MAKING REGULAR RRSP CONTRIBUTIONS THROUGHOUT THE YEAR HAS TAX BENEFITS

The financial experts say there are a few straightforward strategies that allow those with modest incomes to take advantage of the RRSP. The toughest thing is to make the commitment to put aside some money for an RRSP, says Ann David, director of wealth management at Royal Trust in Montreal. "The key is to set aside monthly amounts and to make regular contributions. Don't get discouraged, don't give up, and don't put it off until tomorrow," David says. One strategy is for people to arrange to have money automatically deducted from their pay or from their bank account each month. Financial institutions will accommodate savers so that money is automatically transferred to an RRSP investment, she says.

Some companies offer group plans for RRSP contributions. "Employers are getting on the bandwagon through group plans, where they will withhold amounts from your salary, which is actually a really good way to do it. If you don't see the money, it doesn't hurt as bad," Katz says. By withholding source deductions and transferring the amounts to an RRSP, people get the benefit of the RRSP tax deferral right from the start, instead of having to wait until tax time for a refund or rebate, Katz says.

Individuals who don't have such a group plan at their place of work can still take advantage of this strategy. This option of making RRSP contributions before income tax is levied on your earnings is also generally available to individuals. "[This form of savings] subsidizes you as you go through the year because your taxes are reduced as you're making those RRSP contributions. You are effectively getting your refund throughout the year, instead of getting this lump sum at the end of the tax year," Wood-Tweel says. Individuals can have this type of source-deduction RRSP benefit by obtaining the appropriate documents from Canada Customs and Revenue Agency or from financial institutions that have the CCRA forms available at their branch locations.

INTEREST-BEARING INVESTMENTS CAN BE HELD IN AN RRSP

Another way of putting money into an RRSP is through borrowing, the experts say. Individuals who don't have the free cash right away can usually borrow from a financial institution. Part of the repayment for the loan can be derived from the expected income tax refund. Any borrowing for an RRSP should be based on an individual's ability to handle the loan repayments. "It can make sense to borrow for an RRSP, but you have to consider that your refund is not going to be 100% of what you borrowed, it's only going to be part of it, so you're going to have pay the amount back," David says.

When deciding on individual investments to place in the RRSP, you need to consider what, if any, investments are being held outside the RRSP – the taxable or "open" part of your investment program. If you have sizable wealth outside the RRSP, financial advisers counsel holding the interest-bearing vehicles – such as a GICs, Canada

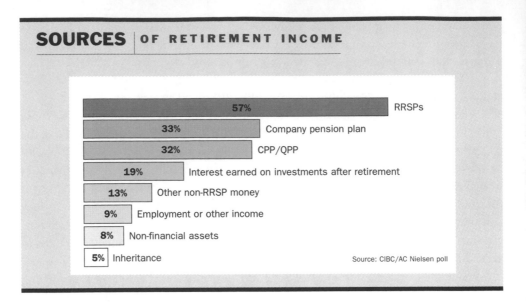

SOURCES OF RETIREMENT INCOME

57%	RRSPs
33%	Company pension plan
32%	CPP/QPP
19%	Interest earned on investments after retirement
13%	Other non-RRSP money
9%	Employment or other income
8%	Non-financial assets
5%	Inheritance

Source: CIBC/AC Nielsen poll

Savings Bonds or bond funds – inside the RRSP and equities and dividend-paying stocks (or mutual funds investing in them) outside. That's because capital gains and dividends are not taxed as harshly as interest income. The capital gains advantage became even greater when the federal budget of 2000 cut the rate to 50% from 75%.

SELF-DIRECTED RRSPS LET YOU MAKE YOUR OWN INVESTMENT CHOICES

If, as is often the case for people still paying off mortgages, your only financial assets are in your RRSP, you will want to include all major asset classes in your plan. That is, equities for long-term growth, bonds or income mutual funds for a stable earnings flow, a small amount of cash, perhaps in the form of money market funds, and maybe some special asset classes such as precious metals or commodities, also available through mutual funds.

The process of asset allocation – deciding on the appropriate mix of stocks, bonds, cash and other assets – is critical. This can be done in consultation with a fee-only financial planner or with a mutual fund broker/dealer or financial planner who makes a living selling "load" (i.e. with a sales charge) mutual funds. Alternatively, you can choose domestic or global "balanced" funds or more tactical asset-allocation funds that let the fund manager decide for you.

Typically, a balanced fund maintains a mix of about 60% equities to 40% bonds, with only minor fluctuations from that formula. A tactical asset-allocation fund makes short-er-term tactical shifts: the fund manager attempts to time the markets by overweighting asset classes expected to outperform and underweighting those expected to underperform.

Whatever the case, you also may need to decide whether to buy a regular "managed" RRSP investing in mutual funds as decided entirely by the issuing institution or a "self-directed" plan in which you can call all the investment shots. Self-directed RRSPs offer much more flexibility in terms of your investment choices.

MAXIMIZE FOREIGN CONTENT FOR REDUCED RISK

Tax planning experts advise taking full advantage of the foreign content allowance in a registered retirement savings plan, which was increased to 30% from 20% in the 2000 federal budget. A reading of history suggests that your returns will be higher over time and your risk level lower with a globally diversified portfolio. Too often, the foreign content component of a portfolio is overlooked.

MAXIMIZE THE FOREIGN CONTENT OF YOUR RRSPS

The ability to diversify RRSP investments to include foreign content is available both for self-directed plans and managed plans. Most plan managers now offer clients a basket of mutual funds, including funds that invest in foreign markets. Those funds provide the opportunity for adding foreign assets to an RRSP portfolio. A self-directed RRSP offers additional flexibility for investment directly in foreign stocks or bonds or other assets. The basic rule is set out in accounting firm KPMG's *Tax Planning for You and Your Family.*

"Generally, only 30% of the cost amount of all property held by your RRSP can be invested in foreign property," the KPMG authors write. "The calculation is performed at the end of each month. Foreign property values over the 30% threshold are subject to a special tax of 1% per month payable by the RRSP. The 30% limit is generally based on the property's cost at the time of purchase, not its market value." KPMG says the RRSP administrator "should monitor" the foreign content "and warn you if it is in danger of going offside."

MARKET GROWTH CAN PUT YOUR FOREIGN CONTENT INVESTMENTS OVER THE 30% LIMIT

"Give yourself a little leeway," advises Adrian Mastracci, a partner at Macdonald, Shymko & Co., a Vancouver firm of financial advisers. He prefers investors to keep in hand a cushion of perhaps 2% as protection against the unexpected. One example of the unexpected can be a capital gains distribution from a mutual fund held within the RRSP that could put the investor offside if the full 30% is used.

Michael Ryan, a vice-president at Leith Wheeler Investment Counsel in Vancouver, warns the cap can affect decisions about the RRSP. For example, it is conceivable that several years of growth in the value of investments held can take the foreign content well beyond the 30% measured by the market value of the RRSP fund. That does not trigger an infraction as content is measured by cost. However, if the investor decides to take his profit and sell some or all of that foreign holding, he will only be able to reinvest up to the 30% cap. Ryan says there can be a tendency for investors to delay taking the profit because they can't find an acceptable foreign replacement.

INCREASING FOREIGN CURRENCY EXPOSURE MAKES RRSP SUBJECT TO FLUCTUATIONS

There are ways of increasing the foreign exposure of an RRSP portfolio above 30% without violating the 30% rule. "Invest up to 30% of the RRSP book value in qualifying foreign content investments and then allocate the other 70% to mutual funds which themselves have 30% of assets in foreign content areas and are also RRSP-eligible," Mastracci says. That means direct investment for the 30% and mutual funds for the balance, which takes the theoretical foreign content limit to 51%. Other strategies for increasing foreign content within an RRSP include investing directly in Canadian companies that operate in US$s or which have shares denominated in US$s. This increases foreign currency exposure. Mastracci cautions against taking on too much foreign currency exposure as currency fluctuations can trigger a gain or a capital loss in the RRSP. He warns that a real capital loss within an RRSP hurts because it cannot be deducted against gains, as is the case in taxable plans.

CARRY FORWARD OFFERS RRSP OPPORTUNITIES

Taxpayers who don't take full advantage of annual contributions to their RRSP have what's known as "tax room." A seven-year limitation on unused RRSP contributions was eliminated in the 1996 budget, creating an unlimited carry forward for unused room. This opened up significant additional planning opportunities, especially for young people. Many people in their teens or early 20s have earned income within RRSP definitions. A lot of that income goes unreported because there is no need for the earners to report just a couple of thousand dollars of casual employment (or self-employment) income, especially if there has been no withholding tax at source. Thus, money earned delivering newspapers, baby-sitting, shovelling snow and other casual work can become the basis for future RRSP contributions, if that income is reported on a tax return.

CANCELLATION OF SEVEN-YEAR RULE MEANS UNLIMITED CARRY-FORWARD OPPORTUNITY

The benefits of reporting have increased substantially, especially for those 18 and older, because of the possibility of getting GST refunds, provincial tax credits and other payments that are income-linked. In fact, generally speaking, there is no reason why anybody with earned income, no matter how low, shouldn't file a tax return – not only for those reasons, but also now to create an earned income base for RRSP purposes. Although this was also the case before the budget, the difference is the cancellation of the seven-year rule, which in most cases would have meant wasting the eligibility because the earner might not have sufficient income within seven years to take full advantage of the carry forward.

The new situation provides more opportunity for income splitting because a parent could make the contribution on behalf of the child without income attribution (each child having reached age 18), giving the child a deduction and a shift of income between generations.

REPORTING EARNED INCOME AT A YOUNG AGE OPENS TAX-SHELTERING DOORS

Even if the child were under age 18, the income-attribution rules wouldn't create a problem – as long as no income came out of the RRSP while the child was under that age. Presumably, a parent would only make such a contribution when the child could actually use the deduction to reduce tax liability, though some may feel that deductibility is secondary to the ability to earn a tax-free return within an RRSP.

If a child had earned $4,000 a year in each of the past four years, for a total contribution base of $16,000, a parent could give the child $2,880 for an RRSP contribution (18% of $16,000). This money could be used either as part of a genuine retirement fund or could be used a few years down the line (with accrued interest) to pay for further education or to help start a business or buy a home.

The bottom line is that reporting earned income even for a fairly young child can open future tax-sheltering opportunities with little or no cost. All that is required is the paperwork ensuring Canada Customs and Revenue Agency has a record of past earned income.

RRIFS OFFER FLEXIBILITY IN POST-RRSP PLANNING

For most of your working years, the pressure is on to salt away as much in tax-free RRSP savings as you can. Eventually, however, you'll be forced to start spending it, and that requires a major change in the way you think about your finances. There are several things you can do with your RRSP savings, which must be "matured" no later than the end of the year in which you turn age 69. One option is to cash in the plan, but this is undesirable because it can result in a huge one-time tax hit on the entire proceeds at your top marginal tax rate. Another option is to buy an annuity, which pays out a guaranteed fixed amount for life but which is based on interest rates, currently at low levels. Or, you can roll your RRSPs into registered retirement income funds (RRIFs), which offer more investment and withdrawal flexibility. It's also possible to arrange combinations of these options.

ALMOST EVERY INVESTMENT PRODUCT IN YOUR RRSP CAN BE HELD IN A RRIF

RRIFs are generally the recommended place for relatively healthy people to put their money because they allow you to invest in mutual funds, bonds and other products that can potentially bring a higher return than current interest rates offer. "There is a definite concern about people outliving their money," says Bernard Roy, assistant vice-president, retirement services with Canada Trust. "If you've been used to a certain lifestyle, you have to consider how you will be able to maintain it based on current interest rates." Generally, almost every investment product that you held in your RRSP can be held in a RRIF. The mix of products you choose should be based on your age, how much income you need to maintain your standard of living, how much risk you are willing to tolerate and what other sources of income you have, if any. "We recommend that you have up to 20% of your RRIF portfolio in equities to really make it worthwhile," Roy says.

MINIMUM RRIF | WITHDRAWAL RATES

Age at Jan. 1	RRIF opened Pre 1993 %	Post 1992 %	Age at Jan.1	RRIF opened pre-1993 %	post-1992 %
65	4.00	4.00	80	8.75	8.75
66	4.17	4.17	81	8.99	8.99
67	4.35	4.35	82	9.27	9.27
68	4.55	4.55	83	9.58	9.58
69	4.76	4.76	84	9.93	9.93
70	5.00	5.00	85	10.33	10.33
71	5.26	7.38	86	10.79	10.79
72	5.56	7.48	87	11.33	11.33
73	5.88	7.59	88	11.96	11.96
74	6.25	7.71	89	12.71	12.71
75	6.67	7.85	90	13.62	13.62
76	7.14	7.99	91	14.73	14.73
77	7.69	8.15	92	16.12	16.12
78	8.33	8.33	93	17.92	17.92
79	8.53	8.53	94+	20.00	20.00

Source: The Rogers Group, Vancouver

MONTHLY PAYMENTS EVEN OUT IMPACT OF MARKET HIGHS AND LOWS

You must withdraw at least the minimum payment by the end of the year after you open your RRIF (see above table). The financial institution that handles your RRIF will calculate its value at the end of each December, and the amount of your withdrawals are based on that value.

If you want to minimize the size of the payments, you can have the valuation done based on your spouse's age, if your spouse is younger than you are. You also can vary the amount of the payments, so long as the scheduled minimum is taken. You also determine how often to take the payments, annually, semi-annually or monthly.

Rob Whipp, branch manager for Fiscal Agents, an Oakville, Ont., deposit brokerage firm, recommends payments be taken monthly to reduce the impact of market and interest rate fluctuations. "Say you have a lot of mutual funds, and the market has gone up a lot" before the yearend valuation of your RRIF. "If you elected to take your annual payment in July or August and the market suddenly dropped, you still would have to take the amount out that is based on your December valuation, which was high." That means you'd have to redeem extra units, which could use up your RRIF faster than you planned, he says.

Taking payments monthly evens out the impact of highs and lows of the market when you're selling off units of mutual funds, Whipp says. It also helps protect bondholders, for similar reasons. Once you start receiving RRIF income, you must pay quarterly income tax instalments. If you take payments annually at the end of the year, that income must be included in your quarterly payments, and you must pay the tax, even if you haven't received the money, Whipp says.

RRIF THEN ANNUITY IS WORTH LOOKING AT

The specter of outliving your money is one that haunts many investors in times of low interest rates. That in part accounts for the equity cult that prompted baby boomers and other investors to stuff their RRSPs with stocks and equity mutual funds. Those already retired face similar concerns. This accounts for the relative popularity of registered retirement income funds (RRIFs), with their RRSP-like flexibility, compared with life annuities, which invest strictly in long-term fixed-income securities.

Ironically, though, one of the chief advantages of a life annuity is precisely that you can never outlive your money. A life annuity is a contract between you and a life insurer, under which you pay a non-refundable lump sum in return for a promise to provide you with a guaranteed income for life, no matter how long you live.

INSURANCE COMPANY ANNUITIES GUARANTEE INCOME FOR LIFE

As York University finance professor Moshe Milevsky explained in an article for *Benefits Canada* magazine, the insurance company can provide a lifelong guarantee because it pools many annuitants' money and makes conservative yield assumptions. Pooling means individuals who do not reach their life expectancy subsidize those who exceed it. Because a RRIF can be converted to an annuity, but not vice versa, it's possible to have your cake and eat it too by using a RRIF early in retirement and switching later to an annuity. The trick is picking the right moment for the switch. That entails making a guess about life expectancy, future interest rates and investment returns.

FINDING THE RIGHT MOMENT TO SWITCH FROM RRIF TO ANNUITY CAN BE A HARD CALL

Making such estimates is no trivial task. Milevsky applies some surprisingly complex mathematics to arrive at a few cogent conclusions about how to maximize the benefits of annuities. He uses what is called a "Monte Carlo Simulation," a computer algorithm that examines all possible combinations of interest rates, equity markets, mortality rates, inflation rates and annuity prices. For most people, Milevsky recommends starting with a RRIF and delaying an annuity purchase until the last possible moment. "Buying an annuity is synonymous with betting that you will live longer than average." He argues the case for what he calls a "do it yourself and then switch" strategy. That means making your own investment calls with a RRIF, then switching at the right moment to an annuity.

PUT OFF SWITCHING TO AN ANNUITY UNTIL THE TIME IS RIGHT

Given the way life annuities are structured, mortality trends and the long-term strength of equity returns, Milevsky says "it makes very little sense for males under the age of 75 and females under age 80 to annuitize any additional non-pension wealth." One would choose otherwise only if interest rates were very high or if you have reason to believe you are much healthier than average, and therefore likely to live longer than most people.

WHEN TO CONVERT | RRIF TO ANNUITY

The potential benefit of investing in a RRIF during the early years of retirement and switching to an annuity later for someone age 69 with a $200,000 RRSP.*

Age switched to annuity	Success probability %		Median bequest $	
	Male	Female	Male	Female
69	100	100	0	0
74	94	97	33,688	19,920
79	89	93	80,825	56,653
84	83	87	141,664	124,166
89	78	81	209,713	240,456
Never	76	79	310,138	683,409

* Annuity payable at age 69 on that amount would be $1,820 for a female and $1,540 for a male. Assumes RRIF is invested in a diversified portfolio with expected return of 13% and volatility of 17%. Mortality assumes IAM 1996 basic rate for life annuities, plus 10%

Source: York University Schulich School of Business, Statistics Canada

ENJOY THE LIQUIDITY OFFERED BY RRIFS WITH DIVERSIFIED PORTFOLIO OF EQUITIES

The accompanying table shows two examples that correspond to the payout a $200,000 life annuity "would have" provided at age 69. This strategy involves consuming from your RRIF the monthly amount that an annuity would have provided and deferring actual annuitization until later. In the first example, a 69-year-old woman stays with a $200,000 RRIF for 10 years, withdraws $1,540 a month (the amount an annuity would have paid), then switches to an actual annuity at 79. She stands a 93% chance of being able to purchase a life annuity paying out an identical $1,540 a month with her remaining wealth. In the second example, a 69-year-old male uses a $200,000 RRIF to generate a monthly income of $1,820. He gets more because males have shorter life expectancies. He has a 94% chance of purchasing a comparable annuity five years from now, and an 89% chance of doing the same 10 years from now.

This strategy depends on investing in a well-diversified portfolio of equities. "Putting the funds in a GIC defeats the point and will likely make it impossible to ever purchase the same annuity in the future," Milevsky says. Among the advantages to the strategy are that the retiree maintains complete control over the funds at the RRIF stage, which means liquidity is maintained. Any emergency or unforeseen cash crunch – for long-term care, perhaps – can be met from the non-annuitized pool. Second, the retiree can annuitize at any future point. "Why pay for something today if, in all probability, you can pay the exact same thing 10 years from now, yet maintain the benefits of the purchase?" Milevsky asks.

A LIFE ANNUITY LEAVES NOTHING FOR YOUR ESTATE

Yet another consideration in putting off the decision to annuitize is leaving an estate for your heirs. A pure life annuity leaves virtually nothing for your estate. Milevsky says it may sound morbid but "the longer you delay annuitization, the greater the chances that you will die prior to purchasing the life annuity, which will mean that your estate gets the proceeds of the RRIF." A less risky alternative is to use Milevsky's strategy alongside a deferred annuity. Not to be confused with his "delayed" annuity strategy, a deferred annuity allows the retiree to lock in a mortality table and interest rate early in retirement, with the payout "deferred" – typically for 10 or more years. A 69-year-old male with $200,000 might use $160,000 in Milevsky's strategy and put the other $40,000 into a 10-year deferred annuity. For a female, the mix might be $145,000/$55,000.

WHAT DOES YOUR COMPANY PENSION PLAN OFFER?

Every year companies that offer their employees a pension plan must send each staff member a statement outlining his or her pension entitlement. Chances are, the employee's eyes will glaze over before getting to the bottom of the first page. While most working people want a pension, few pay attention to the details of the company plan. Yet there are pointed questions employees should ask to get answers that will help inform them about their post-retirement finances. Read that statement, says Janet Downing, lawyer and consultant at Watson Wyatt & Co., pension and benefits consultants in Toronto. And read the booklet about your company pension plan that you got when you joined the firm.

If it's not in plain English, or any other plain language, don't despair. There should be a pension provider, someone at the company or a union representative who can answer questions in a way everyone can understand.

COMPANY PENSION FUNDS ARE PROTECTED FROM BANKRUPTCY

As pension regulations have multiplied, the jargon surrounding pensions has mounted. But the rules protect pension money, even in the case of a company bankruptcy, Downing says. This is because pensions must be segregated from other company funds and will survive a bankruptcy. Paul Love, a partner in the pension services group at PricewaterhouseCoopers, outlines some questions that will bring out the most pertinent information around the company pension.

WHAT TYPE OF PENSION ARE YOU ENTITLED TO?

Traditional defined-benefit plans represent the vast majority of Canadian plans. They come with employer guarantees of a defined income for life. Usually the benefit amount is based on a formula involving years of employment and average or peak earnings. However, these plans are losing popularity because of their inherent complexity and cost, as well as their shortcomings when early retirement is considered. Many smaller and mid-size companies are opting for defined-contribution plans in which the amount of money you get at retirement depends on the amount contributed to the plan and the investment yields it earns during your working life. The employer or employee, or both, contribute a defined amount to the plan, which is managed by a professional investment manager. In some cases, the employee has a choice of how the pension money is to be invested.

Do you have a profit-sharing plan or group RRSP in which employees pool money for RRSP investment? Unlike the more paternal defined-benefit plans, these plans leave the risk – and the investment choices – in the hands of employees. In this sense they are like defined-contribution plans.

Many people welcome the opportunity to make their own investment decisions, says Denise Castonguay, vice-president and general manager of Trimark Pensions, a division of AIM Funds Inc. However, she says employees with these types of plans need some investment education. Many Canadians prefer such safe investments as GICs, which may not grow sufficiently to provide an adequate yield in real after-inflation terms.

ARE THERE PROGRAMS OVER AND ABOVE THE COMPANY PLAN?

Some companies offer supplementary entitlements for anyone earning more than $80,000 (see "Finding the Money to Retire"). Pension plans give up to 60% of income after retirement to those earning up to about $86,000. After that, the portion of earnings received after retirement from a company plan declines. If there is a supplementary plan, check how it is funded, Love suggests. Some of the funding may come from employer profit and amount to little more than a promise.

AT WHAT AGE WILL YOU BE ENTITLED TO A COMPANY PENSION?

What is the normal retirement age? What is the penalty for early retirement? Some firms offer reduced benefits for those who retire early. Others apply tests to determine entitlements.

HOW DOES YOUR COMPANY PLAN MESH WITH YOUR RETIREMENT STRATEGY?

You may want to check out the tax implications of when you begin taking income from your RRSP and other investments. With a pension that's not indexed, you may take little from your RRSP in the early years and let the money grow. When the pension money starts to be insufficient, that may be the time to start using the RRSPs.

FINDING THE MONEY TO RETIRE

John is 53 and has just been laid off from a $100,000-a-year executive position. Is his original goal of retiring at age 63 still realistic? We asked Alain Quennec, financial adviser at Vancouver's Rogers Group Financial Advisors Ltd., to run some projections using a planning package called RRIFmetic for Windows, from Fimetrics Systems Ltd. of Vancouver.

HERE ARE THE KEY INPUTS

• John was part of a defined benefit pension plan before being laid off. That will generate a non-indexed pension income of $30,000 at age 63.

• He has a new job at $50,000 a year, with no pension.

• John has only $60,000 in his RRSP, but has established a spousal plan for his 50-year-old wife, Mary, worth $290,000.

• Mary earns $25,000 a year as a part-time consultant.

• In two years, the couple expects a $150,000 inheritance.

• Inflation averages 4% a year.

• Investment returns average 8% a year.

• Their income goal in retirement is $45,000 a year after taxes (70% of what his executive job paid after taxes).

• They will live 30 years after retiring. The house is paid off, children grown.

HERE ARE RRIFMETIC'S OUTPUTS

John must contribute $6,000 a year to the spousal RRSP plan until retirement. Assuming $4,250 a year of income from the Canada Pension Plan, he will have $25,000 a year after tax, in today's dollars. Mary must contribute $1,500 a year to her own plan. Assuming another $4,250 a year of income from CPP, Mary will have $20,000 of after-tax income.

PENSION EXPECTATIONS MAY BE TOO GREAT

Employees in private pension plans are more optimistic than they should be about their prospects for enjoying a sustainable retirement income. Canadians are going to have to become more actively involved in their retirement planning, chiefly because of the continuing shift from the traditional defined benefit (DB) pension to more portable defined contribution (DC) plans, says Warren Laing, president and chief executive at HRL Funds Management Ltd. of Toronto. DB pension plans guarantee members a set amount of money in retirement. With DC plans, members set aside a regular amount, often in equity mutual funds, and end up with variable and less predictable income.

The next generation of pensioners may be in for a shock when they realize that "investment returns are going to shrink, the cost of living isn't going to go down and people are retiring earlier and living longer," Laing says. He predicts the average pension plan's annual investment returns will continue in the low single digits for the foreseeable future. That prospect is more frightening when one considers investors have become complacent after seeing pension funds generate returns in the mid- to high-teens in the 1990s. Over the long term – 1926 through 1996 – the compound was 8.4% and there is little reason to expect much difference in the long-term average in the 70 years after 1996.

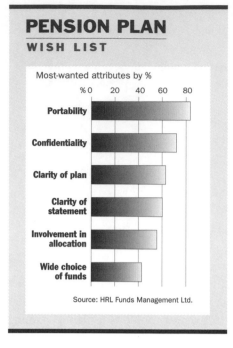

PENSION PLAN
WISH LIST

Most-wanted attributes by %

%0   20   40   60   80

- Portability
- Confidentiality
- Clarity of plan
- Clarity of statement
- Involvement in allocation
- Wide choice of funds

Source: HRL Funds Management Ltd.

MANY HAVE FAITH IN COMPANY PLANS

An HRL-commissioned survey, conducted by Andover Research Associates and IntelliPulse, found that almost half the respondents (48%) were optimistic they will be able to retire at age 65, compared with only 21% who were pessimistic. The study was restricted to people aged 25 to 60 who are in private pension plans. A telling result was that 53% of defined benefit plan members were optimistic, versus only 45% of defined contribution plan members. Nearly three-quarters of high-income earners were optimistic, compared with less than half of all survey respondents classified as baby boomers. Among DB members, 45% believed they could live comfortably even if they retired before age 65, versus only 37% of DC members.

A majority of respondents still had faith their company pension plan would be there when they need it. Nearly two-thirds disagreed with the suggestion firms might reduce or scrap their support for company-sponsored pension plans. "We are amazed" by the level of optimism revealed by the survey, Laing says. "These results raise serious issues."

DEFINED CONTRIBUTION PLANS ARE LESS PROFITABLE BUT MORE PORTABLE

Many Canadians appear to be ignoring the implications of the shift to DC plans. If the trend continues, Canadians will have to "increase their retirement savings substantially if they want to retire comfortably." The survey identified shortfalls of up to 30% between what DC members say is important and how satisfied they actually are with their plans. This gap showed up in every demographic group. "Are DC plans delivering? The answer is a resounding no," Laing says. "The industry has a long way to go before [these] plans meet their needs."

Actuary Malcolm Hamilton of William M. Mercer Ltd. says employees' optimism over their retirement prospects may be misplaced but is understandable. "Investment results have been so good for so long that even if they return to normal it's going to feel like it's bad."

But retiring at age 65 is no great accomplishment, Hamilton says, since few employees will be retiring based only on the investment results of their DC plans. "Many of these people will get Canada Pension Plan or sell their principal residences." Nor did Hamilton interpret the survey as a reason for employees to embrace DB plans again. "DB plans are the least portable of plans," he says. "According to the survey, portability is the No. 1 concern."

DEFINED CONTRIBUTION MEMBERS WANT MORE SAY IN HOW MONEY IS INVESTED

The survey found 83% of respondents want plans that can easily follow them from employer to employer. About three-quarters cited confidentiality about the assets in their plans as important. Two-thirds said it was important their plan and its supporting statements be easy to understand. More than half said they want a strong say in how their contributions are invested. Among DC members, 44% believed it is important to be given expanded investment choices, defined as access to most mutual funds and guaranteed investment certificates.

CPP – A CASE OF EVERY LITTLE BIT HELPS

When you're assessing your retirement finances, don't forget the Canada Pension Plan – it won't make you rich but it can be a good source of supplementary income. And unlike many other income sources, CPP benefits are fully indexed to inflation, meaning they won't lose value over time. The maximum annual CPP retirement benefit for 2001 is $9,300. This dollar figure will increase every January based on inflation for the preceding year. The amount you eventually receive depends on when you retire and how much and for how long you contributed to the plan.

CPP BENEFITS WILL BE BASED ON PREVIOUS FIVE-YEAR PENSIONABLE EARNINGS

Benefits are based on the average of yearly maximum pensionable earnings over the most recent five years. That average was changed from three years in 1998. (See box on the following page for details of premium changes.) According to Malcolm Hamilton, at the actuarial firm of William Mercer Ltd. in Toronto, the benefit reduction stemming from the formula change will be roughly equivalent to the average inflation rate. If inflation averages 2% a year, your benefits will be about 2% less than they would have been with the three-year average.

If you're nearing retirement, you can get a pretty close idea of your CPP entitlement from the Statement of Contributions the government sends you. If you want more details, you can contact your nearest Income Security Programs office. David Conway, national director at CIBC Trust, urges some caution in interpreting future CPP benefit estimates. "The changes being made to CPP now mean there's a greater chance it will exist in future. I just hope they don't change the rules down the road and start clawing back payments."

HERE ARE SOME POINTS TO CONSIDER ON CPP'S ROLE IN RETIREMENT PLANNING

• **Want to split income?** Couples who are both at least 60 and in different tax brackets can "assign" some of their CPP retirement benefits to each other and possibly save on taxes. The amount that you can split with your spouse depends on how long you have lived together while contributing to the plan. For example, if you lived together for 20% of both your contributory periods, you can split 20% of your benefits. (The same type of pro rating formula is applied to the division of CPP benefits upon divorce.) If you retire in the middle tax bracket (about 42% depending on province) and your spouse has no income, the first $538 transferred to him or her will generate a tax saving of $225 annually. Any further transfers would reduce your ability to claim the spousal credit, but even so, you stand to save about 16¢ on each additional dollar. The savings are even greater if you are in the top tax bracket.

• **Thinking about retiring early?** You can start drawing CPP benefits as early as age 60 provided that your income from other sources at the time is less than your benefit entitlements, or you have "substantially ceased working." This requirement does not apply once you reach 65. If you do opt for early retirement, your CPP payments will be reduced 0.5% for every month before age 65 that you begin to collect. So, for example, if you were to retire at the age of 62 (36 months before age 65), you would be entitled to 18% less than your regular benefit. At age 60 the regular benefit would be reduced by 30%.

You also can defer CPP benefits until after age 65 if you wish and will receive 0.5% more benefit for each month's deferral, to a maximum of 30% extra per year if starting at age 70.

YOU CAN WAIT EVEN LONGER BUT WILL RECEIVE NO FURTHER INCREASE IN BENEFITS

• **Change your mind about retiring early?** You can cancel your decision up to six months after starting to collect CPP benefits. You must repay any benefits you have received to date and your future entitlement will be unaffected.

• **Worked in another country?** You may be entitled to a pension from that country for your work. If not, you may be able to have the working time factored into your CPP benefit calculations.

• **Planning to leave Canada when you retire?** CPP benefits can be collected anywhere in the world. If you move to the U.S. Sunbelt and arrange to have the money deposited to your U.S. account, it will even be converted into U.S. funds automatically. However, you should ascertain the tax implications of receiving this government pension in your

---

CPP PREMIUMS GOING UP, | WAY UP

Canada Pension Plan premium payments are way up and are expected to keep going higher in future years. For 2001, the contribution rate was 8.6% of pensionable earnings between $3,500 and $38,300. That rate will go to 9.9% by the year 2003. At the same time, the pensionable earnings ceiling is indexed to average industrial wages while the floor is fixed, meaning the amount of earnings subject to contribution will increase over time. For example, if wages rise with inflation at 2% a year, pensionable earnings will increase from $34,800 for 2001 to more than $36,800 for the year 2003.

The combined impact of these changes would see maximum CPP premiums rise from $1,938 in 1997 to about $3,645 in 2003. Furthermore, since CPP contributions generate only a bottom-bracket tax credit (as opposed to a full deduction as is the case with RRSP or pension contributions), anyone in the middle or top tax bracket will get only a partial offset. For someone currently in the top marginal bracket, the net after-tax cost would be the same as for an RRSP or pension contribution of almost $5,400.

destination country before you move. A financial adviser familiar with the tax regimes of both Canada and the other country could be of great value.

- **Make sure to apply early.** You must apply to receive CPP benefits – they do not come automatically, and the plan administrators may not be able to backdate payments. You should allow at least six months for your application to be processed and for the cheques to start arriving.

PLAN CAREFULLY BEFORE CHANGING COUNTRY

Canadian income tax liability is based on residence, so the date on which an immigrant or emigrant becomes or ceases to be a Canadian resident is a key factor in determining how, and how much, income will be subject to Canadian tax. Generally, the date of commencement or cessation of Canadian residence is the date of the physical move. However, business, financial and social considerations may also affect the factual determination of residence status. It is even possible an individual will be considered to be a resident of more than one country for tax purposes. In such situations, income tax treaties between the countries will usually resolve the residency question.

In the year in which an individual establishes or relinquishes Canadian residence, he or she is considered a part-year resident and is taxable on worldwide income for the portion of the year he or she is a resident of Canada. A part-year resident is also subject to Canadian tax on certain Canadian-source income received for the relevant part of the year.

IMMIGRATION

When an individual becomes a resident of Canada, he or she is deemed to have disposed of and re-acquired each property, except taxable Canadian property, owned immediately prior to establishing residence, for proceeds equal to the fair market value of the properties at that time. Taxable Canadian property includes Canadian real property, capital property used in carrying on a business in Canada, shares of Canadian private corporations, certain shares of public companies and Canadian resource properties.

For properties deemed to be acquired, a new cost base is struck and any gains that accrued before commencement of Canadian residence will not be subject to Canadian tax. Once Canadian residence is established, your world income becomes taxable in Canada at our graduated rates. Any foreign source income received after becoming a resident of Canada will likely be subject to foreign as well as Canadian tax, but to avoid double taxation, any foreign taxes paid in respect of this income generally are eligible for a foreign tax credit in Canada.

THESE RULES GIVE RISE TO THE FOLLOWING CONSIDERATIONS

• If tax rates in the country from which you are emigrating are lower than Canadian rates, try to receive all foreign source remuneration before establishing Canadian residency.

• Review your investment portfolio before establishing Canadian residence. It may be advantageous to sell investments with accrued losses to avoid a future Canadian capital gain combined with a foreign capital loss.

• If marginal tax rates are lower here than in the other country, try to plan the date of commencement of Canadian residence to take advantage of this. For example, if you were to take up residency in Canada in September and earned $30,000 during the remainder of the year, it would all be taxed at the lowest marginal rate; if you immigrated in April and earned $60,000 in Canada, more than half would be taxed at the much higher middle rate.

• If you own significant foreign investments, consider establishing a non-resident trust before becoming a Canadian resident to shelter income from these investments from Canadian tax for up to five years. Consult your tax adviser about this planning opportunity.

• Review the tax consequences of any employer benefits paid relating to the relocation to Canada. Where possible, try to structure the benefits so that they will not be taxable in Canada. For example, moving-expense reimbursements and some mortgage subsidies are not considered taxable, while a standard-of-living equalization payment has been held to be taxable by the courts.

• If you were a member of a foreign pension plan, your employer may be able to continue to contribute to that plan. However, such contributions will reduce your ability to use registered retirement savings plans, registered pension plans and deferred profit sharing plans.

• If you were a member of a foreign pension plan, you may be able to transfer your plan holdings to an RRSP on a tax-free basis.

• You may be able to continue coverage under the social security system of your former country and opt out of the Canada Pension Plan.

• If you own stock options from your foreign employer, it may be wise to exercise the options before establishing residence if the foreign country taxes the benefit more favorably than Canada does.

EMIGRATION

When an individual ceases to be a resident of Canada, he or she is deemed to dispose of all property owned for fair market value at that date. Exceptions to this rule include real property situated in Canada, capital property used in a business carried on by the individual through a permanent establishment in Canada, pension rights (from RPPs, RRSPs and registered retirement income funds), employee stock options and, for certain short-term Canadian residents, property owned when the individual became resident here. This means any accrued gains on non-exempt property will be taxed in the year of departure. However, instead of having to pay the tax immediately, emigrating taxpayers are permitted to post security with Canada Customs and Revenue Agency and pay the tax when the property is actually sold.

If the value of assets you own when you cease to be a resident of Canada exceeds $25,000, you must report their total value and details of each property, other than personal-use properties individually valued at less than $10,000. Once you cease to be a resident of Canada, you are no longer taxed in Canada on your worldwide income. However, if you receive Canadian-source income as a non-resident, such income generally will be subject to Canadian income tax. Certain types of Canadian-source income, such as interest, dividends, rents and pension income, will be subject to Canadian withholding tax at a general rate of 25% (which may be reduced under a tax treaty with your new country).

If you earn Canadian-source employment or business income or sell taxable Canadian property as a non-resident, you will be required to file a Canadian tax return reporting this income and pay the resultant tax. If you are required to report this income as taxable income in your new country, you may be able to claim a foreign tax credit for the Canadian tax paid.

CONSIDER THE FOLLOWING

• Establish the date you became a non-resident and ensure this date can be supported by the facts.
• Make RRSP contributions in the year of departure if you have contribution room. (It is generally advantageous to leave RRSPs in place when leaving Canada, as long as keeping money in an RRSP does not create tax problems in your new country.)
• If you rent out your Canadian home or another property after ceasing Canadian residence, you will be subject to 25% Canadian non-resident withholding tax on the gross rental income. A better alternative may be to elect to file a Canadian tax return, reporting net rental income (after deducting applicable expenses), which will be subject to marginal tax rates.
• If you plan to retain any Canadian bank accounts or investment accounts after ceasing residence, notify the Canadian payers of interest and dividends to withhold and remit the appropriate amount of Canadian withholding tax.
• It may be advantageous to sell property with accrued gains if these gains could be taxed in the new country.

SUCCESSION IN FAMILY BUSINESS CAN BE TRICKY

Who's going to take over the family business when you pass on? It's a question almost every company owner must confront at one time or another, and it can give rise to many problems if not addressed well in advance of the actual event. "The first piece of advice I would give to anyone contemplating a business succession is to start planning early," says Debby Stern, a partner at KPMG in Toronto. "It can take five years or more to arrange a proper and orderly transition. At the least, early planning reduces problems if you suddenly become disabled," Stern adds. "What if the children are too young to take over – do you bring in professional management? Can your spouse cope with the responsibilities? If nobody knows what you want done, the result could be a distress sale. That's to no one's benefit but the buyer."

THERE ARE MANY QUESTIONS TO CONSIDER IN SETTING A SUCCESSION PLAN

Even when you've made a succession plan and have a successor in mind, there may be conflicts and problems to resolve. "You may have children already in the business, but are they up to the task of running it?" Stern asks. "Do they need more training or expertise? How much, and where do they get it?" Timing can be a problem too. Stern cites the example of a client who wants to retire in five years, but has two sons who think they can run the business as a team right away. "This is fairly common. They're trying to pressure him to leave, but he doesn't want to go just yet. He's going to have to resolve this conflict somehow."

What if you don't want to retire completely? Have you made arrangements to continue on in a reduced capacity, perhaps as a consultant or an honorary board member? What if you want to retain control over the company even though you are no longer actively involved? "You have to be careful, because there can be a lot of points of dissension and conflict between family members," Stern says. "The situation can get quite emotional and contentious, so you have to identify all the issues and stumbling blocks, and discuss them with everybody in advance. You have to develop arrangements acceptable to everyone concerned."

IN PLANNING A SUCCESSION, YOU HAVE TO BE FAIR TO ALL FAMILY MEMBERS

Sometimes, for example, an owner wants to pass the business title to a spouse but place the son in charge of its operation. This could result in making the spouse dependent on the son for income to survive – not an ideal situation. One way around this problem is to provide for the spouse separately through life insurance. That way his or her needs can be covered regardless of what happens with the business. The situation can be more complicated if more than one child is involved, especially if the business is your single biggest asset. "What if you have a son who is in the business, and you also have a daughter who wants no involvement in the company?" Gordon asks. "Do you still give them both half shares? This can create tensions for the son, who is doing all the work and getting only half the rewards.

"In planning a succession, you have to think about what's fair for your children and not necessarily what's equitable," Gordon adds. "If you have substantial personal assets, maybe they can be given to the daughter while the son inherits the business. But if not, then again, life insurance can be used to help ensure everyone is treated fairly, without causing problems for the business."

ESTATE PLANNING IS ESSENTIAL

 In the cavalcade of life's pleasures, estate planning probably ranks below trips to the dentist for most people. But the cost of a disorderly estate to your loved ones, your favorite charities and your business (if any) can be enormous. What happens when you die without any preparations – that is, you die "intestate" without a properly drafted will? In general, all your last year's income and any as-yet untaxed assets – including RRSPs and RRIFs, real estate (other than your principal residence), shares and mutual funds with accrued gains – are lumped together in your estate and taxed as income for the final year.

So, for example, the estate of someone with $30,000 in pension income for the year, plus $200,000 in RRSPs or RRIFs and perhaps real estate or other equities with accrued gains of $100,000 could face a tax bill approaching $150,000. And that's just the beginning – your provincial government will take over the estate, perhaps liquidating non-cash assets for fire-sale prices to pay the tax bill and other liabilities, then distributing whatever's left to family members according to a strict formula.

The distribution formula can vary somewhat by province, but generally leaves a share to your spouse and splits the rest between children. If there is no immediate family, it goes to your nearest relatives. If no relatives can be found, the province keeps all. If you happen to own a business, there's more. Your ownership shares will be thrown into the estate pot and taxed as well, before being passed on to family or relatives as per the above list. Without clear instructions on succession, the business could founder or be torn apart by rivals within and without.

There are, of course, lots of wrinkles and exceptions to the above scenarios, but the point is that if you have any wishes regarding your estate, you will have to set them down for yourself. No one will be able to second-guess what you want after you're gone. Despite this harsh reality, though, many people still try to ignore the inevitability of death and final taxes. In her book *You Can't Take it With You: The Common-Sense Guide to Estate Planning for Canadians*, author Sandra E. Foster suggests the top five reasons for not preparing an estate:

1. You like to pay taxes.
2. Your family always gets along.
3. The government will look after it for you.
4. You're not old enough.
5. You will live forever.

Except perhaps for number 4, she notes, the other reasons are hardly legitimate justification for deferring this chore. So what should you do, and when should you start? To answer the second question first, you should start planning your estate as early as possible, if only to avert nasty consequences in the event of an untimely accident. And certainly you should set down your testamentary wishes once you have begun to raise and support a family, to ensure they'd be cared for in your absence.

SOME SUGGESTIONS ON GETTING STARTED

1. Make and update your will. The first step in organizing your estate is to draft a proper will. You can simply write one yourself and have someone witness it – a "holograph" will – but there are potential legal snags that could leave it open to dispute. In most cases it would be better to have a lawyer versed in estate law vet the document. You also should update the will periodically. Most experts suggest once every three years or so. That way you can allow for changes in tax and other laws or in personal or business circumstances. The classic example here is the man who divorces and then remarries without changing his original will, in which case the original spouse could get the lion's share of his assets.

2. Appoint an executor. You will need someone to administer your estate and ensure your testamentary wishes are executed. This individual can be anyone – your spouse, a relative or friend or a professional. But bear in mind that the executor's duties can be numerous and complex. The person you choose will be responsible for making funeral arrangements, locating the will and obtaining probate (many financial institutions will refuse to release assets in the absence of letters of probate), locating and evaluating all your assets, arranging for their safe keeping where appropriate, advertising for creditors, preparing a statement of assets and liabilities, discharging liabilities, liquidating assets in the most tax- and cost-effective manner where required to settle debts or meet the terms of the will, preparing and filing tax returns (there could be as many as three different returns), notifying beneficiaries… and the list goes on. Your spouse probably will be unable to handle all these duties during a period of bereavement. Friends and relatives may understand your personal wishes but lack the necessary skills to do everything in a cost-effective and efficient manner.

For this reason, many people opt for a professional executor or joint executorship between a professional and a friend or relative. The executors' compensation depends on several factors, including the size and complexity of the estate and the duration of the administration. Courts have approved a percentage-based tariff, which is applied in most instances involving an estate of average complexity. Roughly, the tariff invokes an annual charge of 5% of the income earned in the estate plus a management fee of two-fifths of 1% of the assets of the estate under investment. There is also a capital charge equal to 5% of the value of the estate assets, payable as the estate assets are realized and disbursed to beneficiaries or used to meet capital expenditures of the estate. Courts will deviate from the tariff for cause, but you should generally assume executors' compensation will be calculated on that basis, if there is no contract.

3. Assign a power of attorney. This should be done at the same time you draft your will. Basically, the power of attorney provides for someone else to take over your financial as well as health-related matters if you should become incapacitated. Don't assume your spouse could simply take over your affairs because unless a POA exists, your affairs could be frozen until a court or public trustee determines what should be done and allows the spouse to take over.

4. Prepare for business succession. If you own a business, the issue of succession can be highly complicated. As with personal matters, you should start early and give consideration to individual as well as financial implications (see "Succession in Family Business Can Be Complicated").

5. Organize your affairs. You want to arrange your finances to maximize the benefits for those you love, while minimizing taxes. In this regard, there are many strategies you can undertake including:

- Transferring assets to family members or others beforehand.
- Freezing your estate with a trust.
- Placing assets into joint ownership.
- Triggering gains when the tax bill will be lower.

Any of these strategies involve complications, though. For example, some people trying to avoid probate fees will transfer assets while alive, or put them into joint ownership so they pass directly to the co-owner upon death. But this will result in a deemed disposition and unless you're transferring the assets to your spouse at cost – the only person other than certain dependents entitled to this treatment – you may be hit with an immediate hefty tax bill. Joint ownership transfers also mean that earned income from the portfolio will now be divided equally between all joint owners.

LIFE INSURANCE SHOULD BE A PART OF GOOD ESTATE-PLANNING STRATEGY

Some people try to reduce their final tax tab by giving away assets to their children while alive. This may also trigger a large tax liability right away. And the assets revert to the recipients, for them to do with as they please, not an appealing option if you want to keep a rein on a child's profligate ways. Many good estate preservation strategies involve the use of life insurance. When the first spouse dies, RRSPs, RIFs and other assets can be rolled over to the surviving spouse tax-free. But when the second spouse dies, the government takes the taxes deferred on those assets before they are passed on to children or other beneficiaries. An insurance policy can cover that liability with proceeds that are tax free. Proceeds from permanent insurance are most commonly used to pay tax bills when capital gains are realized on death. But many also use them to generate cash for their estate to equalize payments to all beneficiaries or to donate money to their favorite charities.

Another planning point: Many couples have one spouse with a company pension plan and one without, either because they have been out of the workforce or because their job provided no pension plan. The spouse with the pension plan has the choice of a life annuity for a single person only or a joint-life annuity, which extends over the life of both partners but gives a lower benefit. An alternative is to buy a life insurance policy that will provide the spouse with a lump sum that can be invested to provide income. The increased benefits of the life annuity may be high enough to support the cost of premiums. Whatever the case, estate planning can be complicated. It behooves most people to seek professional help in arranging their estate and thus avoid many of the potential pitfalls that await the unwary.

TRUSTS LET YOU CONTROL YOUR MONEY

A trust arises when a person transfers legal title of property to another person (the trustee) with instructions as to how the property is to be used for designated beneficiaries. All types of assets can be placed in trust, including bank accounts, stocks and bonds, mutual fund units, real estate, even private businesses. There are two main purposes for trusts: They let you control how money is used, and they can generate tax savings. Sometimes, too, trusts can help protect assets from creditors.

A trust set up while you're alive is called an inter vivos, or a "living," trust, but you also can also set up in your will a "testamentary" trust, which will allow your wishes to be carried out after you die. For example, a charitable remainder trust allows you to donate a cottage or artwork to charity, generating a tax credit now and allowing you use of the item while you're still alive. Or, you could put assets into trust to support disabled family members when you're gone.

Many small investors may already have trusts and not realize it. If you are putting money into a mutual fund for a child's education, it may be held "in trust" for them. There's no written document but there is an intention to create a trust in that situation, says Sean Foran, vice-president of client services for Trust Company of Bank of Montreal. But this may not cover contingencies such as what happens to the assets upon premature death of the child, so a more formal trust has advantages.

TRUSTS MUST BE PROPERLY DRAFTED TO PROTECT INDIVIDUAL'S WISHES

Because a formal, irrevocable trust cannot be changed, it's essential the trust agreement, or will, be properly drafted and accurately reflect the individual's wishes. The trust agreement should be drawn up by an estate and trust lawyer but any estate-planning expert can help frame the issues and wishes. Typical one-time start-up legal costs are between $2,500 and $5,000, while associated income-tax preparation services can run about $500. There are also recurring annual trustee fees that can run 0.8% to 1% of assets.

CHOOSE RRSP BENEFICIARIES CAREFULLY

Designating a beneficiary for your RRSP or RRIF seems simple enough. But last-minute designations – and even those made more carefully – can produce a minefield of problems. The seemingly fair division of your estate can easily become unfair because there are two types of beneficiaries for registered plans. The first category, i.e., spouses, qualify for tax-free rollovers to their own plans. If you have no spouse, the money can be rolled into a plan for an infirm child or grandchild who's dependent on you or be used to buy an annuity to support a healthy dependent child or grandchild until age 18.

All others fall into the second category. They do not qualify for tax-free rollovers, and that's where unfairness can come roaring in. Since there's no rollover, the institution will treat the transaction as a withdrawal and issue a T4 tax slip – but to your estate, not the beneficiary. Consider the case of a widower who has $200,000 split evenly between an RRSP and some term deposits. He wants to treat his adult son and favorite niece evenly, so he leaves the $100,000 in term deposits to his son through a will and names the niece beneficiary of his RRSP. Unfortunately, the niece will get her full share but the son won't. He'll get only what's left after the estate pays $50,000 income tax on the RRSP cash-out that went to the niece. The only way the niece would be hit for tax is if the estate didn't have enough money to pay the bill. Only then does the law let Canada Customs and Revenue Agency go after the RRSP beneficiary.

A better plan would have been for the widower to leave the RRSP to his estate and name the son and niece equal beneficiaries. They would evenly divide the term deposits and share what's left of the RRSP after tax. But leaving the RRSP to the estate means it might face probate fees – a big concern in Ontario where the levy is $15 per $1,000 of estate value over $50,000 (plus $5 per $1,000 up to $50,000). Some people try to avoid probate by naming joint beneficiaries so the RRSP money will be paid to them outside the estate and won't face probate – unless the financial institution holding the plan insists on it. But this can cause problems too.

NAMING JOINT BENEFICIARIES CAN LEAD TO COMPLICATIONS

Say our widower named his son and niece as joint beneficiaries of the RRSP. The son, who has a child of his own, dies first and his grief-stricken widow soon afterward. The niece will get the entire RRSP while the orphaned grandchild gets far less than the share intended for his father. That's because the niece was the only named beneficiary alive at the time the RRSP was cashed out and, of course, the tax bill went to the widower's estate, reducing the amount available for the grandchild. To avoid this problem, some institutions allow only one person to be named RRSP/RRIF beneficiary. Or, say you have two sons aged 19 and 12. Since the 12-year-old would qualify for a tax-free rollover, you name him as beneficiary of the RRSP and, in your will, leave the other assets of equal value to the older son. Six years later you die without having updated either document. John, now 18, no longer qualifies for a tax-free rollover but still gets the full RRSP, while Sam's inheritance gets reduced because the estate has to pay the tax on the RRSP cashout.

SOME OTHER POINTS TO PONDER

• You can make RRSP/RRIF designations in your will or the plan contracts. If you do both, make sure they match and get updated together.

• Say you name your spouse beneficiary in your RRSP contract and then divorce. Make sure to change that designation – divorce automatically revokes designations in a will but not necessarily in an over-the-counter form. If you remarry, make a new will with a clear statement revoking all previous RRSP beneficiary designations.

DONATIONS IN WILLS NEED A SECOND LOOK

Much personal giving comes by way of bequests in wills – given that most people make large donations only when they are certain that giving away money or other assets will not jeopardize the family lifestyle. However, the tax rules make it important for many individuals to revise their approach to bequests. Thus a review of wills, particularly of charitable bequests contained in them, is necessary.

The key donation-related tax change of recent years is that gifts (including those made through a will) made in the year of death and in the preceding year can be claimed as a tax credit of up to 100% of the deceased's income. This may prompt many people to modify their wills to increase charitable donations. The same change has created a major opportunity with regard to donating money in RRSPs or RRIFs. Until 1996, RRSP/RRIF money paid to an estate was fully taxable and if transferred by will to a charity, only 20% of the amount would be eligible for a tax credit. Now, donations from estates can be transferred to a charity tax-free.

However, a charity cannot be named directly as a beneficiary of an RRSP or a RRIF, so the gift must be made in two steps. First, the money must be paid to the estate, which usually can be done only if there is no surviving spouse or dependent child. Then there must be a will that states the money must be transferred to one or more named charities.

Another change of significance: many wills directed charitable gifts to Crown agency foundations, which provincial governments often set up for certain charities such as universities and museums, because until 1996 only such gifts qualified for a tax credit of up to 100% of income. Now that the 100% tax relief is available for a donation to any registered charity, it may be more desirable to have money bequeathed directly to a charitable organization rather than its Crown agency foundation. If so, the appropriate change to the will should be made.

FAMILY ISSUES IMPEDE TO ESTATE PLANNING

Estate planning is aimed at providing for the orderly tax-effective distribution of your assets at death. Entrepreneurs should embrace the idea since so much of their lives – and their family's well-being – is tied up in their companies. But that's often not the case, says Wally Howick, Toronto-based vice-president with Bank of Montreal's private client services: "The minute you start talking about estate planning, many of them get antsy. They're just not ready to deal with succession; family issues are the single biggest impediment to estate planning."

AN ESTATE FREEZE CAN AVOID A LARGE TAX BILL

The incorporated business owner is caught in a dilemma between prudent tax planning and preserving family harmony, Howick says. Without planning, the harder you work, the bigger that bill. Say your company was incorporated at $100 and is now worth $1 million. If you died today, the tax hit would be about $400,000. Say you continue to build the business to $10 million and then die. The tax would be about $4 million. You can turn off the tax clock by doing an "estate freeze" that revamps the company's ownership. Normally, the entrepreneur converts his or her common shares to preferred shares frozen at today's value. Other family members – typically adult children – get new common shares that grow in value as the company grows.

Howick has found many entrepreneurs understand the tax rationale but still shy away because they're not ready to work out who gets what and are afraid of blowing apart the family. Those who don't plan add to their family's burden during a time of grief and can leave the business vulnerable, he warns. "Your competitors may smell blood and go after your customer base, and even long-time suppliers may want to revisit their relationship."

Tax and succession planning don't have to be done together, Howick stresses. He outlined a way to freeze your tax liability but still buy time to work out the company's future with your family. For simplicity, Howick uses the example of a $1-million business, even though he feels the fees involved make a full freeze worthwhile only for companies worth at least $4 million. As above, the founder's current cost base is $100.

THE PLAN CALLS FOR THREE SETS OF SHARES

• Normal freeze preferred shares for the entrepreneur, valued at $1 million. Though non-voting, they're retractable so he or she can always demand the money.
• Special preferred shares for the entrepreneur. There would be 1,000 valued at $1 each. These would be voting shares.
• New common shares for family members. There would be 100 valued at $1 each.

A discretionary trust is created. If the entrepreneur has a living parent, Howick says it's technically best if the parent creates the trust with a gold coin or other nominal asset that does not produce income. The trust then borrows $100 from an arm's-length lender. Now, the key. Instead of going directly to the adult children, the new common shares are bought by the trust. The trust deed names the children as beneficiaries but does not set their allocations. There might be three trustees: the entrepreneur, a reliable friend and a professional adviser. That caps the entrepreneur's tax exposure but leaves time for the family to focus on succession. The trustees can determine how much the various children are willing and able to get involved in the business.

THERE ARE THREE WAYS THE PLAN KEEPS THE ENTREPRENEUR IN CONTROL OF THE COMPANY

• The retraction feature allows him or her to demand redemption of all or part of the regular freeze preferred shares at any time.

• The special preferreds give the entrepreneur 1,000 votes compared with just 100 for the common shares.
• The entrepreneur is one of the trustees.

"Control is very important to entrepreneurs because they see the business as the key to the family's well-being," Howick says. His example assumes all the children are adults. More complex planning is required if there are minors. Usually, Howick adds, an entrepreneur wouldn't do a full freeze until he or she is over 50, though a younger owner-manager might consider a partial one in certain cases.

A non-profit organization – the Canadian Association of Family Enterprise – can help with communication and other issues and has chapters across Canada.

CHAPTER 9

PERSONAL | PLANNING

- Strategy

- Protecting your credit rating

- Mortgage options

- Buying a home and renting

- Financing your family's education

- Bankruptcy

DEALING WITH THE OBSESSION

KNOWN AS PERSONAL FINANCE | BY JONATHAN CHEVREAU

PERSONAL FINANCE IS NOT A NEW TOPIC, although the recent proliferation of financial Internet sites, books, television shows and repositioned publications seems to suggest it is a brand-new journalistic beat. The reason for this renewed and intense multimedia attention is not hard to fathom and almost too obvious to mention. Money is one of the three gods of modern society, the other two being power and sex. And arguably, money can buy those two. You could more succinctly use the term "My Money" to describe Personal Finance. After all, other people's money is nowhere near as fascinating as your own.

The obsession with personal finance is intensified by the ongoing demographic trends in North America and around the world. This is well documented in such books as *Boom, Bust & Echo* and *The Pig & the Python*. The baby boomers have become affluent and, as they turn 50 in large numbers, they are becoming obsessed with having enough money for retirement. Most boomers are now closer to retirement than they are to the pivotal event of their youth: 1969's Woodstock festival. Few worried about retirement then and they are frantically trying to make up for lost time, taking on perhaps more risk than many are comfortable with.

This generation has bought into the notion that stocks are the best vehicle for growing their RRSPs, to the point they rely on them for retirement income. Hence their keen interest in the stock market and their angst over the outlook for equities. Many also realize that investing in stocks or bonds is best left to professionals, which accounts for their willingness to delegate security selection to mutual fund managers. That willingness has led to a phenomenal growth in numbers of mutual fund analysts and managers.

THERE IS MORE TO FINANCIAL PLANNING THAN GUARANTEEING RETIREMENT INCOME

The generation that has followed the boomers shares their concerns about retirement, if only because it has little confidence the Canada Pension Plan is going to be there for them. While getting a job is their predominant worry, they too see their future in stocks and mutual funds held inside RRSPs. Then there are today's seniors. While saving for retirement is the single biggest topic in personal finance – and the subject of an earlier primer in this series – it encompasses much more than this. In this section, for example, we have primers for the first-time home buyer, how to be a cheapskate, 10 reasons for ditching the car and taking the train and others that originally appeared in *The Financial Post*.

Clearly, the average consumer is suffering from information overload. Apart from what we in the business term "pure editorial," there is also a bombardment of advertising, mostly from the banks and mutual fund companies. Face it, there's big money in personal finance. The journalistic waters are being muddied by pseudo journalists who have a toehold somewhere in the media to flog their personal business interests. Beware the shill in journalist's clothing. There's a difference between the objectivity of full-time journalists on the staffs of newspapers, magazines or broadcast outlets, and those whose real business is public speaking, financial planning, mutual fund sales or computer software.

PERSONAL FINANCE ADVICE COMES IN ALL SHAPES AND SIZES

Before you make a financial decision based on what appears to be legitimate media commentary, you need to understand the nature of journalism and expertise. You need to be selective if you want to find some value in this surfeit of personal finance coverage. At some media outlets, there is a thin line between editorial and advertising. Many Web sites, for example, amount to little more than electronic brochures for various financial institutions. Also suspect are the hundreds of newsletters issued by financial planners. Marketing Solutions has created a package of materials that allows "Joe Planner" to stick his picture on top of a pre-written story and pass off a bunch of pre-written marketing bumf as his personal summary of the great financial events of the day. Some of this information may be good, but be aware that the underlying agenda is to get you to buy more financial products.

The same sort of discrimination needs to be applied in the burgeoning field of seminars. If the speaker is being sponsored by two or three mutual fund companies, how critical is he or she likely to be about mutual funds in general and those particular companies in particular? I'm not saying you should disregard their statements – I myself have given a few such talks – but at least take it all with a grain of salt and doublecheck all assertions afterward. As the conduit between the investor and the financial services industry, the watchword for the consumer of the media's prodigious output on personal finance topics should be "let the reader/viewer beware."

TIPS ON BUYING YOUR FIRST HOME

Thinking of buying your first home? When mortgage rates are low, lots of people realize it's a good time to buy. It was a seller's market in most major Canadian cities during the latter half of the 1990s. That put first-time buyers in a more precarious position than they were in the bargain basement market earlier in the decade. The housing market is notoriously cyclical because developers usually can't resist the urges that lead to overbuilding during boom times.

A friend taking the plunge into home ownership insisted he had no time to read the various primers on the subject, saying "surely it can all be summarized in a single column." It can't really, although you can get publications from local real estate organizations that make the process seem simple. Unable to resist my friend's challenge, however, the rest of this section reflects my personal experience of buying a first home, moving up once and renovating.

The first thing I told my friend was that, like marriage, children and entering a lobster trap, buying your first home is easy to do. But if you make a mistake, getting out is a tricky, costly proposition. Luckily, first-time buyers are shielded from the realities of real estate commissions, which run at 5% or 6% and are paid by the seller. Remember, though, that the selling price will reflect the commission and the buyer is the one who brings money to the table. You should use your own agent because the listing agent represents the interests of the vendor.

You can find an agent at any open house. There's no central place to check out agents' credentials, so don't rush to commit to the first random encounter. Try to get one to share their bible: the weekly updates of the Multiple Listing Service (MLS) covering the district you're considering. They're not supposed to give them out, but you can sometimes snag a copy of the previous week's edition. "Location, location, location" is the well-worn cliche about what's important in a home. Again, the decision is a bit like marriage. You're not just marrying a person, you're marrying into a family.

Same with a house. You don't want to live next to rental properties or crack houses or next to an alleyway. You don't want the traffic noise of a major street steps from your front door or be under airplane flight paths. You do want to be near public transportation, schools, day care, churches, parks and convenience shopping. Ideally, you'd find this all out by renting first in your proposed district – it's like living together before marriage. The corollary of location, location, location is "price, price, price." Obviously, the best locations cost the most and worst locations are cheap.

Young newlyweds may have to get a starter home in a lesser district and later pull up stakes and get the dream home in the classy district. Older first-timers with hefty down payments may be better off choosing their "dream district" right off the bat, even if it entails a slightly larger mortgage. The commission to later sell a $350,000 home would be $21,000. Add moving, legal and other expenses and there seems little point in compromising now and moving to the perfect situation later.

HOUSING OPTIONS INCLUDE CONDOS, TOWNHOUSES AND THE TRADITIONAL DETACHED HOME

There are condos, townhouses and those trendy lofts you see sprouting everywhere. I'm biased in favor of traditional detached houses on real land, where you can grow vegetables in the event of economic cataclysm or put on additions if boom times continue. Condos have maintenance fees, elevators and possibly noisy neighbors. Townhouses have you running up and down three flights of stairs, a negative as you age. Lofts seem an overpriced fad. It may have been a novel thing to have bought a genuine loft years back, but the current wave strikes me as artificial and blatantly commercial. I doubt there are bargains to be had. So we're back to a good old detached home on terra firma. Avoid semi-detached homes unless you're really strapped for cash, and avoid shared driveways. In both cases, the unknown variable is your immediate neighbor. I know a couple who were assaulted by an insane neighbor with whom they shared a driveway.

DECIDE ON YOUR "MUST" FEATURES BEFORE YOU BEGIN YOUR SEARCH

Another basic decision is new house or old. You have to pay GST on new homes, which tend to be out in the suburbs. Consider how you plan to commute to work in this case. New home construction schedules can be problematic and you need to be aware of various unforeseen closing costs. If you like "new" and the ability to customize to your needs, there are hundreds of full-page ads in the major newspapers. Old homes (resales) don't have GST on them but obviously are "used" homes. There are all sorts of potential maintenance problems to check out, such as roofs, furnaces and termites. Resales tend to be in established and more central districts and have lots of fully grown trees. The vendor may be more flexible on price.

Full two-storey houses are better than storey-and-a-half houses, which tend to have chopped-off room corners. A basement doesn't have to be renovated yet, but it should be full height so you can add a recreation room down the road. Many old houses are heated by hot water radiators. If you want central air conditioning, then look for houses heated with forced-air gas. Their furnaces can be later upgraded to air.

Local and regional markets across the country all have real estate listing publications that are freely available. Also, check out real estate listing services on the Internet. Your local real estate board probably has a site and there are other Web services with home listings. It's now common to find real estate listings online with video clips that give you views inside and outside a home.

Understand the concept of tradeoffs. There is no perfect house. If there was, you couldn't afford it. List the "must" features and those you prefer but can live without. You can do a Web search that specifies key features. I suggest leaving out small amenities that can be cheaply added at a later date. What you want is a good solid structure at a bargain price in the district you want, with the potential to later add your dream features. If you plan a major addition, make sure the lot size is large enough to conform to the building permit guidelines.

RESOURCE BOOKS HELP SORT OUT HOME BUYERS' QUESTIONS
Beware the costly glamor features. Pools drown children and are hard to resell, lakeside properties have a $100,000 premium for the privilege of stepping in goose poop, and hot tubs and skylights may be more trouble than they're worth. You need to find out about insurance, lawyers, inspectors and mortgage financing. A good overview is provided in *The Complete Guide to Buying, Owning and Selling a Home in Canada,* by Margaret Kerr and JoAnn Kurtz (John Wiley & Sons, 1997). For mortgage strategies, try Gordon Pape's *The Canadian Mortgage Book.* I don't agree with all of Garth Turner's leveraging advice in *The Strategy: A Homeowners Guide to Wealth Creation* (Key Porter, 1997). But Turner's insights on the type of homes that will sell in the future (i.e. bungalows) versus the white elephants (i.e. 6,000-square-foot monster homes) are well worth reading. I think 2,000 or 2,500 square feet of space is all that the average three- or four-member family needs.

RENOVATING CAN BE CHEAPER THAN MOVING

Renovate or move? The dilemma is a common one for many homeowners. There's an army of real estate agents eager to get you to move, but there's a cost involved in listening to them. In addition to their 5% or 6% commission, there's the difference in price between your old home and your new one, the legal expense of buying one and selling the other and the actual shifting of furniture and other worldly goods. On top of the big costs are lesser ones, such as painting or installing new carpeting in a resale home.

On the other hand, when you stay put and add a bathroom, update your kitchen or build an extension, you pay provincial sales tax on materials and the hated GST on both labor and materials. Having moved into a first home and neighborhood, you can become attached to neighbors who become friends, nearby schools, day care, church, shopping and the whole package deal of home and district.

Real estate agents naturally tend to downplay the loss of community involved in the decision to move. But if you do have good material to work with in your first home – great neighbors, large enough lot, and so on – then renovating can make sense. You can make 100% on your investment in a kitchen and 80% on a bathroom should you later decide to resell. Basement renovations or swimming pools may not be fully recouped but any time you add new space, such as a family room or fourth bedroom, you stand to win on the subsequent resale, says Ross Gilmore, partner at Gilmore & Harris Custom Builders and Renovators.

BEFORE YOU RENOVATE, CHECK THE CONTRACTOR'S CREDENTIALS

If you do decide to stay and renovate, there are plenty of pitfalls in choosing a contractor. You should make a short list of three or four possible firms. Rene Cantin, president of Rosewood Construction and host of CFRB Radio's *Home Improvement Show* in Toronto, says you should always check the references and licences of a potential contractor. Visit the sites of one or two satisfied customers whose projects were of the scope you are contemplating. Check with the Better Business Bureau and call the Canadian Home Builders Association (1-800-387-2422), which can give you the names of provincial and municipal associations that can comment on your proposed contractor. Call your local building department to find out what permits are needed, and insist the contractor obtain them all. Also, make sure they have $1 million or $2 million in liability insurance.

THE LOWEST QUOTE IS NOT NECESSARILY THE BEST DEAL

Get everything down in writing and, if the project is large, have the contract checked by a lawyer. Do not give deposits of more than 10%. You have the right to hold back 10% of value of the project for 45 days after substantial completion. There is considerable variation in the ability of contractors to tackle large projects, Cantin says. "The problem with a reno or an addition is you're tying new into old." Prices can be negotiated but recognize that a contractor has only so much leeway in this tough business. The markup on small jobs may be 20% or 30%, but it may be 15% or less on large jobs.

Watch out for low-ball cash deals from possible fly-by-night operators, warns Kelly Reynolds of the Greater Toronto Home Builders Association. "If the price sounds too good to be true, where they say do this under the table and avoid the taxes, you have nothing to fall back on." But even on legitimate bids, going strictly with the lowest bid could be a mistake. If you leave the contractor with no profit, you can hardly complain if they respond by substituting lower quality materials or skimming on intangibles such as service. "You have to be leery of someone priced really low," says Cantin. "In the commercial business, they say he who makes the biggest mistake in the price gets the job."

RENTING MAY BE SMARTER THAN BUYING

Renting a house or apartment is dumb because after years of monthly payments, you'll have nothing to show for it, right? That's what just about every real estate agent and a large part of the public will tell you. But you won't hear it from Sean Hennessey, an associate professor at the University of Prince Edward Island. Hennessey, who teaches

SHOULD YOU | BUY A HOME OR RENT?

% annual appreciation		Renting wins if initial monthly rent is less than: $200,000 house		$150,000 house	
Funds	House	25% down $	50% down $	25% down $	50% down $
14	5	1,909	1,982	1,361	1,486
	4	1,970	2,038	1,403	1,529
	3	2,016	2,081	1,435	1,560
	2	2,050	2,113	1,459	1,584
12	5	1,600	1,709	1,200	1,282
	4	1,681	1,790	1,260	1,343
	3	1,742	1,852	1,307	1,389
	2	1,842	1,898	1,341	1,423
10	5	1,350	1,402	1,013	1,051
	4	1,462	1,517	1,097	1,138
	3	1,548	1,605	1,161	1,204
	2	1,613	1,671	1,210	1,253

After-tax values compared after 30 years. Assumes 3% inflation and that closing costs equal 2% of house price, mortgage is 8 % paid monthly and amortized over 20 years, property tax equals 2 % of purchase price, repairs and maintenance equal 1.5%, mutual fund capital gains realized only at end and taxed at 37.5%, and first month's rent due as deposit with no interest paid.

personal finance, wrote a paper showing that by retirement an informed renter can beat a home buyer by more than $5 million in Canada – and by more than $2 million in the U.S., where buyers get generous tax breaks. That's after 40 years, with the last 20 years mortgage-free for the homeowner and the renter paying a huge capital gains tax bill.

THE NUMBERS DON'T ADD UP IN THE HOME BUYER'S FAVOR

"I went into the analysis thinking there's no question that buying a home is a good investment because that's what you always hear," says Hennessey, a homeowner himself. "But as I worked through the numbers and logic, I never figured it would come out nearly as bad as it did." Using average housing price figures for North America, Hennessey compared the purchase of a $140,000 home paid off over 20 years at 8% to renting at $950 a month, rising 3% a year. The home buyer's initial $2,800 property tax bill and $2,000 for repairs and maintenance per year also rose 3% annually. He assumed the renter invests the $35,000 that would have been used as a down payment. During the first 17 years, the renter pays less for shelter and invests that difference, too.

THE RENTER'S ADVANTAGE LIES IN INVESTING FUNDS EQUAL TO THE DOWN PAYMENT

"This is a very structured investment approach and you have to be willing to follow it," Hennessey stresses. "If the down payment or the net cost of buying are not invested, the analysis is invalid." Indeed, nearly 80% of the renter's ultimate edge over the buyer is due to compound growth on the down payment. Hennessey assumed this cash and all top-ups go into good international mutual funds averaging 14% a year.

Is that reasonable? Hennessey says the Toronto Stock Exchange 300 index averaged about 12% over the past 45 years and "better-performing mutual funds will get you a much better long-term return than the TSE 300." He assumed a buy-and-hold strategy with no tax until the end of his 40-year analysis period, when he taxed the capital gains at 42.7% – considerably higher than today's top marginal rate on gains.

Eighteen international funds have five-year "tax efficiency" ratings of at least 98%, according to Morningstar Canada's PAL Trak database. A 98% rating means taxable distributions cut the fund's reported returns by just 2%, so an investor averaging 14.3% would net 14%. Hennessey also assumed the home's value will just track inflation at 3% a year. That will startle many but not those who've read *Boom, Bust & Echo*, the bestseller by baby boom analyst David Foot.

WE MAY NOT SEE A HOUSING BOOM LIKE THE 1980s UNTIL 2010

Foot, a University of Toronto professor, suggests the 1980s real estate runup was due to the demographics of the baby boom. But for much of Canada he predicts the baby bust that followed the boom means less demand for housing – at least until after 2010. Tinkering with Hennessey's model, I produced the table on the previous page. It spans 30 years, since I suspect even a veteran renter would likely want to buy a house or condo for retirement. Say you're eyeing a $200,000 purchase with 25% down and accept Hennessey's assumptions of 14% for long-term mutual fund returns and 3% for house appreciation. Renting can match or beat ownership as a long-term investment if you can find suitable rental accommodation for $2,016 a month or less. Housing economist Mary McDonough says the $150,000 and $200,000 house price assumptions have been in line with averages in Canadian cities, "although there are tremendous differences among neighborhoods."

HOME BUYERS LOSE OUT IF THEY ARE FORCED TO SELL BEFORE REALIZING A PROFIT

In consultation with McDonough, I set closing costs and property taxes each at 2% of the purchase price and budgeted 1.5% for repairs and maintenance. I used Hennessey's 3% inflation assumption, but tested investment returns of 10% and 12% as well as his 14%. House appreciation ranged from 5% down to 2%. I assumed a 50% marginal tax rate, which meant taxes took 37.5% of the taxable capital gain after 30 years. "Many households choose to buy a home based on emotional, social and psychological factors and, likely, in the belief that it is a wise investment choice," Hennessey's paper says. "For some, this may be the case; for others, however, it is a mistake from which it takes many years to recover."

For example, by not questioning common wisdom, people concentrate the bulk of their wealth into an illiquid holding that's subject to speculative swings and they become exposed to "extreme unsystematic risk," he argues. Consider the plight of someone forced to sell by marital breakdown, job loss or transfer, a major change in the neighborhood or perhaps because an obnoxious rock band just moved in next door.

HENNESSEY SUGGESTS PROSPECTIVE HOME BUYERS CONSIDER THE FOLLOWING

• Will the house increase in value over time and, if so, by how much?

• Will the house require expensive renovations or repairs now or in the future?

• Do you require greater portfolio diversification than a house can provide?

• Do you have the discipline for a strict investment strategy and appreciate that stock prices fluctuate?

• Is suitable rental accommodation available? Is a long-term lease possible?

• Are there rent controls? To what extent do you face the risk of an unreasonable rent increase?

All these factors can affect the buy/rent equation. But one thing is fairly clear in the wake of Hennessey's analysis: Buying a house simply for investment reasons may not be the wise decision that realtors invariably suggest.

MORTGAGE INSURANCE GETS PORTABLE

The market for mortgage insurance – more accurately referred to as "default insurance" – has undergone substantial change in Canada over the past few years. The changes include the portability of mortgage insurance, the insuring of mortgages held by self-directed RRSPs and the percentage of a home's value that is insurable under a high-ratio situation.

Spearheading this innovation has been GE Capital Mortgage Insurance Canada (known in the industry as Gemico). Neither Gemico nor Canada Mortgage & Housing Corp. – the federal agency that continues to dominate the Canadian default insurance market – offer their products directly to the public. They deal primarily with the large number of financial institutions that lend out mortgage money. The mortgage insurance market began a transition in 1992, when CMHC began insuring mortgages for first-time home buyers who had only a 5% down payment. Previously, the maximum insurable financing for all buyers was 90% of the first $180,000 of purchase price plus 80% of the balance.

INNOVATIONS IN MORTGAGE INSURANCE INCLUDE HIGH-RATIO MORTGAGES AND PORTABILITY

For example, on a $250,000 purchase, the maximum financing previously possible was 87.2%, or $218,000, compared with 95% or $237,500 after the new program took effect. Then, in January 1995, Gemico acquired the assets and operations of Mortgage Insurance Corp. of Canada (MICC), the only other source of mortgage insurance in Canada besides CMHC. Gemico subsequently introduced some innovations, including the ability to insure a mortgage held by a self-directed RRSP. This previously had been available through MICC and was revived by Gemico. It has broadened the appeal of this strategy.

Another innovation is the ability through both Gemico and CMHC to insure almost all of the mortgage amount for homebuyers other than first-timers, compared with the more conservative sliding scale that was used previously. Typically, they will cover up to 90%, depending on the size of the mortgage and other circumstances. For example, they now will cover $450,000 of a $500,000 loan.

Probably the most significant development for the average homebuyer has been the introduction of mortgage insurance portability. In the past, high-ratio borrowers would pay an insurance premium to either CMHC or MICC, and if they moved to a different home, the insurance was lost. That was fine, provided the mortgage on the new property was for a low-ratio loan (covering less than 75% of the property's value). But if they needed insurance on their next property, they'd have to pay another premium.

SELF-DIRECTED RRSP MORTGAGES CAN NOT BE CONVERTED TO A RRIF

Gemico's portable policy, introduced in 1995, provided homeowners with the comfort of knowing that, with some limitations, their original insurance premium was all they would ever pay if subsequent purchases required default coverage. CMIIC was fairly quick to follow suit, announcing a portability feature in April 1996, although it will still not allow you to switch lenders when selling one property and buying another. CMHC coverage, however, does offer some advantages. The National Housing Act, which governs CMHC's operations, allows any borrower to pay off a CMHC-insured mortgage with a maximum of three months' interest penalty after three years, regardless of the number of times the mortgage is renewed.

Gemico, by contrast, operates under the lender's prepayment policies, which vary among institutions. In many cases, the lender will charge a penalty to cover the interest rate differential and require the borrower to continue dealing with them (if a mortgage is still needed) until the current term would have expired. CMHC also will not terminate insurance on a self-directed RRSP mortgage when the time comes to convert the RRSP to a RRIF, allowing the customer to convert the plan in an orderly fashion. Gemico requires full replacement of the mortgage money by discontinuing coverage after the RRSP is converted to a RRIF.

NO ONE PAYS THE STICKER PRICE

Competition has driven down mortgage rates as lenders increasingly show willingness to discount their posted rates. In fact, in *The Canadian Mortgage Book,* authors Gordon Pape and Bruce McDougall "strongly advise" that no one accept the posted rate these days. In most cases, there's room to negotiate up to a full percentage point, depending of course on the length of the term, Pape said. "Negotiating a mortgage has become rather like buying a car. No one pays the sticker price." You can also negotiate away hidden costs such as appraisal fees, which are usually between $150 and $500, survey fees of another $150 to $400, renewal fees, mortgage transfer fees and mortgage insurance in the case of high-ratio mortgages.

The implications for people shopping around for mortgages are clear. If you want a mortgage below the posted rate at your local bank, make it clear that you're aware of what other financial institutions are charging. Comparative rates can be found in the *Financial Post*. If your bank won't budge on the posted rate, then try to get them to waive one or more of the related fees. If that doesn't work, it's time to pull out the heavy artillery. You represent much more than just potential mortgage business to the banks. If you give them your RRSP, credit card and other business, odds are they will be more willing to give you a mortgage below the posted rates.

THE WEB CAN SERVE UP MORTGAGE BARGAINS

For consumers looking to beat lenders' posted mortgage rates, the Internet is becoming a money-saving tool. The big banks enjoy a dominant position in the mortgage market. They have two advantages: a bricks-and-mortar presence on almost every street corner and the ultimate weapon of "relationship" banking. Industry insiders say a two-tiered mortgage rate system developed in the depressed real estate market of the 1990s. One tier is the posted rate the banks would like you to pay, somewhat like the sticker price on a new car. The second is the discounted rate the consumer wishes to pay.

The banks have been willing to discount since 1992, particularly if they think they can also win, or retain, your registered retirement savings plan (RRSP), credit card, commercial banking and other business.

USING YOUR PERSONAL COMPUTER, YOU CAN APPLY FOR A MORTGAGE AND GET APPROVAL
If you are willing to spread your business around and shop for the best mortgage, you should be able to improve on the posted rate by 50 to 100 basis points. To find the best deal, you can go to a traditional mortgage broker or to the new electronic equivalents on the Internet. This exercise may still lead you back to one of the big banks, or it may take you to unfamiliar but aggressive newcomers in mortgage lending. It's now possible to arrange an electronic mortgage from your personal computer. You can apply for a mortgage and have it approved over the Internet without an in-person visit to a branch. A good place to start the search is the Online Mortgage Explorer Web site –

themortgage.com. This allows the prospective borrower to compare rates at several major lenders. You can find out whether you qualify in privacy before having to fill out the online application form.

Posted rates now are just a guideline to what the consumer will pay. More and more consumers are realizing that this is the situation. The two-tiered rate schedule is becoming a problem for long-established financial institutions because the Internet reveals the extent of the competitive alternatives. Virtual banks can post rock-bottom rates because they have "disintermediated" the branch system. That term disintermediation is an Internet buzzword for cutting out the middleman, or woman. New competitors in banking can avoid investing in branch locations and can process documents by secure Internet transmission, e-mail, telephone and fax.

CONSUMERS CAN NOW PURCHASE MORTGAGES, INSURANCE AND MUTUAL FUNDS ONLINE

While Internet mortgage technology is in the developmental stage, all the large banks are actively working on improving their online processes. It's not clear how much mortgage business will eventually migrate to the Net. But all financial institutions are gearing up to provide consumers with the capability to do routine transactions online, from mortgage renewals to insurance to managing a portfolio of mutual funds and other financial products.

MORTGAGE BROKERS CAN HELP YOU FIND THE BEST DEALS

Borrowers not yet tapped into the computer age do not have to be locked out of this mortgage cornucopia. Just as there are real estate brokers, stockbrokers and mutual fund dealers, you can also find a mortgage broker to help you negotiate a better deal. (The bank pays a finder's fee, typically 0.5%.) It used to be the case that mortgage brokers dealt primarily with poor credit risk borrowers who could not obtain loans from the banks, says Rick McGratten, president of the Mutual Group's residential mortgages division. That started to change about 1990 when TD Bank started to use mortgage brokers to win "prime" business.

Consumers can find a mortgage broker by calling the Canadian Institute of Mortgage Brokers & Lenders toll-free at 1-888-442-4625. One such broker, Andy MacDonald of Killian Mortgage Services Inc. of Toronto, says it is becoming tougher to obtain the big rate discounts that were possible until recently. Tom Alton, president of Bank of Montreal Mortgage Corp., says some "dysfunctional pricing" has crept into the marketplace, where people are using price as a primary weapon. He says brokers may be trying to turn mortgages into a commodity. "But if that is all they have to offer, it is the easiest mortgage to steal."

Here is what *Financial Post* reader Morton Katz learned after using the services of mortgage broker Norlite Financial in Mississauga, Ont.: "I have a pretty amazing mortgage and everyone pays way more than me. I am not in any special circumstance – I just did my homework. I figure I have put more equity in my house in 1.5 years than a 7.5% five-year big bank mortgage does in 10 [years]. Tell the others there are millions to be saved."

VARIABLE RATE MORTGAGES GIVE FLEXIBILITY

The mortgage marketplace has changed considerably over the past few years, as lenders scramble for customers. Deals abound, and variable rate mortgages are one recent innovation that can also save you money.

But as always, make sure you understand the contract details. Variable rate mortgages have been around for many years but only became popular among Canadian homeowners about five years ago, when interest rates began a prolonged drop. These most flexible of mortgages give homeowners the freedom to change mortgage terms or switch lenders at any time. They also charge the lowest interest rates, usually the institution's prime lending rate. The rate changes with the prime rate.

INTEREST CHARGED ON VARIABLE RATE MORTGAGES IS OFTEN THE LOWEST AVAILABLE

In its basic form, the variable-rate mortgage has many advantages over its fixed-rate, fixed-term counterparts. It is fully open for additional payments – called prepayments in mortgage lingo – at any time. It is convertible at any time to another mortgage type without penalty or transferable to another institution, also without penalty. Some lenders will insure a variable rate mortgage against default as a high-ratio mortgage (with some restrictions), thus making this mortgage option available to borrowers with lower down payments.

Fixed-term, fully open mortgages are available at most institutions for terms of six months and one year, but also charge significantly higher rates than variable rate mortgages. At times, the difference can be as much as two percentage points between the variable rate and a fixed rate. The only protection afforded by fixed-rate open mortgages is a few extra months at the fixed rate should the prime rate shoot up.

Variable rate mortgages tend to be underpromoted by lenders. For instance, you can pay down a variable rate mortgage at any time during the year, not just on the renewal anniversary. The money enters the mortgage account sooner, and interest costs are reduced accordingly. Over time, this might shave a year or two off the mortgage's amortization, more if substantial prepayments are made. To the lender, however, frequent small prepayments are a big clerical headache when everything else on the mortgage system is automated, save for a once-a-year additional payment. Because it is human nature not to take advantage of a single-shot prepayment opportunity, the fixed-rate, fixed-term mortgage tends to keep mortgage balances – and thus interest payments – at the maximum level.

SOME HOME OWNERS USE THE DOUBLE-UP MORTGAGE LIKE A LINE OF CREDIT

An innovation of the late 1980s was the "double-up" mortgage payment. At the time, some lenders also allowed borrowers to skip a payment, doubling up on a later payment. Many have taken advantage of the double-up option, but it has also turned out to be a blank cheque for spur-of-the-moment expenditures, with mortgage-holders skipping a payment and then having to make it up later. A variable rate mortgage, by contrast, cannot be used as a credit line. Once a prepayment has been made, it's irretrievable. Using the double-up/skip-a-payment combination is like paying off a credit card and then running up the balance again. Prepaying a variable rate mortgage, on the other hand, is like paying off a car loan – the only way to get the amount of the pre-payment back is to take out another loan.

An interesting variation is the capped variable rate mortgage, which charges an "insurance premium" of about one percentage point over prime for the security of a pre-determined ceiling over a long term. These are closed mortgages with terms that vary from three to five years and are convertible to a fixed-rate, fixed-term mortgage at any time. That's an expensive rate premium, although it is somewhat reassuring in volatile times. However, in a period of prolonged rate stability, their appeal is limited.

MANY VARIABLE RATE MORTGAGES LET YOU LOCK IN AT BELOW-MARKET RATES

Another variable rate mortgage derivative is available from FirstLine Mortgages, a sub-sidiary of Canadian Imperial Bank of Commerce. Introduced in 1990 as the "ARM [adjustable rate mortgage] with a Trigger," this mortgage charges an exceptionally low rate, compounded semi-annually instead of the monthly compounding used by basic variable rate mortgages. The borrower gets at least one entire calendar quarter at this rate, plus whatever part is left of the quarter in which the transaction closes. For example, if your mortgage closes Dec. 31 you get three months – the entire first quarter to March 31 – at that rate. If you close Jan. 2, you get that rate for almost six months, until June 30.

The ARM has an impressive array of below-market-rate lock-in options. These options – the longer term rates – are priced as much as one-quarter of a percentage point below posted rates for similar terms. This route becomes even more attractive after the initial term, because the rate is adjusted at the end of the calendar quarter to the Canada three-month treasury bill bid-side rate on the last Thursday of the calendar quarter, plus 1.5 percentage points.

RRSPS CAN FINANCE A HOME PURCHASE

Tapping a registered retirement savings plan to finance a home purchase is an attractive strategy, but you have to have enough money in the RRSP to make the exercise worth-while. You have to weigh the investment return, too. Do the advantages of paying mortgage interest to your plan out-weigh the lost opportunity of investing in potentially more lucrative arenas?

First, the basics. What you are doing is borrowing from your RRSP (only self-directed plans are eligible) to finance a home purchase or to refinance an existing mortgage. "Your mortgage principal and interest payments go back into your RRSP to help finance your retirement," says Leona Tranter, a principal with Canada Trust's financial advisory services group. "These payments generally represent a secure, high-quality investment, usually offering a higher rate of return than other fixed-income investments like GICs."

You may have to sell existing investments in your RRSP to raise the cash to finance the home purchase or refinance your mortgage. What you are doing is selling securities held in your RRSP and using the proceeds to set up a mortgage within your plan. The new mortgage holder – your RRSP – then pays off the home vendor or the current mortgage holder.

THE RRSP MORTGAGE ARRANGEMENT CAN ONLY APPLY TO YOUR PRINCIPAL DWELLING

You do not have to pay income tax on the money that ultimately leaves your RRSP – as is the case with normal RRSP withdrawals – because that money, in effect, is remaining within your RRSP in the form of a mortgage security. You are obliged to repay the debt, with interest, to your RRSP, and that debt is secured by the asset being financed – your home.

Canada Customs and Revenue Agency, which polices RRSP contributions and withdrawals, requires that an RRSP mortgage be set up and administered by an approved lender usually a bank or trust company – and must be insured by Canada Mortgage & Housing Corp., a federal agency, or a private mortgage insurer such as GE Capital Mortgage Co. (Gemico). The RRSP arrangement can only be applied to "non-arm's length" mortgages, Tranter says, "which means you must own and occupy the mortgaged property either individually or jointly."

The terms of the mortgage – interest rate, semi-annual interest compounding and administration details – must reflect normal commercial practice, she says. You must pay your RRSP the same rate a bank or trust company would charge over a similar term. "Any changes to your mortgage during its term must follow your financial institution's regular lending policies and do not receive preferential treatment," she says. "For example, if you wanted to accelerate payments or pay the mortgage off early, you would have to refer to the terms of your mortgage loan." The mortgage payments that will be made to your RRSP in no way affect your RRSP contribution room since each payment's principal portion represents money already contributed to the plan and the interest portion is income paid on the investment.

THERE ARE ADDITIONAL SET-UP AND ANNUAL FEES WITH A SELF-DIRECTED RRSP

Then there are fees. A self-directed RRSP has annual trustee fees of up to $150, although some institutions have reduced or waived this charge. In most cases there is also a one-time set-up fee of $100 to $200. On the mortgage side, the institution that sets up the mortgage for your plan charges fees for the application as well as for property appraisal. You also will have to pay legal or notarial fees, which typically total $1,000 to $1,200, when the mortgage is set up. And if you have a high-ratio mortgage – 75% or more of the property value – you will also have to pay a one-time mortgage insurance premium, generally 0.5% to 2.5% of the mortgage principal (this can be amortized along with the outstanding principal). On the new mortgage's anniversary date, you will have to pay annual mortgage administration fees of up to $200. And finally, many of the above fees are also subject to sales tax.

Tranter says a self-directed RRSP mortgage is suitable only for mortgages of at least $50,000. And do not overlook the RRSP investment angle, she adds. "Your adviser should help you determine the suitability of this type of investment, taking into account your investment objectives, risk tolerance and considering other investments that may yield higher returns. A self-directed mortgage can be a valuable part of a well-diversified portfolio," Tranter concludes, "but it should not be the only investment in your RRSP."

LAWS TRY TO BE FAIR TO CREDITOR AND DEBTOR

After nearly four years of tinkering, Canada's amended bankruptcy laws came into effect in 1997. Bill C-5, which amends the Bankruptcy and Insolvency Act and the Companies' Creditors Arrangement Act (CCAA), tries to strike a balance between a creditor's right to share in a bankrupt's assets and a debtor's right to a fresh start – or, as the legislation puts it, a "balance between rehabilitation and obligation." Some bankruptcy trustees have applauded the changes, saying they should overcome the perception that bankruptcy is too easy an option for consumers. Others are skeptical that widespread abuses by "professional bankrupts" will be curbed.

CHANGES TO THE BANKRUPTCY LAW REFLECT INCREASE IN CONSUMER BANKRUPTCIES

In changing the law the government recognized that business bankruptcies had been relatively stable over the past few years but consumer bankruptcies were on the rise. The new law raises the ante on debtor responsibility with new provisions on payment of debts from surplus income. The Superintendent of Bankruptcy sets standards as to what constitutes surplus income in various situations and regions of the country. If the amount is disputed, it will go to mediation.

The law also provides changes on discharge, which is the process of releasing a bankrupt's debts. Trustees are required to make a report on the bankrupt's conduct. That report now includes a recommendation as to whether the debtor should be discharged, based on the bankrupt's conduct and ability to make payments.

TWO NEW GROUNDS ON WHICH A CREDITOR CAN OPPOSE A BANKRUPTCY DISCHARGE

• If the debtor has failed to pay surplus income according to the bankruptcy agreement.
• If the debtor chose bankruptcy instead of a viable proposal to a creditor – one that would have been accepted by the creditors.

The law is tougher on the thousands of students who abuse the Canada Students Loans program before they've even begun their working life. Students were able to declare bankruptcy even before they graduated. Under Bill C-5, students are not to be released from their loans within two years of declaring bankruptcy, unless a court rules otherwise. Students are aided and abetted by the credit card companies, who, as one insolvency specialist put it, "are just throwing cards at students." But students are already flocking to bankruptcy trustee Chee-Kong Leong with plans to go bankrupt two years from now. "I think it's still too soft," he says. "There's a lot of potential for creative bankruptcy."

THE LAW ENCOURAGES BUSINESSES TO REORGANIZE RATHER THAN LIQUIDATE

Leong sees plenty of scope for continued abuse by high-income professionals who go bankrupt to avoid the biggest creditor of all – Canada Customs and Revenue Agency. The law is designed to encourage insolvent businesses to reorganize rather than liquidate their affairs. Liability protection for company directors encourages this. Previously, directors vulnerable to personal claims were unlikely to rebuild an insolvent firm. It also harmonizes the CCAA with the Bankruptcy Act. Companies now need liabilities of more than $5 million to get access to the CCAA. There are also special rules dealing with insolvency of securities firms and international insolvencies. Bryan Tannenbaum, president of Mintz & Partners Ltd., a trustee in bankruptcy, says C-5 "will go a long way to improve things." He says it will be possible to refine the law over time, unlike many other pieces of legislation.

DECLARING BANKRUPTCY IS STILL TOO EASY FOR CONSUMERS

But some bankruptcy lawyers are skeptical the law will make a difference. "I doubt whether the new provisions will encourage any significant change," says Frank Bennett of Bennett & Co., author of *Bennett on Going Broke.* "It's too easy to go into bankruptcy and likewise just as easy to get out." The Bankruptcy and Insolvency Act was never intended to apply to consumers, Bennett says. The surge in individual bankruptcies has occurred only since the Second World War. Amendments in 1992 intended that consumer debtors would attempt to make proposals or arrangements to pay a portion of their debts in an orderly fashion. "Unfortunately, the laws of going into bankruptcy and getting out are so easy that consumers elect not to make such consumer proposals," he says. "Until Parliament recognizes the problem, I suspect that our bankruptcy statistics will continue to be on the rise for many years to come."

THE INCREASE IN PERSONAL BANKRUPTCIES MAY BE AN AFTER EFFECT OF THE RECESSION

Bankruptcy rates have been rising despite the end of the recession of the early 1990s. That's because of what John Owen, principal of Omega-one, a credit consulting firm in Streetsville, Ont., refers to as "the bankruptcy echo." Today's bankruptcies are spurred by root causes that occurred five or 10 years earlier, such as a foreclosure on a home or the rash of white-collar layoffs at the height of the 1990s recession. Senior managers were initially shielded by generous severance packages. If their joblessness extended longer, they next plundered their RRSP savings. Only after that avenue was exhausted did some take recourse to bankruptcy. Owen says the situation has been aggravated by the rise of financial planners, some of whom advise individuals to "consider bankrupt-cy as just one more element in a comprehensive personal finance plan, as legitimate as making an RRSP contribution to reduce one's tax liability."

10 REASONS TO DITCH THE CAR FOR THE TRAIN

For most families, automobile expenses represent a sizable chunk of the monthly budget. But if you live in or near a major city, do you really need a car? Driving a car to work is an overrated and expensive luxury. As traffic congestion intensifies in big cities and driving manners deteriorate, it may be time for some commuters to re-evaluate their attitude to taking public transit. The government of Ontario's GO transit system experi-enced its first-ever annual decline in ridership in 1992. But it's been rising again recently.

To take a leaf from David Letterman, there are at least 10 reasons to consider com-muter rail, many of them directly or indirectly financial. I base the following observa-tions on my experience of trains on GO's Toronto region Lakeshore West route. But they apply to similar systems in Vancouver and Montreal: B.C. Transit's West Coast Express and the Montreal Urban Community Transit Corp.

HERE ARE 10 GOOD REASONS TO DITCH THE CAR IN FAVOR OF THE TRAIN

10. Save money. You can extend the life of your car and save money on gas, parking and maintenance. The Canadian Automobile Association produces annual reports on the cost of operating a car. You can find the details on their Website at www.caa.ca. The 2000 report pegged the cost at 36 cents a kilometre for a compact that is driven 32,000 kilometres a year. That figure included annual operating and ownership costs. As the accompanying table shows, an Oakville, Ont., resident commuting to downtown Toronto would pay just over $6,000 for the car versus less than $2,000 for commuter rail. That's a big annual saving. Based on this analysis, over a 40-year working life you could buy a house on the savings. A two car family that opted for one car, with each spouse alternating between car and transit, would save thousands a year.

9. Help the environment. Anyone whose only contribution to the environment consists of using blue boxes can feel twice as good by also using commuter rail. A 1982 study found car commuters used as much energy in four years of driving as a transit rider consumes in 40 years. One 10-car commuter train that serves the greater Toronto area carries the same number of people as 1,000 air-polluting cars. If you used transit for a year instead of driving to work, the environment would be spared 13.5 kilograms of hydrocarbons, 100 kilograms of carbon monoxide, seven kilograms of nitrogen oxides and 1,517 kilo-grams of carbon dioxide, according to the Ontario Ministry of Municipal Affairs. To put the last figure in perspective, that level of carbon dioxide is 20% of the amount removed by one hectare of forest. Do you really want all that on your conscience?

8. Health and exercise. The environment is a macro health issue, but transit also can impart direct health benefits to the individual user. The four walks a day involved in

WHAT YOU CAN SAVE | BY LEAVING THE CAR AT HOME

Savings based on 35-kilometre commute at 35.9¢/kilometre, not including parking

Cost of	Car $	GO Train $*	Savings $
Two-way trip	25.14	9.20	15.94
Weekly (5 days)	125.70	41.50	84.20
Monthly (20 days)	502.80	145.00	357.80
Yearly	6,033.60	1,740.00	4,293.60
10 years	60,336.00	17,400.00	42,936.00
40 years	241,344.00	69,600.00	171,744.00

* includes cost savings of GO 10-ride ticket and monthly pass

going between home, rail stations and work can easily add up to the half-hour daily exercise many doctors recommend. The related health benefits may well ultimately save you money.

7. Safety. Driving every day increases the odds of having an accident, which may well result in higher subsequent insurance rates. Recent studies showing the appalling number of red lights being run in Toronto are alone reason to consider public transit. The hazards of drunk driving are equally evident.

6. Reduce highway congestion. Many commuter rail users also own cars and occasionally need to take them to work. No one says you have to take the train every day of the week – if you have a meeting and need the car, take it. A single 40-foot transit vehicle replaces 46 cars in rush hours. If all car drivers used the train just half the time, that would leave the highways that much less congested for those who need to use the car on a particular day. The reduced stress could also help your health and cut future medical expenses.

5. Increase reading and work time. Depending on the length of your commute, you can gain nearly an hour a day of reading time on the train. You may even develop your speed reading skills, as you master the technique of squeezing an entire chapter of a book in during a ride. You can also crunch spreadsheets or do word processing on a laptop computer or make cell phone calls. These productivity gains may translate into increased earning power.

4. Buffer zone. The combination of walking and riding the train makes a nice transition between the leisure of home and stresses of the workplace. In the morning, you can mentally plan your day; at night, you can decompress, without the adrenaline surges involved in coping with discourteous car drivers or the stress and waste of time of traffic jams.

3. Window on pop culture. The train is a great place to check out tastes in popular literature. Seems to be an even mix between trash novels and literary and philosophic classics.

2. Music appreciation. Most motorists aren't really listening to music; they're operating a complex mechanical device that could inflict death at any moment. *Listen!*, a primer on classical music, says that to properly appreciate good music you need to close your eyes and concentrate. You can do this with a Walkman on a commuter train, but it's definitely not recommended for car drivers.

AND THE NO. 1 REASON FOR TAKING THE TRAIN INSTEAD OF DRIVING?

Contemplation and meditation. As transit veterans know, commuter rail cars are the quietest place on earth. Commuters are generally quiet, law-abiding, middle class people who value their privacy and solitude. Conversations on the train are rare. At home, you can't escape the demands of spouse and children and are subject to door-to-door solicitations at any time. If the phone rings, you're compelled to answer. And then there are the incessant demands of the workplace. Only on the train can you grab a few minutes of contemplation or meditation.

BEING A CHEAPSKATE CAN BE GOOD STRATEGY

There are two types of spenders in this world – cheapskates and spendthrifts. If you act under the illusion that you're already rich, spending indiscriminately day after day, you'll end up poor. Conversely, if you act poor, you have a far better shot at ending up rich. While the average consumer tends to drive a hard bargain on big-ticket expenses – going to elaborate lengths to keep taxes to a minimum or shave half a point off mortgage rates – it's the little day-to-day living expenses that really cut into your financial prosperity.

Most of us fritter away at least $10 a day in items we're barely conscious of purchasing. The problem is there are 365 days in the year, which means the habit of daily impulse buying can cost you almost $8,000 a year. That's not a math mistake. In today's overtaxed climate, a penny saved is not a penny earned. In the 50% tax bracket, a penny saved is worth two pretax pennies. If you count consumption taxes such as the 7% GST, an after-tax penny is even more valuable. So $10 in after-tax dollars thrown away every day is $20 pretax.

THESE HELPFUL HINTS SHOW YOU HOW TO SAVE MONEY EVERY DAY

To mangle metaphors further, if you respect these after-tax pennies, the after-tax dollars will take care of themselves. There are plenty of examples of cheapskates who became rich. In his younger days, Sir John Templeton loathed personal debt, including even mortgages. He furnished his early households with used furniture and other bargains, buying things only when he had the cash. Today, the founder of the Templeton mutual fund empire doesn't have to worry about money. But he still tells investors the best time to invest is "when you have the money" and frowns on leverage.

There are some obvious potential cost savings. Take lunch. So-called fast food is neither fast nor cheap and, in some cases, barely qualifies as nourishing food. Bag lunches of fruit, granola bars, sandwiches or microwaveable products such as Lean Cuisine should cut your average lunch bill from about $7 to $3. That's $80 to $100 a month in after-tax dollars saved, which can be applied to paying down your mortgage (priority No. 1 for genuine cheapskates). How much do we waste on coffee? It's $1 a throw, give or take, these days for regular coffee and much, much more if you go to the cappuccino bars. A Brita water filter at your desk is cheaper and probably healthier.

The little consumption items at home also add up. I happen to be an audio buff and used to spend a lot on compact discs. I'd bought in early to the idea the CD sound was superior to old-fashioned vinyl records, and for years happily forked out $20 or more for each CD. I'm not so sure CDs are superior anymore. Their very popularity has led to such volume manufacturing that I find quality has slipped. Second, modern popular music leaves me cold. Third, portable CD players aren't as light and convenient as cassette Walkmans. And fourth, CDs are still expensive. Being a cheapskate, my solution has been to phase out CDs and frequent the few stores that still sell used vinyl records. Until its unfortunate 1999 closure, the best in Toronto was Peter Dunn's Vinyl Museum where you could buy good-quality vinyl from the 1950s to 1980s for $2.50, $3.99 or $4.99 and regulars enjoyed a 20% discount and occasional half-price sales on the cheaper records.

Other outlets still exist where you can purchase almost the entire output of a particular artist for $20 or $30, about the same cost as a single CD. I buy cheap 90-minute cassettes at the Bi-way and record two vinyl albums on each cassette for use in the car or Walkman. Of course if you're a dedicated cheapskate, you can simply go to the library and borrow music CDs or tapes, not to mention books, videos and magazines.

A CHEAPSKATE STRATEGY IS GOOD FINANCIAL PLANNING

Another common household expense is batteries. If you have children, you know how expensive it can be to power the multitude of toys and electronic gizmos that clutter the average home. And if a child ever leaves a flashlight on overnight, as mine has, you know how fast $5 can go down the drain. That's five "after-tax" dollars! The solution is rechargeable batteries.

I used to buy the blue nickel-cadmium batteries sold at Radio Shack, but there's a new type of battery technology out called "reusable alkaline." They are similar to the use-once-and-throw-away alkaline batteries you buy at any convenience store. But you can't recharge regular alkaline batteries, which, apart from being expensive, also makes them environmentally unfriendly.

Rayovac Canada Inc. of Mississauga, Ont., is marketing Renewal rechargeable alkaline batteries. They cost about the same as regular throwaway batteries, work right out of the package like throwaways, but can also be recharged 20 or 30 times. They degrade a bit with each recharge, but hold a charge much longer than the older nickel-cadmium rechargeable technology. Just be warned, rechargers for one type of battery won't work for other rechargeable batteries. There are also a handful of competitors to Renewal.

They're not as widely available as regular alkalines but Radio Shack carries the new batteries and the rechargers.

There are plenty of other cheapskate opportunities out there, too. Don't overlook their value in your financial planning.

DO RESPS ANSWER THE EDUCATION QUESTION?

Which method of saving for a child's education is better: registered education savings plans (RESPs) or equity mutual funds held in trust? While the RESP acronym resembles the RRSP, there is a major difference. RRSPs provide a tax deduction on the initial principal, RESPs don't – they merely shelter the income or growth created by that principal. All capital gains, dividends and interest compound untaxed and become taxable only when withdrawn by the student. The idea is that the student will be in such a low tax bracket that, even though the income becomes taxable, the tax bill will be negligible.

RESP INVESTMENTS ARE INTENDED TO FUND POST-SECONDARY EDUCATION

RESPs come in two main flavors: pooled RESP plans and plans administered by financial institutions or mutual fund companies, which offer flexible and simple "self-directed" RESP plans. The main pooled RESP vendors are Canadian Scholarship Trust, USC Education Savings, Heritage Scholarship Trust and Children's Education Trust of Canada, some of which go back to the early 1960s. You'll typically see their brochures in waiting rooms of maternity wards or retail stores selling children's goods. RESPs were intended to help finance the cost of sending children to universities, community colleges, CEGEPs in Quebec and Canadian junior and technical colleges or universities outside Canada. RESP money can also pay for books, lab fees, equipment, accommodation and transportation.

The 1998 federal budget introduced a grant of up to $400 a year to match an individual's RESP contribution. The 1997 budget doubled the RESP contribution limit to $4,000 a year per child (the lifetime limit remains at $42,000), and other provisions made them more attractive than in past, but they still have a number of warts. For example, pooled RESPs charge large enrolment fees upfront, somewhat like a mutual fund front-end load at the 10% level. If you cancel in the first year or two, you'll forfeit most of that fee.

IN-TRUST FUNDS HAVE SEVERAL ADVANTAGES OVER RESPS

The 1997 budget changes did overcome the single biggest objection to RESPs: the forfeiture of the plans' growth if the child did not go on to higher education. This led to arguments about how much education was needed to keep the RESP earnings. The minimum education requirement allowed by Canada Customs and Revenue Agency was a three-week course with at least 10 hours a week of study and homework. It also insisted the school had to consider the child a full-time student.

RESPs | VS. IN-TRUST ACCOUNTS

	RESPs	In-trust accounts
Availability	Some financial institutions	Most financial institutions
Contribution limit	$42,000 per child	None
Annual cont. limit	$4,000 per child	None
Taxation	Tax-deferred growth in plan Income taxable to child on withdrawal	Interest/dividends taxable to contributor Capital gains taxable to child
Uses	Post-secondary education*	Any purpose at any time

* Federal government allows rollovers into RRSPs, or cashout with penalties.

Source: The Rogers Group, Vancouver

Those arguments are hardly relevant now, since the budget allows parents to take back capital contributions and roll over the income accumulated in the RESPs into their RRSPs to a lifetime limit of $50,000. "If RESPs were a bad idea at $2,000, they're twice as bad at $4,000," says Warren Baldwin, regional vice-president of T. E. Financial Consultants Ltd., though he adds the RRSP rollover may create some new opportunities, particularly for wealthy investors.

The RRSP rollover may also mean the "tontine" aspect of pooled RESPs has been diluted. Under tontine financial schemes, income forgone by plan contributors whose children opted not to go to university was added to the pool shared by those still college bound, typically about 85% of the beneficiaries who started. There is also a 10% a year dropoff between second-year university and fourth year.

"It's a bit of a dilemma," says Tom O'Shaughnessy, senior vice-president of Canadian Scholarship Trust. "Irrespective of what the budget says, the contracts say if you withdraw, you'll forfeit" the earnings. The fund companies do not use the tontine. They also have a simpler alternative that does not use the RESP: the equity mutual fund held in trust.

A Dynamic Mutual Funds advisory argues "astute advisers will find an equity mutual fund properly set up in trust for a child is still more flexible than an RESP and offers greater potential tax savings." Some independent financial planners agree. Vancouver-based Rogers Group Financial Advisors Ltd. prefers trust accounts because "they remain more flexible, especially for longer-term investment horizons."

Pooled RESPs can invest only in fixed-income securities. If you believe stocks or equity funds provide greater longer-term growth, pooled RESPs won't be your best bet. If that's your preference, you needn't have a mutual fund RESP either: just opt for the simpler course of holding the fund in trust for your child.

A FORMAL TRUST LETS YOU SPECIFY HOW THE MONEY IS TO BE SPENT

Capital gains taxes will be paid by the child, but, unless the child is making more than $6,500 a year in taxable income, he or she should have negligible taxable income and will pay no tax. The downside is that while the trustee – usually the parent – controls the assets, the child gains control at age 18 and could decide to blow it on a new car or a trip to Europe instead using it for school. That's why some planners, like Leslie Mezei, an associate with Brightside Financial Services, prefer a formal trust to the informal trusts set up by the fund companies. A formal trust can allow you to specify how the money is to be spent. They cost $500 to $1,000 to set up.

SURE KIDS COST A LOT, BUT HOW MUCH?

Any parent will tell you it costs a lot of money to raise a child, but few people have bothered to count the actual dollars spent. Manitoba Agriculture can tell you right down to the last penny from its annual surveys of child-raising expenses. Taking fads and fashions into account, the Manitoba team has listed the "basic goods and services necessary to maintain physical and social well being." Then they priced each item. As much as possible, they used the Sears catalogue. If the desired item was not available or unsatisfactory, they visited one or more Winnipeg area stores.

BOYS EAT MORE FOOD AND GIRLS NEED MORE IN CLOTHING

They sought well-made items that offered good value, and selections tended to fall between the most and least expensive. In some cases, researchers visited several stores and averaged the prices. As shown on the accompanying chart, total costs of raising a child in 2000 ran to about $9,656 for an infant of either sex. At four years old, the tally was $9,259 for a boy and $9,327 for a girl. At eight years, it was $8,714 for a boy and $8,768 for a girl. At 12, when day care is no longer needed, a boy cost $6,181 and a girl $6,269. At 16, the totals were $7,017 for a boy and $6,724 for a girl. Boys devour far more food and girls need more in clothing.

In May 1997, the federal government enacted child support guidelines for divorce orders, with the figures varying by province and the income of the payor parent. At the average industrial wage, about $35,500, the $3,540 federal standard for Manitoba would have covered about 40% of the estimated cost for a child under 10. At the $45,000 income level, the $4,476 federal standard would have covered about 50%.

HERE IS HOW SOME OF THE FIGURES WERE COMPILED

• Durables, such as clothing, were depreciated over their expected life.
• The food list was based on Agriculture Canada standards for a nutritious diet.
• Health-care costs reflected the difference between single and family coverage under Blue Cross. That category included one annual dental checkup and cleaning, but no eyeglasses or special needs.
• Recreation included a bicycle and lessons in one activity. Significantly, it did not include expensive popular pursuits such as hockey or private music lessons.
• School needs covered just supplies. There was no provision for savings for college or university.
• There was no special weekly allowance. That money came from the categories shown.

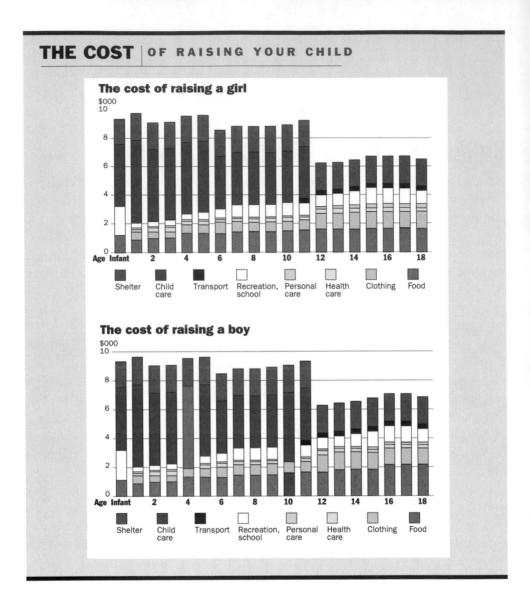

The cost of raising a girl

The cost of raising a boy

• Transportation reflected Winnipeg public transit fares. Manitoba Agriculture says car owners "roughly estimated" that child-related trips and teenage use added about 8.8¢ per kilometre to overall vehicle ownership cost.

• Child-care costs were based on licensed day care in Winnipeg.

The shelter cost reflected the difference between rent for a one and two-bedroom apartment in Winnipeg. Manitoba Agriculture also estimated that each child adds 10% to family utilities bills. Having two children would not double the stated cost because some expenses, such as health insurance, were set per family while others, such as furniture and clothing, can be reused.

MAKE SURE YOUR CREDIT RATING IS ACCURATE

Have you ever wondered what your personal credit history looks like? If you're like the vast majority of Canadians, chances are you've never even glanced at this all-important piece of paper. Even if you're not applying for a loan or a mortgage, you should make it a priority to examine your credit report, if for no other reason than to make certain the information it contains is accurate. And in case you're wondering, it's free for the asking.

I always believed I was in possession of an unblemished credit history, a document festooned with "R1" notations – credit-bureau-speak for credit card balances being "paid as agreed and up to date." But when my eyes gazed upon my two-page credit history, which I had requested from Montreal-based Equifax Canada, you could hear the sound of cartilage on linoleum – my jaw dropped to the floor. I'm the kind of fellow who looks upon debt as a four-letter word. So, you can understand the jolt to my system when I discovered that my personal credit report – the document that banks, utilities and employers use to approve (or assassinate) my character – contained a sprinkling of condemnation.

IT IS WORTH OBTAINING YOUR CREDIT REPORT AND VERIFYING THE INFORMATION

First, there was this Bank of Montreal MasterCard. It was originally activated in December, 1992, my report noted, and was currently carrying a balance of $978. The account had been 30 days past due five times; 60 days past due three times, and 90 or more days past due, three times. There was only one not-so-insignificant hitch. This piece of plastic doesn't belong to me. Other information was awry as well. Gazing on the box listing my former address, my eyes met the name of a street I've never strolled past, much less lived on. And the company I used to work for was listed as being my wife's present employer.

To their credit, a call to the people at Equifax resulted in assurances that the errors would be put under investigation and likely rectified within a few weeks. A telephone representative explained that, based on the evidence at hand, I had been cross-filed with another person of the same name. Somehow my credit and residence history had been merged with bits and bytes of his, and not even Equifax, which is a major player in the consumer-credit information business, knew why. If there is something to be learned from my experience, it's simply this: If you don't know anything about the Equifax and Trans Union credit bureaus – the two largest credit bureaus in the land – you should. They know a lot about you, and sometimes their data are not entirely on the money.

PERSONAL CREDIT RATINGS ARE THERE FOR THE ASKING

A few years ago CBC's *Marketplace* aired a segment in which 100 consumers requested copies of their personal credit reports from Equifax. A staggering 47 found errors. Thirteen reports had errors so significant the misinformation would have affected the consumers' chances of getting credit. "It is definitely a problem, because so much data is being retrieved and entered [by the credit bureaus], errors can easily be made," says Laurie Campbell, a program manager with the Credit Counselling Service of Toronto. "One thing we always ask individuals to do, whether they think their credit rating is good or bad, is to get a copy to check it out."

Yet, for whatever reason, many Canadians look upon credit reports as being documents shrouded in mystery. A national opinion survey conducted for Equifax Canada by Louis Harris and Associates Inc. determined that only 13% of Canadians have seen a copy of their credit report or had the contents of their credit report read to them over the phone. (The corresponding U.S. figure is 38%.) As well, only 56% of Canadian adults believe they actually have a legal right to see their personal credit bureau reports. But there shouldn't be any mysteries about personal credit ratings – credit-bureau information is there for the asking.

INACCURACIES IN YOUR CREDIT REPORT WILL BE CORRECTED BY THE CREDIT BUREAU

By law, personal credit information can be released to third parties only if the person is applying for credit, employment or insurance, or if there's a legitimate business need for this information. (For example, utilities are included under this principle because new customers can run up whopping bills and then skip town.) But anyone can gain access to their own information at any time. And what about those errors? Ken Porter, vice-president and general manager of Toronto-based Trans Union of Canada, Inc., says despite sophisticated information-gathering technology, mistakes are sometimes made on people's reports because amassing data often boils down to "garbage in, garbage out."

Most credit grantors supply the bureaus with information that is accurate and legible. But there are other firms, says Porter, "that give us applications that seem to have been filled out on scrap paper." And that's when mistakes are likely to be made. Michel Globensky of Equifax Canada says hundreds of thousands of Canadians obtain copies of their credit reports each year and Equifax is diligent when it comes to eradicating errors. "If inaccuracies creep in, despite the best of our intentions, it's our job to correct them," he says. "Information is our lifeblood."

Even so, before negotiating a mortgage or applying for a loan or credit card, Campbell of CCS advises people to review their own credit ratings first. "This way, you can correct the inaccuracies before you're sitting across the table from the bank manager," she says. "And if there's any justified black mark on your record that you've forgotten about, at least you know what it's there for."

FINANCIAL PLANNERS DO MORE THAN INVEST

Panicky investors who considered bolting for the equity exits in October 1997 probably have their financial planners to thank for keeping them invested. In such situations, good advice is worth thousands of dollars, while poor advice or none at all can cost you big-time. Financial planners like Jane Baker see their job primarily as keeping clients invested in such situations, holding them to long-term plans made in calmer times. They call this hand holding, something do-it-yourself investors miss out on. But the seemingly simple question of "How do I find a good financial planner?" almost stumped me the other day when a television interviewer posed it.

My flip TV answer was: "Don't worry, financial planners will find you" at the multitude of free seminars that appear as registered retirement savings plan season approaches. I neglected to say there is a free directory available from the Canadian Association of Financial Planners. Call 1-800-346-CAFP or check the association's Web site at www.cafp.org. It contains 800 names of financial planners who have at least a CFP (chartered financial planner) designation or the more rigorous RFP (registered financial planner).

DO SOME BACKGROUND WORK BEFORE CHOOSING A FINANCIAL PLANNER

A CFP designation is restricted to those who pass an exam set by the Financial Planners Standards Council of Canada, a body established in 1995 to set uniform minimum standards. Ideally, financial planners also have an RFP designation, which means they have been in the business at least two years, have liability insurance, have met educational requirements and are bound by the CAFP's code of professional ethics. Keep in mind that, except in Quebec, financial planners are not formally regulated. Financial products are regulated but financial advice about how to put those products together is not.

Based on the numbers for brokers who sell financial products and fund companies that have their own representatives, there must be at least 25,000 people claiming to be financial planners. But the number of RFPs in Canada is less than 5% of that total. The CAFP directory is broken down provincially and reveals degrees and professional designations and how the planner is compensated. Most are paid by commission; but there are some who charge fees and some who use both methods of remuneration.

CHECKING UP | ON CREDIT CHECKERS

Some people believe they actually have to pay so-called credit doctors a fee (typically from $300 to $500) to gain access to their credit history, but it's not true.

Here's how to get the documentation the financial institutions are judging you by for free: Equifax Canada requires photocopies of two pieces of identification such as a driver's licence, birth certificate or passport. Sign the photocopies and include a note indicating current address, former address, date of birth and daytime phone number. Mail to: Equifax Canada Inc., 7171 Jean Talon E., Anjou, Que., H1S 2Z2. Trans Union of Canada also requires photocopies of two pieces of valid ID, as well as a photocopy of a utility bill to verify your address. Mail to: Trans Union Consumer Relations Department, P.O. Box 338-LCD1, Hamilton, L8L 7W2. Information is usually processed in 10 to 14 days and then mailed out. If there are anomalies, call the credit bureau (Equifax: 1-800-465-7166; Trans Union: 1-800-663-9980) and your file will be investigated and, if necessary, corrected. An updated credit report should be on its way to you in 15 to 20 days.

Fee or fees-only means, in theory, you pay a separate fee for advice and a financial plan. Such a planner is supposedly pure and uninfluenced by front or rear loads, trailer fees and other enticements that may compromise objective advice. But you must recognize they have to be paid. There is nothing wrong with being compensated through commissions, as long as this is made clear. Toronto-based planner Jane Baker, for example, charges commissions, a percentage of assets under management and/or fee-for-service, depending on what the client prefers. She spells out each option to all prospective clients.

If you located a planner through a trusted friend or colleague, you are expecting a measure of integrity and competence in the person being considered. But before handing over your life savings, ask for references. The CAFP advises meeting with a prospective planner "to ensure that you get along well." Ask about the planner's education and related experience and establish whether an assistant will be handling your account. If so, ask to meet that person too. Explore the planner's areas of expertise. Where there are gaps, establish how good connections are with accountants, lawyers, investment counselors and other professionals.

YOU HAVE A RIGHT TO KNOW HOW MANY CLIENTS THE PLANNER SERVES

The CAFP does not suggest it, but I would want to know how many clients the planners and their staffs are serving. Ask commission-compensated planners how big their "book" of business is. If it is huge – and many have a book well beyond $100 million – ask yourself how much service you, the small client, are likely to receive. If the book is tiny, is it because the planner is new in the business or has the advice been so bad many clients have left?

Steve Gobel, investors division manager and CAFP president, suggests finding a planner who deals with people with situations similar to your own. You can check the planner's average client asset size by dividing the book value by the number of clients, and seeing how your portfolio size compares. Gobel also says planners should advocate a broad approach to financial planning. This includes clarifying the client's financial situation; identifying goals and making recommendations with regard to cash flow management, retirement planning, tax planning, estate planning, and particular investment products.

SINCE YOU ARE THE SOUGHT-AFTER CUSTOMER, YOU CAN DRIVE A HARD BARGAIN

Products, such as mutual funds, are only one component of a financial plan. If you view the planner as primarily a seller of products, be clear on the nature of these products and how the planner is compensated for selling them. If the planners are primarily fund salespersons, they probably sell six or seven fund families. Find out which ones. Remember, you are the prospect and a highly sought-after customer. Be fussy and drive a hard bargain.

CHAPTER 10

INSURANCE | PLANNING

- The fundamentals
- Home, car and travel insurance
- Group plans
- Disability, critical illness and long-term care insurance
- ABCs of life insurance

INSURING FOR A HEALTHY LIFE

AND AGAINST AN UNTIMELY DEATH | BY JONATHAN CHEVREAU

IFE IS ALL ABOUT RISK. Insurance is the art of hedging against the multiple risks we all face as we move through our lives. "Even the best designed financial plans for individuals, families and their businesses face three fundamental risks," says Bill Strain, executive vice-president with PPIFinancial Group. The family breadwinners may die too soon, become disabled or live too long. He defines insurance as being a "business of risk intermediation."

This chapter explores the various types of insurance available in the Canadian market. These include the traditional big three of life insurance, auto insurance and house insurance. But, increasingly, it's becoming necessary to provide for "living benefits" that kick in not when we die but when we become disabled (disability insurance); critically ill through cancer, stroke and similar calamities (critical illness insurance); and to care for us in an advanced but perhaps infirm old age (long-term care insurance). As Strain points out, there is risk living too long as well as dying young. As he puts it, "increasing longevity increases the risk of outliving your money and incurring greater long-term health care costs."

INSURANCE POLICIES CAN BE TAILORED TO YOUR INDIVIDUAL NEEDS

As insurance products evolve, they are becoming more complex, he says. The pace of innovation in the life insurance marketplace has been particularly frenetic, as products move from concept to delivery in months rather than years. The rise of the personal computer has allowed insurance agents to build many more options into product offerings, empowering financial planners and agents to tailor insurance products to various "what-if" scenarios involving their clients. "No longer does one size fit all," Strain says. Insurance professionals also must accept greater responsibility for keeping clients informed about the risks as well as the rewards of some of the more aggressive strategies.

Examples of this are provided in the articles on leveraged life insurance in the Retirement Planning section of this Investing Guide. Leveraged life plans aim to provide high

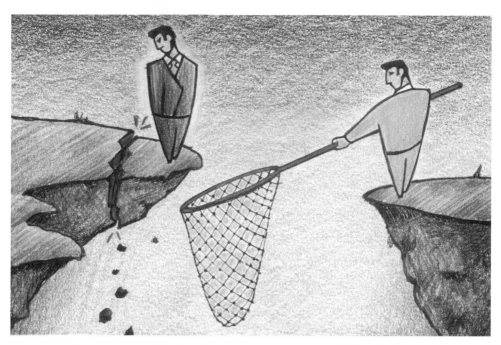

Insurance professionals must accept responsibility for keeping clients informed about the risks involved

net worth investors with a tax-free flow of retirement income. This is achieved through a type of life insurance known as universal life and by using the investment savings portion of the policy as collateral for a series of bank loans. The loans are repaid with the death benefit and, theoretically, a tidy nest egg remains for your beneficiaries. With participating whole life and universal life insurance products, the policyholders assume an underlying investment risk, whether or not they realize it, Strain says

DIFFERENCES IN POLICY PREMIUMS AND BENEFITS CAN BE VAST

Faced with a precipitous decline in interest rates in recent years, disgruntled policy-holders have found the actual returns on their universal life and participating whole life polices have not lived up to the initial promises. This has given rise to "vanishing premium" cases in North America. In either case, Strain and other insurance professionals counsel full and fair disclosure of the assumptions and guarantees laid out in sales illustrations of such products. Insurance is generally available through "group" plans at work or purchased individually to supplement group coverage. There is also a measure of insurance in certain government programs, such as the disability provisions of the Canada Pension Plan and Workers Compensation.

If you want to buy individual insurance, you'll generally have to choose between captive sales people married to one supplier or more independent brokers who try to shop the market for you. Differences in policy premiums and benefits can be vast, as is apparent in the case of automobile insurance in Ontario. In this case, consumer hotlines like the Consumer's Guide to Insurance, can help you choose.

Strain says innovations in insurance will be driven by clients, especially the demographic wave of aging baby boomers. That alone will make long-term health care and related insurance a booming business. The U.S. is well advanced in this market but as health costs rise in Canada, more families here will look to privately financed care through insurance. Strain envisages an era in which well-off consumers build pools of investments through the tax-deferred mechanisms of universal life policies.

INSURANCE POLICIES WILL NOW COVER LONG-TERM CARE, CRITICAL ILLNESS AND DISABILITY
Increasingly, these will be used to fund benefits for long-term care, critical illness and disability. Products may combine various combinations of what to date have been sold on a piecemeal basis. "Rather than using stand-alone products to indemnify a particular risk, tomorrow's products may adopt a more holistic approach," Strain predicts. Such policies would not only insure but "offer the ability to accumulate tax-sheltered supplementary retirement savings" over and above registered pension plans and RRSPs. Even more revolutionary would be flexible multiple life policies that would cover several lives and "introduce the potential for some co-insurance with the policyholder."

ALL YOU NEED TO KNOW ABOUT LIFE INSURANCE

Life insurance is a financial tool whose main purpose is to replace income that is lost when a wage earner dies. It's an efficient way to protect your survivors and dependents against financial hardship and to ensure that they are not burdened with significant debt when you die. Life insurance can also be a useful way of ensuring that your mortgage or tax bill is paid off or be a mechanism for leaving money to organizations or charities of your choice.

HOW MUCH LIFE INSURANCE DO I NEED?
To determine how much life insurance you require, it is important to carry out a financial needs analysis. You can do this yourself, but a trained and licensed life insurance agent can help you conduct a more thorough review. You should take into consideration what immediate financial needs there will be after your death to cover such expenses as medical bills, funeral expenses and estate taxes. Keep in mind also what costs would be involved in a readjustment period for family members or friends who relied on your financial support. Other items to factor in are monthly bills and other ongoing expenses, rent or mortgage payments, day-care costs and tuition fees. A general rule of thumb is that you should buy life insurance that is equal to five to seven times your net income.

WHAT KINDS OF POLICIES ARE THERE?
There are two basic kinds of life insurance: permanent and term. As the name implies,

permanent insurance is best suited to cover long-term and permanent financial needs, such as funeral expenses, income for your survivors and dependents, and capital gains taxes and other liabilities at death. Term insurance, on the other hand, is designed to look after shorter-term financial needs, such as mortgages, education and other expenses when children are young and some business commitments. Permanent insurance provides life-long protection and it is known by several names: whole life, universal life or variable life. This kind of life insurance has several distinguishing features.

First of all, premiums remain level over the lifetime of the policy. Second, reserves in the policy accumulate as a cash value. You may borrow against this cash value, or you may receive it if you surrender your policy. Third, non-forfeiture options

WHO BUYS | INSURANCE?

Age of insured	% of policies	% of amount*
Under 18	17	7
18-24	12	10
25-34	30	38
35-44	22	29
45-54	12	12
55 or over	7	4

Total: 16 million Canadians covered.
* the dollar value of individual policies

Size of policy $	% of policies	% of amount*
Under 15,000	10	1
15,000-24,999	8	1
25,000-49,999	16	5
50,000-99,999	22	14
100,000-300,000	40	60
300,001 and over	4	19

Source: Canadian Life and Health Insurance Assoc.

allow you to use the cash value to pay premiums, to buy a lesser amount of permanent insurance with no further premiums or to purchase an equal amount of term insurance. Participating policies receive their share of the financial success of the life insurance company in the form of dividends that are declared annually and paid to policyholders.

Term insurance provides protection for a specified period of time (one, five, 10 or 20 years or to age 60, 65 or 70) and it pays a benefit only if you die during the term of the policy. Premiums remain level during the term chosen, but they increase when the term is renewed.

This kind of policy does not have a cash value or non-forfeiture options. One form of term insurance, called Term to 100, provides protection to age 100, but generally doesn't pay dividends or include cash values.

Group life insurance is made available by most employers and unions. It is usually term insurance to age 65 and often does not require a medical examination or other evidence of insurability. Care should be taken to determine if your insurance coverage can be converted to individual insurance at the termination of your employment.

WHOM SHOULD I NAME AS A BENEFICIARY?

You can name an individual to receive the proceeds of the policy or you can name your estate or a trust. If you name a beneficiary in your policy, the money goes directly to that person or organization and does not go through your estate, thus avoiding having to pay probate fees or taxes. Another advantage to naming a spouse, child, grandchild or a parent as a beneficiary is the money is exempt from seizure by creditors. You also have the option of naming an irrevocable beneficiary, which means that the policyholder cannot change the name of that beneficiary without his or her consent. This money is also protected from creditors and doesn't become part of your estate. You may also name a contingent beneficiary, in the event that the primary beneficiary you have named is not alive at the time of your death. Otherwise the money will go to your estate. Finally, you can name a registered charitable organization as beneficiary, in which case the premiums can be tax deductible.

WHEN DO I PAY MY PREMIUMS AND WHAT HAPPENS IF I STOP PAYING THEM?

Most people choose to pay their premiums on a monthly basis, often through automatic bank withdrawals, but you can opt for annual, semi-annual or quarterly payments. You may choose to determine the number of years you want to pay premiums, so that at some point your policy will be fully paid up. If you stop paying your premiums for whatever reason, you have 31 days to make the payment after the due date. If you do not pay within that time, your policy will lapse, or terminate. It can be reinstated but this will require payment of overdue premiums, with interest, and may require a medical examination. In most policies there are riders that can help you in the event that you are having difficulties paying your premiums.

HOW SHOULD I USE MY POLICY DIVIDENDS?

If you purchase a participating life insurance policy, you will receive policy dividends (these are not to be confused with regular dividends issued by corporations to their shareholders). You can use them for a variety of purposes: to increase your insurance coverage; to increase future cash values through paid-up additions or bonus additions; or to purchase one-year term insurance. You can also use your dividends to reduce your premium, or you can take them in cash.

Some people choose to leave these dividends on deposit to earn interest or to be invested in a segregated fund, which is the insurance industry's version of a mutual fund.

WHAT IS GROUP CREDITORS' LIFE INSURANCE?

Many people don't realize that your mortgage or car loan may become payable in full if you die. Lending institutions and car dealers sell creditors' group insurance that will pay off these debts in the event of death or in some cases, disability. When purchasing this kind of insurance, pay close attention to restrictions, exclusions or age limits. Also check to see if you own other policies that already offer the same coverage.

SHOULD I BUY LIFE INSURANCE ADVERTISED ON TELEVISION?

As with all purchases of life insurance, before you buy a policy, insist on a thorough explanation of its benefits and read all the fine print for exclusionary clauses. Direct marketing of life insurance is a legitimate business, but a life insurance policy purchase should not be entered into without careful thought and consultation.

HOW DO I CHOOSE AN AGENT?

Selecting a life insurance agent is no different from choosing any other kind of professional adviser. It is important to shop around and to ask the advice of someone you trust. Ask friends or family members whether they can recommend an agent. If not, check the Yellow Pages or call an insurance company. Keep in mind that you are looking for someone who is knowledgeable, who can relate well to you and to your financial situation and who can explain insurance in terms that you understand. Don't meet with just one agent. Take the time to interview two or three.

SOME OF THE QUESTIONS YOU SHOULD ASK YOUR PROSPECTIVE FINANCIAL ADVISER

• How long has the agent been in the business?
• What companies does the agent represent? Some work for only one company, while others, known as brokers, represent several companies.
• What professional designations does the agent have (CLU, chartered life underwriter, or ChFC, chartered financial consultant) and does the agent belong to a professional association (Life Underwriters Association of Canada, Independent Life Insurance Brokers of Canada)?
• Will the agent give you references from other clients?

Once you have chosen an agent, you can begin the discussion of your financial needs and goals. It is important to be open and frank with your agent so he or she can offer you suggestions and options that will truly meet your requirements. Make a point of asking for proposals in writing and be very cautious if your new agent suggests you surrender or replace policies without clear explanations why this is appropriate for you. As with all important financial transactions, read the application form carefully before signing. By signing you authorize the company to carry out a confidential investigation of your medical history. Confirm with your agent that he or she will deliver the policy in person within a specified period and that at that time both of you will review the policy in detail.

WHAT HAPPENS WHEN I APPLY FOR LIFE INSURANCE?

Be sure that you are honest in answering the questions on the application form. Life insurance is a "good faith" legal contract, and if you lie or withhold information, the policy could be null and void. Your signed application allows the underwriting department of the insurance company to verify your medical records and to assess the risks you present, by virtue of your health, age, gender, family history, financial situation and occupation. If you are a non-smoker and can state that you have not smoked for at least a year, you will qualify for lower premium rates. Depending on all these factors, the insurance company may ask that you undergo some form of medical examination.

SHOULD I WORRY ABOUT AN INSURANCE COMPANY HAVING CONFIDENTIAL INFORMATION?

Everyone working for an insurance company must comply with strict and elaborate privacy rules. Your consent is required for any information to be gathered about you, and this information may not be used for purposes other than qualifying for life insurance. Medical information about you can be released only to you and only by your personal physician. You may also request that an insurance company reveal what information it has on file for you. Medical information is shared among some 750 life insurance companies in North America through a non-profit organization called the Medical Information Bureau. The purpose of this sharing of information is to alert against potential fraud. Even though confidentiality is closely protected, you may see if there is a file on you and verify its contents by contacting the Medical Information Bureau at 330 University Ave., Toronto, Ont., M5G 1R7, telephone (416) 597-0590.

WHAT IF I CHANGE MY MIND AFTER I APPLY FOR LIFE INSURANCE?
If you decide that you do not want to go through with your purchase of life insurance after you have applied, you can return your policy to the insurance company within 10 days of receiving it. The policy will be cancelled and your paid premiums will be refunded to you. This is called the "10-day free look" or the "rescission right."

WHAT SHOULD I KNOW BEFORE I REPLACE A POLICY?
If you are thinking about replacing a life insurance policy, do not make a hasty decision. A precipitous decision could result in a loss of coverage, an unnecessary increase in cost or the need to offer proof of insurability through medical exams because of your older age or of being in poorer health. Review your reasons for changing policies and seek trustworthy advice on the pros and cons of other policies. Also explore whether your existing policy can be changed to meet your new needs at a reasonable cost. And by all means ask your agent to assist you in this review of your financial situation and your insurance needs.

If you decide to go ahead and replace a policy, your agent must fill out a disclosure form that explains the pros and cons of both the old and the new policy. Read this document carefully before you sign it. And finally, make certain you do not cancel your old policy until you have the new one in hand. A termination notice must be signed for the old policy to be cancelled.

CAN I BORROW AGAINST MY LIFE INSURANCE POLICY?
You can borrow any amount up to the cash value of your permanent life insurance policy by requesting a loan through your agent or directly by calling your insurance company. No credit checks are required and the interest you will pay on this loan will usually be very reasonable. You can pay back the loan in a lump sum or in instalments. In some cases these loans may be taxable, so check this out before you request the loan. If you die before you have paid back the loan, the outstanding balance and interest will be deducted from the death benefit.

WHAT KIND OF INSURANCE DO I NEED AS AN ENTREPRENEUR?
If you are self-employed or are running a small business, you should look into liability

and disability insurance, as well as group life and health insurance for yourself and your employees. Many insurance companies have very attractive packages of insurance for small companies of five or more employees.

CAN I GET LIFE INSURANCE OTHER THAN FROM A LIFE INSURANCE COMPANY

In many cases you can obtain life, health and disability insurance through membership in professional associations, alumni groups, unions or affinity groups. This is a growing market, so shop around. This kind of plan can also be used to top up your other insurance coverage.

WHAT ARE LIVING BENEFITS?

On a voluntary basis, and upon request by policyholders, insurance companies make available to terminally ill patients a portion of their death benefit, usually up to 50% of the benefit, or in the range of $50,000, although awards can be higher. Your request must be accompanied by medical documents indicating you are terminally ill, and often you must seek a release from the beneficiary agreeing to this prepayment. Living benefits, or accelerated benefits, as they are also called, can make a significant difference in the quality of health care terminally ill patients can afford, and they can also improve the quality of life for people in the latter stages of their illness. Another option for AIDS or cancer patients wishing to obtain an early payment of a death benefit is a viatical settlement company. These are not insurance companies. They sometimes offer up to 80% of the death benefit, but the remainder of the benefit does not go to the beneficiary. Care should be taken in dealing with these organizations and you should check to make sure that they are legal, since in some jurisdictions they are deemed to be trafficking illegally in life insurance.

WHAT HAPPENS WHEN SOMEONE FILES A CLAIM?

To file a claim the beneficiary must contact the agent or the insurance company and provide them with proof of death, a doctor's statement or a death certificate. Claims should be made within 90 days to 12 months after the death. The claim is usually paid within a week to 10 days, unless an investigation is needed to determine the cause of death or if death occurs during the first two years the policy has been in force (the contestable period). Interest will be paid from the date of death. Most beneficiaries prefer to take the proceeds of the policy in a lump-sum payment, although there may be other settlement options for leaving the money with the insurance company.

ARE DEATH BENEFITS TAXABLE?

The death benefit of a life insurance policy is not taxable in the hands of a beneficiary.

WHAT HAPPENS IF THE CAUSE OF DEATH IS SUICIDE?

If death by suicide occurs during the first two years the policy is in force, the claim will not be paid. After that two-year period, the claim will be paid.

WHAT KIND OF CONSUMER PROTECTION LIMITS APPLY TO LIFE INSURANCE?

The Canadian Life & Health Insurance Compensation Corp. (CompCorp) is the industry-funded consumer protection plan. In the event of the insolvency and winding up of a life insurance company, CompCorp provides protection and continued coverage to Canadian policyholders up to certain limits. Coverage is per policyholder, per company, and includes group as well as individual insurance:

- $200,000 for life insurance.
- $60,000 for non-registered accumulation policies and cash values in life insurance policies.
- $60,000 for RRSPs and RRIFs combined.
- $2,000 per month for annuities and disability income policies,
- $60,000 for other health benefits.

WHERE CAN I GET MORE INFORMATION ON LIFE INSURANCE?

To receive more information on life insurance or issues of consumer protection, to talk with a knowledgeable counselor or to request consumer publications, you can call the Information Centre free of charge from anywhere in Canada at 1-800-268-8099 or in Toronto at (416) 777-2344. You can also write to The Information Centre, Canadian Life & Health Insurance Association Inc., 1 Queen St. E., Suite 1700, Toronto, Ont., M5C 2X9

BOOKS TO SURVIVE IN LIFE INSURANCE JUNGLE

Murphy's Little-Known Law of Life Insurance states: "Any product designed to favor the consumer will ultimately be withdrawn or have its rates increased to the level where it favors the company."

That little gem and 34 more life insurance gags come from Richard Gilbert, the maverick president of Megacorp Insurance Agencies Inc. of Mississauga, Ont. Gilbert is a refreshing breeze in an industry that seems to go out of its way to bury simple concepts under a mountain of confusing jargon. Or, as another Gilbert quip goes: "The more complex a policy's language and conditions, the greater the probability that the promises are carved in Jell-O." He warns consumers should never buy a policy without reading the fine print.

Stripped to its essentials, life insurance should be simple. Just don't expect easy or frank disclosure from the insurance companies. A more objective source is a concise primer called *Insure Sensibly* by James Bullock and George Brett (Penguin Books

Canada Ltd.). Bruce Cohen's recently updated *The Money Adviser* (Stoddart, 1997) also has several cogent chapters on insurance. *Insure Sensibly* concedes "life insurance is still sold using a lot of smoke and mirrors; make sure you look past all the fast talk. You need to know what you are buying and why it will work for you. Before you buy, insist on being shown a number of alternatives involving at least a couple of companies and scenarios."

GUIDEPOSTS FOR THE ANNUAL SNOWBIRD TREK

Heading south? Tighter conditions on out-of-Canada health insurance and changing tax rules make it harder for snowbirds each year, but there is help available in making your choices. If you're on the Internet, go to www.snowbirds.org. This association has information on all the topics that interest those who spend winter months in warmer climates. It also has links to other Websites that have tax and medical insurance information.

SHOP AROUND CAREFULLY FOR HEALTH COVERAGE BEFORE LEAVING THE COUNTRY

If you're not on the Net, visit your local Royal Trust branch and ask for their free booklet called *Planning a Winter Out of the Country*. It also deals with tax and customs rules as well as banking. It's on the Net too, at http.//www.royalbank.com. Here's yet another handy information source. The Canadian Life & Health Insurance Association offers a free consumer brochure on out-of-Canada health insurance along with a list of companies and associations that sell the coverage. The list includes their toll-free numbers. For a copy, call CLHIA at 1-800-268-8099 or, in Toronto, 777-2344.

It's more important than ever to shop carefully for health insurance, says Milan Korcok, a Florida-based Canadian who tracks that market. "The process is becoming more exclusionary and there are more pitfalls to watch for," he warns. Korcok's biggest concern involves the medical exclusion questionnaires that are now a standard part of purchasing coverage. "Those forms are now very complex with very ambiguous language," he says. For example, one form asks if you've had dizziness or lightheadedness in the past five years. "What constitutes that, how many times and how dizzy?" Korcok wonders.

PREMIUMS PAID FOR HEALTH COVERAGE QUALIFY FOR MEDICAL EXPENSE TAX CREDITS

A common question asks if you've had a change in medication. Korcok says the insurer may include a switch from a brand-name drug to a generic. Or even a reduction in your prescribed dosage. Also, he points out, doctors advise many seniors to take an aspirin a day for preventive reasons. That's medication but Korcok says many people don't realize that. When buying coverage, remember the premiums qualify for the medical expense tax credit. Also, make sure you take the insurer's toll-free emergency phone number with you. Those lines are run by companies that will arrange or oversee your care. If they're not called within 24 or 48 hours, your plan likely slashes coverage, perhaps to $25,000 or less.

HERE ARE SOME OTHER POINTS TO CHECK WHEN SHOPPING FOR COVERAGE

• Are you already covered by an employer or association plan? To what extent? For leisure trips? Your family or just you?

• Do you rely on coverage from a credit card? Some cover just 17 to 22 days. You can't cover a few weeks with one card and a few more with another; all card coverage starts on departure. Card issuers sell extended coverage but a standalone policy might be cheaper. And does your card insurance only cover trips charged on the card?

• Don't assume all policies have the same exclusions and don't assume the insurer you used last year has the same exclusions this year. Korcok says some plans have widened exclusions to conditions present within the past five years.

• Don't top up one plan with insurance from another. The second insurer may view a problem that developed during the first period as a pre-existing condition.

• More insurers are requiring doctors' statements for certain conditions. Normally you pay for that, but Korcok suggests getting your annual checkup just before your trip so medicare foots the bill.

• Check multi-trip plans if you travel more than once a year. For example, a 30-day plan covers any number of trips, each lasting up to 30 days. If you go south after Thanksgiving, head home for Christmas and then go back, a 90-day multi-trip would cover both stays for one price.

• Save money by taking a high deductible. Check your employer-sponsored coverage, if any. Korcok says the plan may cover the first $5,000 of medical expenses. So you can easily go for a $5,000 deductible on your privately purchased plan. "That's a terrific way to cut your cost by one-third," Korcok says.

• There are low-priced plans that cover just enough care to stabilize you for return to Canada. Check the limit. Some offer only 72 hours of care or $10,000, whichever comes first. Korcok says $10,000 may cover less than two days of intensive care at a U.S. hospital where daily fees run about US$4,000. Some plans have raised their limits to $25,000.

INSURANCE MAY OFFER RETIREMENT TAX BREAK

A little-known leveraged life insurance strategy known as an insured retirement plan (IRP) can be used to generate tax-free income in retirement and leave more for your heirs, according to many investment advisers and life insurance agents. Although these plans have been around for more than a decade, many people have never heard of IRPs, or they think they're too good to be true.

In fact, Tim Henry and Michael Kraik, two investment advisers who are licensed to sell life insurance products through RBC Dominion Securities Financial Services (they are among the minority of advisers who straddle the worlds of traditional investment banking and life insurance) call the IRP "the most effective tax-neutralization strategy that exists in Canada today."

Some insurance vendors, on the other hand, are far less enamored of the IRP concept. For example, Bob Porter, associate broker with Megacorp Insurance Agencies Inc. of Mississauga, Ont., suggests these insurance-based plans are being flagrantly misrepresented by vendors with vested interests. He refuses to sell IRPs to his clients, and suggests they "will come back to haunt" those who deal in them.

UNIVERSAL LIFE INSURANCE

Technically, an IRP is not an insured retirement plan. Rather, it is a retirement plan inside a universal life insurance policy, plus an exit strategy. In addition to life insurance, a universal life policy includes a tax-sheltered cash-value fund that cannot exceed the policy's face value. The policy is funded with contributions well in excess of the cost of the underlying insurance. Deposits are made over several years into investments selected by the policyholder, and an annual premium is withdrawn from the policy to pay for the insurance coverage. Henry and Kraik stress the plan best suits affluent or middle-income people who have maximized their registered retirement savings plan contributions.

LEVERAGING THE CASH VALUE

The key to the tax minimization strategy is to borrow money from a bank on retirement, a loan that is ultimately repaid with a tax-free death benefit. This is also called leveraged life insurance, which admittedly flies in the face of traditional retirement advice to clear all debts. When the policyholder wants to draw on the income in retirement, the accumulated capital is used as collateral for a series of bank loans. These, in effect, provide tax-free income. Interest is tacked on to the outstanding loan balance. The loan isn't paid off until after the policyholder dies, but is structured so the sum of loans plus interest never exceeds 75% of the accumulated investment account. If designed properly, there should be a hefty nest egg left to go to your heirs, also tax free.

PAYMENTS NOT TAX-DEDUCTIBLE

Unlike RRSP contributions, IRP payments are not tax-deductible. But IRP payouts are tax-free, while RRSP proceeds (normally taken through a registered retirement income fund, or RRIF) are taxable. For that reason, people in certain income bands may choose an IRP instead of an RRSP. "You should consider an IRP if you currently own or require life insurance and can wait at least 15 years before you require the supplemental income produced by the IRP," Kraik says. Investment performance of an RRSP or RRIF is likely to be superior because IRPs do not invest directly in stocks or mutual funds. They invest in indexes, such as the Toronto Stock Exchange 300 or Standard & Poor's 500 composite stock indexes, or bond indexes. As the RBC advisers put it: "Life insurance companies can only pay interest on the surplus account values in policies. The companies do, however, have the ability to tie the rate of interest to certain stock market indexes."

WHOLE LIFE | VERSUS UNIVERSAL LIFE

How whole life, universal life policies compare

Policy type	Whole life	Universal life
Period of coverage	Life	Life
Premiums	Guaranteed, usually remain level	Flexible. Can be increased or decreased by policyholder within certain limits.
Death benefits	Guaranteed in contract. Remain level. Dividends may be used to enhance benefits	Flexible. May increase or decrease according to fluctuations in cash value.
Cash values	Guaranteed in contract.	Flexible. May increase or decrease according to investment returns and level of policyholder deposits
Other non-forfeiture options	Guaranteed in contract.	Guaranteed in contract.
Dividends	Payable on 'participating' policies. Not guaranteed.	Most policies are 'non-participating' and do not pay dividends.

Pros and cons of permanent insurance

✔ Provides protection for entire life – if kept in force.

✔ Premium cost usually stays level, regardless of age or health problems.

✔ Has cash values that can be borrowed, used to continue protection if premiums are missed, or withdrawn if the policy is no longer required.

✔ Other non-forfeiture options allow the policyholder various possibilities of continuing coverage if premiums are missed or discontinued.

✔ If the policy is participating, it receives dividends that can be taken in cash, left to accumulate at interest, or be used to purchase additional insurance.

✘ Initial cost may be too high for a sufficient amount of protection for your current needs.

✘ May not be an efficient means of covering short-term needs.

✘ Cash values tend to be small in the early years. You have to hold the policy for a long time, say over 10 years, before the cash values become sizable.

Source: Canadian Life & Health Association

How IRP, RRSP compare
Leveraged insurance can preserve cash flow after retirement

Source: RBC Dominion Securities Inc.

SAMPLE COMPARISON OF IRP VERSUS RRSP

The accompanying chart, provided courtesy of RBC Dominion Securities Inc., shows one example of the difference between making annual RRSP contributions of $10,000 from age 30 to 65 and making annual contributions of $6,000 to an IRP. These amounts are equivalent in after-tax dollars. The total death benefit when the IRP is first set up is $270,000, and is augmented by investment growth and annual $6,000 IRP premium payments. The example assumes a person is in the 40% marginal tax bracket before retirement and in the 50% bracket afterward.

The money is projected to compound at 9% a year, with 3% annual inflation. That return can't be guaranteed, however. Note the RRSP growth stops at age 65 and decelerates when it becomes a RRIF at age 69. The IRP, worth $2.5 million at age 66, is used as collateral to borrow $141,000 each year for 14 years, tax free. At the end you owe the bank $2 million, or $4 million with interest. The cash surrender value of the policy, worth $1.5 million at 65, grows to $5.4 million by age 80. With the $1-million death benefit, the policy is worth $6.4 million in total at the end, Kraik calculates. So after your estate pays back the bank upon your death, your heirs are left with $2.4 million, tax free. Meanwhile, the RRIF's assets have fallen to zero by age 82.

SOME RISKS TO IRPS

There are, however, some risks to an IRP. One is interest-rate uncertainty, says Bill Strain, senior vice-president of Toronto-based PPI Financial Group. The interest rate on the loan will be linked to the bank's prime rate, while the interest earned by the policy's side fund is linked to bond or equity indexes. Strain warns that interest credited on the fund could be as much as two percentage points below the relevant market index. So if the benchmark index is up 8%, you might get as little as 6% interest. That creates the spread the insurance company needs to cover its investment expenses and pay a special 15% federal tax due on investment income credited to exempt policies.

The insurer also might adjust the side fund interest rate because of factors unrelated to investment performance. These include the insurer's expense levels, tax rates, and the accuracy of assumptions on how many people cancel policies early (the "lapse" rate), or die sooner than expected. "You have to look very carefully at just what's guaranteed," Strain says.

CAREFUL MONITORING ESSENTIAL

There is a formula that makes the guaranteed rate a floor rate, well below the rate that would normally be credited. "At any time, the company would have the ability to unilaterally adjust the rates they are currently crediting down to that guaranteed rate," Strain says. So, for example, when five-year money earns 7%, you might find you are receiving as little as 5.4%. Strain says careful planning and ongoing monitoring and management of the arrangement is essential to ensure that the value of the insurance asset is properly matched with the amount of the related debt obligation, no matter how long the insured may live.

THE NEGATIVE VIEWPOINT

Bob Porter, the associate broker with Megacorp Insurance Agencies Inc., is much more critical of IRPs. "Contrary to its name, the IRP is absolutely not a retirement plan that is insured, or in any way secure or guaranteed," he says. "Most are loaded with charges and fees either open or hidden that are not fixed. These are deducted from the policy's premiums with each payment, thus depleting what is available for investment. The name is a disgraceful deception." As for the earnings projections accompanying these policies, Porter calls them "a crock.... It was refreshing to see [the accompanying table] projecting less than 10%, but because of factors such as provincial sales tax and CompCorp levy, the UL's investment would have to return 10% or more just for 6% to be credited to the plan investment fund." CompCorp is an agency that insures policyholders against losses, to certain limits, in the event of a failure of an insurer.

According to one actuary, if UL lapse assumptions are out by one percentage point the costs upon which these assumptions are made will be out by between 18% and 20%. On one policy which had projected annual growth of 10%, the real growth turned out to be minus 3% after three or four years. These UL illustrations are not worth the paper on which they are written.

Richard Gilbert, president of Megacorp, is even more vehement: "These policies are the worst possible buy for the consumer. They contain more fallacies than you can shake a stick at, and are a classic example of why the insurance industry gets a bad reputation. To illustrate [in the accompanying chart] that the IRP, which is no more than a life insurance policy, would have a greater cash value than an RRSP, borders on a criminal act of deception."

EMPLOYERS CO-ORDINATE GROUP BENEFITS

Employers who provide generous group insurance plans or who absorb a significant share of the costs, often wind up covering spouses who should be covered by their own employers. Co-ordination of benefits has always existed but was sparsely enforced. What is new is the strategy used to enforce it. More employers have switched to "positive enrolment." Using this approach, details of dependants, including information on the spouse's coverage, are requested at the time of their enrolment. This way, co-ordination can be applied when claims are processed.

Co-ordination standards are the same for all companies. An employee's claims go first to his or her insurer and the spouse's claims to his or her carrier. Any portion not paid can then be submitted to the other carrier for reimbursement, assuming dependant coverage was selected. When both parents have dependant coverage, children's claims are submitted first by the parent whose birth date comes first during the year. Special provisions apply to children of parents who are divorced or legally separated.

What will it cost you? There is no simple answer, as cost-sharing, rate structures and experience levels vary from plan to plan. You may contribute less and your spouse more, or vice versa. What is certain, however, is that claim costs will be distributed more fairly between employers. Who knows, your employer may be able to share the savings with you.

DISABILITY COVERAGE IS OFTEN IGNORED

Statistically, the risk of being disabled before retirement is greater than that of death. Yet many people fail or refuse to link their health and income, and many insurance agents shy away from selling disability policies because contracts are complex, coverage can be quite costly and there's stiff competition from group plans. That came to mind as I heard about three people, all around 40, who had become disabled. Two of my colleagues at a previous employer were having a hard time pressing claims, while a third was on welfare because she was a contract worker and had no coverage.

Coincidentally, I had just met John Paterson, a Calgary insurance broker who also advises insurance agents across the country on how to sell disability plans. Paterson, president of Paterson Insurance Services Inc., is walking, talking proof of the need for adequate coverage. In 1988 Paterson was a prosperous orthodontist, but then an eye disease ended his dental career at age 34. A top-of-the-line disability plan ensured income for life, but idleness demolished his self-esteem. In 1990 he decided to become a disability insurance consultant.

A DISABILITY INSURANCE CONSULTANT GIVES SOME HELPFUL TIPS

Paterson tells his story in a small booklet called *Russian Roulette: Gambling with Disability*. It's a quick, easy read, albeit very much a sales pitch. In any event, here are some key points to consider:

• On average, it takes at least six months to sell a professional practice. It took Paterson 18 months, even though he worked at the task full-time and eventually accepted a fire-sale price. He later learned that a pre-arranged buy-sell agreement with a colleague "would have eliminated all my effort, time, worry and costs associated with selling my practice [and] I would have received close to its full value."

• Like many self-employed people, Paterson had business overhead coverage to a set limit. That let him keep his staff to help sell the business. Significantly, without realizing it, Paterson had included an "extension of benefit" clause. That let him take, as a lump sum, the difference between his actual overhead costs and the coverage limit. He used that to buy out his office lease.

• Because of their strong cash flows, it's easy for many professionals to get loans. But Paterson says bankers are quick to show concern if the practitioner is sidelined. Paterson's business loans were insured but the demand loan for his house wasn't, and his banker quickly called it. Paterson's disability policy allowed benefits to be "assigned" so, if the bank insisted, the insurer could make the loan payments directly. The contract was sent to the bank's head office and two weeks later the bank manager relented.

• Based on his experience as a broker, Paterson stresses the need for full and complete disclosure when a policy application is made. Disability can mean big-money payouts so claims are investigated thoroughly. In particular, he warns professionals against overstating their income. Also, report any medical condition that might affect your work. The insurer may exclude or limit coverage for that condition, but if you don't report it, the insurer can challenge any claim you make. (A Saskatchewan court upheld an insurer's refusal to pay disability to a man who did not disclose what turned out to be symptoms of multiple sclerosis. Significantly, the man did not intend to deceive the insurer; he just thought he had a temporary condition that was successfully treated at the time.)

• Be careful about fine-print differences among policies. Paterson cites the case of a man whose group plan refused to pay because doctors felt his slow-growing cancerous tumor began several years before his employment. The policy only covered conditions "contracted and commencing" after enrolment in the plan. Paterson says a better clause would have defined sickness as "a disease or disorder which first becomes apparent" after enrolment. Imagine the plight of a dentist who cuts off a finger while doing carpentry. Paterson says one was denied benefits on grounds it was a self-inflicted injury at a time when there was a cash crisis in his practice.

Many group plans halt benefits after two years if you can perform "any occupation" for which you're reasonably qualified. Paterson hastens to point out that "any occ" clauses are based on ability to work, not the availability of a job.

• "Filing a claim can be one of the most stressful experiences of your life," Paterson warns. But there are ways to ease the process. First, if disability strikes, contact your insurance adviser immediately. If he or she is not available, have a lawyer review the policy to make sure you meet all the deadlines and conditions. Ask the insurer to put in writing all requests for action on your part. That avoids disputes over what was or was not said in a telephone conversation.

Make sure the examining physician understands how your ability to work is impaired. "It is easy for a physician to assume a condition may not affect your work if he or she is unfamiliar with the actual duties of your occupation," he says. After your claim is approved, make sure a physician doing a follow-up exam has a copy of the original report. Doctors often use similar yet different technical language, and inconsistent wording can lead to a stressful case review.

NEW CHOICES IN LONG-TERM CARE INSURANCE

Long-term care insurance is a market that's only beginning to attract the attention of Canadian insurance companies. And Canadian consumers are largely unaware such insurance even exists.

By contrast, there is a large and growing long-term care, or LTC, insurance market in the U.S. Paying for long-term care yourself can be very costly. In the U.S., the average price of one year in a nursing home is equivalent to more than $50,000 Canadian. The price tag can be reduced by arrangements for care at home. But the U.S. experience suggests that home care costs in Canadian dollars will be well in excess of $10,000 a year. According to one U.S. study, the single biggest reason for buying LTC is to avoid being dependent on others.

LONG-TERM CARE INSURANCE EASES COSTS OF CARING FOR AGING PARENTS

A big potential market for the product in Canada is a group known as "junior seniors" aged 50 to 65 who want to take care of their aging parents, according to Ian Shaw, president of Oakville, Ont.-based Interplay Consulting Service. It's expected that the giant baby boom generation will gravitate to LTC insurance as it faces the reality that its parents are coming into the long-term care years. Currently, only 8% of the elderly are in assisted-living or LTC programs. The rest live by themselves or are supported by their families.

Since the wealthy can afford long-term care without insurance and the poor can get various government services or subsidies, the middle class is seen as the group most in need of LTC coverage. Measured by the number of days of use, LTC facilities are almost exclusively the domain of those age 65 and over, while about half of hospital use is by this age group.

The families of people who receive LTC are well aware of the emotional cost of providing such care themselves and of the financial cost of hiring professionals. The insurance is not cheap but, should it prove necessary, it could be preferable to wiping out a family's assets or those of a future estate.

SALES OF LONG-TERM CARE INSURANCE ARE SLOW TO TAKE OFF IN CANADA

"The market is huge but sales have been minuscule," says Denis Scodallaro, senior vice-president of ITT Hartford Canada of Burlington, Ont. "It's difficult to convince Canadians there is a need." ITT has an in-home care insurance policy, with riders that can be added for facility care outside the home. However, awareness of LTC insurance may get a boost from the marketing muscle of Toronto-based Commercial Union Canada. In September 1996, the company took the wraps off its Living Care program, which provides tax-free LTC benefits for people requiring home care or nursing home care.

THE COST OF LONG-TERM CARE CAN EAT AWAY AT ASSETS

Like all insurance, the cost rises steeply with age. If you qualify for benefits, coverage is for life, but the insured must be between the ages of 40 and 80 at the time the policy is issued. Commercial Union says benefits are payable in the case of "cognitive impairment" (inability to think, perceive, reason or remember) or if the claimant can no longer perform unaided two of the following five "activities of daily living:" bathing, eating, dressing, toileting or changing positions of the body.

A private Canadian nursing home can cost between $3,000 and $6,000 a month, according to Commercial Union. Even at $100 a day, the cumulative costs of long-term care can quickly eat into savings. At that rate it amounts to $36,000 a year, or $180,000 for five years. Government nursing homes can cost less, but have long waiting lists. Even with government subsidies, ward coverage in Ontario can cost $1,225 a month.

Home care may cost $35 to $48 an hour for a private registered nurse or $70 an hour for an occupational therapist or physiotherapist. Less skilled personal care to help with eating or light housework can run $15 an hour. Government programs may only provide 60 hours a month for home care, or two hours a day.

One advantage of Living Care over other policies is the benefits paid are for a set amount rather than reimbursements for actual expenses. They range from $20 to $300 a day.

THERE ARE SEVERAL COVERAGE OPTIONS AVAILABLE

You can choose between unlimited benefits, or 2,000 times the daily benefit amount selected, or 750 times, with premiums varying accordingly. For example, under a $200 daily benefit and 2,000-times limit, the maximum payout would be $400,000. An inflation option, which carries higher premiums, increases the daily benefit amount by 2% a year for 20 years.

Premiums can be reduced by choosing a longer elimination period, which is the number of days between the commencement of care and the beginning of benefits. For example, a 90-day elimination period results in premiums that are roughly 30% less than if costs are paid as soon as the care begins.

However, Commercial Union's elimination period is based on the number of care days, not calendar days, as is the case with Westbury Life of Hamilton, Ont. So if you needed only three days of care a week, a 30-day elimination period would preclude benefits for 10 weeks. (This feature drew groans from the agents attending the product launch.)

Living Care premiums start getting expensive around retirement age. For $100 a day of benefit, the cheapest premium would be $140 per year for a 40-year-old choosing the 750-times option and a 90-day elimination period. At the other extreme would be a $19,730 a year annual premium to insure an 80-year old for a $100 a day benefit under the unlimited maximum plan and a zero-day elimination period.

A LONG-TERM CARE POLICY CAN BE EXPENSIVE

The policy is a good one but expensive because of the way it is designed, says Dick Gilbert, president of Mississauga, Ont.-based Megacorp Insurance Agencies Inc.

"They're paying for everything: the assessment in the first place, for a co-ordinator to go out and do a whole plan and interview the family and then arrange it all."

Gilbert doesn't expect the product to take off immediately because, when it comes to insurance, Canadians are the "world's worst procrastinators." He foresees a "slow, gradual acceptance" over the next five to 10 years. "Lots of boomers will do it because they're selfish and will want it for their parents. Some wealthier people will buy it for asset protection."

BETWEEN DEATH AND DISABILITY INSURANCE

We all want health, wealth and happiness. But without health, your wealth is going to decline and along with it your happiness. That's why comprehensive financial planning includes life insurance and disability insurance. Life insurance pays your beneficiaries if you die, and disability insurance kicks in if you're unable to work. However, one dreary possibility baby boomers are starting to face is that of a critical but not fatal illness, such as breast cancer, severe heart attack or stroke. It's that netherworld between death and permanent

HOW TWO POLICIES COMPARE

Illness	Canada Life LifeAdvance	Commercial Union LifeCheque
Cancer	excludes stage A prostate cancer. excludes Duke's stage A colon cancer. excludes tumors in presence of HIV or any cancer diagnosed within 90 days.	same as Canada Life. 60-day waiting period before claim paid.
Stroke	states that a measurable neurological deficit must persist for 90 days.	must persist for 24 hours.
Coronary artery disease	only one affected artery necessary for claim.	two or more abnormalities necessary.
Multiple sclerosis	requires two or mor well-defined neurological abnormalities.	needs only one episode of neurological abnormality.
Paralysis	180-day waiting period.	90-day waiting period for accidents 180-day waiting period for illness.
Major organ transplant	five organs (pancreas not covered).	six organs (including pancreas).
Heart attack	death of portion of heart muscle.	same as Canada Life.
Kidney failure	chronic irreversible failure of two kidneys.	chronic irreversible failure of one kidney.
Blindness	covers blindness where acuity worse than 20/200 or less than 20 degrees field of vision.	total, permanent and irreversible loss of all vision in both eyes.

Source: Sean Long Insurance Agencies Inc., company information disablement that pop star Bruce Springsteen described in the song "Jungleland," where inner-city warriors ended up "wounded and not even dead."

Consider, for example, that one in four Canadians suffers from some form of cardiovascular disease and 75,000 a year suffer heart attacks, according to private health insurers Blue Cross Life Insurance Co. of Canada. There are 125,000 new cancer cases reported every year, and one in three Canadians will eventually develop some form of life-threatening cancer. The good news is that these diseases are becoming much less fatal. For example, 75% of stroke victims now survive the initial event. The bad news is that strokes result in high costs, particularly one-time cash drains not covered by basic health insurance plans, such as installing stair-lifts or entry ramps in the home.

A PRODUCT FOR | THE GROUP MARKET

In 1998, Blue Cross's Ontario unit added critical condition insurance, called LifeLink, to its individual or family health and dental plans at no extra cost, and it has also introduced a similar product for the group market, which is also served by Liberty Health, a unit of Connecticut-based Liberty Mutual. LifeLink provides a $10,000 lump sum to individuals or their spouses under age 55 who suffer from any of 18 conditions. Between 55 and 64, the lump sum drops to $5,000.

Andrew Yorke, chief operating officer of Blue Cross Ontario, predicts LifeLink will "be a very popular product, especially with the baby boom generation, which is more concerned about living benefits rather than death." LifeLink does not include breast cancer but does cover Alzheimer's, Parkinson's disease, senile dementia, multiple sclerosis, blindness, deafness, paralysis (if permanent loss of two or more limbs), third degree burns covering at least 20% of the body, coma, liver or lung failure or transplant. Benefits are not paid if the prospective recipient had the condition before taking out the policy.

Critics point out that $10,000 does not go far and that Blue Cross has excluded the age group 64-plus – most likely to succumb to such conditions. "At the very age bands where the prevalence of these diseases is heightened, the coverage is much less," says Fred Holmes, senior benefits consultant with Towers Perrin Inc. "They're catering to the baby boomers aged 30 to 50 who think they may get these diseases. Some will, but they should read the fine print about how badly you must be caught by the disease for a payout."

Mike Guest, a principal at consultants Ernst & Young, agrees the conditions specified in LifeLink are "catastrophic in nature. You have to be down for the count for these to pay out." Indeed, Blue Cross emphasizes that LifeLink covers only the severe medical conditions that are outlined in the contracts. For a heart attack to qualify it would have to be the most severe category defined by the Canadian Cardiovascular Society.

Notably absent from Blue Cross coverage is HIV or full-blown AIDS, although it has been included in some policies elsewhere. Consultants say such policies don't cover situations in which there's an element of human choice – even though, as the Red Cross tainted blood scare demonstrated, AIDS can be involuntarily contracted. Nor does the Blue Cross literature mention Ebola or other deadly diseases of the 1990s.

CRITICAL ILLNESS POLICIES PROVIDE "LIVING BENEFITS"

Advances in medical technology, and the resulting extended lives, have created a need for a new category of insurance called "critical illness" or "dread disease" coverage. While many employer health plans or individual disability-insurance plans will replace income lost in such situations, they may not provide lump-sum payments for such one-time contingencies.

This is the dilemma that prompted Marius Barnard, brother of famous South African heart transplant surgeon Christiaan Barnard, to pioneer critical illness insurance in South Africa in 1983. He found that while many heart transplant patients were able to prolong their lives, they did so at tremendous financial expense. Unlike life insurance, which only pays beneficiaries after a policyholder dies, critical illness insurance is a "living benefit," providing a one-time, tax-free payment. And while the number of life insurance policies sold worldwide is dropping – and disability insurance sales are flattening – since 1993 the critical illness insurance business has been booming.

Since its adoption in South Africa, critical illness coverage has spread to Australia, Britain, Japan, some U.S. states and now Canada. Half a million policies were sold in the first six months in Japan alone, Marius Barnard said when he was in Canada to promote Canada Life's LifeAdvance critical illness policy. Early policies covered the "big five" events of heart, coronary bypass, cancer, stroke and renal failure. This soon expanded to what one consultant calls a "big gruesome list" of 20 or 30 conditions, as new insurers sought to differentiate themselves. Still, the lion's share of claims in 1995 were for female cancer, mostly of the breast. Half of all benefits paid out worldwide are for cancer, heart attack or stroke.

INCREASE IN CRITICAL ILLNESS POLICIES IS FUELLED BY A TWO-TIERED MEDICAL SYSTEM

While it costs more to buy a policy as you age, the average age for critical illness claims is just 41. Sixty per cent of recipients use the money to clear debts (primarily house mortgages), 20% invest it for income, 10% take a vacation and 8% buy new vehicles. Toronto insurance broker Sean Long adds that the rise of critical illness insurance is being fuelled by the emergence of a two-tiered medical system in Canada: the increasingly strapped provincial health care system that entails long waits for care and a system for those who can afford to pay for immediate attention. Long divides all the available policies into two groups: a B list of policies that he regards as lacking in some element of coverage and an A list of just two policies, Canada Life's LifeAdvance and Commercial Union's LifeCheque (see table on page 289).

LONG-TERM INSURANCE MAY NOT PROVIDE FOR ONE-TIME COSTS

Long notes that group insurance covers some drugs but not many of the new experimental drugs required to combat cancer. Long-term disability coverage replaces two-thirds of an individual's salary but does not cover the massive one-time costs associated with surviving a critical illness. The Canadian Cancer Society estimates 67% of cancer treatment costs are indirect expenses not covered by provincial plans. In its coverage, Canada Life lists three types of expenses: lifestyle adaptation costs, such as wheelchairs and walkers; transportation expenses; and home conversion expenses. For example, a lift for a circular stairway costs $13,000 while a home elevator runs between $15,000 and $25,000. A porch lift costs $4,500. Wheelchairs are $4,000 to $6,000, and as much as $10,000 for motorized models. It can take more than $12,000 to convert a minivan for wheelchair compatibility. Home-care companions are paid about $100 an eight-hour shift, and a nurse $240 a shift.

The market for critical illness coverage includes self-employed professionals, stress-susceptible executives, single mothers and, generally, baby boomers worried about an illness striking them or their aging parents. You can buy critical illness insurance that pays out as much as $1 million, but most benefits run between $24,000 and $125,000, paid out within 30 days, according to Canada Life.

IF YOU CLAIM A TAX DEDUCTION ON PREMIUMS, THE BENEFITS WILL BE TAXABLE

Like life insurance, the younger someone is when he or she starts paying premiums, the lower the payments. Coverage lasts until age 75, or more expensive coverage can run to age 100. Smokers pay twice as much and some people, such as cocaine users, may be refused coverage altogether, according to Long. If you die before age 75 without making a claim, 100% of the premiums will be refunded to a beneficiary. The cost of coverage can be comparable with that of insuring a car. For a fit 45-year-old male non-smoker, the LifeAdvance premium is $7.11 for each $1,000 of benefit, or $711 a year for a $100,000 policy. Most people do not claim a tax deduction as a medical expense for the premiums paid, since it would make the benefits taxable. The odds of having a critical illness rise with age. Over 50, the odds for a woman getting breast cancer or a male getting prostate cancer are nine to one, according to Commercial Union Life Assurance of Toronto.

THERE ARE FINE POINTS IN YOUR HOME POLICY

Six years ago, I was nursing my new daughter in a warm cocoon of blankets when I heard a resounding crash. With the baby howling wildly, I leapt out of bed and tried frantically (and sleepily) to insert my contact lenses, dropping one in the process. Finally, I groped my way to the kitchen on the main floor to find water and great chunks of sodden plaster everywhere, and a gaping hole where the ceiling had been. Turns out, a steadily dripping pipe on the second floor was behind all the damage. But when I called the insurance adjuster, I discovered that water damage from a drip wasn't covered under our policy.

If the pipe had burst, we'd have been OK. While the repairs to our ceiling weren't that costly – we did them ourselves – the incident brought home for me the importance of choosing a homeowners policy carefully. All that fine print can have a major impact when the time comes to make a claim. The first thing you need to know when you're choosing a homeowners policy is that they come in two basic types: the "all-risk" (also called comprehensive) or the cheaper "named-perils" (standard or basic) policy. According to Insurance Bureau of Canada consultant John Mitchell, both cover damage caused by a range of things, from storms to fires and theft. A named-perils policy, however, lists all the events that will be covered, and if they're not specifically named in the policy, you can't collect.

Your best bet, and by far the most popular, is the all-risk policy, which basically says you're covered for everything unless it's specifically excluded. This means that if by some fluke the roots of your neighbor's tree, which was previously cut down, burst through the asphalt in your driveway, you're going to be covered unless your policy specifically states otherwise. "That's an example of something you couldn't possibly put in a named-perils policy because you never would have thought of it," Mitchell says.

READ YOUR POLICY CAREFULLY TO UNDERSTAND EXACTLY WHAT IS COVERED

The good news is an all-risk policy doesn't cost too much more. You might pay $670 for a named-perils policy that would give you $200,000 coverage on your home and an additional $120,000 on the contents. But for just $40 more, you can get an all-risk policy that covers you for the same amount, according to Iby Moran, an insurance broker with Toronto-based Consolidated Insurance Brokers Ltd. But don't be lulled into a false sense of security just because you've opted for the all-risk policy. That's what we had, and it still didn't cover that collapsed ceiling.

Which brings me to a key point: look closely at the list of exclusions. Some are standard. You can't get flood insurance in Canada, for example, because floods, unlike hail or lightning, are often predictable. Neither is damage covered if it's caused by mud or snow slides, avalanches, insects and vermin, war, nuclear damage or, as we found out, "continuous or repeated see page" (as from our leaky pipe or a worn roof). "The principle generally is that, as a homeowner, you're expected to take care of your home's maintenance and look for things like that before the situation becomes critical," says Alan Wood, vice-president of IBC's regional office in Edmonton.

COVERAGE VARIES GREATLY FROM POLICY TO POLICY

Beyond those exclusions, you'll find policies vary widely, says Ontario's insurance ombudsman Lea Algar. Some policies won't cover you for damage caused by smashing into your garage with your own car or power surges or outages that result in losses of some kind. Other policies will.

Although they all cover storm damage, you might not be covered for damage caused by snow or ice melting on your roof. And while some include sewer backup insurance as a matter of course, others require you to pay a fee of $10 to $50 a year or don't offer

CONDOS | AND APARTMENTS

If you own a condo, the condominium corporation should have insurance for the common elements of the building (roof, walls, floors and ceilings) and for limited liability. But you are responsible for insuring your personal possessions, plus any changes to the original state of the building (such as wallpaper, carpets or built-in cabinets).

If you're an apartment-dweller, you may think you're covered under your landlord's insurance policy. Wrong. Unless you pay for separate insurance, you won't be able to make a claim if your belongings are stolen or damaged. Nor are you covered for liability. If you inadvertently cause a fire in the building, the landlord's insurance company will come after you to pay for the damage.

A 1991 study found that 40% of apartment dwellers in Alberta had no coverage. Says the Insurance Bureau's Wood: "I think there's a feeling that it's too expensive. And that's just not correct." The average tenant pays $10 to $20 a month, a small price for peace of mind, he says.

it at all. Earthquake-shock insurance is always extra, but how much more depends on a number of factors, including whether your house is made of brick or wood and where you live; in Toronto, you might pay $170 on a $200,000 home, compared with $600 to $800 if you live in southwestern British Columbia.

When deciding on a policy, try to anticipate your needs and situation. Be aware that some companies refuse to insure homes with wiring, plumbing and a roof that are too old. Indeed, if you own an older home, you'd be well advised to pay the extra $10 or so for "bylaw insurance," which allows you to rebuild in accordance with current building codes (a home built in 1920 on wooden pilings, for example, might have to be rebuilt on a concrete foundation at considerable cost to the owner). You'll also want a replacement-cost rider with automatic inflation adjustment. Basically, it says you're covered for the replacement cost of the home and its contents, not just the original cost or the depreciated value.

IF YOU HAVE EXPENSIVE ITEMS IN YOUR HOME, YOU CAN OBTAIN EXTRA COVERAGE
Insurance companies generally divide your belongings into categories and cap the payments for each. Amounts vary, but there might be a $2,000 limit on furs and jewelry, $5,000 to $10,000 for silverware and $5,000 for software. "If you have expensive items – whether golf clubs or home-office equipment – sit down with your insurance broker and ask specifically whether they're covered," suggests Lenore Davis, senior partner with Dixon Davis & Co. Chartered Financial Planners in Victoria. If they're not, you can pay for extra protection through a "personal articles floater." In terms of liability coverage, your insurer may automatically offer $500,000 coverage, but you're better off opting for the $1 million coverage; at just about $10 extra per year, it's easily affordable. And if you have a housekeeper, a nanny or any other kind of domestic help, make sure they're covered, too.

If you want to save yourself some money, don't skimp on the coverage; opt instead for a higher deductible (the amount of the claim you have to pay). Deductibles can range from $100 to $1,000. By accepting a $500 deductible instead of $250, you might shave 10% to 20% off the cost of your home insurance policy. Keep in mind, too, that homeowner insurance isn't like car insurance – your premium doesn't go up every time you make a claim. That said, many property insurers offer a discount in the range of 5% to 15% if you remain claims-free for a specified period of time, while others offer a flat-rate dollar amount annually. You'll lose the discount, of course, if you have to make a claim. On the other hand, if your house is subject to repeated burglaries, the insurance company can opt not to cover you. But more likely it will ask you to install an alarm system.

When it comes to collecting after a loss, your biggest problem is going to be remembering what you had. Try to keep documentation for big purchases and consider doing an inventory of your property room by room. Davis suggests videotaping the contents of your home, so that even if everything is completely destroyed, "you've got a visual record." You should probably have any property worth more than $5,000 appraised. And send a copy to your agent, so if an appraisal goes up in flames when your house burns down, the agent has it on file.

NOTIFY YOUR INSURANCE BROKER IMMEDIATELY, AND KEEP RECEIPTS

To avoid running into trouble with your insurer, there are a few things you need to know. First, says Algar, many policies contain conditions, and if you don't abide by them, you can't collect. For instance, if you're away for more than three to four days during the normal heating season, you must have the water turned off or have a neighbor check on the house daily. "Otherwise, if your pipes burst, you're not covered for the resulting damage." Similarly, if your house is vacant (for example, if you've moved and are trying to sell), you have to let your insurer know and make some arrangements to protect it, or you may not receive a cent if something happens.

You should try to "protect damaged property against any further damage," says Helena Moncrieff, a spokesperson for IBC. Cover a smashed window with a tarp, for example, rather than letting water pour in until your claims adjuster can see it. But keep receipts; there's a good chance your insurer will pay for emergency repairs or hardware needed to secure your home. If you're forced to leave your home and put up at a hotel, hold on to those receipts, too. Most policies will reimburse you for additional living expenses.

Don't launch major repairs without first at least speaking to your insurer. "If it's a sewer back-up, for instance," says Moncrieff, "the insurer will want to come and see your basement to determine whether it's flood water [which isn't covered] or sewage." And if lightning has damaged furniture or electronic equipment, don't simply throw it out. If you do, you will have no proof it ever existed.

As a rule of thumb, keep your insurance broker informed whether you're renovating, operating a home-based business or buying an expensive antique chair. "Talk to your insurance broker every two or three years on the phone, if you don't have time to meet," says Algar. "Communication is key."

CAR INSURANCE: LOGIC DOESN'T ALWAYS APPLY

True story. A driver with a particularly tarnished driving record was facing more than $4,000 to insure his car in Ontario. He found out the cost in Manitoba for the same coverage was less than $1,000. So what did he do? He claimed to live in Manitoba and applied for car insurance there. What's more, he's not the only one. This example, while not necessarily representative of all regional differences, shows the primary beef that most people have with auto insurance is price. Why do Ontario drivers get taken for a ride while people in Manitoba enjoy such discounted rates? As you might expect, the answer can't be framed in simple terms of exploited consumers and fat-cat insurance companies. Contrary to popular belief, insurers – Ontario insurers in particular – are not raking in big bucks from auto insurance.

AUTO INSURANCE RATES VARY FROM PROVINCE TO PROVINCE

The industry has had many years when it lost money on its auto policy business in different regions of the country. And there are other years when the profit is only marginal. Rate increases often are needed just to maintain the status quo against rising claim costs. So what gives? Well, for starters, the type of provincial system in place – private, public, tort or no-fault, the kind of car you drive, your driving record and the hits insurance companies take because of fraud all play roles in determining the premium you pay each year.

It's on the auto claims side – which is divided into two broad areas, bodily injury and vehicle damage – that costs are most sharply felt. As well, insurers are often the victims of unforeseeable events, like the severe winter storms. This is all fine, to a point. But the bottom line, particularly in Ontario, where drivers seem to take the worst beating on price, is that consumers are fed up.

NO-FAULT INSURANCE APPLIES TO BODILY INJURY CLAIMS ONLY

That's why Rob Sampson, Ontario's minister responsible for privatization at the time, spearheaded new auto-insurance legislation in 1995. "We had to stop insurers from holding customers hostage with continuous rate increases and threats of being placed in the high-risk market," he said. "Consumers were afraid to make an insurance claim for fear of rising premiums." Accounting for roughly one-quarter of the general insurance market in Canada, Ontario's auto insurance system acts as a lightning rod for both consumers and politicians. But double-digit yearly increases in premiums weren't the only problem plaguing the system when Mike Harris and his Conservatives took office. A pure no-fault system of insurance – which few understood – proved unable to control costs.

Ontario has experimented with versions of no-fault insurance with mixed results. "We never should have used the phrase no fault in the first place," says Stan Griffin of the Insurance Bureau of Canada. He acknowledges the term has caused confusion among consumers and endless frustration for insurers trying to explain it. No-fault

TIPS | TO SAVE YOU MONEY

1. Don't go with the first quote you get. Shop around. The Ontario Insurance Commission publishes an annual *Guide to Rates in Ontario,* which compares premiums from different companies. There is also a telephone service for comparing rates called the *Consumers Guide to Insurance* (1-900-451-0486, toll charges apply). Several direct telephone insurers can give you a quote in minutes. Check their rates and make sure you are comparing apples and apples.

2. If you don't have time to shop around, contact a licensed insurance broker. Brokers can be a good source of information and can get you a good price. Check with family or friends about brokers they use. Ask the broker about creative ways of saving money, higher deductibles, basic no-frills coverage and how this may affect you in the event of a claim.

3. Wait for your auto insurance policy to expire before you switch companies. Many insurers will penalize you for switching policies midstream.

4. Ask the company or broker about the policy on rate changes after a first claim. Some companies give existing clients a break, but others do not.

5. If you have a teenager who may start driving soon, ask about the insurer's treatment of new drivers. You may be in for an unpleasant surprise when your son is added as a secondary or occasional driver on your policy.

6. Inquire about discounts for joint home and auto insurance policies. Some insurance companies will give you a special rate if you combine the two.

7. Research the make, model and year of your car before purchasing. Insurers have implemented a new historical-claims tracking method for formulating premiums. Some cars, many sports-utility vehicles, for instance, have poor claims or theft records and will result in higher premiums.

8. If you have questions or problems with your policy or a claim, ask your broker for a clear explanation in plain English. Insurance companies have an ombudsman in place to deal with complaints. And the Ontario Insurance Commission recently hired its own ombudsman to act as a last resort for consumer beefs. You can also contact the Insurance Bureau of Canada's Consumer Information Centres across Canada.

9. Ask insurers about value-added programs they offer at no charge. This includes 24-hour assistance and claims reporting lines, support services in case of emergencies and discount cards for other shops and services.

10. Ask the broker or company about the level of service after a claim. Do they use recommended repair shops, for example, or do they provide substitute vehicles following an accident?

insurance applies only to bodily injury claims in auto insurance (fault is still assigned to drivers for vehicle damage claims). Under no-fault, payment to victims of car accidents for injuries is not delayed until blame can be assigned. The tradeoff is that drivers forfeit the right to sue.

Several provinces, including Manitoba, Ontario, Quebec and Saskatchewan, have adopted some form of no-fault insurance to control claims costs. Before the implementation of no-fault insurance in Ontario in 1990, it was estimated that about 30% of claims payments for bodily injuries went to legal fees and court costs, for a total of $500 million in 1989.

No-fault insurance, however, has its own problems, in the form of high benefits and few controls on rehabilitation costs. These problems became obvious in Ontario when Bill 164 came into effect in January 1994. It was an ill-fated piece of legislation that promised generous accident benefits for drivers and tight controls on private insurers. Everyone was to receive what Griffin called Cadillac benefits, even if they were only driving Chevrolets. The system was prone to abuse, especially by private rehabilitation services, and the bottom line reflected this, with average annual premium hikes of more than 10% in 1994 and 1995.

PROVINCIAL GOVERNMENTS TRY TO KEEP AUTO INSURANCE PREMIUMS IN REIN

To counter this trend, the Ontario Tories introduced Bill 59, legislation that promised "rate stability" right in its title. In general, the government sought a balance between no-fault insurance and access to the courts for more serious cases of injury. The legislation introduced a standard level of accident benefits for drivers, with the option of topping up to pay for enhanced coverage. It got much tougher on insurance fraud, raising the fines for those driving without insurance from $500 to $5,000 for a first-time offence. In addition, insurers and health-care providers are working out proper fees and treatment plans for the rehabilitation of car-accident victims to ensure reasonable costs. Early results suggested the legislation achieved its goals, managing to turn back the tide of premium increases. Rates actually decreased by an average 5.4% in the first three months of 1997 and in some cases by as much as 12%.

Auto insurance is legislated by the provinces and there are different schemes across different regions. In British Columbia, Manitoba, Quebec and Saskatchewan, the government has a monopoly on auto insurance, although some of these provinces allow for limited competition on optional coverage and vehicle damage. As the home of medicare, it's hardly surprising that Saskatchewan was first to adopt a public insurance system back in the late 1940s. British Columbia, Manitoba and Quebec followed in the 1970s, frustrated by the inability of the private sector to rein in insurance premiums.

MANITOBA KEEPS COSTS IN CHECK WHILE BRITISH COLUMBIA SEES COSTS SPIRAL

The rest of the provinces have private auto-insurance models. Statistics on rate increases show that government insurers tend to offer lower premiums. Indeed, Manitoba has offered premium decreases to many of its drivers in recent years. Although several government-run programs are stable, others, like the Insurance Corporation of British Columbia (ICBC), are experiencing tough times in the face of rising claims. ICBC is the largest insurer of automobile coverage in Canada because of its monopoly role in the province, which accounts for roughly one-eighth of the national population.

The situation in B.C. is enlightening for many auto-insurance regimes across the country. ICBC endured steadily rising claims costs in the 1990s. At the same time, it faced rising expectations for what auto insurance should cover. In one year ICBC reported that more than 70% of injury claims were from "mostly minor, temporary" cases and the cost of settling these claims was close to $800 million. If you add to this a tort system in which ICBC spent about $223 million in legal costs to resolve claims, you have a recipe for spiralling costs.

ALTHOUGH CARS ARE NOW SAFER, THEY ARE MORE COSTLY TO INSURE

Insurers and regulators across Canada are taking a long look at the high cost of an adversarial legal system on auto insurance, especially when it comes to minor injuries. It is not just the auto insurance system that can affect premiums, but also the kind of car you drive. The types of vehicles on the highways have changed over the years, from two-door cars and family sedans in the 1980s to more sports-utility vehicles and passenger vans. In fact, the number of passenger vans has increased by 37% in the past two years alone. Many of these vehicles have benefited from advances in technology, making them safer and more efficient but, because of their high price, also more costly to insure.

At the same time, insurers are moving to a new system of rating cars based on a system called Canadian Loss Experience Automobile Rating (CLEAR). This system looks closely at the actual claims and theft records of individual makes and models of cars and puts them into rate groups. To date, more than 25 insurers have adopted the CLEAR rating scheme, representing 57% of the Canadian market.

PRACTISING SAFE DRIVING HABITS CAN HELP MAINTAIN YOUR PREMIUMS

Another element that can affect premiums is the kind of driver you are – a prudent person who drives short distances to work or a lane-weaver who speeds from appointment to appointment. Insurers monitor years of driving experience, average amount of driving distance per year, infractions and at-fault accidents very closely and allocate premiums accordingly.

The private-insurance sector in Canada has generally relied on a four-point risk classification system. It weighs the seriousness of infractions, ranking everything from failing to wear a seatbelt to drunk driving. If a driver hits four points, he or she is placed in the residual market, with sharply higher premiums. Insurers are quite well versed in this classification system, but most consumers don't know when they are placed in the high-risk market. Lobby groups such as the Ottawa-based Citizens Forum Advocating Insurance Review have set out to rectify the situation.

In Ontario, the four-point risk classification system is being disbanded. A new system being implemented is intended to be fair and open, giving a driver advance notice of the reasons for being placed in the high-risk market.

For some drivers, the cost of insurance has simply been too high and they have run the risk of doing without it. In a recent crackdown, the Ontario Provincial Police found that one out of every four drivers stopped did not have insurance. Ontario insurance companies paid $43 million in claims last year for accidents involving uninsured drivers. But this represents just one aspect of insurance fraud, a problem that costs the industry an estimated $1.3 billion a year. That is ultimately passed on to consumers in higher premiums.

Insurers have been hit even harder by an alarming increase in accident-benefits fraud rings, which have migrated from the U.S. into Ontario and B.C. These rings stage phony accidents and collect insurance money for supposed injuries.

GLOSSARY | OF TERMS

ALL-OR-NONE

This prevents a broker from filling an order in bits and pieces, which can lead to higher commissions because of a minimum cost for each transaction. The transaction must be for the exact number of shares specified.

AMERICAN DEPOSITARY RECEIPT (ADR)

Shares of foreign companies that trade in the U.S. Banks hold the shares and issue certificates that give the holder a right to take possession. However, the stock of these foreign companies often is not registered for sales through a U.S. stock exchange. This arrangement can allow a multinational company to have an international shareholder base without being listed on several stock exchanges.

ANALYSTS

Brokerage firms employ researchers to follow corporate sectors and report on prospects for companies within those groups. Their reports provide the basis for buy or sell recommendations by the firm and for the advice that registered representatives provide to clients.

ANNUAL INFORMATION FORM (AIF)

This document contains information that must by law be disclosed but which is not included in company reports. Insider shareholdings and executive compensation are among the topics covered in the AIF.

ANNUAL REPORTS

This once-a-year accounting to shareholders contains the formal financial statements for the latest fiscal year and a report on operations from management.

ANY PART

The opposite of an all-or-none order.

ASK (OFFER)

The price sought by a seller for a security.

ASSET-BACKED SECURITY (ABS)

Bundled pools of assets are sold as units and these units are a security that is backed by an asset. Mortgage pools were the principal forerunners of the ABS market and this is now a multi-billion-dollar market in the U.S. More recently, banks in the U.S. and elsewhere have bundled credit card receivable and car loans as ABSs. The general theory is that safety in numbers provides a steady flow of income, usually interest income, while losses from defaults are spread across the pool.

AT-THE-MARKET

Buy or sell a specific number of shares at the best available price. If no buyer or seller is willing to move off the current bid-ask spread, these orders go through at the bid or ask price. Usually, these orders are executed quickly if a stock trades actively.

AVERAGE WORK WEEK

When companies have employees working overtime, it's a good sign for economic expansion.

BANK RATE

In practical terms, the bank rate is a signal from the Bank of Canada on what it thinks is the appropriate level for short-term interest rates. Also, it's what the central bank charges in its role as lender of last resort to the financial system. In its policy role, the Bank of Canada sets a 50-basis-point operating band for the overnight interest rate in the money market. As a backstop to banks and other big institutions, the Bank of Canada is a lender or a borrower. Banking rules require commercial banks to maintain minimum levels of reserves that can be turned into cash on demand. If a commercial bank cannot cover its obligations at the end of the business day by borrowing money from other institutions, it can turn to the Bank of Canada for a loan at the bank rate. Conversely, if a bank has surplus funds at the end of the day and cannot find anyone who wants to borrow, the Bank of Canada will take up the funds at a rate that is 50 basis points, or half a percentage point, below the bank rate. Most days, the banks can find better terms in wholesale markets than they would get from the central bank.

BANKERS' ACCEPTANCE (BA)

A form of commercial paper guaranteed by a large financial institution. Bank issuers collect a premium for backstopping both principal and interest and that guarantee means BAs have lower yields than commercial paper. Standard terms for BAs are one, two, three and six months. Futures contracts on BAs are traded on the Bourse de Montreal, which provides a pricing mechanism for the money market.

BASIS POINT

The common way of stating a spread is in basis points, which is 1/100th of 1%. Thus the difference between 6% and 7% is 100 basis points.

BEARER SECURITY

A stock or bond certificate that is not registered and that is cashable or tradable by the holder.

BENCHMARKS

Pricing in fixed income markets is done in relation to benchmark securities, such as treasury bills and government bonds. The Bank of Canada defines certain government bond issues as benchmarks. A key criteria is the amount in bonds issued for each benchmark. Usually, it's a minimum of $6 billion. The goal is to have enough bonds in circulation so that there will be ample liquidity in the market and no pricing distortions because of mismatches in supply and demand. Generally, the benchmark is the security that has the best credit rating in a given market. Thus, the benchmark is the security that commands the lowest price and other securities would sell at a premium to the benchmark. For example, a corporation might pay 7% to borrow for 10 years when the federal government can get money at 6%. Government of Canada bonds are seen as safer securities because Ottawa has the ability to tax to repay its debts while a corporation is subject to market forces and can go bankrupt. The Bank of Canada now identifies benchmark bonds for terms of two, three, five, 10 and 30 years. Investment dealers will use other actively traded government issues as benchmarks for intervening years out to 10 years but the central bank's list provides the basic benchmark pricing.

BID

The price offered by a buyer for a security.

BLIND POOLS

This is a special vehicle of the Canadian Venture Exchange, which calls them capital pool companies. Essentially, they are an investment in a management or promoter group. Funds are raised by these groups through a shell company, which then searches out investment projects. Thus, the planned use of funds is not known when the investment is made.

BLOCK TRADE

A trade above a specified volume level (the *Financial Post* carries lists of transactions of more than 100,000 shares or a value of more than $1 million). Usually, a block trade is a transaction between institutional accounts.

BLUE CHIPS

These are the shares of large, reputable companies with a long history of profitability and regular dividend payments. The term is thought to come from poker, where blue chips are worth the most.

BOARD LOTS

This is the basic volume unit in which stocks trade on an exchange. For most stocks traded in North America it is 100 shares. But the definition may be different for shares valued under $5 and over $100.

BONDHOLDERS

Bondholders are a specific class of lender and provide part of the long-term capital of the company. Creditors such as banks and other financial institutions provide operating capital to finance inventory and day-to-day operations. Lenders often have a prior claim on assets of the company.

BOND MARKET

Most bonds have terms between two and 30 years and actively traded issues are within this range. Bonds have been issued for longer terms but generally they are not actively traded.

BOND PRICE AND PRICING

Shortly before a new issue of bonds goes on the market, the underwriter fixes the interest rate according to prevailing rates at the time. Then on the day that trading begins, the bond must be priced for sale. If market yields have moved up or down since the rate was set, the price is adjusted. That means the issuer of the bond – a corporation or a government – will get slightly more or less from investors than it would if the bond were issued at par. Take the example of a 10-year bond that pays interest at 6.125%. But market conditions have changed slightly and on the issue day market yield has to be set at 6.176% in order to attract investors. In this example the price would be 99.624 instead of par at 100.

BONDS

Holders of bonds are lenders and receive regular interest, or coupon, income. Governments, utilities and large corporations are the traditional issuers of bonds and most bonds are rated by credit rating agencies that assess the borrower's ability to repay debts. Bondholders generally stand in front of shareholders in any claim on the assets of a corporation when a company is in financial difficulty. Bonds come in many flavors. They often have provisions that make them more attractive to investors, allowing issuers to offer a lower interest rate. Bonds usually are secured by assets owned by the lender, but this is not always the situation.

BONDS WITH WARRANTS

A bond may be issued with a warrant attached. This gives the investor the right to buy a company's shares within a certain time at an attractive price.

BOUGHT DEAL

Traditional underwritings were done on a "best efforts" basis with the investment dealer acting as intermediary between the seller (the company) and investors. The underwriter would use its best efforts to sell the full amount of the issue but there were no guarantees. A bought deal means the investment dealer buys all of the new shares, thus guaranteeing the total return to the issuer. Dealers command higher fees or commissions by taking on the risk of the success of the underwriting.

BROKER

Now a general term for an investment dealer, but historically this term meant an agent who acted for the buyer or seller and collected a commission for brokering a transaction.

BUILDING PERMITS AND HOUSING STARTS

These two statistical series measure the advance stage of construction activity, so changes found in these reports are good leading indicators.

OALL LOAN RATE

This is the commercial market rate for overnight loans between large financial institutions.

CALL

An option that gives the holder the right to buy the underlying security.

CALLABLE OR REDEEMABLE

The issuer can redeem (or call in) the preferred shares. It usually pays a small premium over the initial issue price when doing so.

CAPITAL GAIN (OR LOSS)

The difference between the purchase price and the sale price of a security.

CAPITALIZATION

The share total times the current market price.

CASH FLOW

A company's net income plus non-cash transactions such as depreciation. This is a measure of funds a company has on hand to carry out day-to-day operations.

CASH MARKET

Also called the spot market. Purchase of goods for delivery on the spot. Commodities in these markets are the underlying assets for derivative markets.

CDNX INDEX

A Canadian Venture Exchange index that mainly includes junior companies. Vancouver listings are heavily weighted with junior mining and start-up technology companies.

CENTRAL BANK RESERVES

The Bank of Canada and other central banks have savings accounts that can be used in times of crisis to protect a country's monetary interests. This means the central bank stands ready as the buyer of last resort when others are selling the C$. Since currency value is the result of broad economic forces, central banks in large industrial countries cannot maintain an artificial exchange rate. Central banks may occasionally intervene with purchases or sales from official reserves as a way of sending a signal to markets of its view of appropriate monetary policy. But intervention mainly is done with the goal of taking volatility out of the market when there is a run on the currency. The world's reserve currency is the US$, so the majority of holdings by central banks are in US$s. They also may have significant holdings of euros or yen. Instead of holding cash, central banks hold treasury bills or bonds denominated in those currencies. There are large liquid markets for these securities and they can easily be converted to cash. Central banks also hold Special Drawing Rights (SDRs). An SDR is essentially a central bank currency created by the International Monetary Fund. The value of an SDR is based on the exchange rates of the US$, German mark, Japanese yen, British pound and French franc and the weightings of these currencies in an SDR is proportionate to their IMF quotas.

CERTIFICATE OF DEPOSIT (CD)

Funds deposited with a financial institution for a specific term. CDs are the retail equivalent of money market paper and short-term bonds.

CLASS A OR CLASS B SHARES

Some companies have more than one class of common stock and often these are identified as class A or class B. The usual reason is that voting rights will vary among classes. The origin of this arrangement generally is that an entrepreneurial founder raised funds by selling stock but wanted to retain voting control of the company. One way of achieving this goal was to have voting and non-voting shares, also called restricted shares. Another was to have multiple voting stock, where each share had more votes than the company's standard common stock. Some of these arrangements provided certain dividend guarantees to classes of stock with reduced voting rights. Generally, the voting stock trades at a premium price in the market.

CLOSE

The last price at which a security trades during a trading period.

COLLATERAL TRUST BONDS

Secured by other securities but not property.

COMMERCIAL PAPER

Short-term notes issued by non-financial corporations. Commercial paper is a corporate equivalent of government treasury bills. An example of a commercial paper issuer would be a manufacturer of household appliances that must finance inventories.

COMMODITIES

The raw materials of commerce, such as food products, metals and fuels.

COMMON STOCK (SHARES)

A common stock is an ordinary equity stake in a company. Each share carries one vote in the affairs of the company.

CONSUMER PRICE INDEX (CPI)

This is the most widely used measure of inflation and covers a large basket of consumer goods. The Bank of Canada watches the CPI when setting monetary policy, but the bank's interest is in "core CPI," a definition that excludes energy and food. The theory is that energy and food costs are subject to unpredictable factors, mainly the weather, and price changes for these items are not a true reflection of basic cost pressures in the economy.

CONTRACT

The basic unit in derivatives trading. With stocks, a contract usually represents 100 shares of the underlying security.

CONVERTIBLE BONDS

Bonds that can be exchanged for a company's common shares. Like regular bonds, they pay a fixed rate of interest and have a specified maturity date. Conversion terms are specified at the time of the issue. Convertible bonds combine the security of bonds with the opportunity to make gains from the appreciation of common share prices.

CONVERTIBLE

Convertible preferred shares give the right to convert shares into another class of stock – usually common shares – at a set price.

CORPORATE NOTES

Unsecured promises to pay. As an obligation to pay interest and principal, a note ranks behind all other fixed-interest securities issued by a borrower.

CORPORATE PROFITS

A rise or fall in profits can affect the amount of capital available for business spending and expansion, so profitability is a closely watched indicator.

COUPON VERSUS YIELD

The coupon on a bond is literally the portion of a certificate that is clipped and presented for payment when interest is due but the coupon also is used as a term for the rate of interest a bond pays. Yield is the current return on a bond in the market. As market conditions change, yields on bonds rise or fall. If a bond is bought at par, then the yield and the coupon rate are the same. But if the yield falls, the price of the bond must rise. And rising yields mean falling prices.

COVERED OPTION WRITER

The writer of an option collects premium income and typically the option position is offset by a position in the underlying security so that any loss by the writer in the option is covered by a gain in the underlying security.

CROSS RATES

Foreign exchange values between currencies. Most Canadians think of the C$ in relation to the US$ because the U.S. is Canada's most important trading partner and its most popular tourist destination. But the globalization of commerce and of investing means that security holders must be more aware of currency values. Trading in major currencies now is a huge market and there are futures markets in all the major currencies so that financial institutions and corporate treasurers can hedge currency risk.

CUM DIVIDEND

Stocks trade cum (with) dividend between the time a dividend is declared payable and the date the payment is made.

CUMULATIVE DIVIDENDS

If a company decides not to pay dividends when due, these unpaid dividends accumulate and must be paid before common dividends or when preferred shares are redeemed. With a non-cumulative dividend, there are no arrears.

CURRENCY OPTIONS

Also known as foreign-exchange options, currency options on the C$ trade on U.S. exchanges. Options on other major currencies are traded around the world.

CURRENT ACCOUNT

The accounting of Canada's international dealings. The bottom line is a net number after accounting for exports, imports, flows of investment funds, tourist travel and certain transfers in or out of the country such as pension payments to Canadians living abroad.

CUSIP NUMBER (COMMITTEE ON UNIFORM SECURITY IDENTIFICATION PROCEDURES)

Each security has a unique number, an identification tag that can be useful in identifying securities when doing research.

CYCLICALS

These are shares of companies that are particularly sensitive to changes in economic conditions, usually those changes that naturally occur in the business cycle when the economy is expanding or slowing.

DAY

An order is valid only for the day on which it is placed.

DEBENTURES

Not backed by specific assets. Debentures sometimes are issued by corporations with few tangible assets – such as service companies – or corporations whose assets have already been pledged for another purpose. Some blue chip companies may be able to successfully borrow from investors without pledging assets. A debenture partially backed by some assets is known as a secured debenture.

DERIVATIVES

Derivatives are securities that are "derived" from another security, such as an underlying financial instrument, a stock or a commodity. Also called synthetic securities. Derivatives are contracts between buyer and seller. In the case of exchange-traded derivatives, the specifications are defined by the exchange. Derivative contracts traded over the counter often are tailored to the situation and specifications may vary widely. Futures and options that trade on exchanges are a basic example and derivatives now encompass a broad array of financial products that largely trade in over-the-counter markets.

DIRECTORS

Directors are members of the board and have policy authority over the running of a company, including the power to appoint the chief executive.

DISCLOSURE DOCUMENTS

Details that must be disclosed under regulatory guidelines and rules are contained in the disclosure documents. Reports to shareholders often provide considerable detail beyond the regulated minimum because companies are competing for investor dollars and need to provide reasons why an investor should buy the securities of a particular company.

DISCOUNT BROKER

This term applies to firms that perform a traditional brokerage role as intermediary and do not provide research advice to clients. They charge lower trading fees than the full-service brokers, which include research in their range of services.

DIVIDEND INCOME

The share of a company's profits distributed to a shareholder. Generally, the policy and rate for common share dividends are set by the board of directors. Preferred share dividend rates usually are established in the terms of the issue and can only be suspended under unusual circumstances.

DIVIDEND RECORD DATE

The date on which a dividend is paid, which means the shareholder of record on that date receives the payment.

DIVIDEND YIELD

The annual dividend payment expressed as a percentage of the stock price.

THE DOW

The Dow Jones average of 30 industrials is the world's most widely followed stock index and among the oldest (begun in 1896). It has been expanded beyond the original industrials category and now includes a selection of stocks that is considered representative of the breadth and reach of big business in the U.S.

DURABLE GOODS

Orders for durable goods – products expected to last more than three years, such as business machinery and major household appliances – are a leading indicator because company orders respond to changes in demand. Retail sales of durable goods to consumers are another leading indicator. Because such purchases can be put off during bad times, any increase reflects a changing trend in consumer spending.

ECONOMIC INDICATORS

They are divided into three categories – lagging, coincident and leading. Lagging indicators arrive after the fact; coincident indicators describe current conditions; and leading indicators forecast changes in the economy. Many of these numbers are generated by Statistics Canada, the federal government's central fact-gathering agency. Investors look most closely at leading indicators because economic trends affect prices of securities. Leading indicators include hiring patterns, money supply, corporate profits, housing starts, orders for durable goods, average hours worked by salaried employees and stock market indexes.

EITHER-OR

This is an order to buy one of two or more specified securities. As soon as one order is executed, the others are cancelled.

EARNINGS PER SHARE (EPS)

Net income divided by the number of shares that a company has issued.

EURO

A pan-European currency that came into circulation in 1999. After a three-year phase-in period, it replaces national currencies in Western Europe and will be a potential alternative to the US$ as a reserve currency. The accepted capitalization of the word euro is a formal part of the agreement. It's Euro in Germany and euro everywhere else.

EURODOLLAR

Originally, a market in Europe in US$ deposit claims on U.S. banks. The practical effect of this arrangement allowed these banks to expand their operations outside the U.S. regulatory environment. The market has expanded into other currencies and has become an international financing pool run by the world's largest financial institutions. Generally, the eurocurrency market is beyond the scope of regulation in the home countries of participating banks.

EX-DIVIDEND

Stocks trade ex- (without) dividend after the record date.

EXPANSION

The business cycle has its ups and downs. The good times are called an expansion.

EXPIRY DATE

Futures and options contracts have an end date and the most active trading period usually is within 90 days of expiry. For most exchange traded securities, this date usually is on the third Friday of the month.

EXTENDIBLE AND RETRACTABLE BONDS

An extendible bond gives the holder the right to exchange the bond for a longer-term bond at the same or a higher rate of interest. A retractable bond allows the investor to redeem the bond at par earlier than the original term. For example, a 10-year bond could be redeemed in five years.

FED FUNDS RATE

The U.S. equivalent of the bank rate. The U.S. central bank is the Federal Reserve Board and this is the rate for "funds at the Fed," which are mainly used to cover deficiencies in legal reserves.

FINANCIAL INSTRUMENT

A general term for stocks, bonds, money market paper and currencies.

FINANCIAL STATEMENTS

In the annual report, these are the audited financial results for the year, including a balance sheet, a statement of profit and loss, a statement of retained earnings and a set of notes that explain any unusual items in the reports.

FISCAL YEAR

For most companies, the fiscal year is a January-to-December calendar year, but some companies have different yearends for financial accounting. Retail businesses, for example, tend to have yearends in January or February when inventory levels are lowest.

FOREIGN-PAY BONDS

Some bonds issued by Canadian institutions are denominated in foreign currencies. Foreign-pay bonds are used to raise money in international markets. For example, bonds denominated in yen will appeal to Japanese investors, and those in U.S. funds will appeal to Americans – or they may be bought by Canadian investors seeking exposure to foreign currencies.

FORWARD CONTRACT

Similar to a futures contract, except that a forward contract trades over the counter. Forward exchange rate contracts provide for delivery of a specified currency amount at a fixed exchange rate at a future date. A forward rate agreement (FRA) provides for delivery of a specified amount at a fixed interest charge at a future date. Forwards generally are used by businesses to hedge risk and common terms are up to 12 months.

FUTURES

A contract traded on a recognized exchange in which the seller agrees to deliver a specified commodity or financial instrument at a future date at a specified settlement price. A risk in the futures market is that the seller must pay the price of the underlying security on settlement date, which may be substantially greater than the price on the date on which the contract was sold. Futures are traded on a wide range of farm products, all the basic industrial metals, all the standard industrial fuels, financial market indexes and on several common interest-sensitive instruments, such as benchmark bonds, bankers acceptance notes and treasury bills.

FUTURES OPTIONS

Options on futures contracts for commodities, currencies, stock indexes and other instruments are listed on North American commodities exchanges.

GDP DEFLATER

The national accounts system produces two sets of calculations on economic output. GDP at today's prices is "nominal" GDP. Statistics Canada also calculates GDP using prices in a base year, which is defined as "real" GDP. The difference between real and nominal GDP is inflation and this measure is an implied price index called the GDP deflater.

GROSS DOMESTIC PRODUCT (GDP)

This is the most frequently used measure of Canada's overall economic performance. It's the sum of all the goods and services produced in the economy. A change in GDP represents growth or contraction of the economy. Real GDP is a calculation of national accounts that is adjusted for inflation so that it measures the volume of production, rather than the value. The total value of production is nominal GDP. Comprehensive figures are published every three months and are adjusted to smooth the effects of seasonal changes in the economy. A separate monthly series of seasonally adjusted GDP accounts provides a more frequent monitor of economic activity. At one time, gross national product (GNP) was the conventional measure of economic expansion. The major differences between the two yardsticks are that GDP does not include returns from Canadian investments abroad but does include the returns from foreign capital invested here. GNP includes goods and services produced by Canadians abroad but doesn't include returns to non-residents from Canadian investments in other countries.

GROWTH STOCKS

These are the shares of companies that are seen to have above-average growth potential in revenue so that investors can profit from a rapid rise in market value.

HIGH

The highest price at which a security trades. This usually means during a trading day unless specified otherwise.

INCOME STOCKS

These shares are bought for their dividend potential. Income stocks are of companies with solid earnings records that pay above-average returns to investors.

INDEXES

Indexes are a commonly accepted way of measuring direction of price moves in the stock market. Major indexes contain a representative collection of shares listed on a stock exchange and thus are considered indicators of market direction. Specialized indexes and subindexes of the major indexes are used as benchmarks for stock performance of particular companies within their sectors.

INDUSTRIAL PRODUCT PRICE INDEX

This index measures cost pressures at the factory level.

INSTALMENT RECEIPTS

A securities issue of stocks sold on the instalment plan. Buyers pay for the shares in two or more payments over a specified period. Certificates are issued when the shares are fully paid but they trade as instalment receipts from the time of the first payment. Pricing of instalment receipts in the secondary market will factor in the deferred payments.

INTEREST-RATE OPTIONS

Options on three-month bankers' acceptance notes and on long-term government of Canada bonds trade on the Bourse de Montreal.

IPO (INITIAL PUBLIC OFFERING)

This is a new issue of securities offered to the investing public for the first time.

JUNK BONDS

Historically, bond financing has been used to finance projects with long productive lives, such as railways, roads, industrial plants, pipelines and electrical generating stations. More recently, there has been an active market for high yield bonds, colloquially known as junk bonds. These issues have been used to finance high risk activities and corporate restructurings.

LABOR FORCE SURVEY

GDP numbers take time to collect, so economists look for more recent numbers when assessing the state of the economy. The labor force survey is a good measure of changes in the pace of economic activity. Statistics Canada surveys the workforce every month to assess these changes. A few days after the end of each month, it reports on estimates of total employment and the number of people looking for jobs. There are breakdowns by region, gender, age and whether part- or full-time work is being done. The profile of hiring activity from this survey is a good coincident indicator of economic activity.

THE LANGUAGE OF BOND RATINGS

Rating agencies grade bonds on a letter scale that is designed to measure risk. Among the general principles of rating credit is the rule that the top rating goes to the sovereign credit. That means when Canada is rated double A for bonds sold in foreign markets, no province or corporation in Canada can have a higher rating. As a general rule, bonds rated triple B and higher are considered investment grade. Below triple B is non-investment-grade and the jargon term for this category is junk bonds. Investment dealers prefer the term "high-yield" for non-investment-grade, reflecting the fact that issuers of these bonds pay more to borrow because the lender is unlikely to recover much if there is a default. Each rating agency will have a unique way of stating its rating, so that triple A appears slightly differently. However, the meaning of a credit rating at each level is roughly equivalent. (For purposes of illustration, the triple A section shows different ways of stating a rating.) AAA, A++, AAA: Highest-quality bonds. These offer the highest protection for principal and interest. AA: Superior credit quality, but marginally lower than the highest-quality bonds. A: Good to medium-grade bonds, still considered a good risk with substantial protection of interest and principle. Issuers with this rate may be susceptible in an economic downturn. BBB: Medium-grade quality bonds with adequate protection. Some potential weaknesses exist or issuers in this category are at risk to changes in the economic cycle. BB: Lower-medium grade bonds. These offer uncertain protection and may be considered mildly speculative. B: These bonds are considered speculative with little investor protection, especially during times of economic weakness. CCC: Highly speculative bonds that may be in danger of default. CC: Generally, bonds in this category are in default or have other serious problems. C: In default.

LEVERAGE

The use of borrowed funds to buy securities. Otherwise, the purchase of securities, such as futures or options, that only represent a portion of the value of an underlying security. Use of leverage can be profitable even with seemingly small changes in the price of a security but losses can rise quickly when prices move in the wrong direction.

LIBOR (LONDON INTERBANK OFFERED RATE)

Benchmark rates in the eurocurrency market. These are interbank rates for short-term loans in major currencies.

LIMIT

The maximum bid price for a purchase or the minimum sell price. These transactions may take longer to complete than an at-the-market order, or may never be executed.

LIQUIDITY

Liquidity refers to the ability of a market to absorb buy or sell orders with no unusual distortion in pricing.

LOW

The lowest price at which a security trades. This usually means during a trading day unless specified otherwise.

MANAGEMENT

Under the CEO, management has control over the day-to-day operations of the company.

MANAGEMENT DISCUSSION AND ANALYSIS (MD&A)

A statement from management in the annual report that contains a detailed discussion and analysis of information in the annual information form.

MARGIN

A margin account is a loan facility where a brokerage firm acts as a banker to lend funds to a client for investment purposes. Typically, the broker holds the securities as collateral. Rules on margin lending require clients to provide additional funds if the price of a security falls below a pre-set ratio of market price to cash invested by the client.

MARKET PRICE

The most recent price at which a security traded. If there has been no transaction in a security during the trading day, the list of prices will show bid and ask prices (bid on the left, ask on the right)

MERCHANDISE TRADE

The most detailed breakdown in the current account number is for trade in goods, or merchandise trade. This set of statistics includes breakdowns by categories of goods – from autos, computers, pulp, minerals and so on. Other tables break out the numbers based on trade with each of Canada's national trading partners.

MID-CAPS

The mid-cap group are companies that have grown out of the start-up stage but are smaller than the large capitalization blue chips.

MONETARY CONDITIONS INDEX (MCI)

The Bank of Canada developed the MCI as a guide to setting monetary policy. The intent is to recognize the fact that the C$ exchange value is significant in policy setting because export and import volumes now represent a large portion of the national accounts. A decline in interest rates means an easing in monetary conditions but the impact of a drop in rates can be offset by a rise in the value of the currency. MCI combines these two and a 100 basis point change in three-month commercial paper rates is equivalent to a 3% change in trade-weighted value of the C$. The currency value in MCI is an index based on Canada's share of trade with the 10 largest industrial countries.

MONEY

Most Canadians see coins and bills as simply money, but each has a different status. Coins are a commodity sold by the Bank of Canada in its role as fiscal agent for the government. The central bank sells coins to commercial banks. The difference between the production cost and the face value is pure profit. For large denominations, such as the $2 coin, the profit is substantial. Bills, also called banknotes, are a promise to pay and are carried as a liability on the Bank of Canada's balance sheet. Canada is no longer on the gold standard and the practical effect of the central bank's obligation is to pursue policies that protect the value of the currency in international markets.

MONEY MANAGERS

This is a general term for those who oversee the investment of client funds. Fees vary depending on the type of service and the level of client involvement. A mutual fund is a common money management function and in this situation the manager has discretion on investment decisions with a pre-established set of rules and guidelines. Higher levels of individual service will involve consultation with the client but typically these managers will have minimum amounts for individual client portfolio size, often $500,000 or more.

MONEY MARKET

Securities in the money market are short term, up to a year. Generally, the most active markets are for securities with a three-month term.

MONEY SUPPLY, THE 3Ms

An increase or decrease in money supply is a sign of loosening or tightening credit conditions. The money supply is the total amount of money in the economy available for investments and transactions. Currency, in the form of bills and coins, is just a small part of the money supply. The rest is held in bank deposits. There are several measures of the money supply in Canada: M1: This is the total of all the currency – banknotes and coins – in circulation outside of chartered banks, plus demand deposits at chartered banks (usually money in business chequing accounts that can be immediately spent). M2: This is M1 plus the money in personal savings deposits and most term deposits, such as guaranteed investment certificates. M2+: This is M2 plus deposits at trust and mortgage loan companies, credit unions, money-market mutual funds and life insurance company annuities. M3: This is M2 plus non-personal fixed-term deposits and foreign currency deposits of residents booked in Canada.

MONTREAL MARKET PORTFOLIO

This Bourse de Montreal index is comprised of the 25 most heavily capitalized stocks listed on at least two Canadian exchanges.

MORTGAGE BONDS

Mortgage bonds are secured by mortgaged property. First mortgage bonds are a corporation's senior securities because these bondholders have first crack at the company's assets if the company is liquidated.

MUTUAL FUNDS

Holders of mutual funds are indirect investors. These are pools of money used to buy a variety of securities. A balanced fund will have a mix of basic investment vehicles and there are several types of specialized funds that direct pooled funds into more exotic markets.

NAKED OPTION WRITER

An option writer who does not have an offsetting position in the underlying security is said to be "naked."

NASDAQ COMPOSITE

The National Association of Securities Dealers Automated Quotation (Nasdaq) system is an interdealer market, as distinct from a stock exchange where trades are processed through a neutral intermediary. The Nasdaq composite index includes all shares listed on the senior listings board, which now totals almost 6,000 stocks.

NATIONAL ACCOUNTS

This is the bookkeeping for the country as a whole. The accounts have breakdowns of income and expenditures. On the income side, the broad categories include wages and salaries, corporate profits, interest, investment gains and taxes. Major spending categories include consumer purchases of goods and services, business investment and government buying. On the spending side there are adjustments for changes in inventories and a net calculation of imports minus exports.

NET CHANGE

The change in price from one period to another, usually the latest closing price compared with the previous day's close.

NET INCOME

Money left in the accounts of a business after all expenses and taxes have been paid. Dividends are paid out of net income.

ODD LOTS

Any number shares less than a board lot.

OPEN INTEREST

In options markets, the number of outstanding contracts for a particular series of options.

OPEN OUTCRY (AUCTION) TRADING

The traditional method of trading securities on a stock exchange floor. Transactions are conducted face-to-face. In Canada and the U.S., most stock, bond and currency trading now is done through computer terminals in investment house trading rooms but derivatives trades are still mainly done on trading floors.

OPEN

Also known as a good-till-cancelled order, this remains in effect until executed or cancelled. They are usually orders to buy shares at a specified price and generally a cancellation date is set in advance.

OPTIONS

A right to buy or sell a specific security at a fixed price, called the strike price or exercise price. The holder of an option has no obligation to complete the purchase or sale. Consequently, the risk in buying an option is limited to the purchase price. Options are available on many kinds of investments in Canada and in foreign markets.

ORDER MATCHING ON THE SCREEN

Stock trading systems now allow traders to complete a transaction over a computer network. Elaborate security codes and pre-authorized credit limits are part of the rules for the new digital world of securities trading.

OUT OF THE MONEY

If an option contract expires when the strike price is on the wrong side of the market price, the contract is out of the money.

OUTPUT GAP

When setting monetary policy, the Bank of Canada's goal is to align interest rates with the non-inflationary rate of economic activity. Finding the right mix involves an estimate of the optimum growth rate for the economy. The difference between the optimum rate and the estimated actual rate is the output gap.

PAR VALUE/NO PAR

If a bond or stock has a stated face value, that is the par value. This is the amount that is payable on maturity or liquidation. With bonds, it is common practice to use 100 as par and thus a premium or discount off par is readily seen as a percent. Generally, common stock has no par value while bonds and preferred stock do have par values.

PENNY STOCKS

These shares trade for less than $1, and are usually speculative. The oil and gas and mining industries have a high proportion of penny stocks. In Canada, many of these trade on the Vancouver Stock Exchange.

PLACING AN ORDER WITH A BROKER

The first step is opening an account, at which time the broker will complete a form that includes a risk profile of the investor. When buying securities, investors should be aware of the language of stock orders because sending the wrong signal can be a costly mistake.

PREFERRED STOCK (SHARES)

Holders of preferred shares sit a notch above common shareholders when it comes to payment of dividends or claims on a company's assets. Preferred shareholders are entitled to dividend payments – which can be a fixed or variable amount – before common shareholders get theirs. Like common shareholders, preferred shareholders are part owners of the company but usually are non-voting unless the company falls behind in dividend payments. If a company is dissolved, preferred shareholders are entitled to a share of the company's assets after creditors are paid and before common shareholders receive payments. Preferred shares usually have a par value, which fixes the amount a shareholder gets on redemption. For that reason, the market value of preferred shares may be pegged to changes in general interest rate levels in the economy, much like a bond.

PRICE INDEXES

Measure changes in the cost of a basket of goods over time. Current practice in index design is to use chain-weightings, which adjust for changes in consumption patterns over time.

PRIMARY MARKET

New issues of fixed income securities are simply new loans. Pricing in the primary market is based on yields in the secondary market.

PRIME RATE

At one time, prime was the rate banks charged for loans to their most creditworthy business customers. Now, business financing is much more diverse and the prime rate has become an important benchmark for consumer loans. It's still a rate that applies only to the best credits. Frequently a loan rate will be set in relation to the prime rate – for example, one percentage point above prime.

PROGRAM TRADING

Program trading can apply to any market but often is associated with derivatives. The "program" is a computer program and the existence of massive computing power allows traders to do sophisticated analyses of prices in different markets. A common use of program trading is to find price differences between different markets. An earlier term is arbitrage, which involves buying a security on one exchange and selling on another where stocks are interlisted between two exchanges. Shares of several Canadian companies are listed in Toronto and New York, so currency exchange value is a factor in arbitraging prices between the two markets. Program trading takes arbitrage a step further by trying to find a profit from pricing differences between cash and futures or options markets. Program trading also can be used to change the asset mix of a portfolio.

PROSPECTUS

A legal document that describes securities being offered for sale to the public.

PUT

An option that gives the holder the right to sell the underlying security.

QUARTERLY REPORTS

These documents contain basic financial disclosure on a quarterly schedule plus update reports from management on corporate developments during the year.

RAW MATERIALS PRICE INDEX

Measures costs at the most basic level in the economy.

REAL ESTATE INVESTMENT TRUST (REIT)

An investment trust that holds a combination of real estate assets, including mortgages and property. REITs are structured somewhat like a mutual fund. However, there is one important distinction. With a mutual fund, the potential loss to the investor is limited to the amount invested. With REITs, the issue of liability to the investor is a grey area and there may be an exposure to risk beyond the value of money invested. REITs use the basic trust structure, which provides certain tax advantages to the investors. But a REIT is unlike a standard trust, where the person providing the funds is not the beneficiary. An investor in a REIT also is a beneficiary.

REAL RETURN BONDS
The federal government issues 30-year bonds with interest rates that are adjusted to account for inflation. The base rate is 4.25% and the return is adjusted according to a formula based on the consumer price index.

RECESSION
When things get really bad, it's a recession. The most common definition is two consecutive quarters of decline in real gross domestic product. A recovery begins when the economy starts to move out of the bottom of its cycle, with increasing demand for goods and services, increasing investment and growing employment.

REDEEMABLE BONDS
Also known as callable bonds, they give the issuer the right to pay off – or call – the outstanding debt after a specified date. This allows a corporation to retire high-interest debt when rates drop and borrow elsewhere. Investors often are paid a premium when bonds are called in recognition of the fact they are being deprived of future income.

REGISTERED REPRESENTATIVE OR ACCOUNT EXECUTIVE
These are common terms for brokerage house sales agents who deal with retail clients (ordinary investors) in the buying and selling of securities.

RETRACTABLE
The shareholder can require the issuer to redeem the preferred shares on a specified date at a specified price.

REVENUE
Money taken in from the ongoing operations of a business. Extraordinary items, such as the sale of assets, are not counted as revenue.

RIGHTS
Rights allow the holder to buy more shares directly from the company. Usually, rights are issued at a discount to the prevailing market price, often a deep discount. A specified number of rights allows the holder to purchase a share, usually a common share, as a preset price. Generally, rights have a short lifespan, a few weeks or a few months. Most rights become listed securities and can be traded.

ROYALTY TRUSTS
An investment trust that gets income from royalties. The most common form of income is from owning a stake in an oil or gas well. Royalty trusts have many features in common with REITs.

SECONDARY MARKET
Trading in securities that are already in circulation, which is most of the daily activity that occurs on the Toronto Stock Exchange and other equity markets, is done in the secondary market. When the initial buyer of a security sells, the trade is done in the secondary market. Most of the trading volume in securities markets involves transactions in bonds, stocks, bills and other securities in circulation.

SECURITY CERTIFICATES

Security certificates proof of ownership of stocks or bonds when the name of the beneficial owner is registered. As a practical matter, few investors now take physical delivery of security certificates. Registries are being converted to electronic record keeping and ownership records usually are maintained through an investment dealer.

SETTLEMENT PERIOD

After a securities transaction is executed by the trader, the buyer and seller have a pre-set time limit to complete the deal with a transfer of funds. Settlement periods vary among markets but most transactions must be completed within three days.

SHAREHOLDERS

Shareholders are the owners and the equity stake in the company is represented by stock.

SHORT SALE

The sale of a stock that an investor does not own. The seller uses borrowed shares that are on loan for a fee. The intent of a short sale is to buy at a later date, when the price of a security has fallen, to return the borrowed certificates. If the price rises, the short seller has a loss. Short selling often is done on margin, so a short seller will be forced to "cover" by buying stock if the price rises.

SINKING FUND BONDS

A sinking fund is a sum of money set aside, usually annually, by the issuer of a bond or debenture to be used to repay all or part of the debt by maturity. This provides added security for investors; consequently the yields on sinking fund bonds may be lower than those for other bonds. Redeemable bonds often have sinking fund provisions.

SMALL-CAP STOCKS

These are shares of companies with low capitalization – the number of outstanding shares multiplied by the share price. Small-cap stocks are sometimes defined as having capitalization of $100 million or less.

SPECIALISTS (PROS OR MARKET-MAKERS)

Investment house traders who trade as principals in securities. These traders stand ready to buy or sell and thus ensure there is liquidity in the market.

SPREAD

The difference in interest rates, or yields, between two securities. When the federal government borrows at 6% and a company borrows for the same term at 7%, the spread is one percentage point.

STANDARD & POOR'S 500 (S&P 500)

The Standard & Poor's index of 500 stocks is a broad measure of stock market performance and includes shares of most of the large public companies in the U.S. This index is followed closely by investment professionals because a futures contract based on the index is a key indicator of market trends.

STOCK CONSOLIDATION

The opposite of a stock split. Usually this involves stock of a junior company that is out of favor. Management will consolidate the stock to reflect the reality of the market.

STOCK EXCHANGE SEAT

Some securities exchanges, such as the Canadian Venture Exchange, are structured as co-operatives. Members are the firms that make up the investment dealer community. The seatholders are the member representatives from those firms. The term "seat" stems from the days when stocks were traded by brokers sitting around a table.

STOCK INDEX OPTIONS

In major markets, the option on an index is a driving force in the momentum of the cash market. The most widely followed in North America is the option on the S&P 500 index and moves in the market for this option typically are a leading indicator for the direction of prices in the cash market for stocks in that index.

STOCK MARKET INDEXES

The direction of general stock markets reflects investor sentiment about future profits in the business sector.

STOCK OPTIONS

Exchange-traded puts and calls are available on stocks of most senior Canadian companies and some mid-sized firms. A standard equity option usually covers 100 shares, with an expiry date of three, six or nine months from the day it is introduced. A special class of options, called long-term equity anticipation securities (LEAPS), has a two-year term.

STOCK SPLIT

Literally, a subdivision of a company's shares into two or more new shares. Directors of most companies prefer to have the stock price within a reasonable range of the average trading price on the exchange where the issue is listed. If the price rises to a high level, it will be split to bring the price closer to the average trading price. Stock purchases generally are in lots of 100 shares and pricing is aimed at putting the cost of 100 shares within the budget of a typical retail investor.

STOP-LOSS

An order to sell a stock when its price falls below a specified limit, known as the stop price.

STREET NAME

A security certificate that is held in the name of an investment dealer on behalf of a client.

STRIP BONDS (SOMETIMES CALLED STRIPPED BONDS)

Created when an investment dealer literally strips the interest coupons from the bond. High-quality bonds usually are used for this purpose, often the bonds of provincial governments. Coupons and the principal amount, known as the residue, are sold separately at deep discounts. When bond residue matures, the bondholder receives the principal. Holders of the coupons receive the interest payments, but they can't be collected until maturity. That means there are no periodic interest payments to reinvest. The structure of strip bonds means that they are highly sensitive to changes in interest rates. Thus market prices for these instruments can be highly volatile. Another reason for the volatility is that the majority of strip bonds are bought by investors who hold to maturity and this lack of liquidity in many issues affects the price.

SUBORDINATED DEBENTURES
Corporations will meet their obligations to holders of more senior securities before paying their debts to holders of subordinated debentures. The latter's rights are subordinate to those of other creditors.

TERM VERSUS DURATION
The term to maturity is a simple calculation with a calendar. If a bond is issued at par with a fixed interest rate, the calculation of return to maturity is straightforward. Valuing a bond becomes more complicated if the purchase price is not par because a capital gain or loss becomes part of the equation when the bond reaches par at maturity. This involves the concept of duration, which adjusts the term according to present value of coupon and principal. These calculations involve complex formulas and require computer power to assess the relative values of different bonds at different prices.

TIME VALUE
The amount by which the current normal market value of a right, option or warrant exceeds its underlying value. Essentially, time value is the financing cost of a hedge.

TORONTO 35
An index of 35 blue chip stocks on the TSE. It includes most of the big Canadian companies across the major industry sectors.

TOTAL EQUITY CAPITAL
Total equity capital is the number of shares in circulation.

TRADERS
Persons authorized by a stock exchange to buy or sell. In Canada most traders now conduct transactions over computer trading screens in investment house trading rooms. Exchanges also authorize independent traders, called "locals." The objective in having a large pool of traders is to provide liquidity to the market.

TRADING AS PRINCIPAL
Transactions by an investment dealer for its own account. Traditional brokerage firms only acted for clients when trading stocks but banks and bond trading houses frequently traded for their own accounts in currency and fixed income transactions and now the large investment dealers trade as principal in a broad range of securities.

TRANSFER AGENT
Companies have a designated agent, usually a trust company, that maintains a list of shareholders and records all transfers of ownership in shares of the company.

TREASURY BILLS
Short-term notes issued by a government's treasury. They are short-term loans that provide the government with cash for day-to-day operations. The common terms are three, six and 12 months. T-bills are an important element in the securities market because they provide investors with a way of deploying idle cash. T-bill yields are important indicators of interest rates in commercial lending.

TRIPLE WITCHING HOUR
A slang market term for the last hour of a Friday on which quarterly contracts expire in stock futures, stock options and index options. The big volume on these contracts is on a quarterly basis with March, June, September and December expiry dates. Program traders adjust their positions on those dates and this process can cause volatility in underlying cash markets for equities. Those distortions can have a ripple effect on currency and fixed income markets.

TSE 300
An index of the shares of 300 companies listed on the Toronto Stock Exchange. They are mainly the 300 largest companies, although there are other inclusion criteria, such as length of time listed on the TSE and representation in various industry sectors.

UNITS
Securities can be bundled and sold as a unit. Common combinations are a common stock with a right or a warrant attached.

VARIABLE (FLOATING) RATE
A loan pegged to the prime rate is essentially a variable rate loan because the prime rate, and hence the loan rate, can change when monetary conditions change. Usually, the prime rate does not change frequently but there are other loan rate benchmarks that can fluctuate more frequently as conditions change in money and bond markets. For example, a loan rate may be pegged to an average of treasury bill yields over a specified period.

VOLATILITY
In its standard definition, volatility is a measure of the rate of change in the price of a security over a specified time. The usual yardstick is standard deviation from average price. Volatility also has become a sophisticated security in the over-the-counter market where investors take on the risks of volatility in a security, a process that works much like an expensive insurance policy in high-risk markets.

VOLUME
The number of security units traded during a specified period. With stocks it is the number of shares; with bonds and currencies it is the value; and with derivatives, such as futures and options, it is the number of contracts.

WARRANTS

A warrant is similar to a right, but usually has a lifespan of a year or more. Typically, warrants are issued as part of a stock offering and the warrant is considered an inducement in the sale of the shares. Like rights, warrants will be listed securities and can be traded.

WHOLESALE FUNDS

A general term for transactions between banks, other large financial institutions and big corporations that have active financing operations (such as carmakers that have financing and leasing subsidiaries). Transaction size in the wholesale market generally is at least $100,000 and often much larger. Interest rates in the wholesale markets influence the cost of funds for small businesses and consumers.

WRITER

The creator of an option, a shorthand term for underwriter.

YIELD CURVE

A list of yields for common terms of treasury bills and government bonds that is displayed graphically. In a normal market, the cost of money rises as the term of the investment lengthens and a graph of these yields appears as a curve.

ZERO-COUPON BONDS

Issued without interest coupons. They are sold at a discount to face value, with the difference between the selling price and the face value representing the investor's return.

NOTES

NOTES

NOTES